Dear Chinnu & David,

With love,

Vijaymese

May 17th, 2020

Flashbacks

Stories from My Life and Family

Vijay Yajnik

ISBN: 978-1-7346782-0-8 (Paperback)

Library of Congress Control Number: 2020903489

Book cover design by DiggyPOD
Editing by Meghana Yajnik Doty

Printed by DiggyPOD Inc. - United States of America
Printed by Pothi.com - Bangalore, India

First Edition 2020

Published by: Vijay Yajnik
26 Covered Wagon Lane
Rolling Hills Estates, CA 90274-4822
USA

Email: vijayyajnik@gmail.com

In Loving Remembrance

"Pappaji"

&

"Behn"

"Nobody cares how hard you pedaled,
What matters is how far you moved."

… On effort vs. results

"Just because you will poop again,
Doesn't mean that you don't wipe your behind."

… On making up your bed every morning (the PG version!)

"Always remember what is important,
And never worry about the mouse nuts."

… On priorities

"Instead of ready, aim, aim,
It is better to go ready, fire, aim."

… On having a bias for action

"It is six of one,
And half-a-dozen of the other."

… On equivalence

"Hey, beneath all these growls,
I am just a sweetheart."

… Said with a twinkle in the eyes

"Well, one does need a hint of color..."

… On dressing in flamboyant colors

*... **Sayings of the "CBM" - Crazy Bald Man***
(Selected by Meghana)

v

Acknowledgment

I want to thank Rajkumar College, Rajkot, (RKC) Old Boys Himanshu Jani, Vijay Kaul, Raj Kulkarni, Vinod Raja, Sujan Chinoy, Bharat Avalani, and Rahul Patel, among many, who encouraged me to write. Also, my dear friend, Ron Wilsie, who provided further motivation.

Over many phone calls with the late Madam Rati Cooper, my RKC teacher, and her younger sister, Perin Boga, in Lahore Pakistan, I received valuable encouragement, counsel and inspiration.

I am deeply grateful to Mr. Ayaaz Khan, also my RKC teacher. He sent me a lovely "dua" (*blessing*) to get me going on this whole adventure. It read, "Khuda kare, zor-e-qualaam aur zyada." (*May God power your pen even more.*)

Finally, I want to thank Nilima, my wife, for giving me insightful critiques. She also allowed me extensive time and space in my "man cave" to enable me to take this effort to completion.

CONTENTS

Acknowledgment

PREFACE

Prologue 13
Addressing People in India 17

EARLY CHILDHOOD

A Daring Walk in Dwarka 21
Transfer to Porbandar 25
Villas & Bungalows 28
The New Dodge & An Airport Visit 33
Holidays in Petlad 37
Sakarlalkaka Goes to Petlad 42
Ahmedabad Tales 46
About Family Values 52
Training in "Vilayat" 61
A Monsoon Drive 65
HH Maharani Saheba of Porbandar 68
Rumblings of Rajkumar College, Rajkot 70

RAJKUMAR COLLEGE, RAJKOT

Cross Country Runs 81
"Mere Gale Lag Jaa" *(Just Hug Me)* 85
The Joy of "Live" Performances 92
Primal Fear 101
An Ode to Teachers 108
About Boyhood Dreams 111
A Naturalist 122
Greetings & A Dedication 125
A Match of Pride & Royal Encounters 131

ix

THE JAMUL YEARS

Early Hardships 149
A Boy Called "Vaalji"...153
An Adventurous Train Journey.......................................158
The Blossoming of Jamul..163
Hosting Guests & Visitors...169
A Rhino Hunt...172
A Strange Meeting...176
My First Car Drive...179
Inauguration of Jamul Cement Works.............................183
Four Major Exams in Six Months....................................187

INDIAN INSTITUE OF TECHNOLOGY/KANPUR

Off to IIT/Kanpur & An Unfinished Story.......................197
A Dog Named "Moti"...200
Cultural Events & A Near Disaster..................................204
Meeting the Daughter...208
Tales of Agra & Pavan Nagpal...211
A Terrible Year - 1970...218
Applying for Graduate Studies...222
A Major Decision in Okha..227

A GRADUATE STUDENT

Going to America..233
The Famous "Tea Bag Story"..237
Adrift & The MBA Hustle...242
Looking for a Job..253
Close Encounters of the Third Kind..................................260

EARLY WORK LIFE

The New Working World...273
An Affair to Remember..286
Two "Z" Stories...292
First Return to India..298
San Francisco & Crocker Bank..304
A Performance Review...311

THE LATER YEARS

Adventures with Marv Rich 323
Landing of the Space Shuttle 330
The Kmart Saga 336
Global Experiences 351
Medical Crises in India 372
The Charms of Rajasthan 387

FINI

A Ranking Question 411
Closing an Unfinished Story – Jamul 415
A Nostalgic Sprint – Saurashtra Calling 421
Who Am I? 427

PREFACE

Prologue

It always began with an oft repeated simple question, "Really?"

My children, Neil and Meghana, were very young when all this started. I used to travel a lot at the time so whenever I was home, to have dinner with them and put them to bed, all sorts of conversations and questions would just erupt, out of nowhere. Perhaps I was being tested.

It would start with a query from them about something, and that would trigger in my mind a memory of a person, an event, or a place. I would play this memory back to them verbally in the form of a short story. They were always based on facts, but I would embellish them with comments about the environment, circumstances, history, or a general snapshot of the times in which the stories occurred. Sometimes I added dialogue to make them exciting. They would listen to me with rapt attention, get drowsy, and then fall asleep.

As time went by and they grew older, I would often hear a request, "Dad, tell us that particular story again." I would ask in wonder, "Why?" I would get a cryptic answer, "Because it is amazing!" I never thought much about any of this.

Then in 2010, during a visit to India from the USA, Nilima's brother-in-law, Anal Dalal, arranged for us to visit Rajkumar College (RKC) in Rajkot, my alma mater. He was an RKC "Old Boy" also and drove us there from Ahmedabad. It was my first visit since 1966, when I had graduated and left RKC, after a 7-year stay. The School tour was great, but I was overcome by a flood of memories and emotions. I thought about all the times gone by; my RKC friends and classmates, many lost and some retained; and also, my teachers, many lost and some retained. I felt a pained sense that my youth was gone. On the whole, it was a lovely visit to RKC and Rajkot. It would have stayed that way, except of another development, shortly thereafter.

Rahul Patel, an illustrious RKC Old Boy, launched the "RKC Old Boys Forum", a website on Yahoo groups. In short order, this site began to attract all sorts of old boys, teachers, and many interesting posts started to appear. I wrote some RKC stories and posted them there as well. To my surprise, they were well received and I was encouraged by many to write more. Then, what was even more surprising to me was that I began to receive responses from unknown folks who had nothing to do with RKC at all! They had read a "forward" from somebody of some of my RKC stories. These people, of various ages, were from all over the world. It seemed that something about these stories had resonated with them and their lives. This was intriguing indeed.

I shared this information with my family. Then came a suggestion, filled with gravitas, from my children. They said, "Dad, why don't you compile all these stories into a book? It would make fascinating reading for all kinds of people." I went, "Really?" They replied in one voice, "Yes, really!"

Now, as young adults, they shared a different perspective with me. They felt that my stories were not just some sort of fantasy tales about "good guys vs. bad guys" or some kind of an "adventure". They thought that my stories were about real things and that there were all sorts of learnings in them everywhere. They liked the historical perspective, not only on the Yajnik family, but also on the era in which I grew up in India and matured in the USA. Furthermore, the stories were in "my voice", as it were, and they wanted them preserved that way for posterity.

"Really? Are you serious?" I countered. "Do you know how much work that would be? Also, the costs involved would be huge. Besides, who the heck would want to read my stupid stories anyway?"

They replied, "Yes, we are serious. Lots of people would want to read them, we think."

That was the genesis of this book. It is a collection of stories, based purely upon my memory of actual people, places, events, and situations from my life and family. While I have tried to organize them in a broad swath of a chronological timeline, it is not precise. Also, despite my research, it is by no means an accurate historical record of any sort.

The stories are written in the same manner that I used when telling them to my children. While they are factually correct, I have embellished them to make their reading interesting. A fair measure of the dialogue in them is creative writing, but intended deliberately to capture the spirit of the situation or people involved, as I recall it.

The grammar, expressions, and idioms used in the stories are a mixture of the British English that I was taught in RKC, and the American English that it blended into, over many decades of living in the USA. My natural tendency towards using Gujarati, my mother tongue, and Hindi, which I spoke more often as a young adult, permeates throughout them. I hope that it adds some color and charm to the stories. I have also provided a translation into English throughout the book, to aid your comprehension.

This book is primarily a gift to Neil & Meghana, and secondarily to my extended family and friends all over the world. However, it is my hope that it can be a gift to your children and your extended families as well. Particularly if you grew up in India like I did, but your children were born or raised outside of India, it may have a greater relevance for you.

If this book engages you in some way, raises your level of curiosity about specific things, or ignites a desire to read more about a topic, then I shall consider it a mission fulfilled. Also, if there are any learnings from these stories, that help you in your life or present circumstances, then I shall think of it as the icing on the cake.

Meanwhile, remember that these are just stories. So, relax and enjoy the read. Yes, really!

Vijay Yajnik
Los Angeles, California
October 16th, 2019

Addressing People in India

Addressing people in India properly can be very confusing to the uninformed. In India, the various names with prefixes or suffixes, used to address relatives and others is a rich world unto itself. On the one hand they hold great specificity, and on the other they provide a nuanced statement of respect or endearment. In these norms, the Indian culture is quite unusual, perhaps even unique, when compared to other cultures in the world.

In general, the terms used, distinguish relatives on the paternal side from those on the maternal side. Even the implied reference of endearment is different. This is for some very sound reasons, which may not be obvious at first glance. Since ancient times, India was mainly a patriarchal culture, where men ruled over the affairs in a typical "joint family" within a caste system. Control of all economic and security matters resided with the men of the family. The women were mainly homemakers, raised children, and maintained all the social relationships within the extended family, caste, and community. It was also vital to build and preserve the income and wealth of a family for the well being of future generations. So, the paternal relations were viewed through a prism of the implied formality of economic or social power. On the maternal side, the relations were viewed from a perspective of greater emotional closeness and endearment. A brief story will illustrate this point.

In 1980, I was in Baroda, about to get married to Nilima, when I was introduced to the Vakil family, which was not related to her family in any way. Nilima and her siblings called Dr. Vakil, "Vakilkaka", but his wife was always referred to as "Jayamashi". Further, Dr. Vakil would jovially tell me that he was neither a doctor, nor a vakil (*lawyer*). He had a Ph.D. in Gujarati! Naturally, I was quite confused. So, I asked Jayamashi, "Why do they call you Mashi, and why is he called Kaka?" She gave me a poignant answer and also taught me a lesson, which I never forgot.

She said, "I have known Nilima's family for a long time. When she and her siblings were little, they asked me what they should call me. I gave them a simple answer."

I asked, "What was that?"

She stated, "Kaki kahesho, to agha rehesho, Mashi kahesho, to rasode avasho." (*If you call me Kaki, you will keep a distance from me. But if you call me Mashi, you will be welcome in my kitchen.*)

So, I think it might be worthwhile to shed some light on this somewhat confusing subject. The synopsis below is based on the practices in western and northern India generally, but specifically in Hindu families in Gujarat. They also maybe somewhat specific to the community of Nagar Brahmins, which is my caste. In Muslim families in India, similar concepts are widely present as well. While they are also prevalent in southern and eastern India, the nomenclature is different due to vastly different languages in these regions.

Dada – Paternal grandfather. It can also mean paternal great-grandfather and beyond. For anybody else, it is a term to reflect an age difference of at least two generations.

Nana – Same as Dada, but on the maternal side. Regarded as closer than a Dada.

Dadi – Paternal grandmother.

Nani – Maternal grandmother. Regarded as much closer than a Dadi.

Papa/Pappa/Pappaji/Bapu/Bapuji – They all mean father. The "ji" is a suffix that can be added to any name or term as a mark of respect. In some families, affectionate terms such as Kaka or Bhai are also used to refer to the father. Typically, a father's name was never used by itself or without a suffix, because it was considered a sign of disrespect.

Ma/Ba/Mummy – They all mean mother. In some families, other terms of affection also include Ben, which actually means sister. Unlike fathers, mothers also enjoyed a variety of nicknames in various families as terms of endearment and respect. Sometimes Ba or Ma, either standalone or as suffixes, were also used to refer to the grandmothers.

Kaka – A father's brother. The prefix of "Mota" meant an older brother of a father, while "Nana" meant a younger brother of a father. This should not be confused with the standalone name. For people not related to you, it is a term of respect, when used either by itself, or as a suffix to a name. Typically, this would be used for a person who is one generation older than you. In English, the term is just "Uncle". In some families, sometimes it is used as an affectionate term to refer to the father as well.

Kaki – A kaka's wife. If not a relation, it would be a reference to a lady who is a generation older than you, again as a standalone term or as a suffix to a name. In English, the equivalent would be just "Aunty". But, unlike Kaka, this term would never be used to refer to one's mother.

Mama – A mother's brother. Usually regarded as the uncle who was considered emotionally to be the closest.

Mami – A mama's wife. Also considered quite close.

18

Mashi – A mother's sister. The word "mashi" actually translates to *"someone like a mother"*. So, she was always considered the most affectionate and the closest, after the mother. In many families, this name morphed into "Masi", but that is not lingually pure.

Masa – A mashi's husband.

Phoi – A father's sister.

Phooa – A phoi's husband.

Bhai – A brother. In some families, it is also an affectionate term for a father. For an unrelated person, it is a term of respect for someone who is of your generation or similar in age.

Bhabhi – A brother's wife. In some situations, it may be used as a polite term of respect for an unrelated lady as well.

Ben/Behn – A sister. Also, sometimes an affectionate term for a mother. For an unrelated person, it is a term of respect for somebody who is of your generation, or similar in age, or even a lot older.

Benevi – A sister's husband. Used mainly for introduction purposes to explain relationships. Never used to address a person.

This list is by no means complete. A comprehensive list would be just too large for the purpose here, so it just reviews the principal terms. Well, I hope and trust that these explanations have left you a little less confused about all these names, terms, prefixes, and suffixes.

I thought that this overview understanding would help you enjoy the stories that follow much better. I have not encountered a culture as yet, where names had such specific meanings in family relations, or where the context of their usage could alter their meaning so much.

EARLY CHILDHOOD

A Daring Walk in Dwarka

It happened in 1954 or so. I was almost 5 years old and attending the Pre or Kindergarten School situated within the "colony" of the ACC Cement Works in Dwarka, Gujarat. But before I tell you about this walk, it is important to get a perspective of the environment in which it occurred.

The Dwarka Cement Works (DCW) always held a special significance for my father. He had begun here, in what would be his over 35 years long work career with Associated Cement Companies, Ltd. (ACC), as a young Powerhouse Engineer in the 1930s. Due to its remoteness it provided him, as a single man then, a fertile ground in which to develop his engineering and managerial skill sets. His boss and mentor at the time was Mr. Sumant Moolgaokar, who would later rise to renowned corporate roles at Tata Steel & Tata Motors, including becoming the Managing Director (MD) of ACC.

In this particular posting, his second of three in all at Dwarka, my father had returned in 1952, in the role of General Manager (GM) of the works. In this capacity, he was responsible for not only the functioning of the cement works, but also for the welfare of all the workers, staff, and officers of the works. All the skilled staff members and officers were provided with housing and living amenities in the works colony. It was located adjacent to the cement plant and was practically a self-sufficient community by itself. It had a hospital, post office, bank, schools, general provisions store, sports club, petrol station, auto repair shop, machine & carpentry shop, a fleet of cars/vans/jeeps, and a private PBX telephone exchange, to name a few things.

To add more to the charm of this environ, there was also something else that was just amazing. The planners of the DCW, had also acquired a good bit of land right next to the beaches on the Arabian Sea. It was located about 4 Kilometers or so, to the west of the works and the colony, past the main road to Okha Port. On this spacious property, in a single large compound, they had built three large, two storied, colonial style bungalows. One was for the GM, one for the Assistant General Manager (AGM), and the third was a full function Guest House (GH). There were also additional servants' quarters and garages for cars. The bungalows were grand in design, very British, with paved driveways, and had porches for cars at the front entrances. The GM bungalow, where we lived, was U in shape with a garden in the middle. It had 5 bedrooms with attached bathrooms, drawing room, formal dining room, a grand foyer, and 2 kitchens. The master bedroom suite, on the second floor, had a near 180 degree sweeping view of the Arabian Sea. Quite often, important guests from Bombay or Delhi stayed in the GM bungalow instead of the Guest House. This DCW compound was an address by itself, known to everybody in town. It was just spectacular.

By contrast, the town of Dwarka was a fairly small and crowded place, known mainly for the historic and ancient Dwarkadhish Temple, which is one of the main and highly revered Krishna temples in India, a "tirtha" of the Hindu faith. It is one of the most storied, sacred, and holy temples, that one is expected to visit at least once during one's lifetime. The temple is also the seat of the "Shankaracharya" (Head of the Advaita Vedanta "math" or monastery) of Western India and that raised its religious profile even more.

Almost all business and civic activities in the town of Dwarka revolved around the events happening at the temple. There were some "ashrams" and a few hotels there also, that catered to the tourist and pilgrimage traffic attracted by the temple. Further, since the roads coming into Dwarka were just awful, the main transportation artery was the single "meter-gauge" railway line that passed through Dwarka and terminated at Okha Port, some 15 kilometers away. Daily, two passenger trains pulled by steam engines would pass through Dwarka in either direction and bring visitors and pilgrims. The rest were a few "goods trains" hauling freight to or from Okha Port, which was not very busy at the time.

In this environ, I was enrolled in my school in the colony. Each school day, because of the distance and remoteness of the bungalows, a driver with a car would take me from home and drop me off at school. Later, he would pick me up when the school day finished and bring me home. Sometimes I would ride out with my father in the morning, as he drove himself to his office in the works, but for the return it was usually the driver with a car. My father worked very long hours and he was not always available to bring me back in the early afternoon. I recall the school as being a really fun place. I could play with the other kids and made many friends.

However, it was also quite odd for me. All other kids walked home after school and they could continue to play afterwards with their friends in the colony. But I went home in a car! It was all so conspicuous and in front of all the other kids. I would feel so embarrassed and like a "sissy" of some kind. Some of them wanted to ride in the car for the fun of it, since cars were still quite a rarity in India at the time. However, I was not allowed to offer rides to others. Yet once I was home, I had nobody to play with at the bungalow. In many ways, I thought that my situation was just awful. I would whine and raise all sorts of objections, but my father would not alter "the house rules".

Then came the monsoon season, and the rains were quite heavy that year. On this day, my mother fixed me up with my things and a little plastic raincoat and sent me off. It was a really fun day for us, because it was raining! When school ended, I stepped out and waited at my usual spot near the entrance for the car to pick me up. But the car was a no show. Usually, it was the other way around and the driver would be waiting for me punctually. The teachers were busy with all the other kids, their raincoats, etc. and not worried about me because I was to be picked up as usual. Then, a couple of kids stopped by and said, "Vijay, are you still waiting for the car? You know, the driver may still be tied up in some errand and may come really late today because of these rains and all the flooding going on. Why don't you do what we do? Just walk home. You know the way…" They laughed and took off.

I thought about it for a few moments. Maybe they were just having fun with me, but the suggestion did make sense to me. So, I said to myself, "Why not?" With that, I started walking. I went through the west security gate, but nobody stopped me as they were busy with rain related problems. Then on this lonely road, which went straight to the bungalows, I started to walk on. Yes, there was rain, and strong winds, but I had a raincoat on so I just kept walking onwards. It took me a lot longer than I had imagined. But little did I know what was going on all around me, while I was on this merry walk.

Near hell had broken loose! The driver showed up at the school and I was not there at my spot. He asked the teachers inside the school and they said, "Did you not see him? He is waiting for you." The driver says, "Where? He is nowhere here!" Then the driver goes straight to my father in his office and asks, "Saheb, is Master Vijay here with you? I cannot find him." My Dad calls my Mom at home and asks, "Is Vijay home?" My Mom replies, "No. I am waiting for him. What has happened?"

Now the craziness intensifies. A massive search gets underway for me. Calls, visits, etc. occur to the hospital, police station, colony homes, the plant is searched, the Dwarkadhish Temple is called, etc. All the teachers are traumatized and near tears! So many folks did everything imaginable and more to find Vijay, except for the obvious. Nobody thought to drive on the road to the bungalows! After all, who would be crazy enough to walk in the rain, with local flooding and all, for almost 4 kilometers?

It took me about 1.5 hours to walk home. The hardest part was crossing the main road to Port Okha and dealing with the many flooded patches on the road. It was treacherous, but I was having a ball with it all! I reached home to find my Mom in a near hysterical state. Later, when calm had prevailed and my Dad was home, I thought that I would get the thrashing of my life.

But that did not happen. My Dad looked at me thoughtfully and said, "Today you caused a lot of people immense worry by your actions. You should have at least informed someone... anyone! It was also quite dangerous. Tomorrow, you should apologize to our driver and your teachers."

Then, amazingly he smiled at me and said, "Hey, you know, that was quite brave!" and gave me a hug.

Transfer to Porbandar

In late 1955, my father was transferred from Dwarka Cement Works to the Porbandar Cement Works (PCW). There was an old cement plant already operating there, but a whole new plant was to be built in a totally different location to manufacture "white cement", which was quite a novelty in India at the time and highly in demand all over the country. My father was appointed as GM of both the cement plants.

The old cement works had no "colony" as such and people lived everywhere around the town of Porbandar. It needed a fair amount of attention due its age, and cement production targets had to be met. However, the new cement works was a different story. It was to be situated way out of town, due east in an area which comprised mainly of small farms or fallow land. My father had to deal with the challenges of land acquisition, plant design with architects and engineers located in Bombay, a new colony and all its related facilities, and many more matters. But first we had to move there.

Our relocation to Porbandar from Dwarka became an interesting event. There were no direct roads or railway tracks connecting the two towns, which were only about 100 kilometers apart. There were various seasonal rivers or salt water creeks intruding in the middle. None of them had any bridges of any kind. So, trains clearly were out of the question. If one chose to drive on the awful dirt road, it would soon end at the bank of a river or creek. One would have to cross it by a boat and have a vehicle on the other side available for further travel. This was very difficult to arrange. So, one had little choice but to take a long drive or multiple "meter-gauge" trains from Dwarka, via Jamnagar and Rajkot, a circuitous journey of over 400 kilometers, which could take over a day and night! Perhaps this topic needs some elaboration.

You see, this sort of travel hardship was not unusual in many parts of India in the 1950s. It was a legacy of the decisions made during the British Rule in India, which introduced railways and later motorized vehicles into the land, in the second half of the 19th century. All plans made for railways and roads in India, were intended to mainly support the political, military, and commercial objectives and interests of the British Raj. The needs of the Indian sub-continent and its people were of secondary importance. So, all the major cities of India, which were either ports or centers of political or military control, were connected first by single lane paved roads and "broad-gauge" railway tracks. The secondary cities and towns had soft or partially paved roads and "meter- gauge" railway tracks. The very small towns, with locations of strategic value or "hill stations", had small dirt roads and "narrow-gauge" railway tracks.

However, there were vast swaths of the sub-continent left with no roads or tracks of any kind at all. In these places, one travelled on the centuries' old pathways, by riding on animals (horses, camels, or elephants), or via carts pulled by a variety of beasts of burden. As a consequence, all across India, the transportation network was a patchwork quilt of various types of services, irrational points of inter-connections, and multiple transfers across different modes of travel. The degree of difficulty encountered in any kind of long-distance travel depended very much on where a journey began and where it ended.

All long-distance journeys required careful planning, provisioning of food, water, supplies, etc. and even tents, if overnight stays en route were involved. Safety and security, from wild predatory animals and robbers or looters, were also matters of serious and constant concern. Commercial hotels were a rarity and one could only find a few of them in major cities. Various types of "guest houses", whether private or government run, were sparsely distributed and typically not available to the general public. Most of the "Serai's", (large secure courtyards offering hospitality, supplies, and livery services for travellers) developed over centuries of time for the general public on the main pathways of travel across India, were in quite a decrepit state. Only folks with no other alternative would avail of them. In these conditions, by contrast, we were quite fortunate.

Our journey to Porbandar began on the early morning train from Dwarka. A large crowd of over 100 people showed up at the railway station to see "Yajnik Saheb" off! All our household goods had been shipped off separately by train on the previous day, so it was just Mom, Dad and me, travelling on the train that day with our basic luggage. My older brothers, Kashyap and Ajay, were away already attending the Rajkumar College, in Rajkot. We were booked in a First-Class compartment, with four berths and an attached toilet, which we had all to ourselves.

In those days, the First Class "bogey" (*a railway carriage*) in India did not have a corridor inside with entrances at each end of it, as they do today. In the old design, each compartment had its own doors, directly in and out of the bogey. It was a highly convenient layout, but not very secure or efficient. Also, the bogeys were not inter-connected, as they are on modern trains today. To move from one compartment or bogey to another, one had to wait for the train to stop at a station, get down from it on to the platform, walk over to another, and re-board.

Well, my parents were feted, garlanded, and a small puja was performed by a brahmin from the Dwarkadhish Temple, right on the platform. Then, the "Train Guard" asked my Dad for permission to depart and we steamed out of the Dwarka station. It felt like a royal sendoff! I recall my Mom being teary eyed at having to leave Dwarka.

The train travelled on slowly, at 20 to 30 km/hour, with many stops. We passed Jamnagar and arrived in Rajkot around 1pm or so, and there we disembarked. My father had to pick up a brand new imported Willys Jeep in Rajkot. Our plan was to do that, and then drive the rest of the way, about 180 kilometers or so, to Porbandar. There was no time to visit Kashyap and Ajay at RKC. The manager from Kathiawad Motors in Rajkot (the only Willys Jeep dealership in all of Saurashtra at the time I think) came to pick us up at the station. Dad signed the paperwork and we set off on the drive.

The brand-new Jeep was totally open! The canvas back cover and doors had been shipped off separately to Porbandar. So, the three of us were in this open Jeep, with the wind lashing at us, throughout our cold 5 hour or so drive to Porbandar. Dad drove in right seat, I sat in the middle near the gear shaft, and Mom was on the left side. I recall it as being a very cold and dusty drive, with half of it being in the dark. We reached our destination very late, and I was hustled off to bed promptly.

But there lay another surprise for me, which I did not discover until the next morning.

Villas & Bungalows

I woke up in the morning to an amazing sight. The prior night, after a long, dusty, windy, and freezing drive, I was just exhausted and had promptly fallen asleep when I was put to bed. But on this new day, it was just "wow!" I could not fathom what my eyes were seeing!

There were some 12 or so villas built right smack on the beach in Porbandar, literally a stone's throw from the Arabian Sea. You could just walk down the backyard to the beach which was protected by a long breakwater off in the distance. We were housed temporarily in Villa # 4, a beautiful and comfortable building. As one looked out west towards the ocean, to the left past Villa # 1, there was a gorgeous and pristine beach that seemed to go on forever. One also had a clear view of the "Porbandar Palace", the residence of HH (His Highness) Natwarsinhji, then Maharaja of Porbandar. The grounds of the Palace, which looked like the Versailles Palace near Paris, were very ornate and just flowed magically into the beach. It was just spectacular. But to appreciate this truly, perhaps a brief recap of recent history of India is in order.

Post 1947, after independence from the British Rule, the heads of all the "Princely States" in India, an old patchwork quilt of some 550 or so large and small States, had retained many special privileges. These were granted to them by the "Accession Agreements" with the new Government of India, to form a federal union, named officially as the "Republic of India". In essence, they handed over their States to create a large unified modern country in the form of an elected parliamentary democracy.

The structure of this newly minted Republic was based on the British model. It came to life on January 26th, 1950, and comprised of a Constitution to guarantee the fundamental rights of all citizens, an independent Judiciary, and elected State & Federal legislatures. The political party with a majority or "control" of the legislatures was invited by a titular President or a State Governor, to form ruling Governments. All political power was vested in these governments at the State and Federal level. This power gave them control over all the civil and administrative services, military and police, taxation, and treasury. It was a massive change in every manner all across India and it took a measure of time to secure its foothold in the minds of its people and all governing institutions.

But what about the Princely States and their royal families? In return for their contributions and relinquishing political power, they were given many things. Well, for one, they were awarded "Privy Purses", which were annual tax-free grants from the Government of India, in perpetuity with inheritance rights. They retained all their "Royal Titles" by law, and ownership of most of their personal real estate and other chattel properties. So, even without political power, the royal families of these Princely States retained a vast amount of economic and social power. Also, because of their Titles, in the minds of their former "subjects" or local folks, they were still thought of as rulers or kings.

In most places, the royal families were highly revered and accorded immense respect by everybody due to their status and continuing patronage of various local causes, institutions, arts, and charities. In general, the royal family members were well educated, in many cases in England, well-traveled, and highly connected with other royal families through various marital and other relationships. Their world is a fascinating subject by itself and a simple summary of their ways and lifestyles just does not do it full justice here in a short story. But it is a subject rich in Indian history, traditions, events, and is worth exploring in depth.

As I had been told all these things by my parents, I always looked at the Porbandar Palace in sheer wonder. I wanted to go inside and have a look, but that was not an easy thing to achieve. I would have to wait a bit longer. However, in the proximity of the Palace our life in the Villa # 4 was wonderful during the year or so that we stayed there. I was enrolled in the elementary school at Navyug Vidyalay, a local school with Gujarati as the medium of instruction.

As a result, over time, my spoken Gujarati morphed from the pure Sanskritized Devanagari Gujarati spoken at home, into the Kathiawadi Gujarati spoken at school and all around us in Porbandar. This latter version of the language is a rich world unto itself as well. Its peculiar idioms, literature, expressions, accent, and a "sing song" tonal quality make it a charming, affectionate and humorous dialect of Gujarati. In those years, whenever we travelled to Ahmedabad or Petlad, for either a holiday or a family function of some sort, everybody would actively engage me in conversations. They just loved my spoken Kathiawadi Gujarati and I would make everybody laugh constantly with it. At the time, I never quite understood why. But later on, after joining Rajkumar College in Rajkot, and being forced to learn and switch to English, my natural usage of this lovely dialect of Gujarati sadly just faded away.

At the Villa, we had memorable visits from Ramankaka, my father's cousin, who would occasionally show up from Rajkot to spend a few days with us. Also, Kiritbhai, my eldest cousin, came once during his Gujarat University holidays. I recall Pappaji teaching him to drive in the Jeep. He somehow managed successfully to get into a "fender bender" during a lesson and everybody used to tease him about it.

Our temporary stay at the Villa came to an end in about a year or so and we moved to the ACC bungalows compound, a short distance away. This compound was similar to what we had in Dwarka. There were three lovely bungalows built in grand British designs. One was for the GM, the second for the AGM, and the third was a Guest House. The shared compound had lovely gardens, driveways to the entrance gates, garages, and various staff quarters. The bungalows were all very spacious and beautifully appointed. We stayed there for about 5 years or so. In this time, there were countless visitors, amazing parties, and many memorable events.

The AGM bungalow held an interesting past for us, as I found out. When my father got married to my mother in 1940, he was the AGM of the Porbandar Cement Works, and actually living in that same bungalow! He took a week off from work and went away to Ahmedabad for his wedding. It was held in Petlad, near Anand, where my mother's family lived. There was no such thing as a "honeymoon" in the customs of India at the time, so a wedding did not require more than a few days' worth of time at most. Well, when he returned, he was received by a huge crowd of well-wishers at the Porbandar railway station. They had a brahmin priest, marigold garlands, sweets, and all manner of things to welcome him and his new bride. However, he disembarked from the train all alone. There was no bride! Utterly surprised, he explained to everybody that my mother had to stay behind for a few days to attend to some things and would come later. Not only was everybody disappointed, but many were left wondering if he had actually gotten married at all!

So, a couple of weeks later, when my mother arrived, my father had to throw a party at the AGM bungalow on that very day to convince everybody and allow them to celebrate as they had planned earlier. Mom was very tired after all the hectic activities of the wedding and its aftermath at her home. She was raised in dire poverty in Petlad, as her father had died suddenly at a very young age. The family, comprised of a mother and seven children, was left with meager means of financial support and this made for some very hard times. She used to tell me that there were days when there was not enough food for everyone to eat at dinner. So, the younger kids were fed, while she and her mother would drink a glass of water and go to sleep. As the oldest single daughter, my mother had to carry the burden of running the household and raising all her younger siblings. To do this, she was pulled out of school in the 8th grade and all marital prospects were also deferred for her. When she married my father, she was 21, which was considered quite old for a girl at that time. She had not left Petlad in years and knew very little about the world outside, or its new and modern ways.

So, arriving in Porbandar by train in First Class, being driven in a car to the AGM bungalow, and getting immediately immersed into a celebration party with all these strange people and surroundings, she was left totally bewildered! After a while, she said to my father, "Chalo, apde gher jaiye..." *(Come, let's go home now.)* Pappaji replied, "Tu gher chhu. Aa apdu ghur chhe." (*You are at home. This is our home.*) She was shocked out of her wits at learning this! For her, it was a Cinderella story coming true. All her life, when referring to my father, she would tell others, "Aa to mara Mahadev chhe." (*He is my Mahadev, meaning Lord Shiva.*)

It is truly amazing that this lovely lady, who grew up with every imaginable strike against her, and little formal education, would one day play hostess to Pandit Jawaharlal Nehru, and later his daughter, Indira Gandhi, when both of them were respectively the Prime Minister of India.

At the GM Bungalow, when I was done with school, I had little to do and nobody to play with. In those days, there was no television in India and radio broadcasts consisted mainly of news and some music programs. We would listen to the Vividh Bharati music programs, but everybody loved the weekly broadcast of Binaca Geetmala on Radio Ceylon, because of its wonderfully humorous host, Amin Sayani. But the time of day that I really looked forward to was the evening. This is when we would go to the Sports Club nearly every day. My father was a great athlete and loved to swim, play cricket and tennis. On many occasions, when he played tennis, I would be assigned as the "ball boy", which was great fun for me. My love for this game started here. My parents also played a lot of Contract Bridge with others at the Club and participated in tournaments. Whenever Kashyap and Ajay were home from Rajkumar College, Rajkot, I would get to play table tennis or billiards with them also. They were both good athletes and won many tournaments in various sports at the Club.

One afternoon, I was loafing around aimlessly behind the bungalow and was spotted by Ila, the daughter of our driver, who lived in the staff quarters with her family. She was much older than me. She was sweet, jovial, and also quite athletic as I found out. She asked me, "Vijaybhai, shu karo chho?" (*Vijaybhai, what are you doing?*) I told her that I was doing nothing and was just bored. So, she said brightly, "Cycle shikhvi chhe?" (*Want to learn to ride a bicycle?*) I replied, "Ila, mari pase cycle nathi..." (*Ila, I don't have a cycle.*) Then she went, "Mari pase chhe." (*I have one.*) I was quite surprised when she brought forth her father's bike!

31

In those days in India, bicycles were the main mode of local transportation for a lot of people and even small families. They were sturdy, but heavy and expensive. Each bicycle had a large soft seat with springs in it for the main rider. The front and rear wheels had mudguards. The chain drive was a single gear design with a metallic chain guard as well. All controls for the front and rear brakes were with mechanical rods and linkages. There was a flat stand on top of the rear wheel mudguard for carrying things or sitting on and sometimes a basket above the front wheel mudguard as well.

It had a reflector tail light and a headlight in front of the handle bars, powered by a small spring-loaded generator. At night, with a release, the spindle wheel on top of the generator made contact with the side of the rear tire. As one rode the bike, the rear tire powered the generator which in turn powered the headlight. It was a working design, but one had to be moving to get any light! At times the crossbar of the frame also had a little seat for a child to sit on and the handle bars always had a little mechanical bell on it. While there was also a version designed for women, with a curved frame crossbar, all bicycles came in one size … "Adult"!

I stood next to Ila's bicycle and was horrified to see that the seat was level with my eyes. I asked her, "Ane hun kevi reete chalavu? Bahu moti chhe." (*How can I ride this? It is too big for me.*) She replied, "Arrey, ama kayi nathi. Hun tamane shikhvadish..." (*Arrey, there is nothing to this. I will teach you how to ride it.*) So, my lessons with Ila began.

Every day in the afternoon, Ila would teach me to ride for an hour or so. The first step was to kick off, stand up on the lower pedal of the cycle, and just balance it, till it came to a stop. She ran behind me to help me learn to balance it and to avoid the usual falls. After I mastered this, I was allowed to kick off repeatedly and continue for longer distances. Then came the turns, to the left and right, also on a single kick off. Then she taught me to go, stand up on to the chain guard and mount the seat. Then finally, after mounting the seat, to push both the pedals near the top of their respective arcs to provide little bursts of power to keep the bike going. To dismount, I was taught to just ride a pedal down to the bottom of its arc. It was just amazing. Ila taught me to ride a full adult bike without hurting myself seriously.

With this newly acquired skill, and later when we found and borrowed a lady's bike for her, we went on many bike rides togther. However, in due course, Ila got married and moved away. I did see her a few times after that, but sadly, with passage of time, I lost contact with her.

To this day, whenever I ride a bike, I think of sweet Ila and the gift that she gave me.

The New Dodge & An Airport Visit

It was a very exciting morning. Pappaji had just informed me at breakfast that we were going to receive a brand-new car that day, a 1957 model Dodge! The car was purchased and imported from the USA by the ACC Head Office in Bombay and was destined for use at the Porbandar Cement Works for both the old and the new cement plants.

At the time, I used to be fascinated by American cars and had a large collection of photos I had cut out from various magazines. I used to look at them in total wonder. The cars were huge in size, spacious, and very ornate with tail fins and lots of chrome plating. I used to find their dashboards immensely fascinating. I would examine all the gauges, knobs, and controls in great detail in the photos.

Also, I was just amazed that they had radios in them! This was a very big deal for me. The radios in most homes at the time were all huge in size, very much like a large ornate box, and had vacuum tubes in them. Transistor based radios had not arrived in India as yet. They had medium wave, short wave, and long wave frequency bands and it took a few minutes for them to warm up before any sound came out. The manual tuning dials were also quite large and in varied designs. Many were circular, but some were horizontal as well, depending upon the manufacturer and model. Brand names like Marconi, Phillips, and Grundig were quite popular and their radios were almost like a piece of furniture in the family or living room. They all needed long external antennas to pick up a signal and tuning them to a particular radio station required some skill. It is from this era that the expression "London looking, but Tokyo tuning..." originates. It was a sly way to refer to somebody who was cross-eyed! So, a radio inside a car was a very big thing indeed. How novel to listen to a radio while driving around in a car! I could not wait to experience it.

You may be wondering why were cars imported from places so far away? Well, this was due to the fact that in India at that time, there was no domestic manufacture of cars. After Independence, the Government of India had licensed some "joint ventures", such as with Fiat in Italy, Mercedes Benz in Germany, and some British companies for manufacture of cars and trucks in India. But these actions had yet to yield results of any significance, so a lot of motorized vehicles were still imported from Europe and the USA. Our new Dodge arrived in Bombay by ship from the USA and then it was transported on a train, in a freight bogey, to the Porbandar railway station. It was to be received in the station freight yard.

In response to a tantrum on my part, my father relented and allowed me to miss school and accompany him to the railway station to take delivery of the Dodge. I was in awe of what I witnessed. A "shunting" steam engine huffed and puffed and slowly pushed the freight bogey up against a long sloping delivery ramp.

In those days, only steam locomotives were available to provide power to railways in India. They were huge. They had a water tank and a coal car attached to them. They came in two basic flavors. One was for pulling trains, and the other was for local use in a railway station yard. The latter assembled or separated various types of bogeys for different purposes locally within a station yard. These yards could be enormous, depending upon the importance of the station. Porbandar was not only a major station, but also a terminus with a sea port nearby, so it was a very busy place and a center of major commerce.

After some official ceremony, which I did not understand, the bogey was positioned and finally opened. I got my first glimpse of the Dodge and was excited beyond belief. They used winches and pulleys with steel wires to pull the car out of the bogey and down two slides for tires on each side and then down the sloping ramp. Then came my real disappointment.

I thought that we would just drive the Dodge home, but that was not so at all. The car could not be driven. It needed all sorts of onsite maintenance before anything could be done. It needed petrol, various oils, proper tire inflation, and various electrical and mechanical things done to it before it could be even started up. All this would take the trained mechanics in attendance more than a day. My Dad said, "Well, there she is!" I consoled myself in being allowed to touch it all over and sit in it for a while, but that was it.

A day later, the Dodge arrived at our bungalow. She was so shapely in form with fins, black in color with light grey leather interior, and riding in it felt like one was riding on water! All my tantrums were forgotten and I just fell in love with her. On all our long drives in it, I would stand off the rear seat, clutching the back of the front bench seat, watching the driver and the road ahead for hours on end without tiring. My parents always joked about this peculiar behavior of mine. We had some very memorable times with this car over the years.

Then, this day when I had just returned from school, my Mom said, "Vijay, get ready quickly. The Dodge is almost here and we have to go to the aerodrome immediately."

I asked, "Why?"

She replied, "Pappaji is returning from Bombay on a flight." I was really surprised.

I went, "A flight? You mean by an aeroplane? Where? How? We don't have any aeroplanes!" It took a while for my Mom to explain to me what was going on in the face of my relentless questions. It became a memorable afternoon.

While I knew about them, I had never seen an aeroplane in my life. At the time, Indian Airlines, a Government of India enterprise, had started a new passenger service from Bombay to Porbandar. There was a single roundtrip flight from Bombay to Porbandar, only on three days of the week in the late afternoon, I think. The Porbandar aerodrome was a small little airfield, with a single paved short runway that had a windsock at one end of it. The taxiways and apron were just areas cleared of trees and shrubs, with painted stone markers placed on rolled but unpaved dirt. There was just one tiny building that housed the control tower and a lounge to handle passengers and baggage. I was fascinated by all this because it was so different from a railway station.

There were few people there and I ran around in excitement all over the place asking a million questions of my Mom, who was steadily tiring of it all. Just then, an Indian Airlines official came to her rescue.

He asked cheerily, "Hello, Mrs. Yajnik. Is this your son, Vijay?"

My Mom said, "Yes. As you can see, he is terribly excited and full of questions."

Then he asked me, "Would you like to go to the control tower? Want to talk with the pilot of the aeroplane that your father is flying on?" Just bursting with excitement, I replied, "Ohhh, yes!" My Mom smiled in relief, as I was taken to the control tower located on the second floor. What happened next was beyond my imagination.

I was seated next to the radio operator. He called the pilot of the flight which was still 20 minutes or so away. He said, "This is the Porbandar Tower. Do you read me?"

An answer came back, "Roger, Porbandar."

Then he told me to ask my question, and in pure imitation, I said into the microphone, "This is Vijay. Is my father, Mr. Yajnik, on the aeroplane with you?"

After a few moments, back came an answer, "Affirmative. Mr. Yajnik is onboard this flight. Over."

Then I blurted out, "Can I talk to him?"

Again, after a few long moments and various shuffling sounds, I hear, "Yajnik speaking. Is that you, Vijay?"

I breathlessly replied, "Yes, Pappaji, it is me!" Then, my father said, "It is nice to hear your voice, but you should not be talking like this on this radio. Now, thank everybody there. I will see you soon."

Needless to say, I promptly forgot to thank anybody, and raced downstairs to tell my Mom what had just transpired!

In a few minutes, we went outside and watched the Dakota DC-3 aeroplane approach in descent and land on the runway. It had twin engines with propellers. Beneath it there were two huge wheels and a small baby wheel below its tail. On the ground, the aeroplane was sloping at a steep angle with its nose pointing towards the sky. Its engines made a deafening roar, and as it came to the apron it kicked up an incredible storm of dust and wind which almost blew me off my feet.

Pappaji emerged from it along with other passengers who all seemed to know each other. Everybody seemed to be aware of and much amused by my antics.

My father thanked everybody at the airport for their sweet gesture and later gently admonished me to not repeat such behavior in the future.

Holidays in Petlad

Our holidays in some summers in Petlad were quite memorable because our extended family usually went there "en masse". They were also a time of some trepidation for me. On the one hand, it felt very exciting because it was so different, but on the other, it felt like we were off camping in the boonies.

The town of Petlad, where I was born, is in the heart of the Kheda District of Gujarat, an area known for its good and fertile soil. Its original and ancient name was Prahladpuri. But somehow this name got morphed at first into Petladpur and then into just Petlad. Farming and related work was the main economic activity around town. But it also had an illustrious and highly educated Nagar Brahmin community residing in it, a college for higher education post matriculation, a large civic library, and many lovely Hindu temples. It also had a great bazaar for handicraft products and a large marketplace for various goods going to and from the port at Khambhat on the Arabian Sea.

My mother's and my paternal grandparents' families were from Petlad also, so we had extensive ties to various extended families everywhere in town. My grandfather, affectionately called Sakarlalkaka, had an old but lovely house there that he had inherited from his Dhanlakshmimashi *(better known as 'Moghimashi')*. She had become widowed at a young age and had no children. So, my great-grandfather, Jhaverilaldada had suggested that she legally adopt Sakarlalkaka, his middle son, to take care of her. She did, but in her family, folks also wanted Sakarlalkaka to change his last name from Yajnik to their's. He refused to do so and there was a huge fracas about it. He felt that his father had educated him through law college, etc. and it would not be right for him to give up his family name. Regardless, he took care of her for her entire life. Jhaverilaldada was quite interesting as well. He was a teacher who had worked in many places in his career. Among them, he had taught at the Alfred High School in Rajkot. Actually, one of his students had been a boy named Mohandas K. Gandhi, who later went on to become Mahatma Gandhiji, father of the new idependent India.

The house was in the "Moti Brahmpole" (*a large, old world style, street where brahmins lived*). In the old and rural Indian towns, there were all sorts of "poles" (*streets*) everywhere, of many flavors, for various caste-based communities. A "pole" was like a secure street, with controlled access and exit points, within an area of the town. It had two to three story houses on both sides. They all shared either common walls or walls that touched each other. Each house had a heavy and highly secure main entrance door with steps leading up to it a few feet above the street level. The upper stories had balconies that overlooked the street and everything going on in it. Once you entered a house through this main door, you typically faced a whole another world.

All these "pole houses" had a fairly standard design. While there were many variants built also, in general, they were all similar from a functional and structural standpoint. From the entrance door, you came into a large room called the "khadaki". It would have seating furniture, a swing, stairs to go to higher levels in the "medi" with the balconies above, and a toilet for the comfort of all visitors. This is where most guests were received and seated. Past this room, one entered an inner open courtyard, called the "chawk". It was open to the skies, surrounded on all sides by the multi-storied house and a protected hallway. Around this courtyard were the bathrooms, water stations, various living and other rooms, the "mandir" (*temple*), and obviously many more swings. But here was the most fascinating part.

The entire courtyard had a false floor! Below the courtyard floor, there was a massive water storage tank! Rainwater from the roof during the monsoon season was guttered or piped into it to fill it. It also had in a corner a three-foot-wide opening like a well, with a waist high wall around it and an ornate metallic cover on it. The water tank was called the "tanku" (*literally, a tank*) One could draw water from it using a rope and large brass or copper jugs designed with a neck on them for the rope. Due to lack of any sunlight, nothing could live or grow in this tank.

Beyond the courtyard, was a room called "parasal" and it usually had the kitchen attached to it. Beyond this was the "orado", (*a large inner room*) and finally the "vado" (*an open shed like area*) which was used for storage of grains, hay, coal, wood, and sometimes to house domesticated animals. Furthermore, the house also had a large basement below its rear wing for storing all sorts of food, vessels and things. The overall construction materials used, the thickness of the walls, and the natural ventilation provided by the courtyard, created an environment which was shaded and cool in the hot summers and warm for the relatively mild winters. By any measure, this ancient design was simply brilliant for India and its climate.

Well, except for one, a measure called Vijay. After all the modern comforts of the ACC bungalows, I used to find everything in Petlad just appalling. This lovely Petlad house used to totally freak me out! Initially, there was no electricity, so we used oil and kerosene lamps. After it was electrified, things got better, but not by much. The floor of most rooms had a paste of mud and "chhaan" (*dried cow dung*) applied to it almost weekly. It was always fresh, had antiseptic qualities, and got rid of all kinds of insects and such. But it had a peculiar odor. I could never get used to it.

Oh, and the toilets! They were in fact septic tanks, but with a difference. You actually squatted on "two tile footprints" atop a 30-foot hole in the ground below you. I was just terrified of it! I thought that either something sinister was going to crawl out of it and bite my privates, or that I would just fall into that hell hole! So, I would throw all sorts of tantrums and refuse to use them. Many times, my mother would just send me off with a "lota" *(a small jug)* of water to the nearby open fields to do my business.

Everything about Petlad was the "old world" of India. At the railway station, there was no motorized transport. We would hire several "ghoda gaadi" (*a horse and buggy*) to go to the house with all our luggage. At the entrance door, it was always a major event to get the huge rusty locks opened. Since there was no public sewage system at the time, the street was always had the stinking effluent from all the houses. One had to unload bags with great care and watch one's step. Once inside the house, it would take a whole day of cleaning everything just to make it livable, and a few more to make it comfortable. There was no telephone or radio. Forget TV, because it had not arrived in India as yet. Shortly after our arrival, the visitations would begin. All sorts of people ranging from relatives, friends, neighbors, etc. would call in to welcome us. An often-used refrain, which I always detested, went something like, "Aa, Vijay chhe?" (*Is this Vijay?*). "Arrey, meh to tane nago joyelo...!" (*Arrey, I have seen you naked*!). I guess this expression was a proxy for saying that they had seen me as a little baby, but I could never get used to it.

The house was large and full of all sorts of interesting and peculiar things from times gone by. I would spend my time exploring all the rooms slowly and discover many fascinating things. There were paintings and old photos from the days of my great-grandfather. I found small glass vials containing long rice grains with shlokas (*poetic stanzas in Sanskrit*) from the Geeta carved on them. I discovered small statuettes made of carved sandalwood which were still quite fragrant. There were some very old pieces of furniture which were mind boggling in their design.

I remember one large wooden, waist high, storage chest in particular. It was called an "iskotero". It was wooden and heavy with two large wheels, but also had wide metallic bands around it and a great big tough lid. Nobody knew how to open it! There were no discernable locks, keyholes, or latches anywhere on it. It took us days that one summer to finally find an old locksmith who came to the house to help us open it. He told us that he used to make them in his working years. In a very methodical manner, he went about finding all sorts of hidden and movable parts, to open various hidden compartments with hidden rods and links, which eventually led to opening the lid. Everybody was excited when he finally got it open and there was a huge expectation of finding some sort of lost treasure in it. But alas, it just had a few old cooking utensils. Then, as a surprise, he opened a few more compartments in the wall of the chest from the inside, and there we discovered some items of gold and silver, and some jewelry as well.

Life in Petlad during those summers could be enjoyable in many ways. The fruits and vegetables one found in the Chavadi Bazaar were so fresh and tasty. The air always seemed clean and the water was soft and sweet. Sakarlalkaka would dispatch me nearly every afternoon, in the peak of the heat, to go to the local post office on foot and mail his endless postcards. All food was cooked on open fires with coal or "chhaan" patties and the resultant meals were so yummy and tasty. These were flavors that one could not find in the cities of modernizing India.

The afternoons were somewhat lonely and boring for me. Sometimes I would go outside the front door, sit near the steps, and try to chat or play with other kids, if they were around. One day, I went to sit outside with a fresh ripe banana in my hand. I was looking around in a distracted manner and did not spy one of the local cows, wandering around the street, taking a direct aim for my banana. She slowly walked up, took the whole banana out of my hand, swiftly ate it, and gave me a lick of thanks on my hand! I shrieked in fear and ran inside. It took a while, and another banana from my mother, to console me.

Sometimes I would get into fights with my cousin Shridevi (Motiben or Baby or Shri). She was Munikaka's daughter and was 10 months older than me. In our family, like in most Nagar Brahmin families, there was a tradition that a person who was younger in age always served the needs of those who were older. This would span things like servng water or tea, fetching or putting away things, doing errands, and so forth. However, in matters of food or choosing things, it was the opposite. The youngest always went first.

Shri would use this tradition to her advantage and order me around for the sheer fun of it! One day, I had had enough of this, so I grabbed her and pinched her hard on her hand and waist. She let out a loud yelp and my father heard it. He came around and saw that Shri had tears in her eyes. When he heard from her about what I had just done, he gave me a sound walloping right there! Shortly, I began to cry out of pain.

Then, Pappaji sat me up and said sternly to me, "We never raise our hand or hurt a girl. We never do that. Do you understand?

I nodded.

"Good. Never forget it. Now, go wash your face."

This episode was soon forgotten. Shri and I resumed our usual mischief. But I never forgot that lesson my entire life. If I was really angry with somebody, who was a girl, I would do something entirely different. I learnt that also from another unusual event in Petlad.

One evening, Sakarlalkaka and Munikaka got into a debate about something. They were sitting on two separate swings near the "chawk" facing each other. What started out as a discussion with different points of view about something, soon deteriorated into a heated argument between father and son. It then morphed further into an angry shouting match. Even that did not pacify their anger. So, both of them then proceeded to shout at each other and slap their own faces! One would not actually hurt the other, so they shouted at the other and slapped themselves! To me, it was like a Charlie Chaplin or a Three Stooges movie, except that it was now getting totally out of hand. My father shortly intervened and put a stop to all of it. He calmed them both down and ended the debate. However, to me it seemed like an amazing way to handle extreme anger. I confess to having done it myself a couple of times.

However, such episodes aside, in the evening, after all the chores were done, time was spent in reading, visits, and conversations. I enjoyed these hours the most, because they were full of informative discussions and learning. Topics ranged widely from politics and current events, to science, poetry, literature, philosophy, history, religion, and so on. Everybody, including the ladies, most of whom were highly educated, would participate animatedly. Everyone would answer my endless questions with great patience. I would often hear, "Damayanti, aa taro chhokero bahu bole chhe." (*Damayanti, this boy of yours talks a lot.*) My mother generally sighed and agreed, but then always gave me a hug.

When the holidays in Petlad ended, it would be a sad time. The whole arrival process would be reversed and there were many "goodbyes" to be said.

We would leave Petlad and take wonderful memories along with us.

Sakarlalkaka Goes to Petlad

(As told to me by Pappaji)

"It was a heated conversation, which had an explosive end." Pappaji said.

I was sitting with him on the swing in the family room in Nikunj, our bungalow in Ahmedabad. Somehow, this morning over tea, our conversation had taken a turn towards discussing the temperaments of various Yajniks, past and present. The focus of the moment was on Sakarlalkaka, Pappaji's father, and my grandfather.

"So, what happened?" I asked, filled with curiosity.

"Well, it began as a simple discussion about something he wanted to do in Petlad. It was nothing urgent in nature, so I suggested that it could wait till we all went there for the summer holidays. But he misread me completely. He felt that I was implying that he was incapable of undertaking this trip by himself. It all went downhill from there."

Sakarlalkaka said, "So, all my sons, Surendra, you, and Muni, you all think that I am too old, infirm, and cannot travel by myself anywhere anymore. Not even to Petlad!"

"Not at all, Kaka." Pappaji responded in a gentle manner. "We all know that you can do anything that you set your mind upon. But you must think this trip through very carefully."

"What is there to think about? I will go to Petlad, as I have done for many years, and return after my business there is finished. There is no problem at all." Kaka stated.

"But Kaka, please consider this. Who will assist you, if there is a need? In Petlad, where will you stay? You know, the house is closed. Where will you get your meals, cooked by a brahmin, that you always insist upon? How will you manage the daily transport that we arrange for you when we are with you? And what will happen, God forbid, if there is a health emergency of some sort? Who will run to assist you? These are quite relevant and serious concerns for all of us."

"Nonsense. This is all meaningless. I am done arguing with all of you and your attempts to control me. Nobody will ever control me or my life. I am leaving right now. There is a train in an hour from the Maninagar station. I will be on it. NOBODY IS GOING TO STOP ME!"

Well, as Pappaji explained to me, Sakarlalkaka was a bright, articulate, rational, knowledgeable, and gifted jurist with a prodigious memory. He was tall, athletic in his build, nearly Caucasian fair in his complexion, and strangely had little streaks of blonde color in his hair. He had lived a hard life, but had accomplished amazing things including being appointed a Judge in the Civil Courts of British India. All this was from a start with a meager background and built upon sheer hard work and merit. He had great street savvy and suffered no fools.

He was highly conservative in his values, a devout Hindu Nagar Brahmin, and quite religious in his habits. He hated the British, was fiercely independent in his thinking, and most of all, incredibly stubborn. But he was driven, had a bias for action, and was somewhat of a pit bull in achieving results. In short, a tough but lovable man, who could be difficult beyond belief. Actually, Pappaji and I agreed that many of these traits had generally permeated our family in some measure all around and in all the generations!

In short order, Sakarlalkaka stormed off to the Maninagar station. He put on his coat over his shirt and dhoti, grabbed his "topi" (*a cap*), his walking stick, his purse, and simply set off on foot. Everybody in Nautam Nivas (Kaka's home) stood by watching all this in dazed state. What should be done now? Nobody had any answers.

Then, Pappaji said, "Well, I think we should let him do what he wishes. But just to be safe, I will follow him at a safe distance, out of his sight. If there is any trouble, at least I will be there to assist him." So, he left very quickly as well, in hot pursuit of Sakarlalkaka.

While Kaka was certainly showing signs of aging, he was still very much in control of his faculties. He walked to the Maninagar railway station, bought a ticket for himself on the next train, and went to the platform to await it. My father followed closely behind him, but nearly out of sight at all times. The train arrived, and Kaka boarded it. Pappaji boarded it also, but still out of his sight.

Now, in those days, in order to get to Petlad from Maninagar, one had to change trains at the Anand Junction Station. This involved crossing the railway tracks to get to the opposite platform. Since there were no overhead crossing bridges at the time, one had to walk to end of a platform, down a sloping ramp to the ground, and then cross the actual tracks at a designated crossing. It was designed with embedded railway ties to facilitate the crossing for not just the passengers, but also the luggage carts, etc. Once on the opposite side, one walked up the sloping ramp and onto the opposite platform. It took some effort, but it was quite functional and generally safe.

Well, that is, as long as there were no trains going through the station. But in overcrowded India, even then, there was always train traffic in both directions at all times, often with few visible or discernable early warnings. This is where things got interesting at the Anand Station on this day.

Kaka started to cross the double tracks. As he was part way across the first set of tracks, loud cries rang out from the platforms, "Dada, train ave chhe!" (*Dada, a train is coming!*). Sure enough, a goods (*freight*) train was coming on the next set of tracks. He stood between the two sets of tracks wondering what to do. Should he go back? But just then, another train appeared on the tracks that he had just crossed! Now, he really did not know which way to go. Going either forward, or backward, there were approaching trains on both sets of tracks. He was standing between them and feeling quite confused, amid all the crazy screaming going on all around him. My father saw all this, and quickly jumped in from the platform and stood next to him.

"Kaka, I am here. It is alright." Pappaji said.

"Arrey, Viru! Tu kyan thi?" (*Arrey, Viru, where have you come from?*)

"Kaka, I have been with you all along. I was just out of your sight. But let's not talk about that now. My left arm is already around this tall sign pole. Please let me put my right arm around your shoulders. I will lock my hands, but just hold on with me. There will be intense winds, dust, and flying debris, so let's close our eyes and protect them by keeping our heads down. We will just stand here, till the trains pass. Nothing should happen to us in between these tracks."

The thundering trains, with their huge puffing and hissing steam locomotives and screaming whistles, passed with twin massive and long roars. Between the tracks, the ground shook and they kicked up quite a windstorm with shockwaves and turbulance, which caused all sorts of stones and debris to fly turning them into small projectiles. A few hit Pappaji on his bald head and he bled a little. But they were both generally okay. Then, my father escorted Kaka slowly to the opposite platform. There were loud cheers from folks all around the platforms, joyous at an averted potential tragedy.

Kaka now became reflective and quiet. He sat down on a bench on the platform and said nothing to Pappaji. My father was silent as well. Both father and son said nothing to each other at all for a long time. There were no comments, statements, or even any suggestions. Just plain old silence. Eventually, Kaka spoke.

"Viru, mari moti bhool thai. Mane maaf kar." (*Viru, I made a big mistake. Please forgive me.*)

"Have mare Petlad nathi javu. Chal, gher jayiye." (*Now, I don't want to go to Petlad. Come, let's go home.*)

Pappaji brought Kaka home safely on the next train. There were no further discussions about this whole episode. There were no retributions, "I told you so" comments, or "put downs" of any kind from anybody.

There was just a nice "arati" *(a ritual prayer)* at the mandir in Nautam Nivas in the evening, a delicious meal of Kaka's favorite "khichadi", and lots of jovial laughter all around about many things. Kaka was full of smiles also.

Then, Pappaji said to me, "That was the way the Yajniks approached and dealt with events in their lives at the time. If you give it some thought, you may discover interesting things in it for yourself."

Ahmedabad Tales

The Yajnik Bungalows

We got off the train at the Maninagar station in Ahmedabad and hailed a "ghoda gaadi" (*a horse and buggy*) to take us to Nautam Nivas, the bungalow built by my grandfather, Sakarlalkaka. It was about 1 kilometer away and now home to Motakaka, my father's older brother. It was just my mother, father, and I, and we had our basic luggage, which fit in it nicely. When we reached there, the driver asked for what would amount to double the normal fare. My father was surprised, and asked him, "Mari pase thi atla vadhare paisa kem le chhe?" (*Why are you asking for so much more money from me?*)

Without missing a beat, and with a smile on his face, the driver said, "Saheb, tamari pase thi na layiye, to koni pase thi layiye?" (*Saheb, if we do not take it from you, then who do we take it from?*)

Pappaji was impressed by this answer, so he laughed and paid him the cash. Then he turned to us and said, "Yes, I can already tell. We are in Ahmedabad."

"But why did you pay him in full when he was clearly overcharging us? Also, you did the same thing with the coolies (*porters*) in the station!" I asked him.

"He has a family to support and also his horse to look after." Pappaji replied. "Besides, folks like coolies, hand-cart pullers, shoe polishers, dhobies (*laundry workers*), domestic workers, and so forth, all have something in common. They all engage in physical labor."

"So?" I wondered.

"You should always be large hearted with anyone who serves you by engaging in physical labor. They are not begging for anything or expecting any charity from you. Any kind of work involving physical labor is a very noble thing. You should always respect it and be more giving towards people who engage in it."

"They may not have been fortunate enough to acquire other skills, but there is great dignity and honor in what they do and the role that they play in our society. Yes, one should be fair, but always generous, with people who engage in physical labor."

A sense for business or commerce runs in the very veins of every citizen of Ahmedabad. The legend is that it is due to something in the water of the

46

Sabarmati River, often referred to as "Sabar Cola", which flows through the city. All facets of life in Ahmedabad involve intense and seemingly endless negotiations, and eventual gloating over perceived one-upmanship or "a win". Let me illustrate this with a quick side bar story.

On a rainy day in Ahmedabad, an old man stopped by an umbrella vendor and asked for the price of an umbrella. The vendor replied, "twenty rupees."
The old man then asked, "Will you sell it to me for ten rupees?"
The vendor looked at him aghast. Then he thought, "Oh, well, he is an old man, and it is raining. If something happens to him, because he got wet, I don't want that to be on my conscience or to affect my karma in this life." So, he replied, "It will hurt me, but okay, you can have it for ten rupees."
The old man promptly asked, "Will you sell it to me for five rupees?"
The vendor looked at him in sheer disbelief and near shock! He said, "Dada, at ten rupees, it was a sale at a loss for me. And now, you want it for five? Look, it is raining and I don't want you to get wet and fall sick. So, why don't you just take an umbrella for free? Consider it a gift from me. No charge to you for this umbrella."
And again, the old man promptly said, "Will you give me two umbrellas for free?"

But such stories aside, the nearly 800 years old Ahmedabad, in various forms and names, was always an important and significant center of commerce, industry, education, law, arts, civic leadership, and government in the western region of India. It had a rich history and it was socially, culturally, and religiously quite diverse. When the railway trains from Bombay became fully operational around 1870, it had a great impact on the direction of growth in Ahmedabad. Various residential and other communities sprang up around both sides of the new railway tracks.

Maninagar was one of them and it was located about 4 kilometers south of the Ahmedabad Junction railway station. Around late 1920's, Sakarlalkaka bought four adjacent plots of land in Maninagar in a new housing society. On one he built his home and named it "Nautam Nivas", after his wife and my grandmother, Nautam Ba. It was a lovely two-story bungalow with a large basement, big front and back yards, and a car garage. Sakarlalkaka lived his retirement years there with Motakaka, his eldest son. It passed on to him after Sakarlalkaka's death. Years later, in the early 1960's, Munikaka and Pappaji built bungalows as well. They were both two storied bungalows, spanning the other lots of land which they had inherited. They named them "Swati" and "Nikunj", respectively. So, all three brothers had a bungalow each, right next to each other, and that proved to be very valuable in their retirement and later years. Locally, they were given the moniker of the "Yajnik bungalows" and were at times used as a point of reference when giving directions to people.

Since Swati and Nikunj were built much later, most of my childhood memories happened and are associated with Nautam Nivas, when Sakarlalkaka was still living. Whenever we visited Ahmedabad, Nautam Nivas was home for all of us.

Poojas & Rituals

L ife in Nautam Nivas was a reflection of the values and norms of the old and recent past of India, and especially Gujarat. The long shadow of Sakarlalkaka fell everywhere. He was the ruling patriarch and everything was done according to his exacting demands. If anybody held a different view on something, he could not care less. It was his castle and they were his rules. If you did not like them, you were free to leave. He was a retired judge, accustomed to passing rulings, and quite used to prevailing in most matters.

Kaka was a conservative and devoutly religious Hindu man, who walked the talk of living a true brahmin life, per the scriptures. The mornings, regardless of season, began with a mandatory bath for everybody. There were no showers and one had to make do with a bucket of water and a "lota" (*a small metallic jug*). Then, a Pooja (*a ritual worship service*) had to be performed at the Mandir. The person assigned to do this, if a male, had to wear a "solu" or an "abotiu" (*a silk dhoti*) for it. If female, a certain type of a silk sari was required. A typical Pooja lasted an hour or so and one had to perform all the rituals required in a specific sequence. Whenever I was assigned to this task, typically I had an audience, which made sure that I did it correctly since a lot of it consisted of prayers recited in Sanskrit.

All meals were vegetarian and served in the kitchen itself, with everybody sitting on the floor. There were more rituals with each meal and one was not to drink any water during it. Water from a "matlee" (*an earthen water pot*) was permitted only after 45mts from the end of a meal. It was believed that it was not good to dilute one's digestive juices with water. On specific days, various types of "fasts" were observed and on others "mini-feasts" were held.

Another curious practice was to ostracize from the kitchen, any lady who was menstruating. I would be told, "The crow has touched your mother, so she cannot come into the kitchen and have a meal with us for 3 days. She must eat separately outside." I never understood any of this, but I do remember that I used to hate the goddamn crows.

There was no concept of snacking between meals. The evening dinner would not begin till twenty minutes past the arrival of the "Fast" (*an express or a fast train*) in the evening from Bombay. We could see the tracks clearly and hear all the trains from the house veranda. This was a precaution, in case an unannounced guest showed up on the train from Petlad or that region. This was actually something that happened with considerable regularity.

Also, if some good news had been received during the day about something, Kaka would insist on a visit, prior to dinner, to the Manikarnikareshwar Temple (*a Lord Shiva temple*) near the major Char Rasta (*Four Roads*) intersection in Maninagar. He would insist on walking to it and take all the men along. If nobody was available for whatever reason, I was drafted to be his companion by default.

I recall that it was a very small temple with a tiny Shiva Linga (*the classic representation of Lord Shiva*) in the center of it. Along the way, Kaka would tell me some of the legends of Lord Shiva and also remind me that He was our "Ishta Deva" (*Supreme Deity*). All good things happened under His blessings.

One such beneficiary clearly was Kiritbhai, Motakaka's son, and my eldest cousin. Because of him, I would have to visit this temple frequently. Kiritbhai was studying at the Gujarat University in Ahmedabad. He was just amazingly bright and a genius at anything he touched. He was tall, fair, and very handsome. Each year, he would be the "Topper" (*Valedictorian*) of his class and would rank as "First Class First". We always received the exam results a day before they were published in the newspapers, because the photographers would show up at Nautam Nivas to take his photograph. Every FCF student had his picture published. These results would be joyously celebrated in Nautam Nivas and I would be promptly dragged off with Kaka to the temple.

Kites & Ice Cream

I cannot remember the year, but it was Uttarayan (*Jan 14th or Makar Sankranti, when the Sun starts to move northward in the Indian zodiac*) and for some reason we were in Ahmedabad. In Gujarat, this event is celebrated in a big way with the flying of paper kites during the day. At night, the kites are flown with paper lanterns containing lighted candles hanging from the kite string (*Tookkal*). It is a special sort of a festival which is celebrated with great enthusiasm.

Kiritbhai loved flying kites and battling others with them. I knew very little about all this, so he told me that he would teach me. He bought a bunch of kites, firki's (*rolling pins of special strings, with glass shards*), glue, and some "agarbatti's" *(thin incense sticks)*. He taught me to use them to string up a kite properly and attach it to the string line rolled up in the firki. I would help him with the kite lift-off and then was in charge of the firki. He was excellent at flying them and we battled others flying their kites from rooftops all around us with great vigor.

We cut many kites, with lots of shouts and hoots, and then our kite got cut! I still remember that kite just floating away, dragging its long string with it. Well, the string got hooked in the thorns of the huge "thor" *(cactus plants)* marking the boundary of the land next door, where Nikunj was eventually built. I was promptly dispatched to retrieve it before anybody else got there and took it.

Sadly, not only did I lose that kite, but I returned with thorns stuck in my legs and arms. Kiritbhai felt terrible about it, but to his relief, my Mom said to me, "You are actually lucky. These thorns are easy to remove and you will heal fast. I was more worried about those awful strings with the glass shards in them. They are very dangerous for your fingers." I know of no place in the world that flies kites quite like they do in Gujarat. One must experience the real thing, at least once in life.

During the summer heat, everybody craved something cold. Nautam Nivas did not have a refrigerator at the time. They were not easy to get, were expensive, and Kaka was totally against even the idea of having one. He thought that it was a British gadget intended to seduce Indians. But he would relent when the "shaved ice" carts came along. Shri and I would take huge advantage of it. He would let us go forth and buy this shaved ice, with all sorts of flavored syrups poured on it, just as a summer treat.

Then there was ice cream! Oh, my God, I have never seen such mania around ice cream. Everybody was just plain nuts about it. There had to be a celebration to justify it. The occasion could be anything at all. An evening would be selected for an "Ice Cream Party". Everyone would gather at Nautam Nivas. Shashiphoi and Anilphooa would drive over all the way from across town, on the other side of the Sabarmati River, with their sons Manoj and Pankaj.

Ice cream was brought in "kothis" *(steel cylinders)*. They had been sealed and manually cranked around in wooden barrels containing ice and brine for quite some time in order to change the liquid contents inside them into ice cream. Typically, there were several kothis of different flavors of ice cream.

To offset the sweet creamy taste, there were loads of all sorts of savory items. Everybody would gorge on all this, till the ice cream was gone. Since there was no way to preserve it, one had to finish it all!

When I think about it today, I still feel that it is humanly impossible to consume so much ice cream in one sitting by any group of people. But amazingly, we actually did.

About Family Values

O ne day, Neil and Meghana asked me an interesting set of questions, backed by their keen observations as growing young kids in the USA.

They asked, "Why are we so different from other Indian families we know around here? In so many ways we are similar, and yet we do many things differently. Why?"

I replied, "I am not sure what you mean."

"Well, we don't go on regular visits to any Temples around here. Almost all our friends go to "Baal Vihaar" (*Hindu religious schools in USA*), Church, or Temple services on weekends, but we do not. We celebrate Christmas and also Diwali & Raksha Bandhan *(the Hindu thread tying ceremony)*, while many of our friends do not celebrate both. You tell us that we are Brahmins or priests by our caste, so by religious doctrine we are not allowed to smoke, drink alcoholic beverages, or eat meat. But you do all of these things and we eat meat. Further, when we visit India, we see that so many members of our extended family there are pure vegetarians, religious, and quite against doing any of these things. Gosh, just look at Dadi Ba! She is so traditional in every aspect of her life in Ahmedabad. All this is awfully confusing."

Then, I said, "Both of you have raised a fascinating topic for discussion. Your questions are quite valid. Each generation in the history of mankind, at one time or another, has asked the same or similar questions of the older generation. The answers are a bit complex, but quite interesting. You see, there is no right or wrong in them, because they are based on an evolution in the values of every family."

Thus began a series of conversations with my children, as I attempted to clarify things for their perhaps puzzled state of mind.

Grandfather's Generation

I ndia was a very different place in the times of my grandfather, Sakarlalkaka. It was under British rule, the economy was largely agrarian, and commerce focused mainly on trading in various commodities. Manufacturing activities were largely confined to local handicrafts and the industrial revolution was still beyond the horizon. All lucrative jobs were either in the government, political or social services, or the military. The prized profession was the practice of law, which required considerable formal education and various certifications. In all towns and

52

villages of India, people lived according to the prescribed ways of their religious faiths, castes, and communities. These aspects, despite periodic upheavals, had not changed much for well over a few thousand years.

In the Yajnik family and our extended Nagar Brahmin caste generally, life was lived according to a strict religious code of behavior and conduct. Even the calendar followed was not the Roman or Gregorian calendar. We followed the Vikram Samvat calendar, which was totally different and 57 years ahead numerically. It was luni-solar and had Sanskrit names for the months and seasons. There were all sorts of special days and festivals when different rituals had to be performed, fasts undertaken, and temples visited. Further, there were many widely accepted beliefs prevalent at the time and most of them were based on sound practical reasons. They were diverse in lots of ways, so let us examine this subject a bit more.

All food consumed was strictly vegetarian and had to be cooked fresh. With a lack of any refrigeration capability, leftovers were considered "vashi" *(contaminated)* and never kept. Any excess food was either given away to others, such as the domestic help, or fed to the wandering cows and animals which were always present everywhere. One was never allowed to eat outside the home for the fear of eating something that was either contaminated or cooked by someone of a "lower" caste. So, eating at a street side stall or vendor was forbidden. While this minimized the risk of getting sick, to a great extent it was also for reasons of religious purity.

Any surprise guest, or "atithi" *(literally, a person without a "tithi", or a date, for their arrival on the calendar),* was regarded as a divine presence, and had to be looked after with great care. In poorer families, a guest would be fed before the folks in the home could have their meal. Perhaps this custom originated because any type of long-distance travel in India was full of difficulties, uncertainties, and any sort of communications were nearly impossible. Further, daily baths and cleanliness, in the home and in one's person, were greatly emphasized, with strong religious overtones.

Any type of Western or British ways, whether in food, drink, or clothing, were frowned upon. Everybody, including the women, was taught and learnt not only the pure Devanagari Gujarati, but also Sanskrit. Many were fluent in both and could read or translate the classical Hindu scriptures with ease. One exception was the English language, which many had studied in school and spoke quite well. Another was English literature, which was widely read and discussed frequently.

Curiously, there was a strong prejudice against travel to foreign lands. This was often referred to as going to "Vilayat", meaning England, or Europe in general. The USA was at the time regarded as a third-rate and provincial wilderness in the minds of most educated people in India.

It was widely held that any exposure to the European cultures would simply pollute and corrupt the pure male Brahmin mind. This would manifest itself in the men learning "tamsik" *(impure or carnal)* things such as drinking alcohol, smoking, and eating meat. Furthermore, they would be beguiled by the white, blue eyed, blonde, western women, who showed little modesty, and would entrap them with their charms.

Oh, and obviously, there were no such worries regarding the Brahmin women! God forbid, because sending them to Vilayat was simply unthinkable and totally out of the question!

There was simply no possibility of debating any of this. It was the way it was, and one had to simply suck it up and live with it. Sakarlalkaka embodied most of these values as the patriarch of the extended Yajnik family.

In this environment, my father decided that he must go to Vilayat, if he was to further his young career at Associated Cement Companies Ltd. (ACC). He had graduated from the prestigious Engineering College, in Pune, with a Bachelor's degree in Electrical & Mechanical Engineering. Further, he had done his Masters at the Institute of Sciences, in Bangalore. After a short stint at a textile mill in Ahmedabad, an experience which he totally hated, he had found an adventurous opportunity through an advertisement. He had applied for it, been hired as a Powerhouse Engineer by ACC, and placed at the remote Dwarka Cement Works. At this stage, he was feeling good about his future career prospects.

ACC was a British company, born out of a major set of mergers in the early 1930's. Its mission was to lead the development of the young cement manufacturing industry in India. Its major shareholders, the entire Board of Directors, the Managing Director in Bombay, and the General Managers at its cement plants all over India, were all British! There were no Indians in any position of substance or power anywhere.

The Board had noticed this vacuum in local inclusion as well and decided to send a few promising young Indian men to Europe and England for a year, to train them in the processes & technologies of cement manufacturing and general management skills. It was a highly coveted opportunity, and there were many applicants for it from all over ACC.

Pappaji applied for it and got selected! But there was a catch. The start of this training was a year away and the trainees had to make a "retention deposit" with the ACC Head Office, by 30 days prior to departure from India. These funds would be returned with interest, upon completing 3 years of service, after the return from the year of training overseas. If you left ACC within 3 years after your return, for any reason whatsoever, you forfeited your deposit and all accrued interest.

My father had saved some money, but he did not have enough to meet the deposit requirements. So, he approached Sakarlalkaka for financial help. Pappaji was joyous and looking forward to this whole training program. With excitement, he explained it all to Kaka.

"Tare Vilayat javu chhe?" *(You want to go to Vilayat?)*, Kaka thundered. "Viru, tu gando thayi gayo chhu?" *(Viru, have you gone crazy?)* Then, it all turned into a complete heartbreak for Pappaji. Years later, in retirement, he would cry profusely when re-telling me this story. It hit him so hard, that he could not get even a little bit of help, for that which mattered to him so much. What made it worse was that it was not due a lack of financial resources. Kaka certainly had the resources. No, the brutal truth was that those who had the economic power, exercised it ruthlessly, to protect and preserve their "family values".

Sakarlalkaka was angry, adamant, and just shut my father down. Kaka felt deeply that his children should never to go to Vilayat. If they insisted on doing so, as adults without his approval, then they should find their own resources and stay away from his home, Nautam Nivas. He would simply not tolerate any British pollution or its evil ways in his home. This episode changed Pappaji in fundamental ways, and forever.

My father returned to Dwarka deeply disappointed, depressed, and resumed his work. He did not visit Kaka at all for the next 10 months. In the 11th month, while on his way to Bombay, he stopped in Ahmedabad to see Kaka and Nautam Ba. Kaka was aloof, but Ba was sweet to him as always and fussed all over him. Finally, Kaka asked him about the Vilayat training and the required funds. Pappaji informed him that he now had the funds. Kaka said, "Show me your bank passbook." Pappaji did, and gave him proof that he did have the money. Then, Kaka fell totally silent. He had lost his duel, based on his economic power, with his son in these changing times.

Pappaji's year in Vilayat is a story by itself, so I will save that for later, because this one is not finished yet. In 1939, when Pappaji sailed from Bombay, on Kaka's orders, nobody came to see him off. There were no celebrations, garlands, or a send-off of any kind at the Ballard Pier. When he returned nearly a year later, the same exact thing happened. His itinerary was well known, but there was nobody present to receive him. His dear friend in Bombay, T.D. Dave, or Davekaka to all of us, who worked at the ACC Head Office, helped him out with an overnight stay. Next day, he simply took a morning train to Ahmedabad, and just showed up at Nautam Nivas in the early evening.

Shashiphoi, who was not married at the time and just adored Pappaji, noticed him approaching the house and started screaming wildly, "Virubhai avya! Virubhai avya!" *(Virubhai has arrived!)* Nautam Ba rushed out to see and hug her son. But then, Kaka boomed, "Koi Viru pase jasho nahi! Prayashchit karvanu chhe." *(Nobody should go near Viru! He has to perform a ceremony of repentance.)*

Pappaji was made to sit outside in the front yard, with his luggage, for some time. A priest was procured, and he was made to perform this ritual ceremony of repentance and purification, before being welcomed into the house.

It was then, after almost 2 years, that Kaka came up to Pappaji, and gave him a bear hug with tears flowing in his eyes. While there were many words of mutual endearment exchanged, Kaka had not changed one bit.

But Pappaji certainly had, and in so many ways. It took the whole family a long time to figure it all out.

Father's Generation

My father was an amazing mix of the old and the new in his values. He had retained many of them from his upbringing, but he had added others, and morphed many. He did remain a devout brahmin, in the sense that he would not smoke, drink alcohol, or eat meat. He practiced many of the brahmin rituals, but also left many out. He was very progressive in his thinking and highly tolerant of the diversity of the Indian diaspora in its faiths and customs.

He firmly believed that it was this "conservatism" in India that was at the heart of what had left it conquered and economically under developed. He defined it as a social resistance to change, a disdain for experiencing or learning new things, and a general inability to step out of one's "comfort zone". In a century of rapid technological development and its economic impact worldwide, these traits along with the parasitic grip of Colonial Rule, had caused India to be left behind significantly. In essence, he felt that one should not only preserve the old and good, but also consider and adopt the new, and move with the emerging times.

However, these were highly contradictory and controversial concepts to a lot of people for a variety of reasons. He faced many a challenge to his strongly held views over the years.

An early episode to reflect all this occurred in the Sevalia Cement Works (SCW), in Gujarat. My father had been promoted to AGM and the plant was in its Phase II & III expansion mode. Pappaji was working like a dog with brutal hours across many work-shifts and all-night stints. The GM was Mr. Burgess, a British man, whose family lived mostly in England, not in India. He was bright, highly skilled, and a mentor to my father. They got along very well, but differed in certain things. Mr. Burgess liked his evening "sundowner" (*a drink of gin and tonic water with quinine in it*), but my father did not drink alcoholic beverages. He liked to hunt wild fowl, especially pheasant and peacock, in the countryside with his shotgun, but my father did not believe in hunting. He liked to eat fresh meat, but my father was a strict vegetarian.

Despite these differences, Pappaji always found him "Rajwadi" *(royal)* cooks, bearers, and butlers to cater to his lifestyle. He would also join him often, but stick to his own food and drink habits. There was great mutual respect of one another and their ways.

Then one day, Mr. Burgess decided to retire and return to England. Pappaji was promoted directly to the GM position. He was the first Indian to be appointed GM in the British ACC, and that was a very big deal indeed at that time. He stayed in frequent contact with Mr. Burgess in England over the ensuing years. But sadly, a few years later, Mr. Burgess died. Apparently, he succumbed to long term effects of certain toxins in the peacock meat, which it turns out are harmful to humans. Nobody knew this at the time.

The GM bungalow, at any ACC cement plant, was an astonishing place. It was always a beehive of activity and all sorts of visitors came there and they had incredible demands. My mother had to learn to deal with all of them.

The British guests wanted alcoholic drinks, elaborate non-vegetarian meals, and western desserts. The Indians wanted the same drinks, but on the sly, and had crazy dietary requirements. My mom figured it all out and set up two separate kitchens, with separate sets of crockery and cutlery, and took care of all of them flawlessly. She also trained the staff to serve everybody with great precision. A popular compliment went, "Mrs. Yajnik (or Damayantiben), you are a superb hostess! We really enjoy our visits with you here!"

The fact that my parents could adapt to this world and succeed in it is a testimonial by itself. They were incredibly successful in balancing their "family values" with the requirements of Pappaji's job.

My Generation

So, how did all this affect me? I was in a bit of a trap. On one hand, I had family traditions and values breathing down on me. On the other, my parents, while progressive and adaptive for many things, were still strict and conservative in a lot of their thinking and habits. But there were many other and different influences working on me in my life as well. The very first was Rajkumar College, Rajkot (RKC).

When I joined RKC, I was placed in the "vegetarian" group in the "Mess" (*dining hall*), where we had our meals. While I am sure that they did their best, the food was just boring. At the next table though, where the "eggetarians" sat, things were tastier. And two tables over, where the "non-vegetarians" sat, the food on any day was just delicious to my palate! Well, slowly and on the sly, I started eating the egg dishes, then bits of meat curry, and then pieces of meat itself. Soon, I forgot all about being a brahmin, and just dug into the delicious food. Thus, began my transformation. Selecting my dietary inclusions was just the beginning.

RKC was an astonishing world in every imaginable way for me. I made lots of friends, played sports, learnt many things, shared amazing experiences, and much more. In terms of family values, I never thought about anybody's caste, religion, or station in life while at RKC. We were all just kids in a school, we were all the same, and we had similar problems. What distinguished us were our individual abilities, talents or skills, and a committed team spirit. Our teachers were just superb and so dedicated to us. My 7 years at RKC affected me deeply, and its many splendored education changed my life forever.

My years in IIT/Kanpur were also highly formative, but in a very different way. It was 5 years of an intense scientific and technical education. But in my view, the value of it all was different for me. Yes, it taught me to compete academically. But most importantly, it taught me how to learn things that I did not know. However, the grades in various classes is what mattered the most. They were everything. If you got anything less than an "A-", you were an idiot or just plain rubbish. When you are in a world class school, studying with the "best and the brightest" of India, it is actually quite easy to feel stupid. I felt that frequently, because I had many more diverse interests and IIT/Kanpur was not designed to cater to them.

Then I came to the USA. It was not because of some grand plan or an amazing foresight. It was the only thing one could really do at the time, because there were hardly any jobs for a graduating class in India. Studying abroad offered a path to bigger things in a shrinking world and perhaps that could facilitate a meaningful life back in India eventually. At least, that was the conventional wisdom at the time.

But the USA in the early 1970's was a tough place, as many an IIT/Kanpur graduate lucky enough to get there, discovered the hard way. Academic success was usually easy for them, given the formidable training in India. But success in jobs or work was not so certain. Most had no training really in actual work, because of a more theoretical and bookish grooming in their studies. For many, the realities of actual engineering work in the USA proved daunting. So, a lot of them took the option to pursue a Ph.D. degree in some esoteric field, and move towards a life of teaching or technical research.

My life turned out to be a bit different. I explored the many opportunities available in the USA and jumped headlong into a set of choices full of risk. It was fraught with pain and uncertainty. I made many mistakes, but I was also tough enough to recover from them.

A key and most critical ingredient in all this was my ability to fit into any situation I found myself in. I know of hardly anybody of my background who could do this successfully.

I achieved success by many a measure, but it altered and morphed the "family values" that I was raised with.

That is a large part of the price I paid.

Epilogue

So, what does this multiple generation stuff really say about family values? If you recall, that is where this story began. The narrative above was intended to crystallize a few things for you to think about. Now, let me summarize the essence of it.

You see, in my view, "the values" in any family are not a fixed or constant thing. The only thing constant about them is change. What causes this change? Well, many things.

About Family Values

A large part of our family values is inherited from the family we were born in and where we grew up. These will be certainly determined greatly by the religion, caste, or community to which the family belonged.

However, there is another major part. It has a lot to do with the level of formal education pursued. This is usually complemented by various resulting experiences in our lives. They have a huge influence upon us and can be highly formative as well. Usually, they broaden our base of knowledge, develop critical incisive thinking, and question many an assumption in our social lives and norms.

But on top of this foundation, most importantly, our family values reflect the choices that we made in our lives. They were almost entirely up to us, regardless of our circumstances.

As I mentioned before, there is no right or wrong in any of this. There is a poignant and profound lesson in all of it. Perhaps therein, lies the answer to your insightful questions.

In life, you make your choices, and live with their consequences.

Your family values will always reflect those decisions.

Training in "Vilayat"

(As Told to Me by My Father)

On a sunny morning in early 1939, Pappaji sailed from the Ballard Pier in Bombay aboard the P&O Lines ship, SS Strathmore. He had five other ACC colleagues with him and they were a group of single men. While all the others had a big "hoopla" around their sailing, my father had nobody to see him off. It was his first overseas sailing and everything about it was new for him.

All international travel was done on steam ships, which were at the time the essential means of transportation, unlike the modern cruise ships which are meant to provide exotic holiday experiences and entertainment. The ships leaving Bombay, sailed through the Arabian Sea, Gulf of Suez, and entered the Suez Canal at Port Suez. At Port Said, at the north end of the Canal, they entered the Mediterranean Sea. The class of travel they were in was not opulent, but functional and reasonably comfortable. They enjoyed the ship's amenities, which were few, and passed their time playing cards, walking around on the decks, or reading. The food aboard, if you were a vegetarian, was edible, but nothing to write home about.

They disembarked in Italy and their travels began in earnest. They had a detailed and well-planned itinerary. In each city or town, regardless of the country, they stayed for a few days and visited various cement plants nearby. These visits were backed by lectures and discussions about the processes and technologies involved. There were many focused discussions on plant design, construction, and operations. They were also given materials to read and absorb.

But, an implied part of this training also was great exposure to different cultures, languages, lifestyles, diets, religions, values, and history. They also got a taste of how India was viewed externally, with all its demeaning stereotypes. One quickly became aware of what was going on in the world at large and what that may portend for the future in India.

They covered many countries. From Italy, they went to Switzerland, Austria, and then to Germany. In Germany, Adolf Hitler was the Chancellor. The political environment was highly polarized and toxic. German nationalism was at a fervent pitch and rumblings of war were everywhere. Pappaji's group generally stayed below the radar during all this and continued their training, but there were some close calls.

One day, on a train from Warnemunde on the Baltic Sea, to Berlin, the train was suddenly stopped in the countryside. A whole team of Nazi SS Officers and soldiers boarded it and began a detailed search. Pappaji's group had no idea of what was going on. An SS Officer flung open the door to their compartment, took a slow and careful look at each one of them, and then told the other soldiers, "Indisch schwartzas!" *(Indian blacks!)*. The journey resumed shortly, but my father never forgot the racial insult.

From Germany, they headed via France to Denmark. Pappaji simply loved Paris and all its ways. They visited various places, caught the burlesque show at the Lido, and also saw many films in theatres. He just adored Maurice Chevalier and Greta Garbo, and would tell me about their classic films many times over.

In Denmark, they had one very memorable weekend, at a beachside resort on the North Sea. On this Sunday, while his whole group was there, the star of the beach was Pappaji! Now, try to picture this in your mind. He was 5ft. 11in tall, very muscular and buff, brown in complexion, with dark hair all over his body beyond belief, but totally bald! He was simply an amazing sight to behold! The Danish girls on the beach that day, who were all lily white, blue eyed, and blonde, found him incredibly fascinating and alluring. He had a tough time surviving that day!

England was the final country where the group spent many months. They saw a lot and did a lot. Pappaji was placed in a house with a British landlady to look after him. She was sweet, adorable, and took care of him with great affection. Their training progressed, but then WW II seemed very likely. Life in London became very confined, restricted, and many shortages began to appear. Major war preparations got underway and then the war actually broke out. My father could recount all the key radio broadcasts of the time, including the ones by the stammering King George VI, because he was there and listening to all of them, on the radio with everybody else! Then, London was placed under nightly watch for the German bombers. There were even some actual air raids, with bombing runs that were attributed to secret practice missions by the German Luftwaffe.

But amidst all these happenings, Pappaji's training continued. His biggest problem was food. It was almost impossible to find decent vegetarian food in England. If you asked for it anywhere, all you got was a salad, bread, and some cheese. Nobody can live on that for long. Pappaji decided that he must do something for his survival and health. He tried meat gravy, some meat, a little fish, some eggs, and so on. After all the tastings, he concluded that he could accept eggs, but not meat or seafood of any kind. They were things that gave him "sug" *(nausea or revulsion),* so he decided to not eat them. But he developed a taste for eggs, especially the way the British ate them. His order of preference went from soft boiled, to poached, to scrambled, to fried, and finally to an omelette. He would often carry hard boiled eggs with him as an energy snack when he was travelling, a practice which he continued lifelong, even later in India.

Pappaji never took to smoking or tobacco in any form, unlike his mother, Nautam Ba. She used to consume tobacco in her "paan" (*betel leaf*). Drinking alcoholic beverages was another hurdle for him. Many in his group enjoyed drinks, because they were used to them in Bombay. Pappaji was not, but he tried various spirits, beer, and wine. The only acceptable thing for him was wine. He did not like the feeling of a "booze buzz", so he decided not to drink regular spirits. Years later, in India, he would sometimes take a shot of "Drakshaasav" *(a spiced Indian sherry)* as an antidote for a cold, or to just feel warm on a cold winter night.

The group had a limited social life after the work day. But they went to pubs, dance halls, theatres, and so forth. One of his colleagues met a pretty British girl during all this and fell in love with her. He wanted to marry her and take her to India. He was a Parsee man and felt that his progressive and broad-minded family would not object to it. It took days to talk him and her out of their spontaneous and passionate idea.

Soon thereafter, the war efforts intensified in a big way. The group was told to return to India quickly, because its safety could not be assured in London any more. They were hustled off to Southampton and put aboard the P&O Lines steam ship, SS Strathaven, which sailed promptly for Bombay.

Their return voyage was very scary and extremely dangerous. They had to sail south and then pass through the Strait of Gibraltar in order to enter the Mediterranean Sea. This strait was the most dangerous body of water in the entire world at that time, because many German U-Boats lay in waiting to sink any Allied ship passing through.

While they did have an escort of two Royal Navy destroyers, their ship had to switch all lights off at night and go totally dark to prevent external detection. No music or dancing was permitted to avoid any sonar pickup. Nobody slept the night when the Strait was crossed, because everybody was so tense, and expected a torpedo to hit at any time. Once they were in the open Mediterranean Sea, there was a collective sigh of relief, but still a lot of tension remained.

It was only after they reached Port Said and entered the Suez Canal, that everybody finally felt safe and the celebrations began. My father would describe this voyage, particularly the crossing of the Strait of Gibraltar, to me in exhausting and minute detail many times over. It was obvious that this crossing and voyage held a very special place in his heart and mind.

He arrived in Bombay and disembarked at the Ballard Pier in the late afternoon. While others got a near royal welcome, there was nobody there to receive Pappaji. He took a taxi to the flat of his dear friend, T.D. Dave. He stayed the night with Davekaka and took the next morning train to Ahmedabad.

He reached Ahmedabad in the late afternoon and took a "tanga" (*horse and buggy*) to Nautam Nivas. He was tired, but also looking forward to some lovely Indian tea and great home cooked food later. He heard Shashiphoi screaming at sighting him and laughed happily. He was glad that his near 1-year trip had finally come to an end.

Well, he thought that, but his trip was not quite over. Not yet, because unknown to him, one more thing still remained to be done, before he could step into his home.

A Monsoon Drive

"Sir, let's find a picnic spot. I think Vijay and the ladies need a break and it is also time for lunch." Mr. Joshi said.

My father replied, "Quite right. But, what should we pick? There are so many lovely places in this area."

It was during the monsoon season. We were on a road trip from Dwarka to Jamnagar, I think. I am not certain about the destination. My father and Mr. Joshi had some business to attend to there, and the rest of us were just tagging along in the ride for the sheer fun of it. By the rest of us I mean my mother, Mrs. Joshi, and myself. Pappaji was driving and so we had no driver on this trip. We were in a sturdy Jeep station wagon, so there was no cause for any alarm.

Mr. Joshi, who was a bit younger, was the AGM reporting to my father, who was the GM of ACC's Dwarka Cement Works. We lived in adjacent bungalows in a shared compound in Dwarka, facing the gorgeous Arabian Sea with all its lovely sunsets. The Joshis were Chitpavan Brahmins (*a brahmin caste of people with fair complexions*) from Maharashtra, a state of India, and Marathi was their mother tongue.

It so happened that my father was fluent in Marathi, because he had spent many years studying at the Engineering College, in Pune, Maharashtra. So, our families grew close not just due to physical proximity, but also because of social and cultural similarities between us. They had a lovely daughter named Neelima. She was very pretty, had green eyes, and studied in a boarding school for girls in Southern India. She was younger than me and during the summer holidays, she would many times come over to our house in the afternoon to play or read my vast collection of comic books. On this drive, she was away at school and so not with us.

After various discussions and debates, a suitable spot was identified, and I was sent off to haul all the picnic baskets, food, drinks, etc. over to it from the jeep. My mother and Mrs. Joshi laid down a beautiful "dhurrie" (*a cotton rug*) on the ground on this grassy knoll and setup all the things I had brought from the jeep in a very attractive manner. When we finally sat down, I looked around and could not believe the beauty of all the sights around us.

We were on a small hilltop. Behind us was a range of hills, with our little road near its base. In front of us, there was another range of hills at some distance, but with a lovely valley just before it. In this valley, there was a riverbed at its bottom, for what appeared to be a seasonal river. Then, in the middle of the valley, there was this structure that looked like a tall and wide earthen wall. To its left was the bone-dry riverbed, but to its right was an astonishing sight. There was a huge wide lake and it seemed like this wall in the valley was responsible for holding back the water and creating it. The lake had all sorts of flora and fauna all around it and was simply beautiful. But on the other side with the dry river bed, it looked like a desolate world, nearly devoid of life.

"Vijay, here is your sandwich", my mother offered.

"Oh, thanks, Behn." I said. "But, Pappaji, what is that huge wall in the center of the valley? It looks very strange."

"Ah, you are observant!" he replied. "That wall, as you call it, is actually a dam. A siphon dam."

"A siphon what? A dam? That does not look like a dam. There is no huge concrete wall, or power station, or buildings, or flowing water. It looks like a tall and great big dirt wall, with grass growing on it!"

"But it created a lake, did it not? It stopped and gathered the water from a flowing river, so that wall is a dam."

"He is right, Vijay," Mr. Joshi chimed in. "That is a fine siphon dam indeed."

"Good grief, you say it is a dam. But it seems like a dirt wall to me. And, since we are discussing it, what exactly is a siphon dam? I have never heard of it," I asked, with a puzzled look. They both had a hearty laugh at my expense.

I was just beginning to show my annoyance at all this, when my father explained, "Vijay, a siphon dam is one of the oldest designs for a dam created by man. You can find thousands of them, not only all over India, but all over the world, especially in places where conserving water is essential for man's very survival. They all, more or less, look like this one. The side with the lake looks pretty, but on the side, which is dry, one must be careful and ever vigilant."

"Why is that? I mean, look, there are people walking their herds of goats around on the dry side, right now."

As Pappaji began to give me an answer, he stopped abruptly, and turned towards the dam. Some curious and strange sounds had started emerging from it suddenly. They rapidly grew louder. They seemed to start with some erratic hisses and gurgles, then wavy water ripples, then a series of loud "booms", and then the deafening "roar" of water gushing out of a dam.

I simply froze at the sight. I felt delighted, but also scared. I watched the goatherds skillfully drive the herds of goats to higher levels as the dry riverbed filled rapidly with massive torrents of water.

"So, what happened just now? I asked Pappaji

"Oh, the dam did what it was supposed to do! We are very lucky to be able to witness it. You see, inside that earthen wall, there are large pipes that are set up as siphons. When the water level on the lakeside rises too high, the siphon is naturally completed and it activates. The dam releases the excess water till the lakeside water level drops back and the siphon shuts off. So, this dam regulates the lakeside water level within a range. It needs no power, has nothing mechanical in it, needs no attending staff of any kind, and it just preserves the water on the lakeside all by itself."

"Wow, that is amazing!"

"But on dry side of the dam, one has to be ever vigilant. It is hard to predict when the siphons of the dam may activate. But when they do, as you can see right now, they release a massive volume of water. If you are in the wrong place in the riverbed, you can get washed away or even be killed by the rushing water. The moral here is that one should never picnic in the dry riverbed near a siphon dam. It could badly ruin your day."

Well, we wrapped up the picnic and resumed our drive. By now the dry riverbed was filled with water which flowed onwards forever it seemed. Over many miles of travel, I could see that the dam was still operating at a furious pace. The experience was just awesome.

So, I developed a huge interest in siphons, much to the distress of my parents. I played with siphons everywhere. In the bathroom, I had tubes stuck inside buckets and outside I made them in water storage tanks using garden hoses. Initially, I would suck on the tubes to start the siphon. I did not know any better.

Then one day, I sucked in a lung full of water, and that led to a lot of drama in our home. I got sympathy and a shellacking, in equal measures, for my stupidity. All my siphon tubes, etc. were taken away from me, and I was forbidden to experiment with siphons.

If you are curious about what sort of drama, well, that is yet another story.

HH Maharani Saheba of Porbandar

(Original Posting: RKC Forum - February, 2015)

From the ever-gathering fog in my memory, I want to add my 2 paisa worth of input, which I know is perhaps totally irrelevant, to this discourse. Now, I may be in the proverbial outfield, but it may be interesting for you to learn that I actually met quite a lot and knew well the Maharana and Maharani of Porbandar, albeit as a little kid.

In 1955, when I was 6 yrs old, my Dad was transferred to Porbandar as the GM of the ACC, Ltd. cement plants. One was in the old town and a new plant was to be built near the road to the new and fledgling airport. For a year or so, we lived in the "Villas" near the beach. There were some 8-12 of them and they were just beautiful (I don't know if they are still there today). Then we moved to the ACC bungalows.

It was a charmed life. During this period, we would be invited quite often to various functions at the Maharana's Palace, probably since my Dad was the GM of a major employer in town. What I remember is that I was told to get properly dressed and behave, since we were going to the Palace (it was sort of like being "presented at court" before the monarch). I used to really dislike all the getting dressed up stuff, but I could not disobey the orders of my parents. They too used to dress up in their fineries. It seemed often like the 'upper crust' society of Porbandar was in attendance at the Palace, for whatever was going on that day.

I was a mischievous and somewhat difficult kid who had learned to survive in the local Gujarati School, Navyug Vidyalay, in Porbandar (I don't know if it is still there today). So, I would to be up to my usual mischief, Palace or not, much to the embarrassment of my parents. However, what I remember is that wherever all of us kids were, Ranisaheba was always there!

She loved kids. She would play with us, laugh with us, scold us, give us treats to eat, and did not give a hoot about what anybody thought. She was British, and all of us thought, just stunningly gorgeous. Not just physically, which she certainly was, but as a person and as a maharani. I had this odd habit of charging towards her! She would sweep me off my feet for doing that and then proceed to sternly discipline me. She was just wonderful and all of us kids thought the world of her.

It was Ranisaheba first, and Ranasaheb next, who told my father that I should be sent to RKC. When my Dad pointed out that my two older brothers were already there, they were just delighted. In fact, Ranisaheba told him to not lose even one year and to dispatch me to RKC immediately. She even offered to assist in the admission process, whatever that may have been at the time (I learnt all this from my Dad many years later).

For what it is worth, from my viewpoint, the Maharana and Ranisaheba of Porbandar, like many other Indian royal families, were truly a breed apart. They certainly had their share of troubles, controversies, and trials that were at times quite public. Regardless, I was lucky enough to experience first-hand at a very young age, their culture, kindness, progressive thinking, and grace.

Rumblings of Rajkumar College, Rajkot

It happened in 1959, during the summer holidays in Petlad. It was evening and a raucous family debate was underway. I was merely a spectator sitting on the sidelines. It was all quite intense.

"Virubhai, you are making a very big mistake.", Munikaka said. "With Kashyap & Ajay, it was another matter. Your circumstances were different. Why do you want to put Vijay through this, now?"

"Virubhai, he is right. Munibhai is quite right." Shashiphoi chimed in. "This is not the right kind of education. Vijay will suffer seriously because of your decision. It is a huge mistake!"

Then, the various Kaki's and Mami's present, they all weighed in. "Virubhai, we think it is a terrible mistake as well. How can you let go of your child, yet again? To a boarding school no less, where there is no love? Don't you have any feelings or any heart for him? This is just awful!"

Motakaka somberly said, "I agree with all of them."

But Sakarlalkaka, my grandfather, was strangely totally silent.

My father was put on the defensive. He explained yet again and pleaded with everybody about the real value of a Rajkumar College, Rajkot, education. But they all remained fiercely opposed to it.

Then various voices sprouted up, and said amazing things in varying tones. Comments such as "That school teaches British values, and we do not want that kind of an education anymore." "Oh, at his tender age, Vijay's values and thinking will change vastly." "How will a nice Brahmin boy, live with all those Kshatriya boys and Rajwadi princes?" "Oh, you know, many of them are Muslim!" "In that school, he will learn only violence and waste his time playing all their sports." "And Oh, God forbid, he will learn to eat meat!". "This is all just terrible. It is a bad idea."

My father was overwhelmed by all this, but he did not budge. He put a stop to it by saying, "Okay, I will give it more thought."

The next day, in the afternoon, Sakarlalkaka approached me. I was goofing around on a swing and he came up and sat next to me. He smiled, and said gently, "Master, kem chho*?" (Master, how are you?)* "Master", meaning a bookish person in Gujarati, was his affectionate name for me.

I said, "Dadaji, I am fine, I guess."

Then he asked, "Are you concerned about the discussion last night? If you are, I would not blame you. In fact, I would understand."

So, I asked him, "Dadaji, what should I think? What should I do?"

Kaka then said, "They all mean well for you, because they love you. And your father loves you more than anybody. This is hard for him too. But, my question for you is, what would make you happy?"

I replied, "Dadaji, I don't know."

And he went, "Quite right. It is a tough school, but also a good school. It is different, but it will open your eyes and mind. I had to learn many of these lessons the hard way. I never had such an opportunity."

"So, you think I should go there?"

"I think you should follow what your father decides for you. He has also learnt many things the hard way." Sakarlalkaka replied.

In a day or so, my father announced to everybody that he was sending me to Rajkumar College, Rajkot, in July. There were many protests and loud whines all around, but my father just closed the discussion.

Only Dadaji sought me out, and gave me a bear hug, something I had never seen him do to anybody before. Then, he caressed my head and blessed me.

Epilogue

It was 1987. My parents were visiting us in Walnut Creek, California, from India to help us after the birth of our daughter, Meghana. Kashyap, my eldest brother, lived nearby in Pleasanton. One evening, during a discussion, Kashyap suddenly asked my father, "Pappaji, why did you send us away to Rajkumar College, Rajkot, at such a young age? Why did you do that?" It was quite direct and somewhat surprising.

Pappaji smiled and said, "I am surprised by your question, after all these years. I thought that you had understood by now. But anyway, since you have asked it, I will answer it."

"When all you boys were little, giving you a good education, with any kind of continuity, was quite difficult in India at the time. In my job at ACC, I was transferred to different locations almost every 3 to 5 years. If we had kept moving all of you with us, your education would have suffered gravely. So, your mother and I had to make a very difficult choice."

"We decided that a public or boarding school education for all three of you was the only real option for us. It was very expensive and difficult to afford, but it was also a matter of serious concern for your future.

71

"Luckily, we could secure admissions for you and Ajay in Rajkumar College, Rajkot, initially, and later for Vijay, when you graduated."

"It was financially really hard for us through all those years, and we had to give up or forego many things in our life to do this for you boys."

Kashyap pursued further, "But did you not miss us? Did you not love us?"

Pappaji said, "Of course, we missed all of you terribly and sorely. And yes, we loved you all very much as well."

"Now, give this some thought. Sometimes, letting someone go is a bigger act of love than clinging on to them."

Pappaji & Behn - 1940

Behn – As a newlywed - 1940

Pappaji – Early 1930's

*(l to r) Sitting: Pramudaphoi, Pramodkaki, Nautam Ba, Vilaasben,
Sakarlalkaka, Pramodphooa, Girikantphooa
Standing: Snehalataphoi, Shashiphoi, Pappaji, Motakaka, Munikaka*

Pappaji at Versailles Palace, Paris, France - 1939

Sakarlalkaka – 1930s

Kiritbhai – 1957

*Pappaji & Mr.
Burgess in
Sevalia – 1950s*

*With Mr. Burgess
& Davekaka*

*The Yajnik &
Dave Families
in 1950s*

A Family Photo
Mid 1950s

Kashyap, Ajay, & Me
Porbandar-Mid 1950s

My favorite Dodge car

*With Behn &
Kumudkaki – Near
Petlad – 1950s*

*Kiritbhai &
Nikhilbhai sail
abraoad –
Bombay, 1958*

*With Anilbhai in
Porbandar – late 1950s*

The Family in Ahmedabad – Early 1950s

*Outdoor Function
at Sevalia Works*

RAJKUMAR COLLEGE, RAJKOT

Cross Country Runs

(Original Posting: RKC Forum – April, 2012)

Question: Years after leaving Rajkumar College (RKC), have you ever had an experience or achievement, directly related to some aspect of your training at RKC which you had long forgotten? This question is not in the context of a job, business, family, academics, or lingual skills, but in terms of "life experiences". I have had this happen to me many times, in things ranging from the trivial to the sublime.

Rainy Afternoons & Cross-Country Runs

At RKC, in my days, when the monsoon rains came down hard in the July-August timeframe, the games in the afternoon would be cancelled. The whole wing (in my case, the Junior and later Senior) would be organized into troops and we would set out on a cross-country run all around the city of Rajkot. We would run, three abreast, for a while and then get a walking break. After a few minutes, the run would resume. It could last from 1 hour to 2 hours, depending upon the weather situation. Typically, the run was in the rain. Everybody would be soaked totally during the whole thing. We would come back, clean up, dry out, and go to dinner.

Now, I used to hate these runs. I thought they were a waste of time. I mean, we ran at PT and during the games, etc. every day, so why not take a rainy afternoon off? Besides, I shuddered at the thought of getting soaked to the bones. I would have to fight my mind even to lace up the shoes. Well, at RKC there was no choice in these matters, so I would start grudgingly with my troop, with a perfectly rotten attitude towards it all inside me. However, to my amazement, soon after we got going, it would actually become enjoyable and a lot of fun! The body warmed up, the rain was cool, and the air felt good. So, it would always end in a lovely way, but it was never ever something I could get really excited about at its start.

Well, I graduated from RKC and soon thereafter I forgot about these runs. Oh, I liked running, and over the ensuing years, in fact I did a lot of it. I ran races for competition, charity, fun, etc., in many gorgeous locales all over the world. But, if it was raining, it was always a day off for me.

This poor attitude of mine stayed with me stubbornly for years. Until one day...

Afternoon Thunderstorm in Hong Kong

The year was 2001. I was posted in Hong Kong on an Expat assignment at a British company. We lived on the main Hong Kong island, in a beautiful setting in the high hills overlooking Happy Valley. Our apartment was on the 17th floor of a high rise building in the Parkview residential complex.

It was August and the monsoon season was in full swing. My family was away and I was all alone. It was afternoon on a Sunday and I was totally bored in the comfortable ambience of a fully air-conditioned building. Outside it was very hot, unbearably humid, and utterly miserable. The de-humidifier machines were working at max capacity and the weather looked ominous in every way. I decided to deal with my boredom by going out on a hike. I thought a good physical workout, with a large measure of sweat, would surely cure my blues.

Now, it may surprise you, but Hong Kong is a great place for nature walks and hiking. Away from all the glittering lights, fast city life, and the mega urban sprawl, there exists a well-preserved natural environment within the high granite hills which are everywhere. It is wilderness. There are trails carved out all over that can show you sights, flora & fauna, and historical landmarks that are just thrilling. Tourists never get to see this side of Hong Kong - only the locals do. Also, the mountainous nature of the terrain creates microclimate zones which are highly volatile and unpredictable. So, a whole sub-culture exists around all this, with festivals, food fairs, races of all sorts, marathons in many variations, etc., dating as far back as when the Brits fought China and grabbed Hong Kong in the end in a one-sided treaty.

I set out on my favorite hiking trail. I traversed a high range with a sharp ridge and dropped into a lush valley which held a huge water reservoir far down below. As I began my descent into the valley, I sensed that a thunderstorm was developing. The trail was steep and narrow, but opened up into a small clearing in a lovely meadow further down. The clearing had a few abandoned rusty old sheds that surrounded many weed covered artillery gun placements from WW II days. I noticed that I had company. There were young couples and a few families with little kids that were also on the trail a bit ahead of me. Just then, Mother Nature decided to show her power in full glory.

The thunderstorm started with that familiar vertical breeze. It picked up strength rapidly and everybody realized that rain was imminent. People raced for shelter, any kind of shelter, in all directions. I raced too and found a place under a broken awning of a shed. The rain started in mere seconds, an intense downpour as the heavens opened up, accompanied by harrowing thunder and lightning. The wind was now at a howl. Umbrellas snapped and were blown away. Everybody cowered behind or under something and waited wondering what would happen next. That is when it happened to me.

I had a flashback to the cross-country runs of my boyhood from many years ago. A movie played in my mind with scenes of rain hitting my face, running through the localized flooding at places in Rajkot, and stomping with both feet in water puddles sending splashes of water far and wide, to mention a few. The flashback was vivid and so joyous. I felt a rising wave of elation in my heart, and on a pure impulse, decided to re-live those experiences. I simply smiled to myself, and discarding the protection of the awning, just stepped out into the rain! I was soaked in an instant, but I did not care. The rain felt just wonderful, the wind was like a divine massage, and I started jumping around, dancing, and frolicking all over the clearing like a little boy! Then something else happened.

Some six or seven little Chinese and Japanese boys and girls, who had been keenly watching my crazy solo act, suddenly tore free from the clutches of their Moms and raced forward to join me! They were perhaps between 5 – 7 years old. I held their hands and started dancing in circles and in various other formations.

In barely a minute or so, seeing their happy faces full of laughter, and hearing the shrieks and squeals of delight, one by one, their Chinese/Japanese Moms (who are normally very reserved in a public setting) began to join us. Our circles and pairs grew bigger. Then everybody egged the Dads on and soon, one by one, they joined us too. Finally, all the coy couples (mainly Brits, Aussies, or Kiwis), who were out on "hiking dates", came along also. People did folk dances, jumps, twirls, and played little games. There was loud and raucous laughter everywhere. And all around us, the thunderstorm raged on in all its fury. But nobody noticed it. Everyone was lost in the fun of this impromptu party!

In about 15 minutes or so, it was over. The rain stopped, the thunder and lightning ceased, and the wind dissipated to a gentle breeze. There was a surreal silence. And then, with a slow gurgle here, a soft hiss there, the water runoffs began their show. Little rivulets and waterfalls started and soon turned into larger ones as they picked up volume and speed with all the water flowing down from the high granite hills.

In a few minutes, it all turned into a deafening roar and we saw some 100 to 200 waterfalls of various sizes, shapes, and heights going at full force! It was an incredible sight perhaps seen by people rarely. We all watched in awe for the brief time that it lasted.

The social dynamics of the group after this show were also amazing. Despite the different nationalities, languages, backgrounds and so forth, the whole group was laughing freely and talking animatedly in the universal "language of the heart". Then, all of us hiked a few miles over to a tea stall at the trailhead. Some had green tea, some had Earl Grey, some had jasmine tea, and I got to have a lovely "Indian masala tea".

To this day, whenever I think of that afternoon in Hong Kong, I think fondly about our dear RKC and those cross country runs. Every time, I feel truly grateful and blessed. Yes, crazy as it may seem, now I actually await rainy days so I can go out for a soaking wet run or walk, a pattern of behavior that my friends and family find incredibly strange and quite odd.

Perhaps this little vignette strikes a chord within you.

Vijay Yajnik
(1959 – 1966)
Mayne House

"Mere Gale Lag Jaa" *(Just Hug Me)*

(Original Posting: RKC Forum – September, 2014)

It has been a while since I sent out an RKC Flashback to the group. It was about cross-country runs on rainy afternoons. Perhaps some of you remember it. I did not want to overdo it so I refrained from writing more of them.

But this recent spate of emails about our RKC teachers, the names in the lists, Teacher's Day in India, PM Modi talking to kids via TV, etc., brought back a flood of memories. In my case, and perhaps because I do not live in India, it is about more than memories or nostalgia. Specifically, I thought about this teacher who, with some tough love, taught me something that proved priceless for me years later.

So, while we celebrate and thank all our RKC teachers, on this Teachers' Day, this RF is for him. And the "him" here is none other than the late Mr. Bharat Singh, our gym and swim teacher, in my days at RKC.

What is an "RKC Flashback"? It is written deliberately in the format of "a short story". Please forgive me if it seems a bit long. I hope you enjoy it and also obtain some learnings from it.

Fasten your seatbelts, it may be a bumpy ride!

Acquiring a Vital Skill

I was 9 years old when I joined RKC in 1959 and was placed in the Junior Wing with Mr. Lavkumar as our Housemaster. I did not know English and spoke only Gujarati. This sudden immersion into the world of RKC, with no ability to communicate except with sign language, was traumatic, to put it mildly (Gujarati was verboten and this was strictly enforced. It cost you at the tuck shop). RKC at the time was chock full of "princes" from various states in Saurashtra and elsewhere in India. They were rich, handsome, athletic, regal in their manner, loved sports, and had royal "titles"!

In contrast, I was this gangly awkward kid from Porbandar who knew just about nothing and I was certainly not "royal" in any way at all. Also, I was skinny. It would be accurate to say that I was reed thin. My nickname in the Gujarati school in Porbandar was "khad-makadi" *(grasshopper)*. Others called me "gavar shing" *(string bean)*. You get the picture! But this was RKC, a school designed mainly for the children of the Indian royalty or Brits. Physical abilities were not just a good idea, they were required. They were mandatory. If you could not compete, you just did not fit in and your life turned to shit very quickly. Everybody understood this unwritten code.

In my very first week, I was assigned to my swim class. There were maybe some 10-15 other kids with me. We were called the "non-swimmers" and were to learn to swim. Soon, in every class, someone or another would learn the skill and go swim a "breadth" at the deep end of the pool. This event would be celebrated in a big way by the entire class, much like a pilot getting his/her "wings" after the first solo flight. One by one, most of my classmates became "swimmers", and now there were only the three of us, I think, that were left still paddling away like idiots at the shallow end. It was humiliating.

Then, this day at the end of the class, our teacher, Mr. Bharat Singh, who I will now refer to as "BSir", asked me to wait after everybody had left. I was mortified! I mean BSir to me was in one word... terrifying! His huge body, his muscles, his strength - and he was tougher than a "drill sergeant". He wanted me to stay behind? This surely meant death.

BSir asked me to sit down. He wanted to talk with me. He said, and I am paraphrasing here, "Tu tarata kyon nahi hai?" (*Why are you not swimming?*) "Tu darta hai." (*You are afraid*) "Tu paani se darta hai." (*You are afraid of water*) "Tu aaj is dar ko maar de gaa." (*Today, you will kill this fear*) This was not a conversation, but it swiftly got the point across.

Then he continued, "Dar kya hai?" (*What is fear?*) "Dar shuru se nahi hai, dar anjaam hai." (*Fear is not there from the beginning. It is a result.*) Now I am thinking, is BSir a student of philosophy also? This was most unusual from a man who I thought could kill Superman with ease. Then he said, and these are pearls of wisdom, again paraphrasing, "Aam tor par, jung mein, log darte the." (*At the front, in a war, folks were afraid.*) "Main kaheta tha, jab bhi koi musibat aaye, ghabrao nahin. Pahele socho. Phir samana karo." (*I used to tell them, whenever any trouble arrives, do not panic in fear. First think, and then confront it.*) At the time, I did not think much of this lecture actually. Little did I know.

BSir asked me to go straight to the deep end. At the pool in RKC, in those days, there was a parapet at the water line. It was like 8" below the pool deck. You could hang on to it. Water flowed over it into a channel and into the filtration system. Everybody used to spit into it. BSir told me to go in and hang on to the parapet at the deep end. I was totally petrified about this. But you did not argue with BSir! So, I went down the steps gingerly, facing the wall, with great fear, and then slowly turned and faced the water. BSir was right there in the deep water, treading it. He was maybe 3 feet from me. But amazingly, this Hercules of a man was smiling at me! He only had soft kind words of encouragement! There was no shouting, anger, or any aggressive theatrics. He was sweetness itself! Then BSir said, "Ghabrao nahin. Pahele socho." (*Do not panic. First, think.*) "Phir bus, mere gale lag jaa." (*Then, just hug me.*)

Now this provoked serious thought in my mind. I thought, "Let's face it, you really have no escape from this, ... but he is barely 3 feet away! A kick off the wall should get me 2 feet and my arms at least another 1.5 feet. He has a neck like a tree trunk, ... he is huge, ... he cannot possibly move much. This should not be as difficult as it appears. Once I grab him, he can drag me over. It seems like pretty good odds." All this and more went through my mind for a few seconds. I decided to go for it and lunged for his neck. All I found was water! I kept hearing "Paani khinch, ... ghabrao nahin, ... pahele socho, ... shabash!" (*Pull the water, ... don't panic, ... first think, ... well done!*) When I came up for air the first time around, BSir was still right there! He was still only 3 feet away and repeating his words. Since I could not find his thick neck, I grabbed the water and pulled. In a bit, I looked up and BSir was gone! I panicked! Where was the thick neck? He was standing on the steps, grinning like a Cheshire cat. I turned my head a little and the opposite wall was in front of me. I never found the neck, I never got the hug, but I had just swum my first "breadth". I was now a "swimmer"! And I felt bloody good about my new found status.

BSir did not let me off easy. He made me swim at least 10 breadths that day. Each time he was farther away from me and my confidence grew exponentially. I realized that I had known how to swim all along. I was just afraid of the deep water. The last breadth, and I will never forget this, he sat straddling the diving board that protruded over the deep end, dangling his massive legs on either side, smiling and teasing me about my speed. When we finished, he again said to me, "Aaj tu ne dar ko maar diya. Shabash!" (*Today you killed the fear. Well done!*) "Par yaad rakhna. Jab bhi koi musibat aaye, ghabrao nahin. Pahele socho, phir samana karo." (*But always remember. Whenever any trouble arrives, do not panic in fear. First think, then confront it.*)

Little did I know then, that this bit of advice, which I would summarily forget after leaving RKC, would one day end up saving my life.

A Memorable Weekend in 1982

It all started out as a simple idea for a fun weekend among four friends who were also work colleagues. We were all in our 30's. Our group comprised of Jim Jones, Mike Sczuka, Steve Niles, and me (The names have not been changed, in order to identify the guilty). Jim, our captain, owned this 40-foot sailboat. She was a beauty. She was ocean going, had all the sails, all the navionics, an incredible galley, an inline V-8 diesel engine, and could sleep 12. But the best part was that she was rigged so that just one person could sail her from the cockpit! She was seriously high tech in terms of sailing boats at that time. Jim adored her more than anything, a notion his wife, Maria, just hated. She also hated sailing.

Mike was divorced and single, very eligible, and a player, who liked chasing women. Steve was happily married, with kids, and a homebody. I was the recently married one and still trying to figure out my Indian wife and her joys and sorrows. In short, we were a motley crew of friends that was looking to have some fun, away from the realities of our lives. We all thought that Jim's sailboat would provide that for us over a weekend.

We shoved off early on Saturday morning from the San Francisco Pier 39 marina and sailed all over the SF Bay. The weather was perfect and the day was a blast. Food and fun were at the max. A 40-footer is also a "chick magnet", so Mike was in his element. The next day, around mid-day, we found ourselves off of Paradise Cove, near Tiburon. It was a hot day and we were anchored off the beach in about 20-foot deep water. It was the kind of day when everybody says, "Gosh, it is so hot, ... I need a cold beer." (In reality, this is just crap. It is simply an excuse to drink one too many). Well, as we relaxed, we noticed some bikini clad women sunning on the beach. They had noticed the boat as well and soon offered to swim out to us, which Mike encouraged wholeheartedly. Now, Jim, Steve, and I had mixed feelings about this. We thought, "It sure seems like fun, ... so it has to be bad for us." Then, Jim comes up with the lamest excuse I have ever heard in my life. He says, "Mike, don't be crazy. The water is too cold for their swim." Well, that set everybody off with hoots of laughter. Mike responds with, "Man up! I can swim in this! And sure enough, then followed the typical alcohol fueled male macho bravado of "No, you cannot...", "Yes, I can...", "I bet you 10 bucks...", "No, make it a 100...", "Pollocks cannot swim...", "And Towelheads can?..." and so on (I think every RKCian knows exactly what I am talking about here!). Well, with four adult boys, nearly hammered after too many beers in that hot sun, it went all the way. Partly to show off to the women, who were by now standing on the beach with binoculars trained on us, Mike got to the edge of the boat's deck, screamed and thumped his chest like King Kong, and leapt off!

There were screams from the beach. Not of joy, but of concern. We also rushed to the edge of the deck and scanned the water surface. In a second, Mike broke surface and shouted, "Shit, get me outta here!!" He dashed to the stern and we hauled him in. He was shivering hard with chattering teeth, but still buzzed. He says to me, "Ok, Towelhead, your turn, or are you chicken? And where is my C note?" Well, an RKCian does not pass up a dare, no matter how crazy it may be. It is just not in our DNA to admit fear or failure. So, yup, like an idiot, I took the bait. I went to the edge of the deck, threw a nastygram at Mike, and leapt off.

Now, for those that may not know, SF Bay waters are very dangerous. An Arctic cold current feeds the Bay and the water is ice cold. Within 10 minutes, usually hypothermia starts to set in. Also, given the natural topography of the SF Bay, there is always a current of around 5 knots everywhere. In the main channel, it is 9 knots. It is nearly impossible to swim against or even at an angle to this fast-moving massive body of water. That is why, back when, Alcatraz was considered a prison from where nobody escaped alive. Then, there are the huge whirlpools in the main channel. If you get sucked in, you may not be found for days, if at all. Past them, one could easily get washed out under the Golden Gate Bridge and out to the Pacific Ocean. And for good measure, just outside the GGB, are the breeding waters of the Great White Shark (yes, as in the movie, "Jaws"!). In short, it is a very bad idea to try to swim in the SF Bay. All four of us knew this.

Against my sun heated skin, the ice-cold water hit me with the sting of a whip lash. My body jerked hard as I went below the surface. My torso shook so hard that I dislocated my right shoulder (At the time, I had an old ski injury which had left me with a partially torn rotator cuff in my right shoulder. This would cause anterior dislocations easily in certain arm movements. It has since been surgically fixed.). As my descent into the water stopped, I sensed the motion caused by the current. I was bone cold and then I felt the searing pain in my right shoulder. I checked my right shoulder and felt the bonehead. My whole right arm was just limp and totally useless. All this happened so fast. I tried clearing my head with, "Where am I? Let's see now, ... you are 6 feet below surface in SF Bay, ... there is a 5 knot current dragging you away to the main channel, ... it is crazy cold water, ... you have 10 minutes to the start of hypothermia, ... the pain says your right shoulder is dislocated, ... and nobody on the boat knows your condition. Overall, this situation is not good, ... in fact, it sucks!"

As my mind began to comprehend the danger I was in, the panic attack started. I felt it welling up inside me. That intense sense of fear and foreboding started to develop rapidly. And this is when it happened. This is when I had my flashback.

Suddenly, from way back in time, a booming voice shouted in my mind," Jab bhi koi musibat aaye, ghabrao nahi. Pahele socho, phir samana karo." *(Whenever trouble arrives, don't panic in fear. First think, then confront it.)* It kept repeating, getting louder and forceful. It overtook my panic attack. I began to think. In microseconds, I worked out a plan and went straight into execution mode. I took my limp right hand with my left hand and laid it across my stomach. With my right-hand fingers, which still worked, I gripped the left side of my waist and stabilized the arm. That reduced the pain. Next, I kicked to break surface. As soon as I broke surface, I rolled over onto my back and with my left hand and legs tried to swim a backstroke towards the boat. The boat was already 20+ feet behind me as I had drifted away. Then I shouted repeatedly toward the boat, "Dislocation, ...dislocation!!" Luckily, amidst all the revelry on board, Steve heard me. Then I heard urgent shouts on the boat. "Hey! Vij, ... in trouble, ... raise anchor, ... get the vest, ... ready the rope, ... get up on the bow, ... stern ladder down, ... raise the main, ... fire motor!" I knew that help was on the way.

The whole gang swung into action. I could hear the clanking of the heavy chain as the anchor was raised, the shrill whine of the main sail's motorized winch winding its sheet, and then with a menacing growl the diesel motor came to life. Under power and sail, I was rescued, but it was 300 yards from where I had jumped in and just 150 yards or so from the main channel. We returned to Pier 39 and I was taken to the hospital to get fixed up. Then, after making a solemn pact that we would not ever talk about our weekend, we all went home sheepishly.

We certainly got a walloping from our families. But the story also leaked at work, so we got raked there as well. We were told or asked, "Are you all nuts?"... "You could have died!"... "How utterly immature!"... "Grown up little boys"... "Arrested development, no doubt", and so on. The embarrassment went on for weeks.

Epilogue

Many years have passed since that weekend. Steve is now retired and living up in Idaho with his family. Mike met the love of his life (in our HR Dept.!), married her, and later retired in Calistoga, Napa Valley, California. He died a few years ago of cancer.

Nilima (my wife) and I, met Jim and Maria a while ago during a trip to San Francisco. We met after many years and had dinner at a restaurant. After we settled into our table, I casually asked, "So, how is the boat?". Maria happily replied, "Oh, we sold it. Jim does not sail anymore!" Nilima nodded to this thought in full agreement.

After a lovely evening, as we were leaving, the ladies went to the powder room. While Jim and I stood waiting for the valet to bring the car, Jim asked me, "Do you remember anything that day after that crazy jump?" I replied, "I remember you guys coming for me, but not the details. I was in serious pain."

Jim went on, "It was hard to catch up with you, and luckily, you did grab the rope we threw over your chest with your left arm. But what was harder was getting you in the boat. With the current, I had to hold her at near full throttle, in reverse, with the sail down. Also, I was worried about the two screws slicing somebody's legs. Especially, since Mike and Steve had to jump into the water to help haul you aboard. And then, going back to the Pier, the wind kicked up crazy and the Bay had white caps everywhere. I don't know how we made it back. You know, by the time we got you to the ER, you were blue in color and hyperventilating? We were really scared."

Jim then turned and asked me, "Tell me something, because I have always wondered about this. That day, when you were below the surface, with your shoulder popped out, how did you control the panic? If you had not, you know, it might have been fatal."

I replied, "Jim, as a young boy in India, I was blessed with the opportunity to attend a great school with great teachers. And I was blessed even more by having an incredible swim teacher. I used to be very scared of water. He taught me to handle panic."

Jim goes, "Yeah, but you were 6 feet under, in the frigid SF Bay, how did..."

And I went, "Yes, I know what you are wondering about. Now, you may not believe it, but down under, in the ice-cold water on that fateful day, he was there with me."

When I finally got the chance to visit RKC some years ago, I met ASir (Mr. Ayaaz Khan) and later LSir (Mr. Lavkumar). However, BSir had passed away a little prior to my visit. I was deeply saddened to learn that, because I always wanted to tell him this story.

If I could have done that, I feel that after all these years, without a doubt, he would have been filled with joy. In spite of his painful arthritis and the wheelchair, I know that I would have finally gotten that promised hug!

The Joy of "Live" Performances

(Original Posting: RKC Forum – October, 2015)

This past Summer of 2015 was special for me. Madam Cooper and her sister, Perin Boga, came from Lahore, Pakistan, to the USA on a tour organized by the amazing Rahul Patel. I was lucky to participate and had the opportunity to host them for a week in Southern California and environ. I saw them after 50 years! It was just wonderful. We strolled down the memory lane and caught up on our lives. We also had some lively times, shared experiences to be treasured, and made new memories together, to add to the very old ones. It was simply priceless for me and my wife, Nilima.

One of the things I was able to do with them, during a nearly 1,000-mile road trip, was share with them a flashback of mine. They got quite a kick out of it. I thought that you might enjoy it also. So, here it is for all of you.

"Detention" with Madam Cooper, Richard Burton, & Claire Bloom

Soon after I joined RKC in 1959, I was placed in Form IV. The class had some 5 students in it and our teacher was the young and lovely Miss Rati Cooper. While I dabbled a bit here and there, it would be accurate to say that I did not know English. Well, Miss Cooper (Madam) had no tolerance at all for students that did not know this prized language, so I was someone she focused her attention on considerably, much to my chagrin. I was given extra prep work and drilled in English relentlessly. My mistakes in everything, whether written or spoken, were promptly identified, explained, corrected, and also forgiven. However, what was never ever forgiven was a lack of effort or dedication to learning. These were cardinal sins and would elicit Madam's wrath visibly. And that was never a pleasant experience.

In this new and strange environment, I made a friend. He was in my class. His name was Shahid Siddiqui. We became "best buddies" over our RKC years and beyond. Shahid (Sid) and I (Yaggy) bonded even more because we used to travel by train together from Rajkot to Bombay when RKC closed for the holidays. The school was mostly empty by 11am, because many students were picked up by their families after breakfast. Our train was at 2pm or so. We would go by a "tanga" (*a horse and buggy*) with a teacher to see us off at the Rajkot Junction railway station. During the train journey, Sid and I would fight like cats and dogs at various train stations in our quest for the latest comics on Superman, Batman, etc. At issue was always, who would buy what? Who would get to read what first? However, the one thing we both looked forward to was the arrival of the Ahmedabad Junction station. This would be after a change of trains from the smaller "meter" gauge to the bigger "broad" gauge at the Viramgam Junction station, a process which we found to be very exciting (Does this still occur today? Does anybody remember this? I wonder.) At Ahmedabad, our small RKC group was joyously greeted by the radiant smile of Mr. Ayaaz Khan (ASir). He was always there! It was great and we adored him (He was not yet a teacher at RKC at the time. He had yet to join the school staff.). But to us, he was handsome, fit, eloquent, caring, and so funny! We would talk super excitedly, share some "bhajias" (*deep fried vegetable fritters*), drink something, catch up on RKC life, etc. as quickly as possible. It would all be over in 20 minutes and the "goodbyes" would follow. Sid and I would be sad after Ahmedabad went by and then it was time to sleep. In short, Sid and I became very close through such shared experiences.

Then, during school one day, Sid and I engaged in some serious mischief in the Junior Wing. And we were caught. In fact, we got caught red handed! Furthermore, to add insult to injury, and we thought we were being very clever, we proceeded to lie about it all! Our tall tales did not work. The evidence was overwhelming. Justice was administered swiftly, we were found guilty, and sentenced to detention on Saturday.

I had no idea what "detention" was or what it meant. Sid explained it all, and then confidently told me to not worry because he was going to get us out of it! The film in the quadrangle that Saturday evening was "Prisoner of Zenda", or "Ivanhoe", or "Robin Hood", or some such thing, and Sid was not going to have us miss it. It was all going to work out wonderfully, until we learnt Saturday evening that detention later on was being held by Miss Cooper! Both of us just froze! Matters had decidedly taken a turn for the worse. I was just beside myself and I blamed Sid for everything. Was it not enough that I had to do all that extra prep work given out by Madam? Now, even on a Saturday night, I could not have any fun, I wailed. But our goose was cooked. We had no choice and so, with a heavy heart, we decided to make the best of it.

We went up the stairs to Madam's apartment slowly and quietly. At the door, Sid whispered, "Yaggy, ask for permission to enter." So, I took a deep breath and said, "Madam, can we come in?"

93

Back came a very sharp and clear retort, "You can. But you MAY not."

Sid elbowed me and said, "Use may instead of can." So, I tried again, "Madam, may we come in?"

Now came back a sweet and melodious reply, "Oh, yes! You certainly may!"

Madam had everything laid out. The record player, records, books, cushions, etc. She was beaming with joy! She cheerily announced, "Tonight, we are going to listen to a play. And you will love it, I am certain." She told us about how she had secured recordings of some wonderful plays and how we were going to listen to them and learn some amazing things. This particular one was a Shakespearean play (I forget which one, ... maybe "Taming of the Shrew"). But what I clearly do remember is that it starred Richard Burton and Claire Bloom! At the time, I had no idea who they were, except that I liked the sound of their names. And foremost, I remember that pair of theatrically trained voices that left me mesmerized.

The evening that followed was magical. We listened to the records and followed the play along in the books. Madam pointed out things like "enunciation, diction, pauses, tempo, emotion, projection, modulation, etc." It was all about the proper and theatrical way to speak. Then, at the end, Madam said something else. She said, and I am paraphrasing here, "You have just listened to some gifted and skilled professional artists perform. But you should experience what it is like to see or hear them perform "live"! It is even more amazing! You see, unlike a recorded performance, a "live" performance is unique. Each one is unique. It is all between you and the artists for that one particular time. Is it always perfect? No. Each performance is different. Artists have good days and bad, mistakes are made, unexpected things happen, stage hands get it wrong, music is off at times, and so on. But the professionals show their real skills and artistry in handling and recovering from all these things, to deliver a grand performance. That is what makes it unique. And it is a thing of beauty!"

That evening, I recall leaving detention in a very reflective state of mind. What I had just heard was incredible, but I could not get my head around it. "Live" professional performances? Where? When? How? In the ensuing years at RKC, I did recitations (at annual Prize Givings) and school plays ("Toad of Toad Hall", etc.). I was in great company in all these activities. Buddies like Sid, Himanshu Jani (Jans), Vijay Ram (Golsy), and many others, in a long list of names come to mind. We all performed in something or another together over those years. And of course, there was always our annual Tattoo. Throughout all this at RKC, and later on, even through the university years, I was able to experience many aspects of the performing arts, but "live" professional performances remained elusive for me. Where my family was posted, and also in Kanpur, the opportunities were very limited. And I could not see much more than "folk shows" or a few timid "nautanki" type recitals.

I never fully understood what Madam had meant that evening at detention, until many years later, in a different time and at a different place.

A Play in Beverly Hills, California

(Noel Coward's Play, "Private Lives", starring Richard Burton, Elizabeth Taylor, Claire Bloom & George Segal)

It was a Sunday morning in September, 1983. With a cup of coffee in hand, I opened the Calendar section of the San Francisco Chronicle and there it was! A quarter page Ad announcing a very limited engagement of a theatrical play in Los Angeles. In fact, only 7 shows, one per day. But that was not all. Headlining the show were Richard Burton and Elizabeth Taylor! Supporting them were Claire Bloom and George Segal! I could not believe my eyes!

I said to Nilima, "Hey, hon, we gotta go and see this!" The cheapest way to LA at the time was a 7+ hour drive from San Francisco, which is where we lived. So, this meant that over two days we would have to drive 14+ hours and stay overnight in LA. So what? To me, this was no big deal, a piece of cake, and nothing to worry about. My suggestion was instantly rejected.

I pleaded with Nilima. I talked animatedly about RKC, detentions, Madam Cooper, etc. It was all to no avail. She said, "I feel bad saying this, but that was your childhood in a British style public or boarding school. I attended a Catholic school, as a day student. It is hard for me to relate to your experiences. Now, if this show had Amitabh Bachchan, or Rajesh Khanna, or even Jeetendra, or Dharambhai, performing "live", I would be there in a flash." Well, after much ado, in the end, she decided to let me win and gave in. She told me calmly, "Look, we have seen many shows with famous stars. But I know that these stars are special for you. So, ok, let's go see them, while we still can. However, in spite of your excitement, this is still after all just another theatrical show with some famous actors."

Now, this comment of hers made me think. It certainly was a perspective, quite different from mine, and it was conveyed with honesty. And yet, ...yet somehow, ...I felt that she had missed the point. The essence of it, ...the realm of possibilities in grand theatre, ...an opportunity to witness highly skilled artists, ...with a lifetime of training, ...at the "top of their game", as it were. A game, where anything can happen!

Noel Coward was a celebrated British author, among many other things, of the 20th century. His play, "Private Lives", was written and performed in the 1930's, in London and New York, with celebrated stars of that era. It was a smash hit. It has been made into films also. Since then, the play has been revived, reprised, adapted, translated, and so forth, in countless ways. Its allure lies in its story, and all that it can and does imply. It is a comedy, with drama, verbal fights, surreal dialogue, and a social commentary on its times. It is also stylish and quite "avant garde". Major theatrical/film stars have been drawn to it repeatedly, in its various incarnations, over the decades.

In essence, this 3-Act play is about a divorced couple that has found new spouses who are much younger. At their honeymoons, to their utter surprise, they discover that they are checked into the same resort as their "ex-es". Furthermore, they are in adjacent suites! Then all sorts of stuff happens.

Well, this story obviously had huge commercial appeal for Richard Burton and Elizabeth Taylor, who had in real life by then, been married and divorced twice! This was art imitating life and it was irresistible to the audiences and the media. All 7 shows at the Wilshire Theatre in Beverly Hills (in LA) were sold out promptly. The "premier" show brought forth all the big Hollywood celebrities and the scene at the theatre entrance was better than the red carpet on Oscar night. It had national, live, TV coverage. The sheer wattage of the stars present in the audience could blind anybody. *Private Lives* had become hyped as a must see (... or be seen at) event in Hollywood. Amidst all this glitz and glam madness, I managed to score two tickets to the 5th show, with great difficulty. They were monumentally expensive, and I wondered seriously if I had made a mistake.

From the opening curtain, it was clear that "Private Lives" was a superb production. All four stars, who comprised the entire cast, were greeted with long ovations upon their first stage entrance. Richard and Liz were clearly the objects of all the star-struck adulation and curiosity. Claire and George were superb in every way also. The play was great fun and everybody was enjoying it enormously. And then, it suddenly happened, ...surprisingly, ...and out of nowhere!

The scene was intense. Liz, at up-stage center, was working herself up into a major frenzy towards Richard and Claire was behind her at mid-stage right. Liz hurled a major verbal insult at Richard. Everybody drew their breath expecting a nasty response from Richard, ... but nothing came back! He just stood there at mid-stage left, quite still, and looking totally lost! He mumbled,

"Oh... uh... wh-what's going on?" Liz and Claire also stood still, maintaining their positions and postures, and gave a steady look at Richard. Many seconds went by, ... yet nothing. A hush fell across the theatre with everybody wondering what was happening? Something was clearly not right. Even the orchestra seemed to be lost and drifted off into silence. Suddenly, my mind flashed back to that RKC detention evening with Madam Cooper from so many years ago. I recalled Madam's words in a rapid burst of mental flashes, "Each "live" performance is unique... skilled professionals... highly trained in their craft... things do go wrong... unexpected things happen... handling and recovering... a thing of beauty!"

Then it dawned on me! In a snap, I realized what was going on! Richard, ...the great Richard Burton, ... was having a "hard blank"! All theatrical performers experience "blanks" at various times in their lives. These "blanks" come in two basic flavors. The "soft blank" is one where, for example, an artist momentarily forgets a word/phrase/line and has difficulty recalling it. His memory is jogged by other cast members or an off-stage prompter. The lapse is corrected, and the action continues. A "hard blank", the rarer flavor, is one where an artist loses orientation, context, character, and dialogue, totally and completely. The mind simply goes blank, like a clean slate. It is a frightening experience for the artist. Nobody knows what causes it, how to predict it, or how to prevent it. It remains a mystery. Also, it ends very unpredictably. Nobody can predict its duration, or how or what causes it to end. But when it does end, it is as though it never happened! The restoration and recall of the mind are instantaneous and complete. So, the challenge for the artist afflicted, and the cast on stage, is in dealing with the episode and the possible damage that can be caused by it. Professional artists are trained, grilled, rehearsed, etc. in various techniques about how to deal with a "hard blank", if it should happen to you or a fellow cast member, God forbid.

Note: What follows below is purely from my distant memory. The events and their sequence are accurate. But as to the words, I have taken poetic license to try and make the reader feel how I felt when I experienced it. I can only hope that I achieved that purpose.

The tension in the theatre was now palpable. Richard was still bumbling around at his spot with incoherent grunts or silence. Liz and Claire were standing still looking at him. The audience was getting uneasy, sort of with a sense of "Hey, what the f**k is going on?" (Hollywood audiences often have no class at all, and little patience.) Then suddenly, everything changes!

Liz takes a graceful step to her left and steps out of her character, Amanda. She walks around up-stage and starts chatting with the audience about her private life with Richard! "Oh, such a relief to be out of Amanda! You know, this here Dickey is always full of surprises. When we were married, did you know this? ... Ah, yes. ... When we were married, ... you know, ... he loved the bottle. He just loved it. He loved it more than me! And he was such a dreamer, ... he was always dreaming. Were you not always dreaming, darling? Dreaming about me!" Then, Claire steps out of her character with a similar graceful step to the left, walks up-stage, and starts bantering with Liz!

"Now, now, Liz, you must get a hold of yourself. It is not Dickey's fault that you have gone over the hill, shall we say? Things are now sagging, ... still nice, ... but in need of a lot of support, eh, mon cherie? You know, Cleopatra was a while ago. And that, dearie, was such a dream! ... Oh, that Anthony and you, ... what a dreamy pair! But don't knock him now. He still loves you and dreams about you. Well, ... at least that is what I am told!"

"Why, you little hussy! How dare you? Oh, ... but is it true what I hear, Claire dear? That you have had it bad for him for a while now? And that he is quite enamored of you! He fancies you, does he not? And in your dreams, you want him too, don't you? Trollop!"

The catty and wicked banter continued. The "zingers" then began flying at Richard from both of them. The audience was still clueless, but now in hysterics with laughter. Liz was on a roll, in her superb "improv" mode, and just crackled with her evil laugh and earthy humor. Claire "played" the demure defender of Richard, but was sharp as a tack as well. Then, I noticed something. Both of them moved on stage, but within a limited space. In their loud and crass banter, there was a constant theme about "dreaming" and 'being loved or wanted". Also, after every zinger or two, both of them would pause, look at Richard steadily for a bit, then turn away and resume their banter. Their jokes were raunchy, private, personal, tender, vicious, and more, but always returned to their theme at the end. The "improv" build, timing, and execution were flawless. It all looked and sounded like the play. By now, the audience response was like loud thunder after every zinger, and I am sitting at the edge of my seat wondering where all this was going. Suddenly, things changed again!

Richard's "hard blank" resolved itself! Some 3 to 4 minutes had passed (in theatrical terms, if you are on stage, that feels like several eternities). Richard now had total and complete recall of what had just happened. So, he looks confidently at Liz and Claire, smiles broadly, takes a graceful step to the left, steps out of his Elyot character, and is now himself! Then he says, "Well, well, Elizabeth and Claire, you have had your fun with Dickey. Richard will now deal with all the lies that you two harlots have been telling my friends here!" The audience roared its approval! But I was fixated on the stage. This just cannot be! The whole cast on stage was "out of character"! Where was the play? What next? How does one get back? To where? I had never seen anything like this in my life! In my gut, I sensed that I was about to witness a major theatrical disaster.

Then I noticed the furtive looks, glances, and quick low whispers between Richard, Liz, and Claire, throughout the raucous noise from the audience, which was still giddy about Richard. As the audience settled into quiet, Liz projected beautifully across the theatre. "Pickup... Top of 31... On Count ... Five... Four... Cue Music... Three... Two... One!" Then, simultaneously and with surgical precision, Richard, Liz, and Claire took a graceful step to their right and entered their respective characters, in mid-scene.

Liz whirled around and snarled at Richard, "Elyot, you still want me, don't you? Admit it. You have always wanted me. I am the one and only. You want me..."

Richard gave Liz a charming smile, a shrug, and said, "Amanda, not in your dreams, love. Not ever... not even in your dreams!" Then he walked over towards Claire.

Action resumed. Nothing seemed amiss in the play.

It took a while to sink in. The audience slowly realized that they had just witnessed something incredibly awesome. Most did not know exactly what, but they knew enough to sense that it was special. Then the applause began. First as a ripple, which grew into a wave, and then into roaring breakers. As full realization set in, it became loud as thunder. Everybody was on their feet. On stage, the play action stopped! By now, George was also on stage. The entire cast froze in acknowledgement of the long applause. Through it all, I noticed that nobody in the cast broke position, posture, or even facial expression! There was just no movement, period. As the applause died down, the play action simply resumed.

There were five curtain calls. Richard, Liz, Claire, and George were uber loved! The stage was splattered with thrown flowers and bouquets. Each star was handed something floral by somebody very young from the audience. The whistles, hoots, shrieks, and applause just went on... and on. The star cast gave each other a kiss on the cheek and blew kisses at the audience. The audience chanted, "Liz, Dick... Liz, Dick..." Sensing the fervor, Richard again gave Liz a nice kiss on the cheek. Liz turned and gave him a full hug and a kiss on the lips in return. The whole place just went nuts!

Locally, it came to be known as "The Performance". The critics, media, theatre guru's all weighed in with a common theme the next day. "No words can describe fully what occurred last night at the Wilshire Theatre. Let's just say, it was one of the finest moments in the theatrical arts."

Epilogue

S trangely, within a year of the show we saw, Richard Burton passed away, quite suddenly and at a rather young age. Liz lived a long life for many years after Richard. She was often seen around LA at various "show biz" events. Local legend still persists in whispers that, till the end of her life, she kept a picture of Richard Burton near her bed. Claire and George continue to have successful careers.

In 2006, Sid and Shehnaaz, his wife, visited us in LA. I regaled him with this story, among many others. He loved every bit of it. He too had not lost his love for the theatre. In fact, he was playing "Jahangir" in a local group production in Bangalore! Little did we know then, that Sid would fall gravely ill soon thereafter. We saw them again in Bangalore, in December 2007, when Nilima and I went there to visit them. His illness was too advanced. We shared precious moments together. We received news that day that Sid was going to become a Grandpa! And then I had to bid "adieu" to my very dear friend. He passed away 4 months later. With him, a piece of me died as well.

Among the many things I could tell you about Madam & Perin's visit this summer, I think Nilima said it the best. She said, "Now, I understand why you have talked about her so much all these years. I met her only for a week, but I just fell for her too."

Madam and Perin made their visit with us memorable in so many ways. I will give you one small example. The first morning, after they arrived, I asked Madam, "How would you like your coffee?" She smiled brightly, and in her theatrical best, said, "Black as the night, ... Hot as hell, ... and Sweet as love, Vijay!" Honestly, how can anybody top that? We wish them a healthy, long and joyous life.

I humbly dedicate this story to Madam Cooper and all my fellow RKCians, who developed a love for the performing arts, under her tutelage.

Primal Fear

(Original Posting: RKC Forum – October, 2016)

F riends,
It seems that this forum has lately gone low key or fallen entirely silent. The reasons, I do not know. Perhaps it just reflects the collective moods within the countries.

In India, you have the "Currency Crisis" that is making life miserable for everybody, even if it is temporary. Here in the USA, we have the "Election Crisis", as nobody can figure out how a rich, red necked, thin skinned, misogynist, racist, and inexperienced wacko got elected President! I am bewildered and at a total loss also. The theories about why all this happened are endless. To me, it seems that this country is just turning more stupid by the day.

In these trying times, perhaps some kind of distraction and levity are in order to make sure that we all maintain our collective sanity. So, I have written something for all of you. I hope that it makes you forget your troubles for a little while, brightens your day a little bit, and perhaps even makes you smile.

As is said in the Gita, "... And this too shall pass..."
Enjoy & Happy Thoughts, Always,
Vijay

A Troubled Night

A few nights ago, I went to sleep in a somewhat perturbed state of mind. Then later on, something happened, which woke me up, startled me quite a bit, and provoked some old memories. Let me explain.

You see, I live in the Palos Verdes area of Los Angeles. Out here, everything is quite rural, quaint, understated, and most of it is your true American "horse country". Oh, one can go riding horses of all sorts here (Arabians, Thoroughbreds, Quarter horses, etc.). They all need to be exercised every day and the horse farms welcome riders of all skill levels. You select the horse, choose English or Western saddle, the route for the ride, etc. and all rides are free. Also, it is a nationally known place for horse shows, sales, and "stud services". By local law, there are few street signs, if any, no street

101

lights of any kind, and at night, it is all very dark. It is also quite easy to get lost (GPS does not work here, due to a lack of signal) and, to make things a bit more interesting, there is also plenty of wild life around. But, on the whole, for those of us who choose to live here, it is a charming place.

Before I go on, I should remind you that my memories of RKC, as a young lad especially in the 1959-62 years, are quite similar to all this. The school was quite dark at night, as I recall. There were stairways, hallways, nooks, and other sinister looking places, that put some real fear in a kid like me at night. The lights were low wattage, luminescent types (the old yellow bulb!), as opposed to the fluorescent (the lovely white tube light!). On dark moon nights, the Quadrangle looked to me, from the Junior Wing arches, like some kind of a scary huge black pit with demons and goblins running around!

Perhaps it was all the fertile imagination of a young boy, but I was not alone. Then we had this "Phantom" episode (Does anybody remember it?). There was this guy, who came to RKC in the middle of the night, dressed all in black, and stole things while scaring the students in many ways. He terrorized the entire school! I recall kids in my dorm who refused to go to sleep, because "the Phantom was coming!" The key teachers, ASir (Mr. Ayaaz Khan), LSir (Mr. Lavkumar), and Rogey (Mr. Rogerson) organized a posse of some kind, and in a few days, they caught this crazy dude. I think they beat the crap out of him before turning him over to the authorities. Apparently, this guy used to work at the Gaisford Theatre near RKC, and would come to the school after the late show. It was a very scary episode, to say the least. Well, it was in this frame of mind, that I went to sleep on this night.

I woke up suddenly and for no explicable reason. It was around 3:00am. I was in the bedroom above the garage, with the window open. I was about 10-12 feet above the driveway and about 8 feet off its sides. There were bushes, shrubs, and trees all around it. I heard loud and ferocious growls, strained hisses, and scuffling. With it, I also heard loud squealing. I became alert very quickly. I went to the window and strained to see. Outside it was pitch black and I could not see anything. Based on the sounds, I sensed that a "hunt" of some kind was in progress. Should I use the LED torch? Should I go down and investigate? After some thought, I decided to let it all be. It was nature doing its thing and it was not my place to interfere. But, in all honesty, I was also afraid.

Next morning, I thought about it. Yes, I had been afraid that prior night. But why? Surely, it was a fear of the "unknown". But what if it was something "known"? What would that fear be like? I thought about it for a while. And then, I recalled a few events in my life where I had, in fact, experienced just such a fear. I decided to call it the "Primal Fear". Here are a few short stories that you may enjoy and possibly even relate to.

Visit to Sasan, Gir Forest, India in 1954-55

It was late in the evening and getting dark. My Dad, our Chief Chemist (CC), and I, were in an open Willys Jeep driving on a terrible dirt road through the dense Gir Forest. We were headed towards the Government Circuit House (or Guest House/Dak Bungalow, etc. I forget the name it was called at the time) in Sasan, at the center of the Forest. (Is it still there? Maybe they tore it down and built something else?) My Dad was driving, I was in the middle seat, and CC was in the left seat. Suddenly, we hear a "…hissss …and … thump … thump … thump…" My Dad brought the Jeep to a stop and said," I think we have a puncture in the front left tire." As he shut down the motor, head lights, etc., an eerie silence fell upon all of us.

Then suddenly, we hear snarling, scuffling, and all kinds of growls from about 30 feet away to the left of the road. In the dim and fading light, we see a pride of lions feeding on a "kill". At 5-6 years of age, I was scared out of my mind! And then CC started chanting "Om Namah Shivaye...", because he did not know what else to do.

This is when my Dad said to me, "Vijay, listen. Yes, there are lions there, but do not be afraid. If anything comes near us, just turn this switch and push this button. That will start the engine. This switch turns the lights on, and this one is the horn. They do not like light or sounds, so we should be fine. Just watch out for them, while I change the tire." I said, "okay", but I did not believe it. My fear was "Primal". The fear of knowing that you were not at the "top of the food chain" any more, in your current situation.

Dad went to work quickly. He got the spare tire out, jacked up the Jeep, changed the tire, and then put everything in place in the back. When he walked around and got into the driver's seat, I heaved a sigh of immense relief. As he started the engine and turned on the headlights, a full-grown adult lion passed from the left to right about 6 feet in front of our Jeep! I think CC choked on his chants, I went comatose in raw fear, and my Dad said, "Let's go now. But he is a beautiful creature, isn't he?"

We got to the Sasan Circuit House in a short while. It was a classic British style "hunting lodge", the kind found all over the world, especially in India, South Asia, or Africa. A nice big full-service building, with 4-5 bedrooms, built 2-3 feet off the ground, surrounded by 8-10-foot verandas with wooden canopies, on two sides at least. There were lovely wicker furniture sets everywhere and steps that led down to the ground which was just dirt. There was a clearing of about 20 feet all around the property, but no paving, parking spots, compound walls, gates, etc. You walked down the few steps from the veranda into the cleared area, and then into the wilderness and its dense foliage. There was also very limited electricity and for a very short time, mainly for emergency needs. Lanterns were used for light mostly.

That night, there were two British families and one Parsee family there from Bombay. The "Khansama" (that was I think the title of the Chief of Staff of the place!) was serving "Sundowners" when we arrived. Shortly, a sumptuous dinner was served and then they "set up for the night". The Khansama explained that the building had to be totally secured at night because of the presence of wild animals. And we were smack in the middle of a large wilderness area. They stacked up all the veranda furniture, secured all the doors on the inside with padlocks, in case somebody left something open accidentally. Then, the world went dark, except for the occasional oil lamp. It was quite scary all around.

Around 2am or so, I woke up and wanted a drink of water. The water station (your basic clay "matlee", because there was no fridge of any kind) was down the hallway, past a large window. I walked over and at the window, I froze. Outside, on the veranda, sat a huge lion and a lioness! I could only see them in silhouette, but they noticed me and turned their heads to look at me. Except for the slight protection of the thin glass window, I was only about 3-4 feet from these big cats and I was terrified! I felt the adrenaline rush of Primal Fear. I began to struggle with the ambivalence of the "fight or flight" response to mortal danger. Then I did something quite prevalent in the face of mortal danger in the animal kingdom. I pee'd in my pajamas!

When my Dad told others about all this the next morning at breakfast, they all laughed with great affection. They thought it was all so cute. The Khansama just smiled at me and said, "Oh, they are regular visitors here. We even have names for them and their cubs. Did you see the cubs?" I pouted and said, "No! And I am done seeing lions now for a long while."

I have not been to the Gir Forest since that memorable trip so long ago. Hopefully, one day I get to see how things are today. I am told that the preservation programs for the Asiatic lions are now quite advanced and well organized. Perhaps the RKC Alumni continue to be a part of these efforts even today. If so, I wish them continued and much success in their endeavors.

Kruger National Park, South Africa – Summer of 2000

I t was in the month of June, when it is Winter "down under". I was on a safari trip to this famous park and wildlife preserve with my family. It was all the more special for my wife, Nilima, and me, since our children were young enough to come with us, and old enough to remember it all. With a much lower level of foliage in the winter, it was a great time of the year to see wildlife in their natural environment.

We were driving from the Sabi Sabi Game Reserve to the Mala Mala Game Reserve in the Kruger National Park, as we had split our time between these fabulous places. We were in an open Land Rover jeep driving on dirt roads, which were more like wide pathways. At a T junction, the Ranger turned left and suddenly right in front of us we see a herd of giraffes! There were some 30 of them and they were very close to us! I asked him to stop the jeep so I could shoot some photos. As the jeep came to a stop, I jumped out on the left side with my camera at the ready. Immediately, the Ranger jumped out also, with a gun he grabbed from the gun rack. I heard him load the magazine and cock the rifle. He stood right next to me with his gun ready for trouble! Then he said gently, "Vijay, never ever do that in this Park. You do not know what is 3 feet from you in this foliage. It can and has been fatal for many folks over time." I was incredulous! I said, "Really?" And he said, "Yes. And, do you know that giraffes are a favorite food for large cats? There could be anything near us right now. And, with a herd as large as this, a hunt could begin at any moment." Well, I quickly took my shots and got back into the jeep fast. During the rest of the trip, I kept thinking about what the Ranger had said. Such mortal danger? In such a serene and beautiful scene? It was hard to imagine.

Next day, we set out on our daily open jeep safari drives. There were two each day. One in the early morning and one in the evening and into the night. We were headed to see a herd of rhinos, when suddenly our tracker, who sat on a special chair, called out to the Ranger, "Eh-hey...Ngonyama!" The Ranger gently brought the jeep to a stop. He spoke in a low whisper, "Shhh... everybody! Shhh... keep quiet! Look, on the left, 4-5 feet away, a male lion!" There were 6 of us in the jeep. Everybody looked and slowly, one by one, they began to see the lion. All, except me and my son, Neil! Both of us strained hard, but all we saw was natural foliage, no lion anywhere! Then suddenly, Neil whispers, "Holy crap, Dad! He is huge!" And I am going, "Where? Jeez, beta, somebody show me this goddam lion!"

The camouflage was perfect. All I saw was yellow foliage. Then, as sometimes happens, the mind is picking up data points, but it cannot form the full picture. And then all of a sudden, it does! My mind did just that and suddenly the lion snapped into its form and came into sharp focus. And I went, "Oh, Dear God!" An African lion, a full-grown adult, is a sight to behold! And when he is that close, it is surreal. He was gazing straight at the Land Rover with his huge tongue hanging out! I again felt that rush of Primal Fear. Thank God, I was in this vehicle! Then, I understood what the Ranger had meant the prior day.

Later that evening, we encountered 3 lionesses! As we came up on them, they were quite still and gazing at something ahead of us. The Ranger whispered, "… Shhh... be very quiet… and stay still... watch... a hunt is in progress!" He shut down the Land Rover's engine and headlights. By now night had fallen, but the moon was out and we could see them clearly about 30 feet away. Then, the lionesses began to split up. One went to the right, one in the middle, and one to the left towards our Rover. She walked very slowly and stealthily towards us and then stood by the side. But her gaze was locked onto something up ahead in the dark. She was so close to me that I could have reached out and down and caressed her back! But I was just beside myself in raw fear. My heart was in my throat and Neil gripped my arm tightly and silently mouthed, "Dad, I am scared." Then, as if on some cue, all 3 lionesses charged. I have never seen an animal so large go from zero to a speed of perhaps 30-40 km/hour, in barely a second or two. All three went off like bullets. Then, in the distant moonlight, I saw an adult impala leap clear across the entire road. We waited quietly in the dark, but there was only silence. The Ranger said, "They missed." It took 2 hours and 3 drinks to calm my nerves down that evening. Even Nilima had 2 glasses of wine.

Next day, at the evening dinner, we were treated to a feast with live African "Zulu" and "Xhosa" entertainment, and to introduce us to a "boma". A boma is round structure, about 40-50 feet in diameter, and is made of a single wall made out of bamboo. They lash bamboo sticks together with natural plant strings into 6-8-foot segments. Then they lash these segments together and set them up vertically in a circle. One end of the bamboo is shaved to create a very sharp spear like point, while the other end is flat and placed on the ground. The wall ends overlap to create a natural gate. It is a very sturdy structure, but it is light in weight and easy to move. Once built, in the center of the circle, a bonfire is created. It is used for cooking and heat at night. There is no roof, but everybody inside a boma is protected from the wildlife outside it. It is the oldest known form of a structure used by man for living since his nomadic days. It is simply brilliant.

As our gala evening in the boma ended, we were all told that we would be escorted to our cabins by Rangers with guns. The Game Reserves in Kruger National Park have no compound walls or gates and wildlife has open access to all the grounds. Basically, at night you do not move without an armed escort. After our Ranger saw us off, I decided to linger outside our cabin door and smoke a cigarette. (I gave up this filthy habit 11 yrs. ago. The hardest thing I have ever done.)

That entire evening, a large herd of elephants had been making a loud racket near the riverbank. Just then, they decided to cross the river, and it got really crazy. All their trumpeting, fighting, and thrashing around got quite loud and frightening. I was listening to it all when I heard a low frequency guttural growl from maybe about 15 feet away behind a tall hedge. I froze instantly! Whatever it was, it sounded large and ferocious to me. Maybe it was moving away from the crazy elephants? Again I felt that Primal Fear. This time, the "flight" response kicked in. In a flash, I stubbed out the cigarette, yanked open the cabin door, got in, slammed it shut, and put on all the deadbolt locks. My family looked at me in wonder with expressions that asked, "What's going on?" I was panting hard, but said, "… Shhh, … there is something big, ... just outside!" We all stayed silent and listened intently, but we heard nothing. So now everybody starts making fun of me and calling me "chicken" or "fattu" and other such choice words.

Well, in my defense, the next morning, we saw that there were "pug marks" (*paw prints*) of a large cat all over near the cabin door! Even my crushed cigarette butt had been pushed 8 feet away to the bushes. Later on, the Ranger looked at them carefully and said, "Yes, you certainly had a visitor here last night. Actually, it looks like there were four of them. Different sizes though, it seems. Ah, well, that is Kruger Park for you!"

It was an incredible trip. We made a boatload of wonderful memories, little or large, to cherish for a lifetime. I am sure many of you have done similar trips as well and have similar stories.

I love these national parks, wherever they are, and whatever wildlife they help preserve. I try and do my share to support them however I can. They are after all the heritage of our planet.

It is good to experience Primal Fear sometimes as well. It also reflects a connection to our past and evolutionary heritage. A connection that is vanishing faster than we realize the world over.

An Ode to Teachers

(Original Posting: RKC Forum – April, 2017)

Thanks to Pradeep, ASir, Bharat, Vijay Kaul, et. al on the wonderful comments about our "unsung teachers". I could not agree more with all the comments made, especially regarding the late Mr. H. Yajnik, who was related to me. Let me elaborate a bit, with your permission.

Mr. Harvadan Yajnik, was my father's paternal second cousin (my great grandfather & his grandfather were "sagga" brothers). But to me, he was "Harukaka". He was my teacher at RKC also and my "guardian" in Rajkot. He was a very humble, unassuming, and gentle person. He was also a very learned man and very proficient in not only Gujarati, but also Sanskrit, which he spoke fluently. He had a characteristic limp in his walk which was due to polio he had at an early age, and which he survived. Outside of school at family gatherings he was just a delight to converse with on so many literary topics, of which he was a lifelong student.

As an example, I remember one discussion wherein he taught me that, the key in all great writing was the ability of the author to use a literary tool called "context". This tool was used in the sense of supporting a narrative, characters, situations, etc., to give life to the written word and could take many different forms. It could be used by its presence and placement in various ways, or by its absence as well! This had never occurred to me. He said further that the same tool is used in the more modern media, such as films, by gifted directors, who tell a great story in the visual medium. He said that they may not realize it, but it is the same tool! If you think about it a bit, you will notice that it is a profound observation. He was a remarkable man in many unsung ways. I was very fond of him.

While on this subject, let me mention two other Yajniks who were also my uncles that you may or may not know about.

Dr. Ramanlal Yajnik, was the Principal at the Dharmendrasinhji College in Rajkot for many years. The "Yajnik Road" in the Jagnath Plot area in Rajkot is named after him. He was my father's much older paternal first cousin (His father was my grandfather's older brother who died of the Black Plague in Bombay at the dawn of the 20th Century. So, he was raised by my grandfather.)

To me, he was just "Ramankaka". In his retirement years, he lived in Rajkot also, just like ASir. He had done his Ph.D. in English Literature at Cambridge or Oxford (I forget which one) in the UK, he was fluent in

Sanskrit, and was a lifelong educator. He started several colleges in East Africa and India.

While he was in Rajkot, in the late 1950's before I joined RKC, he would often visit us in Porbandar. I used to hate these visits! Why? Because each day, before dinner, he would demand that I recite all the "Shlokas" he had taught me, and also "Aank" (Maths Tables in Gujarati) from 1 to 20, before him and my parents! This was required of me in order to get my dinner!

During one visit, after my recitals were finished rather poorly by me before dinner, I asked in sweet innocence, "Ramankaka, tame kyaare javaanaa chho?" (*Ramankaka, when are you leaving?*) My parents were horrified by my question, but Ramankaka laughed heartily, swept me off my feet, gave me a big hug, and said, "Tu kahe tyaare!" (*When you tell me to.*) But all my silliness aside, he was a fascinating man, who was always teaching everyone around him something from his life experiences and knowledge. Oddly, even to this day, whenever I have to do arithmetic mentally without a calculator, I find myself doing it in Gujarati!

Indulal Yajnik was Ramankaka's older brother. He was a contemporary and colleague of Gandhiji, Pandit Nehru, Sardar Patel, and all the great Indian leaders in the fight for India's freedom from the British Raj. He was sent to jail with all of them in Ahmadabad, and later to the Yerwada Jail in Pune. He lived a tumultuous and controversial life during major political upheavals in the fight for India's freedom. Later, he was a leader in the fight to create the State of Gujarat from the old Bombay State (or Presidency) and was also an MP in Delhi from the Ahmedabad constituency for 5 terms.

His relevance here is that, while he was not a teacher or an educator in the traditional sense, he was a journalist and a prolific author, who made a huge contribution to literature in general, and the modern history of Gujarat, in particular.

He founded the Navjivan Press in Ahmedabad, which he then placed at Gandhiji's feet. He wrote plays/novels/poems/stories, and the magnum opus which is his autobiography. Written in Gujarati in 6 volumes, and later translated into English and published by the Gujarat Vidyapeeth, this work is a masterpiece. I highly recommend it, if you enjoy history. While his personal story, which is lively and colorful, is not lauded as much, it is his narration of the events, customs, and the ambiance of the times he lived in; the social and political climates; and the massive currents of change sweeping India at the time, that make it just amazing writing. His keen sense of observation, perspective, and emotional response, make it all a highly enjoyable read. But all this aside, to me he was just "Indukaka".

He was 6'4" tall, had a booming megaphone like voice, and was lanky in his frame. He lived like a "fakir". He kept no money, possessions, or property. Whatever he got, he donated it away promptly to somebody who needed it more. He did not care for material things and lived very simply. He had no family, children, or a home, except for his "ashram" in Nenpur, near Ahmedabad. I believe that it is a school today for the children of low-income families. He was a prodigious reader/writer, a very bright intellectual possessing a photographic memory, and he was firm in his belief that India's way out of poverty was through the education of its people. He always sided with the poor and the disadvantaged in everything, in particular for access to education.

One day, he walked up to our home in Ahmedabad, clear out of the blue! My parents and I were surprised and jumped up to receive him. He stayed with us for the night. My memories of that visit are vivid because I had never met anybody like him in real life!

The conversations, in their breadth and depth, all evening long were just incredible! They spanned topics like the Central Government budget, industrial priorities, education from Standard 1 to 12, infrastructure needs, literature, economic development of the Bhil people of Gujarat, tobacco, import/export regulations, foreign exchange controls, barter trade with the Soviet Union (Russia), national fiscal policy, and on and on. He arrived around 5pm and by 7pm, we had a house full of some 30 people engaged in intense discourse with him. His knowledge of the facts/statistics, grasp of complex issues and conflicts, and logical articulation of national policy with simple clarity, left everybody just mesmerized!

He ate simple food and slept on the floor, even though beds were available in the bedrooms. Strangely, the next morning was exceptionally cold and there was frost on the grass which was quite unusual for Ahmedabad. My father offered Indukaka a long woolen coat. He accepted it and we stood waving goodbye to him as he walked out of the gate at the end of the driveway.

Outside the gate, we noticed an old man with a little girl shivering in the morning cold with a small fire lit before them. As Indukaka walked up to them, he stopped for a brief chat. In a moment, he took off the woolen coat, and draped it over the old man. And then, he just walked on!

I consider myself fortunate to have been born in a family with such learned men, who valued education more than anything else in the Nation's quest for freedom, prosperity, and social equality.

I believe that, whether they were well known, or "unsung", they were all fundamentally great teachers.

About Boyhood Dreams

(Original Post: RKC Forum – July, 2017)

In our formative years at RKC, in any era in time, nearly all of us had some kind of a "boyhood dream". Maybe it was to play cricket someday with the great masters of the game, or to climb a tall mountain, or to go on a long motorbike ride (e.g. Kumar Shah), or to become a famous actor/singer/performer, or whatever else. While most of us just dreamed about these sorts of things, and eventually outgrew them, there are some of us who actually followed through, and somewhere in our later lives, lived out those dreams. Within these folks, lives something that I fondly refer to as the "Spirit of RKC"! May this spirit live long and forever, in each generation of RKCians, the past, present, and the ones to come.

I dedicate this posting to all those RKCians, who in spite of grave doubts from others, against formidable odds, and many difficulties, lived out their boyhood dreams, on their own terms.

Zamperini Airfield, Torrance, California

I met a friend the other day at the celebrated Zamperini Airfield, here in Torrance, California. He is, as they say, a "fly boy". He is a pilot and flies single engine airplanes all over locally, for business and fun. Well, actually mostly for fun, but with a hefty "tax write-off" as an added benefit. It is an exciting and a thrilling pursuit, if you have a taste for danger. And the danger here is one where you can easily just... well... just die! For a private pilot in the USA, the constraints on what you can and are allowed to do are many. The lifestyle and legal restrictions are severe. The science & technology involved are intense and complex, and you really have to be dedicated to perfecting and maintaining your skill set. Any or all of these variables can come together, in some way and at any time, to determine the difference between joyous exhilaration and tragedy. This activity is not for the faint of heart, frivolous in attitude, or lacking in discipline. But out here, many idiots and zealots pursue it. I was one of them, until some time ago.

Now, you may wonder, what the devil does all this have to do with RKC and this forum? Well, as you may know by now, all my stories on this forum have some basis that goes right back to our lovely school, my formative years there, and many a flashback. These are also some of them, strange as it may seem to you.

The Senior Wing "Club"- Mr. Ayaaz Khan & Mr. Pettigrew

I had just graduated over to the Lower Senior Wing in 1962 or so. I am not sure of all the designations, but I believe that Mr. Ayaaz Khan (ASir) was our House Master. Mr. Pettigrew (PSir) probably was the House Master of the Upper Senior Wing. Anyway, they were the two teachers that I remember so well from that time, and for very different reasons. ASir, because he was just amazing in every sense of the word. He taught me in classes and encouraged me to read. He played field hockey with me, yelled at me, punished me, comforted me, and was always there for me in everything, especially when I was not sure of myself. Even today, I do not know how to value it all. It was priceless. I was blessed to be in the care of a truly gifted human being, and an incredible all-round teacher. And then there was PSir. I was in awe of him. In the Senior Club, he would do slideshows of his Himalayan and other trekking/camping trips which left me just astonished. PSir showed all of us how to dream about bigger and greater things and to experience the "joy of life", even with its many dangers. Well, ASir and PSir were the reasons that I found myself in the Senior Wing Club a lot at this time. And that led to a strange discovery one day.

In the Senior Wing Club, I stumbled across a book. It was about airplanes, how they were built, and how they were flown! It was rather simplified, but it had pictures, concept illustrations, and featured a single engine, fixed landing gear, land aircraft, like a Piper or a Cessna. I was amazed! I read and re-read the book countless times to try and fully understand what it said. But the more I thought I understood it, the more questions arose in my mind. And the book did not have the answers. The book explained, in pictorial terms, the "what" and the "where" about the airplane. But it never addressed the "how", the "why", and "when" about airplane flight. I remember being frustrated by the lack of answers in this book. These feelings stayed with me for many years till I studied "Fluid Mechanics" and "Thermodynamics" at IIT/Kanpur. In these courses, my "tube light" got switched on, and I went, "Aha!"

However, as we all know, studying something is one thing, but doing is quite another. For example, let's take our favorite national sport, cricket. Oh, one can read books on it, see films, study the techniques of the masters, examine the role and skills of various positions, etc., endlessly. But it is not really cricket for you, until you get before a wicket on a pitch, with some pads on, a bat in hand, and face a bowler with a shiny red ball in his hand. Then the beauty of the game comes home in its full context. It is a totally different perspective. So, just like many a kid in India, who yearns for the day when it is his turn "at bat", I too awaited my turn at experiencing the world of "flight".

It took a lot longer than I thought. What follows below are some stories from my "love affair" with the world of human flight.

Pre-Flight School - An Ode to Rex

It was 1976. I was 26 years old, working and living in Detroit, Michigan, the auto capital of the world at the time. The city was known for its engineering and manufacturing prowess and its strategic location in the area of the USA called the "Great Lakes" region. The state of Michigan itself is chock full of freshwater lakes everywhere and touts itself to tourists as the "Water Winter Wonderland"! The summers are hot and humid. The winters are snowy, brutally cold, and miserable. There is a saying there, which goes, "If you think it is cold... wait for 15 minutes... it will be colder!" At times it was so cold, that I have actually had my eyes start tearing, and then had the tear drops freeze on my cheeks! So, you may ask, why would anybody want to live there? Well, if you liked cars, it was the "mother lode" of all places for them. Also, and not as well known, if you liked flying airplanes, you could not find a more thrilling environment! Michigan offered you every kind of flight challenge imaginable around the whole year! So, there were many flight schools, lots of airfields of every shape, size, and type, and also a major US Air Force presence to seriously mess up your flying life. In this lovely place, I determined to experience what I had seen in that book at the Senior Wing Club in RKC a long time ago. I decided to learn to fly an airplane.

I joined the Beech Aircraft Flight School in Pontiac, a suburb of Detroit, Michigan (Yes, the same name as the car!). On day one, I met Rex, my flight instructor. Rex was from Texas, a veteran US Navy fighter pilot who had done 2 tours of duty aboard aircraft carriers during the Vietnam war. Also, he was a graduate of the "Top Gun" naval combat flight school at the Miramar Naval Base in San Diego, California. (Yes, it is not just a movie! It is a very real combat flight school in the US Navy.) In short, Rex was a "jet jock" and the word "fear" was not in his dictionary. At our first meeting, Rex checked me out, and with disdain in his blue eyes, he asked me, "Son, you read all the books yet?" I said, "No, not yet. I just got them." He then said, "Forget it. Save your cash. Read all the stuff you got, take the tests, and when you know something about flying and airplanes, then come see me." He cancelled my class promptly and just left, muttering something like, "Crummy civilian kids!". He was tall, handsome, and very fit. His manner and swagger reminded me of our late Mr. Bharat Singh (BSir), in his prime, in many ways. As I

113

would learn later, just like BSir, Rex also had a "lingua franca" that was all his own.

It took me about 4 months of patient and methodical self-study to go through all the materials and pass the FAA (Federal Aviation Administration) written tests. It was a hard study because I was not familiar with most of the subject matter. Things like airplane classes & design, electrical/mechanical systems, aircraft engines and classes, landing gear, navigation, FAA rules and regulations, communications, meteorology, flight maps, airport classes and design, medical emergencies, life support systems, and on and on. Also, it was all hardcore practical information and little of the theoretical things that I had studied in engineering school. It was a real and very rude awakening.

When I finished, I went to see Rex again. He was surprised to see me! He said, "You finished all that stuff and the tests? Son, most kids just give up! Well then, let me ask you a few things. You ever get carsick, seasick, or airsick? You in shape? Ever go to the gym or workout? Ever booze much? Do ya scare easy?" I answered, "… No… Somewhat… On weekends, I run… A few beers on Fridays... and I don't know." He said, "Ok. Good enough. Let's go to the little bird and feel some air." And thus, began an amazing journey for me, in the company and under the guidance of a true battle-hardened taskmaster. I felt like I was wonderfully back at RKC, in so many ways!

Flight School

Rex wasted no time at all. The "pre-flight" check was done quickly and efficiently. He verified that I knew how to do it. Then he subjected me to hard labor. I was ordered to "Remove the wing lines... pull the chocks... let's shove her (the plane) over… put some juice in her (aviation gasoline) … hell, just top her off." When we were done with all that, I was already sweating like a pig in that August heat and humidity. Rex then smiled, for the first time, and said, "Son, always do that yourself. All the attendants in these airfields just suck. You can't tell who's really gonna mess you up with your juice." We got into the Beechcraft Sundowner 150 airplane with the ID Number ending in "78S" on its fuselage. It was a 4-seater with low wings, so the cockpit was above the wings. It had a full instrumentation package for a training aircraft of that era. I was put in the left "pilot" seat and Rex took the right "co-pilot" seat. We had dual flight controls. Rex took me through the startup checklist, we started the engine, and taxied out. Rex introduced me to the techniques of taxi, stopping, turning, etc. and made me do them right off. He had the radio and handled the airfield tower. He spent a lot of time just drilling me on the "pre-take off" checklist, including engine run up and so forth, and then we rolled for take-off. Rex flew us out of the airfield and got us up to 5000 ft. altitude. Then the crazy stuff started.

Starting Off: Rex said, "You have the plane." As I took control of it, he added, "Ok. Fly her due North at 5000 ft., level flight." I got it pointed to the North after much fumbling around, only to realize that I was now at 3000 ft! And we were still descending! So, I climbed back up. When I reached 5000 ft., I was now flying due East! I turned again, only to end up at 4000 ft. I just could not do what he wanted. So, Rex says, "Son, you are not flying her. She is flying you!" After 45 minutes of repeated attempts, I was a miserable failure. We returned and Rex sat me down. "Son, you gotta learn to multi-process up there! You gotta have eight eyes, six ears, and four hands. Get it? Listen, your Mom could take care of you and your siblings, cook dinner, hear the doorbell, answer the damn phone, and change diapers, all at the same time. See, she was skilled at multi-processing! And you're just fumbling around with one thing at a time!" So, Rex trained me in multi-processing. He would bark, "Altitude, Climb Rate, Heading, Speed?" I would have to answer in rapid-fire responses. In a couple of lessons, my learning curve really picked up. Then, he says, "Get a feel for her. You gotta feel her. Now, tell me what's happening without looking at the instruments. Vocalize, and mentally get ahead of her behavior."

Under very exacting and repeated tough instructions, my training continued, one hour at a time. I started flying the plane and making it obey my will. I learnt to take off, do controlled turns, stalls, slips, and all the required maneuvers. I was now coming up on 6 hours of dual flight training. So, we focused on runway approach and landing skills. This was really difficult for me.

Landing: For the love of God, I just could not do it! Rex taught me the airfield pattern (downwind, turn to base, final approach, etc.) and all the rituals that go with these stages, but when it came to "the flare", I was just awful. This is when you are above the runway markers, you chop the engine to idle, bleed airspeed, and gently touch down. Sounds easy, doesn't it? I failed repeatedly and miserably. Then on this particular attempt, I hit the runway real hard, bounced back up 50+ feet, and then dropped back down like a stone, at a near stall. I was badly shaken by this episode. In fact, I got very scared by it. I broke out in a major sweat, started to tremble and shake uncontrollably, and I could not even taxi the airplane. Rex got us over to a holding area.

He said, "Hey, that was a doozy! You're lucky we didn't stall!" So, I said in a bit of anger, "Why did you not do something?" Rex calmly replied, "Son, that was a first for you. The first of many to come. Right now, you are feeling scared, aren't ya? Good. You gotta learn what "that fear" is like. I can't teach it. You just have to experience it, all by yourself. When you feel it, then you will learn to handle it." Then I said, "Ok, all that is good to know. But I think I am done for the day." At this, Rex just exploded and turned into a monster. "… Whaat? You wanna get done? Hell, no, Son! We are going right back up and you are gonna shoot that same damn landing again, right here, and right now. You hear me? And not once, but twice. We gonna fix that fear of yours, right now!" We shot not 2, but 7 landings after that! I did get the hang of it. The 7th one was my best. Rex said, "Hell, yeah... softer than cotton on a baby's butt!" I considered that to be a compliment.

"Solo" Flight: Every student pilot wonders about when he will get to do his "solo" flight. Typically, it occurs somewhere between 10 to 15 hours of "dual" flight training. This is when the flight instructor decides to leave the airplane, asks you to take off, run the airfield pattern, and land back, all on your own, obviously including all the tower communications. By design and tradition, the student pilot does not know when this will occur. There is no fixed date, timetable, or even any warning. It is all up to the judgment of the flight instructor, and can occur at any time, on any training day. It is a seminal event, and upon completion, it is celebrated gloriously by all the student pilots, flight instructors, and the flight school. They even cut the student's tie or shirt and pin "wings" on it!

On this day, Rex decided to give me "soft field" landing and takeoff training. This is where you land on unpaved fields or dirt, then turn around, and execute special take off maneuvers. Then, he wanted me to shoot landings at air fields with very short runways or obstructions, such as tall trees, water tanks, power lines, etc. He knew where all of them were located. Well, that day, I was "on", and having a great time with all this, when Rex says, "Hey, I forgot. I've gotta be someplace. Let's get back." I returned us to the Pontiac airfield, and as I was taxiing back, Rex grabs the mike and calls the tower, "Tower... Seven Eight Sierra here… student solo flight... request clearance... over." The Tower responded, "Roger… Seven Eight Sierra." I was still trying to figure out what was going on, when Rex says, "Pull over at the holding area... and idle the engine." As I did so, he says, "Son… take your solo flight... pick me up on your taxi back... and remember... Pops is right here... watching your every move... you can always see me… right here by the runway... God Speed!"

Then, Rex opened his door against the propeller air blast, and got out of the airplane with great effort. I felt a massive rush of adrenaline! On the radio, I heard the Tower clear the entire airspace around the Pontiac airfield. Some 5 inbound flights were put on hold or waved away. All departing flights were placed on hold and the fire engine trucks drove up close to the runway. All this attention made me feel really important. (Little did I know at the time that it was all for the safety of others, not mine.) I did my solo flight, picked up Rex at the holding area, and we taxied back to our hangers. Then big celebrations broke out! After so long, I felt the first real sense of accomplishment in my quest to learn to fly an airplane.

Flying Around Michigan & Indiana

I did my solo flight at around 11 hours of dual flight training. Then I had to fulfill various solo student flight requirements to be eligible for my private pilot license flight test. All these student flights required approval and supervision from Rex. But he would not let me go without some additional dual training first. His words were, "Ok, so now you can fly a bird. Fine. But you need to know some other things, which can make all the difference between life and death." I wondered, "Rex, what do you mean?" He said, "Let's go up and I will show you."

The training that followed was beyond my wildest imagination. He did things like shutting off the gas tank at 5000 feet and telling me, "Ok, you are out of gas. Find a dirt field and land it. You got 2 minutes, maybe..." He took me out on night flights. In the brightly lit Detroit metro area, he would say, "Ok. Where is the Pontiac airfield? Find it." Or we would fly out to the countryside, where it is nearly pitch black, and he would say, "Find the field and land it. Oh, the lights are out on the runway." He gave me "hood" training. This is when a hood is placed on your head, so all you can see are your cockpit instruments. You fly by the instruments and your feel for the airplane. Rex said to me, "I know that you are not gonna be flying IFR (Instrument Flight Rules), but this training may save your life one day, if you get your butt in a ringer, especially in the Michigan weather." As it turned out, every bit of all this training actually came to my rescue many times over later on.

A Scary Cross-Country Flight: As a part of student pilot training requirements, one has to complete several three-point triangular cross-country solo flights. In each one, you fly from the Home airfield to Field A, then to Field B, and then back Home. Each airfield must be at least 100 miles away from the other two, one must land at each one and get the "log book" stamped at the General Aviation terminal, and all three segments must be completed on the same day. Also, one must use Visual Flight Rules (VFR) with a filed

117

FAA flight plan. This meant that the student pilot must navigate using maps and landmarks on the ground. A radio transponder was allowed only for aircraft identification. (In those days, there was no GPS or "auto pilot" technologies available in training aircraft.) In short, you flew by the seat of your pants, your maps, eyes, ears, and your brain. The triangular flights ensured that you faced all the different wind conditions on a given day to really test your navigation and flight skills.

Well, on this partly cloudy day, Rex authorized my flight plan. I was to fly from Pontiac to Grand Rapids, Michigan, then on to Fort Wayne, Indiana, and then return. Each segment was about 1.5 hours in duration. I was feeling pretty good, but Rex warned me, "Son, stay a little scared, keep your wits close by, and don't screw up. I don't want a call from the FAA about you. God Speed!"

With such a sendoff, I started out. I got to Grand Rapids just fine, but the weather was deteriorating. I checked the Fort Wayne weather, and it was still fine, so I took off. En route, I learnt that Fort Wayne weather was now Marginal VFR, meaning borderline for someone like me. As I got closer, it got worse. I felt moderate rain hitting the airplane at 7000 feet, thunderstorms appeared in the distance, and then visibility became very poor. Now I was scared about finding the airfield. I radioed the Fort Wayne Approach Control for help with my situation. The AC asked, "Seven Eight Sierra, have you had any hood training?" I replied, "Yes. 2 hours." AC said, "Roger. We have light traffic right now. So, I can talk you in. But you do exactly as I say…" I pushed away my maps and began flying by the instruments, with razor sharp focus, under strict AC & then Tower guidance. After 40 minutes of turns, zigzagging, and very slow descent, the Tower said, "Seven Eight Sierra... heads up... cleared for landing!" I looked up and right before me, under a huge canopy of black ominous clouds and barely 1-mile fuzzy visibility, I saw the runway slab, welcoming me with all its lights fully ablaze! Just as I landed, a thunderous downpour began. The airfield closed for all flights. As I taxied to Gen Av terminal, in my mind and heart I said, "Thank you, Pops!"

US Air Force Encounter - Selfridge Air Force Base, Michigan: During all my flight training at Pontiac, Rex would always tell me, "Son, stay the hell away from that Air Force Base! You hear me? Don't you even get lost in that direction. Them fellas don't like anything that flies that ain't theirs! They don't play games, and they got no sense of humor at all!" The Selfridge Air Force Base was a truly sinister place, not only by reputation, but also in fact. In all flight maps, it was shown as a "restricted airspace", which meant that without proper clearance, nothing was allowed to enter it or fly in it. There was no information about it anywhere at all. It was just a big large "blank blob" on all the maps. Later on, I found out that it was one of a select few Air Bases that were a part of NATO's Strategic Air Command. It handled all kinds of military hardware and ordinance, including nuclear payloads, etc. for the USA and NATO forces. In that airspace, there was constant inbound or outbound traffic 7x24 hours. Huge B-52 bombers, C-5 & Hercules transports, variety of fighter & other aircraft, etc. could be heard, but rarely seen. They all did "military" takeoffs and landings, which typically are very steep and executed fast. Well, on this day, like a total idiot, I invited trouble, without even realizing it.

I was headed to the airfield of a cute little town named Bad Axe, in Michigan, on a cross country training flight. There were strong cross winds at 8500 feet, my cruising altitude. I was busy, with my small slide ruler, trying to calculate my ETA (estimated time of arrival), when suddenly all hell broke loose!

A fighter jet came up from below my left wing, roared past me in a steep climbing left turn, and blasted me with his exhaust! My plane yawed and rolled around violently and I desperately tried to get control of it. I had barely steadied it, when another fighter jet came up from below my right wing. It also roared past me in a steep climbing right turn, and blasted me with his exhaust! Now, I was really desperate and struggling hard to regain level flight, in the midst of all their frightening wake and exhaust turbulence. When I finally managed it somehow, I looked all around, up and down, wondering what all that was about? I could not see or hear the fighter planes anymore or spot anything. Their screaming engine roars had vanished and there was no other sound besides my own little engine. It was very strange and I had this eerie feeling about it all.

I was rechecking all my airplane instruments for any problems, when I noticed that the fighter jets had now slowly risen up silently from below me and were flying 50 feet off my wingtips on both sides! We seemed to be in a formation flight, because no matter what I did, they were both always at my heading, speed, altitude, and always 50 feet from me! I could see the helmets of both the pilots clearly through their canopies, but there was total radio silence. Then, I got the hand signal to land immediately. I rocked my wings to say, "Yes." One fighter jet led the way and the other followed me, but both were now at a good distance and their "after burners" had been turned off. I was "guided" into a near formation landing on the very scary and simply mammoth main runway of the Selfridge Air Force Base. To use air force jargon, "The bogey had been intercepted and landed".

As I taxied to an apron, the fighter jets just melted away. My little plane was promptly surrounded by armored vehicles and soldiers bearing all sorts of guns in assault positions. Over a loudspeaker, I was ordered to shut down, get out very slowly, and keep my hands open and in sight at all times. I was frisked, handcuffed, arrested, and thrown into a holding cell. A team of people swarmed all over my little Beech Sundowner 150 airplane with all kinds of high-tech gear. Nobody would say anything to me, or even speak to me, and I was petrified out of my mind!

In about an hour, I was taken into an "interrogation room" and faced 3 stern and very tough looking young men. Over the next 3 hours, I was asked about my entire life history, what I was doing in the airplane, why was I in restricted airspace, etc. It was very formal, direct, and recorded.

Then suddenly, they stopped and left. Soon, a man in a suit appeared. He was much older, but with piercing grey eyes. He smiled at me, and asked if I wanted some coffee. I said, "Oh, yes, please..." As he got me some coffee, another man, who looked like a very senior officer, walked in.

He asked roughly, "Is this the civvy kid?" He took a chair, studied me for a bit, and sighed deeply. Then he said, "Look, we are kind of busy. I would like to help you out, but I don't know how. Can we talk to anybody right now, who can vouch for you?"

My eyes lit up and I said, "Yes. My instructor, Rex, at the Beech School in Pontiac."

Then he also smiled, and said, "Rex? Rex Reed? He's teaching you? Well now, ...that figures, ...because he sure has done a shit job!"

So, I asked, "Do you know him?"

He laughed heartily, and said, "Oh, yes! In more ways than I care to admit. We flew missions together in Nam."

Rex came over and rescued me from my nightmare. He was also allowed to fly my airplane out back to the Pontiac airfield, on a special clearance, but without me. After I drove Rex's pickup truck back, I was ashen faced, and really fearful about what would happen to me.

Rex was pensive, looked at me for a while, and then softly said, "Son, do you know that you were 6+ hours overdue? The FAA has been burning up the airwaves. Your flight plan was still open, and today, nobody had seen "78S" anywhere, on any airfield, around here."

"There was a Search & Rescue mission underway with 2 choppers looking for your wreckage. They were even wondering if you might have hit the drink in some damn lake. Jeez, you scared the crap out of me! Oh, and the Air Force Base? The crosswinds must have blown you over into their airspace. But, hell, in their crazy world, they follow rules. And they don't tell nobody... nothing... ever!" I was just too stunned to respond.

Then, Rex said simply, "Son, wanna have a beer?"

I said, "Sure. But what happens now?"

Rex replied, "Oh, nothing. I took care of it. But you learnt your lesson... the hard way. Come on, I'll buy 'em for us."

End of My "Love Affair"

Soon after all these events and many others, I got my private pilot license. For me, it was one of my proudest achievements and an RKC "boyhood dream" realized. Oh, I had some "lively" times with a pilot's license, but those are all very different stories, for another time and another place.

Then it so happened that, within a few years, I got married, settled down, and started a family. With that, my flying days regrettably came to an end. You see, I was admonished repeatedly, by most friends and certainly all my relatives, with, "Vijay, now you have responsibilities. You must live in a rather sensible, and a more mature manner. After all, flying around in a little airplane is just such a foolish thing to do!"

Rex left the Beech Flight School soon thereafter also. He had a highly successful career as a commercial pilot, flying private and corporate jets. He ferried around the rich, powerful, or very famous people, all over the world!

And that Pops of mine, did he have stories? Oh, my goodness... unmatched... about stuff... that you just would not believe!

A Naturalist

(Original Posting: RKC Forum – March, 2018)

Seeing Himanshu Jani's post on this forum regarding the death anniversary of Mr. Lavkumar, I became a bit reflective, and thought about some of my memories about him and the impact that he had on my life. It is hard and painful to realize that he is no longer with us. But he is very much alive within me. I am sure that this is true for many of you as well.

Delayed Realizations

Mr. Lavkumar (LSir) was my Housemaster in the Junior Wing, when I joined RKC in 1959. He never taught me in classes, but this association over 3 years in the Junior Wing, was incredibly impactful for me. At a very tender age, he imbibed into me and so many of my schoolmates at the time, various teachings about life, nature, philosophy, history, music, and our great Indian culture with all its diversities. All this occurred over many events and occasions. At the time, I must admit, I did not care for much of it at all. I mostly whined and complained in various ways and was generally oblivious to what was being imparted to me. Many years later, as I grew older, I came to understand and appreciate what this teacher had indeed gifted to me. To put it simply, it was amazing. So, from a trove of memories, on this occasion, I would like to share with you just a couple to illustrate my sentiments.

A Long Overdue Meeting

The first is about my finally meeting LSir, nearly 45 years after I had left RKC! With the arrival of the internet and emails, contacts long lost were reestablished. It began in 2009, when I had a lovely meal at the home of the great Ushakant Patel in Ahmedabad. In attendance also that day were, Vijay Kaul, Mr. & Mrs. Mathur, and others. LSir came up in the conversations and I expressed a strong desire to meet him. Years went by, phone calls occurred with LSir, who remembered me well, but no meeting. Then, on a rare chance in 2011 or so, we finally met. I was in Ahmedabad again, and Ushakant Patel was having brunch at his farm house (Harmony Farms) with him and invited me to join them.

We spent an unforgettable 3 hours together. LSir, despite the years, was in great form. He still had this lovely ability to convey something swiftly, with acupuncture precision, and with a clever, but graceful, smile on his face.

Upon seeing me, he says, "Vijay, taru pet vadhi gayu chhe. America ni charabi utaar. It is not good for your health." (*Vijay, your tummy has grown. You should reduce this American fat.*) I was trying to respond, but he adds, "Kem, tu daaru bahu piye chhe? Ochhu kari nakh." (*Why, are you drinking too much? Reduce it then.*)

And thus, it began. We had a meal of fresh rabadi, thepla, ganthia, and marcha. It was all washed down with a delicious "chhash"(Ushakant is a great host). Then, LSir turned a bit serious.

He said, "Vijay, come back to India. Anhi tare mate bahu kaam chhe." (*There is a lot of work here for you.*) All my pangs of long felt guilt welled up within me in seconds. I was at a loss for words, because he had nailed a key sentiment felt by most expat Indians. He sensed my discomfort and promptly changed the subject.

He said, "I have a gift for you." I replied, "Sir, what? A gift for me?" He said, "Yes. It is something you will cherish." He gifted me an RKC T-shirt with the school insignia embroidered on it. Well, in front of Ushakant and other guests, I shamelessly ripped off my shirt and put on this T-Shirt immediately. It did not fit, because even at the largest size, it was woefully tight on me. But I did not care. Ugly as I may have looked, I kept it on. LSir was just delighted by my behavior! With a gleam in his eyes, he said, "I can see that the emotional ties are still very strong!" Then, he turned to others and said, "Ane kahevaye 'prem na bandhan'!" (*This is what is called the 'bonds of love'*) There is a photograph of us together on that day, before the shirt came off.

It was a lovely time together, we caught up on our lives, and he invited me to visit him in Manali at "Vasishtha" (I think that was the name of his home there.) In the ensuing years, we stayed in touch actively. He used to enjoy my periodic writings on this forum and would send me endearing personal notes about them. He was particularly touched by the stories on Mr. Bharat Singh (BSir) and Cross-Country Runs in Hong Kong. He gave BSir a lot of credit for the "mystique" of RKC. But, alas, the Manali visit was not to be. This turned out to be my one and only reunion with LSir. Before I could visit him or even meet him again, he passed away.

A Sad and Unusual Day

The second, is about the day I learnt of LSir's passing (I wrote about this in the Condolence Book for Nrupendraji & LSir's extended family.) It was morning in LA when I got the news. I was quite upset and distraught. It was odd, but it felt sort of like a loss in one's family. By some weird instinct, I sought refuge in nature, which I felt would help me deal with my feelings and emotions. I drove out to the Redondo Beach nearby, and sat outside on a crop, staring at the Pacific Ocean on this lovely sunny day. Then, something curious and strange happened.

I noticed a California Bald Eagle (a white plumed eagle, an endangered bird here, and a rare sighting) circling above me, soaring about 200 feet or so overhead. Then, some seals came up out of the water and onto the beach, with a huge sea lion accompanying them. This was unusual. And then, about 200 feet into the ocean, I see a school of a dozen or so dolphins playing around very actively just in front of me. Then suddenly, with loud "whoosh" sounds, I see the water spouts of a few migrating whales further out. One whale even did a partial breach directly in front of me!

Now, each of these events, taken individually, is not an uncommon sight around here. But all of them together, on this morning, in front of me? That was very curious, odd, and peculiar indeed! In about 15 minutes or so, they were all gone.

Was it nature, celebrating the life of a man who loved nature? Was there a divine message here, that LSir's soul was now free and in a truly happy place? Or perhaps, was it all just a coincidence? I guess, we will never know. But, to my amazement, I did feel a sense of peace develop within me.

LSir was not just a gifted teacher and mentor, but a remarkably knowledgeable man as well. Perhaps his greatest strength was in his freely admitting, "I don't know. Tell me about it."

Among many things, I attribute my love for nature, outdoors, classical music, history, and my innate curiosity about things I do not know, to his teachings and lessons in life. On his death anniversary this year, and every year for that matter, let us all celebrate his life, and the gifts that he left within all of us, in his own special way.

Greetings & A Dedication

Mrs. Bharucha

(Original Post: RKC Forum – August, 2018)

Dear Farzana,

It is such a joy to learn from Madam Cooper & ASir (Mr. Ayaaz Khan) that your mom will turn 90 shortly. A grand milestone! I feel compelled to write to you because of a few memories, that we made together, which were very impactful for me. I doubt if you remember them. So, let me elaborate a bit.

It was 2010, I believe. Anal Dalal had arranged a visit to Rajkot & RKC for me and my wife, Nilima, who did not know much about RKC, or my upbringing there at the time. I was returning to our beloved school for the first time since 1966, when I had graduated and left. Perhaps I had changed more so than our lovely school. But I recall the visit as being filled with a very strange mix of feelings, as we began.

We had a grand tour of the ole' school; we visited the dorms, sports fields, pavilions, and had lunch at the Principal's bungalow. It was "nostalgia at the max" for me. I remembered so many of my mates/buddies, teachers, events, our highs and lows, etc. Only to realize, in the end, that time moves on for all of us. It was so strange to realize that all teachers from my time at RKC were gone from Rajkot! Well, except for ASir, who I was going to visit shortly thereafter at his home in Rajkot.

I was feeling quite sad, and just then, we accidentally met. I was told by somebody that, "This is Farzana Mehta. She is the daughter of Mrs. Bharucha, who you may remember..." And I was just besides myself with joy! I was like, "Remember her! Are you kidding? We loved her! Is she well? Where is she?" I babbled on without a break, and then you said to me very simply, "Come, why don't you meet her?"

It was just wonderful. I got to meet and hug Ma'am Bharucha after all those years! She did not teach me, but she was always around Madam Cooper so I had many an interaction with her. Also, for me, she seemed to be the last person of continuity with the old past, who was actually at the school, and that made it all so very special. Well, Farzana, thank you.

So, Ma'am Bharucha, (Farzana, please read this to her... if she cannot, or all else fails...)

On this momentous occasion of your 90th birthday, I want to first convey my "pranams" to you. Then, I want to wish you many happy returns of the day, and a long life of health, happiness, and joy with your family and friends! God Bless...

Also, in this season, my best wishes for a Happy Navroz to you and all your loved ones!

With affection,

Vijay

The Amazing "Cooper Crepe Myrtle Tree"

(Original Posting: RKC Forum – September, 2018)

Dear RKCians,

There is a lovely Crepe Myrtle Tree near the entrance gate to where I live in California. I see it several times a day, on my walks, jogs, or just driving in and out of our residential community. This has gone on for many years. I have always adored this tree.

With it, I have felt the seasons change, sensed the passage of time, and lived through personal highs and lows. I have sat near it, thought about things in its shade, and also felt a sense of comfort from it. Furthermore, what is also interesting is that, no matter the season or climate conditions, this tree always shows strength, resilience, and fortitude, but without losing any of its beauty or grace. Without showing any outward signs, unlike so many other bigger trees, it has successfully fought off insects, water controls during droughts, marine fog damage, and various parasitic and other forms of bio attacks. Year after year, the tree simply goes onward and forward in the cycles of its life, and continues to spread joy to all who experience it.

A couple of weeks ago, while on a walk, I noticed it again. Suddenly, I was reminded of Madam Cooper! I feel that this tree embodies, in so many ways, so much of what Madam Cooper truly is as a person. The lessons she imparted to me and countless other students at a tender age, and also in her service to our lovely RKC, are reflected in this tree.

So, Nilima (my wife) & I have taken the liberty and christened this tree, "The Cooper Crepe Myrtle Tree" (I hope that Madam does not object to this somewhat unilateral act on our part.). Every year, towards the latter part of summer, this tree blooms magnificently. The floral peak is reached in the second half of August, typically. This year was no exception.

Attached below is a photo of this tree from some days ago. Have a look! In it, perhaps you too may see a reflection of your inner self or sentiments.

With much love to Madam Cooper & best wishes for health and happy thoughts, always,

Vijay

Madam Cooper

(Original Posting: RKC Forum – January 6th, 2019)

It is Saturday evening (January 5th) here in LA, but it is the 6th, AM hours, in Lahore. And there, it is now Madam Cooper's birthday!

I just got off the phone with her and Perin in Lahore, sharing with both of them all the greetings for this lovely occasion. And lovely, it is so very much. We reminisced and talked about so many things. Madam is a fantastic conversationalist. She does not miss a beat. Her memory is amazing, her grace in the smallest of things is unmatched, and her attitude towards life is infectiously positive. Her values are steadfastly solid and her capacity for love is immense. I am discovering that every interaction of mine with her is a lesson in some aspect of life for me. I feel truly blessed, that regardless of age, she continues to remain my teacher. She has given me so much and I cannot help but feel that I have not done enough for her in return. Now, this is not a mathematical or social equation, but an emotional equation, if you get my drift.

So, by way of a small written word, to support the earlier and larger spoken one, I want to wish Madam, on this Birthday in 2019, the following:

- A Long Life of health and happiness
- A Year of hope and adventurous travel
- A Month of warmth and good fellowship
- A Week of glorious celebrations
- And a Day of smiles, shrieks, candles, and a lovely glass of wine

Madam, Happy Birthday! And best wishes for many happy returns!
With happy thoughts, always,
Lots of love,
Vijay

Epilogue

In a short while after this posting, to my surprise, Madam Cooper fell ill. She seemed to be doing well in her recovery at the hospital and there was even talk about going home. Then without a warning, on March 8th she passed away quietly and peacefully. She was 89 years old.

When I heard the specifics from Perin, in a phone call to Lahore a bit later, I could barely hold myself together. How does one sort through a set of intense emotions and deliver a succinct assessment of how one felt? I was not experienced at this. I felt lost, about this incredible loss.

So, I asked myself, "What did you lose? And why do you grieve?" It took me a fair measure of time before I could answer these questions.

"I lost a beloved teacher, who did more to develop me than anybody else in my life." I replied to myself.

"Well, were there not others? Surely, you miss them too! Shall I name them?" an inner voice would not let it go.

"Yeah, you can name them all. But for me, there was none like Madam Cooper."

"Why do you say that?" the inner voice persisted.

"Well, she gave me the gift of the English language, literature, and culture, at a formative age. She taught me to speak on a stage, or in a public setting, which built my confidence. She taught me manners, etiquette, and grace. She showed me right from wrong, with some tough love. She taught me to appreciate the performing arts. And most of all, she also taught me compassion and humility. She affected greatly what I later became as an adult."

"Yes, she was amazing indeed. But is that all?" the inner voice asked.

"Oh, no! I met her and her sister Perin, after 50 years, for an amazing week in Southern California in the Summer of 2015. We had a reception for them at my home, spent time seeing sights in LA, and visiting National Parks over a 1000+ mile road trip. It was a week that I could never have imagined. We lived some lively times together and made grand memories."

"When it came time to leave, I went with her and Perin all the way to their airplane gate. We hugged, kissed, and she left me some incredibly endearing hand-written notes, which I cherish to this day. And then, they were gone!"

"I wanted to see her again, but sadly that was not meant to happen. As a US citizen and being born in India, it was not deemed safe for me to travel to Lahore, Pakistan."

"Yes, that is unfortunate, Vijay." the inner voice said. "But you and your RKC buddies had great times with her over the years, did you not? So then, what is the reason for your grief?"

129

"It feels very close." I replied. "In many ways, for a whole lot of us over the years, she was like our RKC mother. That includes everything, from tender to tough, that goes with that label."

"Oh, that seems intense." the voice offered.
"Yes." I continued, now in a somewhat curt manner. "If you were not lucky enough to live it, you will never understand it."

A Match of Pride & Royal Encounters

(Not Posted on RKC Forum)

Embracing a Sport

It happened in late 1965, as best as I can remember today. While the precise dates may be a bit fuzzy in my mind, the events that occurred around them are crystal clear to me.

Like all RKC students, I too played all the sports. It was mandatory for everybody. The list included cricket, football (*soccer*), basketball, field hockey, gymnastics, swimming, tennis, track events, etc. I liked all of them and enjoyed playing them. But, in the intensely competitive environment of RKC, I was not what you would call a "star athlete". I was average in most sports. Well, this was simply not good enough in RKC.

In this school, with its tradition of royal students, it was all about winners! It loved winners and did not give much of a damn about losers. It was the regal way, or the way of the "kshatriyas" *(warriors)*, if you will. Now, there was nothing mean or indecent about any of this at all. It was wrapped up nicely in traditions and rituals. Royalty was expected to be better than a "commoner" at anything, and so it must also be in sports of any kind. It was a widely held belief at the time, and no offense of any kind was intended or implied towards anyone. However, it did affect the sense of self-worth for many an RKC student over time. Sadly, in some ways, I was one of them.

Out of all the sports I played in RKC, I began to excel somewhat in one of them. It was tennis. This was due to some unusual reasons, that most folks at the school did not know about. They had nothing to do with RKC. You see, my father was very fond of tennis! He was also an all-round star athlete and had played at the varsity level in many sports as a college student. He was a jock and excelled in cricket, in particular, as a fast bowler and a batsman. Anyway, Pappaji had the tennis courts at the Porbandar ACC Sports Club, and later, he had a tennis court built on the grounds of our bungalow in Jamul, in Madhya Pradesh! He played regularly in all these places. He was gifted at this sport as well.

During the summer holidays during my RKC years, when I was home in Jamul and totally bored, my father would encourage me to play tennis. I would, whenever I could find somebody to play with. That was not very often. Then one day, in a throwback to our days in Porbandar, Pappaji drew two lines on the side wall of our car garage and had someone paint half a tennis court on the pavement in front of it. The lower line was the "net". The upper line marked the level above which my serve would go outside of the "box" on the other side and be a "fault". Pappaji then said, "You need nobody now. Go there and practice. Just serve and try to hit between the lines consistently. Outside of that, practice your backhand the most. It is usually the weakest for most folks. And perfect your cross-court shots." Suddenly, I had found my calling! I proceeded to spend my hours of boredom, for days on end, just banging away at this wall. I did not realize it at the time, but the level of my game improved by several quantum measures! Actually, I became good at it. I won a few interesting tennis matches at the Jamul Sports Club as well. But those are different stories.

One day back at RKC, soon after this summer, I found myself playing against Mr. Basant Singh, who taught tennis to RKC students in my time there. In the past, I had been quite forgettable for him. I was just like many other students. But now, I gave him a run for his money! He was surprised and a bit startled.

"Vijay, your game has changed." he said. "I am pleasantly surprised. What has happened?" So, I explained it all to him. He said, "Okay, Sunday morning, 9:00am, singles match with me. Let's see what you really are all about."

Gosh, for me it was "game on"! I was determined to wipe him out. But he was awfully skilled and I was quite naïve. We fought hard and long in this 3-set match. It was "mano a mano" (*man to man*), as they say, in this 'hand to hand' combat. We went over 10 games in each set, but in the end, he won. He was more mature and could control his emotions, even in the face of adversity. By contrast, I was all over the place, frequently angry with myself, or emotionally quite out of control. I was heartbroken that I had lost.

"Vijay, you should not be disappointed today at all," Mr. Basant Singh said. "You played a great match."

"Oh, Sir, thank you," I replied. "But I feel that I am just terrible at this game. I get angry with myself and cannot seem to figure a way out to ever win."

"No, you must not think of it that way," he went on. "Listen, next month, we have a whole group of students from King George's College, Chail, visiting us. We are going to have all sorts of inter-collegiate sports events with them. One of them is a singles tennis match. I have to pick a student to represent RKC. Our top two players are Shahid, and now you, at the moment, I think."

"Oh, Sir, please pick Shahid. He is way better than me at everything. Also, he is the Head Boy. He will make RKC proud, I know." I said, in earnest and honest support for my dear friend, Sid.

"Yes, I probably should do that." Mr. Basant Singh said. "But no, I am going to pick you. Do you know why? I think you are hungrier for the win. It takes that passion and drive. Right now, you seem to have them. But I need to teach you to channel them properly and to control your emotions. So, we start daily practice every evening, starting tomorrow. Vijay, I can promise you that it is going to be a hard journey. But I also know that you will make your school proud of you. Agreed?"

I gushed, "Yes, Sir!" in complete delight. I was also totally clueless about what I had just committed myself to with Mr. Basant Singh. I had no idea at all about the toughness of his training. It was not only physical, but it was also intensely mental. The man was relentless and tough. Actually, I must confess, this training helped me a lot in my later life in other ways too.

The Tennis Match

It turned out to be a major event! I had no idea about what it would end up being, and to say that I was shocked would be a gross understatement. At nearly the end of a week of inter-collegiate games of all sorts, on this evening, they had scheduled this singles tennis match. The ambience of it all, got me both excited and quite anxious.

The match was to be played on the Main Court next to the Gymnasium. There were bleachers and chairs set up on the far side of the Court, across from the Gymnasium steps. The entire RKC school, some 300+ students, was in the audience, along with the visiting student group from KG, Chail. All the RKC teachers, many Old Boys, and a variety of local dignitaries were also in attendance. The Chief Guest for the event was even more special! He was HH Thakore Saheb Shri Pradyumansinhji of Rajkot! He was highly regarded by everybody, was a benefactor of RKC in many ways, and a lover of sports. He arrived with his entourage, with much fanfare, and that added massively to my already frail nerves.

I started to tremble and Mr. Basant Singh, who was nearby with me, noticed it immediately. He steadied me and said, "Vijay, forget this crazy setup. This is just our match from last Sunday. So, how are you going to beat me?" It certainly distracted my mind for the moment. Well, I tuned out all the announcements, greetings, and brief speeches on the PA system, and in short order, I found myself on the Main Court. The match was about to begin and I was still quite nervous. I had never felt so much pressure placed upon me ever before! I was playing solo and representing RKC in front of the entire school. It felt like I was carrying the entire school on my back! It simply was unacceptable for me to fail. In the annals of RKC and its royal heritage, fear or failure were just not an option. These were serious matters, particularly when it came to competitive sports. It was all about pride and commitment. And, good grief, I had the HH of Rajkot himself in the audience!

The match began. I started out miserably. I was having a hard time getting over my nerves. I heard occasional cheers from the largely friendly audience, but the player from KG, Chail, was playing much better than me. He broke my very first serve game and put the heat on me. At this moment, I lost it and got angry. But as Mr. Basant Singh had taught me, I channeled the rage into my play. In my mind, I said, "Hell with the damn audience! Who cares anyway? But I am going to whip this KG twerp. I am going to work him hard. I am going to obliterate him from the face of this Court!" And then, with all that, I actually started to play tennis.

It was a tough match. We were nearly even in our skills and the required physical endurance. The air was hot and humid. It was an uncomfortable and a sweaty environment. However, there was also a huge difference in our perspectives towards this match. For my opponent, it was perhaps just another tennis match. But for me, it was my self-worth, pride, and life itself in RKC! He could afford to lose without many consequences. But I could not afford to lose at all. For him, a win would be nice, but for me, it was everything. It all showed up in how we played.

I was aggressive and relentless. I would make him work in every point. I forced his errors. Also, I played with strategy and finesse at times, or with brute force and speed on other occasions. But he was a worthy opponent. The excitement about the match continued to grow with each game and set, as we proceeded towards a full 3-set match. For the audience, it quickly became a truly entertaining match, because the balance of victory kept shifting constantly throughout the games with many "deuce/advantage" points. I must admit though that the RKC crowd did cheer me much more than they did my opponent. However, in the end, I did prevail. There was a long and raucous applause. The chief cheerleader for it was the HH of Rajkot himself! Mr. Basant Singh was very pleased.

A prize was shortly given to the RKC Team Captain, with some fanfare, for the win in the tennis match. I was still sitting by the courtside, when the ADC (aide-de-camp) of HH of Rajkot walked up to me. He said, "Thakore Saheb tamane bolaave chhe!" (*Thakore Saheb is asking for you!*) I was astonished!

I went up the Gymnasium steps with Mr. Basant Singh and bowed to the HH of Rajkot, prior to introductions. (The Indian Royalty had titles and privileges in those times. By law, these customs had to be followed.). He smiled broadly, shook my hand, and said, "Dikara, tu aje Rajkot satu gajabnu jhajhumyo!" (*Son, today you fought valiantly for Rajkot!*) He thanked me profusely for my "fight for Rajkot" and said that he had enjoyed the match immensely. In return, I reflexively thanked him for all his support for our RKC.

It was indeed special for me to be introduced to the distinguished HH of Rajkot. I did not think much about it after the match evening ended. But in a few days, to my utter astonishment, I received a gift! It was from the HH of Rajkot and it was delivered at RKC by his ADC. It was a brand spanking new Slazenger tennis racquet, with the insignia of the Rajkot State embossed on it! The net was made from a rare "cat gut" and it had a press and a cover with it as well. I was used to playing with cheap, crappy tennis racquets at RKC and at home. So, this was something spectacular for a young tennis player like me. I was just thrilled! I showed it off to everybody around me.

However, in a few days, this special racquet went missing from my cupboard. My friends and I looked everywhere for it, but it was gone! Perhaps it was stolen by a collector of special things, or maybe somebody took it to sell it for cash in the markets, or possibly it was taken to be given to somebody else who needed a racquet. I never found out what happened or why. It just vanished from sight without a trace!

Later on, someone suggested that I contact the ADC of the HH of Rajkot and tell him what had happened. Maybe they will replace it! It was possible, but I just did not have the heart to ask for a "repeated gift" from such gracious people, who had been so nice to me already.

A Royal Farewell

Soon, life got very busy and serious for all of us with the upcoming Senior Cambridge exams. Then, one day, Mr. Basant Singh approached Shahid and me and asked if we would represent RKC and play an exhibition doubles tennis match in Jamnagar. It would occur sometime after our exams were finished. We looked at each other in great delight and agreed immediately.

The exhibition match was scheduled for some time in Jan-Feb, 1966. Sid and I were preparing for it in earnest on Sundays. Alas, then came the saddest news imaginable. The revered HH Maharaja Jam Saheb Shri Digvijaysinhji of Navanagar, had passed away. All of RKC was in a state of total shock. Sid & I had met Jam Saheb many times in the Principal's Bungalow, when he was visiting RKC or just passing through Rajkot. He was a huge patron of RKC, President of its Governing Council, very knowledgeable, and so impressive. Meeting him for any occasion was always an unforgettable experience.

On a couple of occasions, I even recall meeting his wife, Maharani Gulab Kunwar Ba at RKC as well. She too was an amazing lady. But on this day, I remember feeling a profound sense of grief and loss at the passing of our Jam Saheb. It was a first for me. It was also very personal in its impact on me.

Instead of a tennis match, Sid and I, along with others, went to Jamnagar to attend Jam Saheb's funeral, as the representatives of the students of RKC. The funeral procession was just unimaginable in its pomp and grandeur. It looked like something out of a Hollywood movie! It was accompanied by a genuine public outpouring of uncontrollable grief from the citizens of Jamnagar, who loved their departed monarch so very much.

When they lit his funeral pyre, which was made of sandalwood, with "homemade ghee" poured on it, I lost it also and cried uncontrollably. Sid and I met and hugged so many ordinary folks, and also many dignitaries, who were just weeping for the loss of their Jam Saheb. I have not seen or experienced anything quite like this in my life since that time anywhere.

I could go on a lot more, but such were a few of the aspects of my final academic year at RKC. As my dear mother used to say, "Rang na to chheeta hoy, kunda na hoy!" (*It is sprinkles of color that are liked, not buckets of them!*)

This rich and somewhat vivid mural, is left incomplete, quite deliberately. It comprises only of tennis matches, a royal gift, and a royal farewell.

However, this mural is also reflective of my growth as a person, and as an RKCian. All of which defined my life in countless ways, not only in the years that followed, but in fact, forever.

1961-62

Left to Right   MAYNE HOUSE
Sitting : Vijay Yajnik, Shahid Siddiqi, Arunkumar Patel (Ca...
Girirajsinh Dabhisi, Vinodchandra Vagher

Seated (l to r): Me & Shahid
Standing (3rd from l): Himanshu
1961

My Recitation – Prizegiving 1963

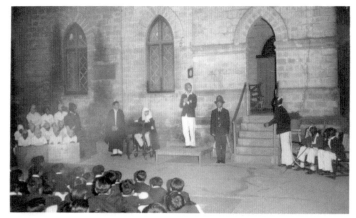

*"Toad of
Toad Hall"
– A Play
1963*

*Himanshu, Vijay Ram
& Me – Recitations
1964*

*Interludes – Tattoo
Himanshu, Shahid, &
Me
1966*

Shahid & Me - Inspection, Tattoo 1966

At March Past – Tattoo 1966

Mr. Freeman, UK High Commisioner and Mr. Rogerson

Mr. Basant Singh & Our Tennis Team
1965-66

My RKC Class of 1966

Prefects of Class of 1966 with HH the Jamsaheb

My Amazing RKC Teachers – 1965-66
L to R: (Seated) Mrs. Kulkarni, HH the Jamsaheb, Madam Cooper
1st Row: Mssrs Lavkumar, Pancholi, Kulkarni, Rogerson, Basantsingh, Bharatsingh,
Jadeja. 2nd Row: Mssrs George, Siddhan, Dalpatsingh, Pettigrew, Chhaya, Yajnik,
and Ayaaz Khan.

Lioness "Ganga" & Lion "Bhiliyo" in Sasan, Gir Forest – Around 1955

Kruger National Park
South Africa - 2000

The Three Lionesses - Kruger National Park

Living Out Boyhood Dreams - 1976

With Mr. Lavkumar - 2011

With Mr. Ayaaz Khan - 2016

Ronald Reagan Library, Getty Museum, Hollywood Walk of Fame & Las Vegas - 2015

RKC Reception for Madam Cooper & Perin Boga
at my home in Palos Verdes (LA) - 2015

Bryce Canyon, Zion, & Grand Canyon National Parks

Madam Cooper's All Time Favorite Park – The Grand Canyon National Park

The "Cooper Crepe Myrtle Tree" near my home

THE JAMUL YEARS

Early Hardships

My parents were transferred from Porbandar to Jamul, in Madhya Pradesh, in the Autumn of 1960. My first visit there from RKC was a while later, so I was spared the days of early hardships. But later, my parents told me lots of stories about those days.

ACC's Jamul Cement Works (JCW) had been envisaged as the "crown jewel" in the network of its cement plants all over India. The Jamul area had enormous deposits of limestone, a key raw material for the manufacture of cement. Also, nearby was the Bhilai Steel Works (BSW), a public sector steel manufacturing plant, set up in collaboration with Russia which had provided the needed technology and expertise. It was gigantic, and it had next to it a huge planned residential community for all its managers, Russian families, administrative staff, and skilled workers.

The key link between these two entities was something called "slurry", a byproduct of the process of making steel from iron ore. It was a waste product for BSW, but a vital raw material for JCW in making cement. So, the proximity of the two plants was of great synergistic benefit.

The BSW was well built up and already in production, when my parents arrived to setup JCW. They got a huge surprise, because in Jamul there were none of the comforts of the bungalows of Porbandar. In fact, they had to start on simple barren land, which was just wilderness.

There was little staff on hand and only a few key senior managers were present. They all lived on the plant site in military tents, in very rustic conditions. As GM, my father was offered nice accommodations in a lovely hotel in the BSW colony, but he declined. He felt that he and my mom should live right along with his team, in the same level of discomfort. Nobody could believe this decision, including the folks in the ACC Head Office in Bombay. So, this and more, became the stuff of many a legend.

It was a truly spartan existence. The entire JCW property was secured with a barbed wire fence and had physical markers within it designating various sections and their purposes, including a huge area for the cement plant itself. In the residential colony area, there were a dozen or so military tents for living and a few more for administrative functions.

The work priorities were very clear. First, build the infrastructure to bring in power and water, provide drainage, and remove sewage. Next, create the basic roads and start to build the permanent housing in the colony. Without housing, people could not come to live there and without them, nothing could progress forward. Also, basic structures, for things such as a general store, bank, and post office to support a nascent colony had to be built.

Everybody was highly motivated and my father was driven like a military general in a battlefield. Work progressed rapidly. Within 6 months, my parents and other senior managers, moved into the newly built "C" level junior bungalows, and their vacated tents were occupied promptly by other new arrivals. And so, it went on. The "B" level & "D" level buildings came next and a whole community started to come into existence.

It took over a year to achieve critical mass, and then work began also on building the cement plant and its required infrastructure. On the whole, it was a remarkable achievement, given that all things moved at a snail's pace in India. This was usually because of some inane regulations or procedures, which had no bearing on anything real. It could also be due to a government official, who would stand in your way until his ego was suitably catered to in some manner. But, all this aside, there were many serious and simply wild challenges at times that the team had to overcome as well.

A famous one was the "milk episode". One day, all the wives of the managers and staff onsite, just revolted! They were sick and tired of not being able to get, on a regular basis, something as basic as milk. They marched into my father's office tent and demanded that something be done about it at once. My Dad was thinking, "I am here to build a cement plant, not to deal with all your whining about milk supplies." But he did not say any such thing. Instead, he smiled and calmed all the ladies down, and promised that he would find a solution for this crisis.

He had not the foggiest idea of what he should do. So, he went out for a walk to think about it, among all the laborers who were toiling away all over the place. During this walk, he encountered a few men and women from the Jamul village, and they launched into another tirade against him! They were upset that the JCW plant site had cost them critical fields close to their village to graze their cows and buffaloes. Now, they had to go away far and that was hard for so many families. Then, my father hit upon an idea. He asked to meet with the "Panch" *(the village council, comprising of 5 elders, with legal powers)* of the Jamul village.

At this Panch meeting, attended massively by everybody in the Jamul village, my father made a proposal. He said, "I have heard of your grazing difficulties. So, I will permit you to graze your cattle anywhere on the plant grounds. But you must keep them in a stockade, which we will build for you, at night. When the plant is built and grazing will not be possible, we will provide you with feed for your cattle in the stockade. In return, we want you to sell your daily milk production to the plant colony general store first, before anybody else. We will agree to pay the daily fair market price for your milk." The entire meeting exploded in joy and the Panch accepted the proposal immediately.

The Panch and the village people had no formal education, but they were not stupid. Further, they tested my father to see if he was good for his word. They were very satisfied, because my father did much more for them than what he had promised. So, he became revered as the "Yajnik Saheb" in the Jamul village and we were invited to all sorts of functions and festivities around the year. According to my mother, she also received "marriage offers" for Jamul village daughters for me! But all these wonderful things aside, after that the JCW colony never had a shortage of milk.

Then there was this fracas about the merchandise at the colony general store! All the ladies of the colony simply hated everything sold in that general store. The fruits and vegetables were never fresh, grains were of awful quality, "dal" *(lentils)* of any kind was terrible, and the needed basic spices were never in stock.

It was also interesting to note that this poor general store was being run by an accountant, who was actually the "store keeper" of the cement plant, but also doubled as the store's purchasing agent. He was single, did not cook at home, and always disliked having to waste a day going to Raipur, some 40 kilometers away, once a week to make a buying trip. And, no matter what he did, he could never please these ladies of the colony.

So again, the ladies arrived "en masse" at my father's tent. "Mr. Yajnik, the general store is terrible! We cannot buy basic necessities. You have to do something." My father explained the whole setup to them, and they replied, "Yes, yes. But it is not working for us. You have to do something."

So, Pappaji thought for a bit, and said, "Okay, are you willing to help the general store? Will you help with the purchasing activities of the store to make it better for the whole colony?"

They said, "We don't understand. What do you want us to do?"

He amplified, "A truck goes to Raipur every day for work purposes. Usually, it is only half full. If one of you goes with it, you can make purchases of fresh food and other products daily, and keep the store properly supplied for everybody. You can share this daily duty among yourselves and make proper shopping lists for what should be bought for the store each day. What do you think?"

He made the sale promptly. The ladies of the colony became the "purchasing agents" of the general store and nobody complained about the merchandise ever again.

In fact, it became one of the finest food shopping destinations in the area over the years.

A Boy Called "Vaalji"

It was around 1956 or so. We had moved recently into the Porbandar GM Bungalow. That evening, Pappaji had just come home from work and was having his British style tea service. Shortly, Gaju, the butler, came by and told him that an elderly man was at the gate asking to see him. This was not unusual. Many people came to see him unannounced in the evening for all sorts of reasons. Pappaji always welcomed such visitors without any hesitation, if he was not preoccupied with something urgent.

Gaju showed the man in. He was in his mid-fifties, but looked a lot older. He had a gentle but proud manner about him, and it was apparent that times were hard for him. He wore a coat over a shirt and a clean dhoti. He was accompanied by a young boy. My father asked him to be seated on the sofa, but he said that they would sit on the rug instead, an obvious gesture of politeness reflecting a lower social status.

He began, "Saheb, mare musibat na divaso chhe." *(Saheb, these are days of difficulty for me.)*

My father gently asked him to describe his problems. He explained that his younger brother had recently passed away in Porbandar and the responsibility of raising his two orphaned sons had now fallen upon him. He had managed to place the older son in a laborer's job at the port, but he was worried about the younger boy who was with him. He introduced him to Pappaji. His name was Vaalji and he was 11 years old. He was groomed well, and wore a clean shirt over a pair of khaki shorts.

Pappaji said, "He is only 11 years old. He should be in school."

The man replied, "Saheb, kharacho posato nathi. Ane amare etli avak nathi." *(Saheb, I cannot afford the expense. And we do not have enough income.)*

In the conversation that ensued, the old man pleaded with Pappaji to find some kind of employment for Vaalji. He said that Vaalji was a good, hard working, trustworthy boy and would do any job well. Pappaji was in a predicament. Vaalji was too young for any sort of work in the cement plants and at his age he had no useful skills. He was just a nice young boy, who actually should be studying in a school.

My mother had been listening to the whole conversation. She told Pappaji that perhaps Vaalji could work as a domestic helper in the bungalow. That morning, the lady who did such work had suddenly bolted for Rajasthan due to some kind of an emergency in her family, and the timeframe for her return, if it happened at all, was unknown. So, Pappaji asked the man if Vaalji would be willing to work as a domestic helper in the bungalow.

He replied, "Saheb, tame kahesho te badhu kam sari reete karashe. Ben pan khush thashe. Tamane mara Garasiya na lohi ma lakhi apu." *(Saheb, he will do any work for you very well. Ben will be happy. I can write it down for you in my Garasiya blood.)* This was a strong statement filled with emotion and pride. The Garasiyas of Saurashtra were like the Rajputs of Rajasthan. Their whole community, clans, and various castes were the stuff of local legend. They were "kshatriyas" *(warriors)*, who were a hardworking, trustworthy, and proud people with a rich and noble heritage. Pappaji was very touched, and along with my Mom, they hired Vaalji immediately. The old man expressed sentiments of life long gratitude to them.

True to the promise made by his uncle, Vaalji turned out to be just amazing. For his age, he was muscular and strong. He was always working, doing something or another. He had a cheerful disposition, a wonderful attitude towards doing any kind of domestic work, and a radiant smile. My mother quickly became very fond of him and would spoil him in all sorts of small ways, particularly in matters of food that he liked to eat. I was about 7 years old at the time and mischievous in many things. So, Behn asked Vaalji to keep an eye on me and all my antics. He was great fun and would even play with me when time permitted.

I did not care much for studies in the elementary school and would goof off at any opportunity. So, my parents hired a tutor for me. Mr. Trivedi would come by for an hour or so 4 days a week. He would teach me to read and write in Gujarati initially and later a little bit of English. Vaalji became very interested in these tutoring sessions, so my mother made a decision. She told Vaalji that he could join me in these sessions, if he had finished all his chores. In actual fact, mother changed things around in a way so that Vaalji would always be free for these sessions. She also got him writing supplies and a nice big slate.

Vaalji took to these sessions like flies on dog poop. He was very bright and had a great memory. He absorbed things quickly and in any spare time, I would find him studying and practicing things he had learnt in these sessions. He started with the Gujarati alphabet and soon began to read and write. Then he began to do the same thing with English. He did not speak English so this part was much harder for him. But he was relentless in his pursuit of knowledge. He would ask me to switch on the radio and tune it to an English broadcast on All India Radio or BBC and he would listen to spoken English with rapt attention and try and repeat the words out loud. I showed him the Gujarati and English dictionaries that we had and I would often find him going through them searching for words. Steadily, his vocabulary grew. He got pretty good with Gujarati and began to speak broken English words and phrases as well. When he had any free time at all, I would find him reading Gujarati magazines such as Akhand Anand with great delight.

On our summer holidays most years in Ahmedabad and Petlad, my parents would bring Vaalji along. He was priceless in the speed with which he cleaned up things and got those homes in good working order. He did not need much direction. He would figure things out on his own and handle all sorts of problems, large or small, with great initiative. After these years, Vaalji was hardly thought of as domestic help anymore. He had become a part of the Yajnik family and was treated with great respect by everybody. My parents also assisted his family financially and in many other ways.

In 1960, there was a major crisis for Vaalji. My father was transferred to Jamul, in Madhya Pradesh, a place which was far away from Porbandar. What was Vaalji to do? There were no guarantees that the new GM would keep him in his job at the bungalow. The old uncle came to see my father again.

He said, "Saheb, take Vaalji with you." Pappaji was shocked to hear this.

Pappaji explained, "Kanjibhai, Jamul is very different from here and quite far away. There is no cement plant there as yet and no housing of any kind. It is wilderness. We will be living in tents for quite some time. This may not be well suited for Vaalji."

Kanjibhai replied, "Saheb, you have chosen to go there, have you not? If it is good enough for you, it will surely be good enough for him. I am not worried about Vaalji at all, as long as he is with you and Ben. I am certain that you will find good use for him over there."

So, Vaalji went with my parents to Jamul. While he was of immense value to them in countless ways and in many things, there was no bungalow for Vaalji to work in. But there was a ton of work of all kinds to be done and there were staff shortages in all areas. One big problem was finding drivers for the company vehicles, since the Bhilai Steel Works had taken away most of the available licensed drivers. A few who could have been hired, would not accept the job because there was no housing available in Jamul for their families. It was a vicious cycle.

Then, one day Vaalji approached my father and said, "Saheb, could you have somebody teach me to drive? I am already here and I can help with the driving duties in addition to working in the colony tents."

Pappaji thought about it for a while and said, "It is a good idea, but we have nobody available to teach you. Everybody is very busy. Well, I could teach you, but only at the end of our long working day. Will you accept that?"

"Saheb, that would an honor for me. Yes, of course." Vaalji replied smiling.

So, Pappaji began to teach Vaalji to drive at a pace of 30 minutes per day. He was amazed by the speed with which Vaalji mastered the skills of driving. He had excellent motor reflexes and control. Not only that, he began to read all the car manuals in his spare time, with his basic ability to read some English, and became highly knowledgeable about all aspects of the vehicles. He became very adroit soon, at all solving all sorts of maintenance problems with the vehicles as well. It was all self-taught.

Pappaji could not believe Vaalji's overall progress which had occurred with lightning speed. So, he decided to promote him into a job grade for "skilled workers". Vaalji was relieved of all domestic work duties and was now a member of the pool of skilled staff workers. He got a huge pay raise, a hardship allowance because of the Jamul location and its primitive conditions, and was now eligible for company provided housing, when it was built.

As major construction work for the remaining housing colony and the cement plant commenced, other needs cropped up. The Jamul Cement Works took delivery of huge construction vehicles. These included earth movers, graders, road rollers, excavators, cranes, and large dump trucks, many with hydraulic lifts and steel plated belt drives for propulsion, much like army tanks. These were all highly specialized in their purpose. They were all imported and designed for heavy duty industrial use. Operating any of them required highly specialized training on site and in classrooms. The ever vigilant Vaalji saw another opportunity and applied for these jobs. He was selected and given extensive training. Upon completion, he was promoted to the highest skill level grade with a huge increase in pay. Now, he could operate or drive any machine on the plant site and he also knew how to maintain them in good order. The arc of his career at Jamul was simply astonishing!

After a few years, with the Jamul Cement Works officially now in production, Pappaji was transferred to Dwarka again. Vaalji was by now married, with a young family, and well settled in Jamul, which had transformed into a lovely thriving community. He came to visit my parents upon hearing the news.

They shared lovely laughs over tea and reminisced about the past. My father advised Vaalji that he should not move back to Gujarat, just because he was being transferred back there. He had acquired highly desirable skills in Jamul and there was a huge demand for them in many other places. Dwarka was an aging plant just like Porbandar and the future there would not be as bright. Vaalji took the advice and stayed in Jamul.

Shortly thereafter, ACC won a major contract to build a huge cement plant in Jeddah, Saudi Arabia. There were many highly lucrative jobs there with all sorts of special allowances for skills, hardships, home visits, and so forth. Payments would all be made in Saudi Riyals. Vaalji called my father for advice. Pappaji's short answer was, "Go. Don't miss it."

Vaalji went to Saudi Arabia for 7 years. He sent his family off to live in Porbandar. He would visit them twice a year, when on "home leave". He was always a frugal man, had no bad habits, and lived rather simply. He saved all his money and sent it home. In Porbandar, he bought a total of 3 homes and situated his entire extended family in good housing. He received a handsome pension at retirement from ACC and with his additional savings lived a comfortable life in his later years in Porbandar.

After Jamul, I did not get to meet Vaalji again. But my father told me that once Vaalji showed up at the Nikunj bungalow in Ahmedabad on a surprise visit. My parents were just thrilled to see him. Pappaji, who was now retired, asked him to sit on the sofa. But Vaalji chose to sit on the rug near them, just like a long time ago. Now, he was well off and happy, still had that radiant smile, but he never forgot his humble past and the people who had helped him and given him opportunities.

This story of Vaalji illustrates some simple truths. All around us, there are always opportunities knocking and brass rings passing by. The key is to learn to recognize them, assess the risks involved, make informed decisions, and then grab them without fear or hesitation.

There is no point to living a life of regrets.

An Adventurous Train Journey

The platform at the Rajkot Junction railway station was nearly deserted. The Kirti Express, the last daily passenger train, had arrived from Porbandar a bit early at 9:50pm. The passengers getting off at Rajkot had already disembarked from the train and were long gone. All the passengers boarding at Rajkot for the overnight journey towards Mehsana had already done so and settled into their compartments. Most of the vendors, who would normally be walking around on the platform and calling out to sell their wares had closed up shop for the night. Even the stray dogs, normally seen prowling around the platform, had settled down somewhere for some sleep. Except for the hissing of steam from the train engine, all was quiet.

"Munikaka, thanks for seeing me off, but I think you and Ushakaki should go home now. I have done this journey once before, so there is nothing for you to worry about." I said.

Munikaka had been posted in Rajkot six months earlier, and had been designated as my local guardian at RKC.

He replied, "That's alright. The train leaves at 10:20pm and that is only five more minutes from now."

Just as he finished, we heard a public announcement that the Kirti Express departure was delayed by 20 minutes, due to some rail traffic congestion up ahead.

I had arrived at the Rajkot station a lot earlier from RKC in a "tanga" (*horse & buggy*). Other students had come along in their tangas also. Our whole caravan of tangas to the station had been escorted by a teacher. The school had closed for the holidays earlier on this April day after breakfast. Most of the students from Saurashtra, who were being picked up by their families, had left by 11:00am. The Bombay/South India groups, that I used to travel with before, had left by the 2:00pm train. So, we were the last stragglers to be sent off on this late-night train. We were the North India/Other category of a group. The interesting part was this "Other" category. It was new for everybody at the time, but it had a rich history.

After Independence from British Rule in 1947, India was furiously playing catch-up with the world on every imaginable front, with limited capital resources. This was particularly evident in the Indian Railways network. This legacy network, born in the 19th Century British India, comprised of tracks of three different gauge sizes, their respectively different rolling stocks, and a vast patchwork network of stations and junctions to provide connectivity. All trains, within a gauge sub-network, went from their point of origin to the destination entirely intact. It was the passengers who had to get on and off, and change trains at many places, to travel around the country.

Well, in the early 1960's, the Indian Railways started introducing a novel concept, adopted from the European railway networks. They began introducing "destination bogeys" that travelled from a station of origin to a destination, over long-haul distances, within a gauge sub-network. This meant that the bogey would be detached from one train and attached to another train, according to its routing and train schedules, and the passengers were left free to relax and travel in settled comfort. In these bogeys, the "train changing business" was left in the hands of the railways. It was a great concept and it was well received by the travelling public. But like most anything in India, its adoption was full of fits and starts.

After a pause, I said, "Really, Kaka, you should go home. I am well settled in my berth and will just go to sleep. I am sure the train will leave soon. It is a very early morning train change for me in Viramgam in order to catch the 'Howrah Bogey'."

This new Howrah Bogey (HB) originated at Viramgam in the west, with Calcutta's Howrah Station as its destination in the east, crossing most of central India attached to a diverse mix of trains. It was a highly desired service for many people.

After a little discussion, Munikaka relented and said, "Well, you do seem well settled, and there is nothing further to be done here at this station. So, okay, we shall return home, as you suggest." We shared affectionate goodbyes and then they left.

I returned to my berth and laid down on my bedroll to sleep. I was dozing off a little, but I was also waiting to hear the rhythmic sounds and feel the motion of a moving train. They always put me to sleep promptly. But the train did not move for a long time. It was well past midnight when I woke up because of a sudden jolt. I looked outside the window and noticed that we were just departing the Rajkot station. The Kirti Express was running over 2 hours late.

Throughout this night, I had disturbed sleep. The train stopped many times, for long periods at random places, typically in the middle of nowhere. All stations that we passed, or had brief stops at, were just deserted. Occasionally, I would hear people, outside near the tracks, engaged in animated conversations, but I could not understand what they were saying. Then it was morning. We had still not arrived in Viramgam.

On the last trip, when we were on time, the Viramgam Junction had arrived around 4:00am. One side of the platform had "meter-gauge" tracks, but the other side had "broad-gauge" tracks. There was a train waiting on the broad-gauge tracks side. It was the Saurashtra Express, which originated at Viramgam and was destined for Bombay. It looked so huge to me compared to our train from Rajkot, which looked like a toy train.

When I had disembarked, pulling my steel trunk and bedroll with me, I had discovered that the Howrah Bogey was just across the platform, less than 50 feet away! In minutes, I had checked in with the conductor and boarded. My assigned berth was a corridor side upper berth, which was just fantastic. In the daytime, I could sit down below and I had access to two wide windows. And with an upper berth assignment, I could climb up and take a nap anytime I wished. Given the length of my journey home, this arrangement was simply awesome.

The Saurashtra Express would leave Viramgam at 5:00am. Around 7:00am we passed Ahmedabad, around 11:00am we passed Baroda, and we reached Surat around 2:00pm. Here the HB would be disconnected from the train and positioned on a "siding" with a short standalone platform. There would be no electricity inside the HB. All bogeys had electricity only when they were connected to trains. So, for this duration, there were no lights or fans operating, which made life inside the HB very uncomfortable, especially in the hot weather months. Everybody would just spill out, find some water and shade to stay cool, and just wait till the HB was re-connected to a train.

That would happen around 6:00pm when we were connected to the Tapi Valley Express to Bhusaval. It was called an Express, but it moved like a local train and stopped just as much. Bhusaval was a major junction station on the main tracks from Bombay to Calcutta. We would arrive at 3:00am, be detached, and get re-connected to the Howrah Mail (HM) from Bombay at 4:00am. This HM train was something to experience!

The Howrah Mail was a daily train from Bombay to Calcutta. At the time, it was one of the oldest and most storied trains of India. From way back in the 19th Century, it connected Bombay, a critical center of commerce, with Calcutta, the seat of the British East India Co. government. The train had bogeys for all classes of travel, including the new "Air Conditioned" (AC) class. It had a dining car, meal service in bogeys, and it was fast. A behemoth of a steam locomotive pulled it.

It had track priority over everything, because its very creation was based on the critical need to move the Royal Mail fast. It stopped only at key junction stations which were about 30 to 50 minutes apart. It travelled at maximum speeds allowed on the tracks and stopped at stations only for a few minutes. Longer halts were made only to pick up water and coal or change steam engines at specific yards.

After travelling for the entire day on the HM, I would reach the Durg station, in Madhya Pradesh at 6:00pm. The HM stopped there for just 3 minutes and I would disembark and be met by my parents. From Rajkot to my home in Jamul, it was a journey of 2 nights and 2 days, at that time.

However, this morning in Viramgam was very different. The Kirti Express had arrived 4 hours late and the Saurashtra Express, with the HB, had departed a long time ago. I sat down on my trunk on the empty platform wondering what to do. My few fellow RKC students were debating their options as well, but they had a simpler task before them. All of them had to go to Bombay regardless, and any number of trains could take them there. But my journey home was via Surat, to Bhusaval, and then to Durg.

How should I do this without the HB? I did have a valid train ticket to Durg. I may not have the HB, but I could aboard the next available train at each junction on my route and just keep going forward. I had enough pocket money for food, so surely, I would eventually get there. Well, after some thought, I decided to act on this plan.

That is exactly what happened. I boarded the next train at Viramgam for Surat. Once there, I had a long wait for a train to Bhusaval, so I went off to see a film at a theatre near the station. I still remember that it was a film starring the young Indian movie star, Saira Banu, who I thought was so pretty. The film was "April Fool". Well, my journey was in the month of April and I felt a bit foolish that day as well! Then later, I took the slow train to Bhusaval. Since I was so very late, I just waited there for the Howrah Mail and took it to get to Durg. I reached at 6:00pm, exactly 24 hours late. There was nobody there to receive me. My parents were nowhere in sight. Now what should I do? Again, I thought for a bit and then decided the next step.

I went to the Durg Station Master's office and introduced myself. I asked if anybody there would kindly call my father to arrange for a pickup since I had arrived a day late. Their response was simply overwhelming!

"Where have you been? Are you okay? My God, we all have been so worried. Nobody knew what had happened to you. I will contact your father at once. You parents will be so relieved."

An hour later, my parents came to the Durg station to pick me up. There were lots of hugs, kisses and words of relief all around me. After hearing my story, my mother slowly recovered from her state of near hysteria.

My father said, "See what RKC training is all about? His training has taught him at a young age to be confident, to think, and to take proper action to solve his problems. And he did just that!"

Later I learnt that my father had not been as brave as he had portrayed to everyone. Phone calls, telegrams, etc. had gone out all over to people in Rajkot, Ahmedabad, Baroda, Surat, Bhusaval, Nagpur, Railway Police, etc. with the same question, "Do you know where Vijay Yajnik is? Have you seen him or heard from him?"

Well, it had not occurred to me to call or inform anybody in any town. What would I say? I did not know how to do any of that anyway. But I knew my route, I had a valid ticket for it, and a little pocket money. RKC had taught me to never be afraid, and to think, especially in the face of adversity.

As the saying goes, "All is well that ends well."

The Blossoming of Jamul

In 1960, when my parents arrived in Jamul, the old village was about 3 kilometers away. Adjacent to it, ACC had acquired huge swaths of land for building a massive cement plant with the latest technologies, a housing colony with various modern support services, and vast quarries to mine the limestone. All this had occurred with assistance from the State and Central governments during the previous 5 years or so. Now it was time to actually build the Jamul Cement Works and bring it to life. That was my father's strategic mission. It had to be accomplished beneath the long shadow of the Bhilai Steel Works, a behemoth of a public sector enterprise undertaken with Russian assistance, about 10 kilometers away.

Jamul was a sleepy old village which had not been touched by much of anything over time. It was a simple farming community like so many all over India. So, the development of a major industrial complex nearby was a matter of great trepidation and fear for everyone living in it. They were all concerned about what it would mean for their simple lives.

Pappaji sensed this very quickly and concluded that it was vital to win the minds and hearts of the people of Jamul, if things were to go forward smoothly. So, he asked to meet the Panch *(the village council of 5 elders with political power)* of the Jamul village in a public setting. A meeting was organized and moderated by the Sar Panch *(the head of the council)* himself. The language spoken was Hindi and luckily my parents were fluent in it. Pappaji was astute in his understanding of human relations and perceptions, so he did many things carefully and deliberately.

He drove his Willys Jeep right into the village's central crossroads himself, with the driver seated next to him. Everybody noticed that he was driving it himself. He parked it and then walked all around the village greeting people and introducing himself, in fluent Hindi. He was dressed in his work clothes. He had on a shirt tucked into his khaki shorts with a leather belt. He had calf high grey woolen socks and brown leather wingtip shoes. He wore a British style Pith helmet over his bald head and carried a thin whip like riding stick, also made of red leather, in his hand. The whole village was aghast at this formidable sight, presented by an Indian! It got everybody's attention immediately.

Pappaji began the meeting by introducing himself and briefly reviewing for everybody all the activities that were going on in the Jamul Cement Works site and the plans for the near future. Then he opened it up for a Q&A session quickly. He encouraged the generally shy crowd of people to feel safe and ask him about anything on their minds. They started in an uncertain way, but shortly warmed up. No question was deemed trivial or stupid. In his response, my father would not only answer the question, but also provide the context for it, so people could understand the thoughts behind it. The meeting lasted for over 3 hours!

It became a seminal event in the history of the Jamul village. It also affected its future and fortunes in many ways. A feeling of trust began to grow after it between Pappaji and the Panch, and this had far reaching consequences for a lot of folks over time. The elders in the Panch, while not literate or formally schooled, were not stupid people at all. They listened and learned things quickly.

At times, my father found that he was negotiating matters with himself. On the one hand he was trying to help the Panch and the Jamul village, but on the other he also was the GM of the Jamul Cement Works. By temperament and in his values, he was highly civic minded, believed strongly in education, and economic improvement for all. He was secular in his thinking, embraced diversity, and harbored no prejudices of any kind. He was progressive, honest, and fair to all in making many tough decisions. These traits were tested repeatedly in the ensuing years.

Some consequences of the meeting became apparent very quickly. The colony "milk crisis" was solved. That led to asking the Jamul farmers to supply fresh fruits, vegetables, eggs, and meat to the colony general store first, before taking them to other distant markets. The villagers were happy to oblige since the general store paid them a price which was a bit above the market and saved them transportation costs. Soon, an economic bond began to take hold. Then, Pappaji did something else that surprised many people.

He offered tours of the Works site to the people of the Jamul village. He would frequently accompany small groups of men, starting with the Panch, on a full-blown tour of the Works grounds. He would explain all the activity going on and the future plans to all of them. Shortly, my mother started to do the same thing with the women of the Jamul village, starting with the wives of the Panch, and then others. She was often joined by the wives of various managers in the Works.

An old saying goes, "Familiarity breeds either love or contempt." The tours removed any mystery surrounding the Works in Jamul, and bred love. Everybody saw the potential of what was happening and it was all a very positive and welcome addition to their lives. But then, Pappaji went even further.

He told the village that when the construction work for the cement plant began in earnest, there would be a great need for a large labor force. He would offer a job to at least one member from every family in the village, man or woman, to make them a part of it. In jobs requiring some skills, he was willing to offer them skills training as well. He received a tumultuous response, so he began hiring immediately from the village, all the laborers needed even for the construction of the housing colony. Action always spoke louder than words to simple people.

One day, during a meeting with the Panch, my father asked them about what they did with the funds given to them by the government and ACC regularly, per the land acquisition agreements. He was shocked to learn that they were just distributed away per the Jamul village formula. My father suggested that instead the Panch should consider investing them in improving the conditions in the village for the good of all. It was after all their home. They were very intrigued by his suggestion. Thus, began a multi-year project to lift Jamul out of poverty and put in on the map of India.

Plans were developed for electrification, water supply, roads, and a sewage system. Pappaji accompanied the Panch to the Collector's Office in Raipur for government approvals and prioritization in resource allocations. A suggestion was made that many important people from Delhi would come to the inauguration of the cement plant in a few years and that would present a great opportunity to "showcase" an improved and modern village in the changing India. So, all government development plans were greatly accelerated for Jamul.

Under Pappaji's guidance, the Panch constructed permanent buildings for schools, hospital, its temples, and even a mosque. Soon, a post office with a telegraph opened. It started offering banking services as well which were novel to everybody. The Panch also created a proper "Sabji Mandi" *(a vegetables and grain marketplace)* and this made Jamul an important center of commerce in the region. Jamul was transformed from a backwater village into a modern town in a few short years.

However, throughout all these changes, some things still remained the same. India's caste system, its endemic cancer, would not go away and would hinder progress on many occasions. Jamul at times suffered from communal or caste-based conflicts. These issues would spill over into the construction activities in the Works. For instance, many laborers would refuse to work alongside a person from a lower or an "untouchable" caste! My father would confront these issues head-on and aggressively. He tolerated none of this "caste nonsense", as he called it. But these things were all too real in the minds of the local people.

It was often said, "Sahib nahi samjhenge. Woh to brahmin hai. Maas bhi nahi khate." *(Sahib will not understand. He is after all a brahmin. He does not even eat meat.).*

Sometimes this "brahmin caste" status went in his favor as well. Being of the highest caste, most folks would listen to him and respected him by default. On occasion, he would use this leverage to teach others by example. He would not hesitate to join a group of "untouchables" for a meal at the Works canteen or even in their homes in Jamul. He would join Muslim families in their Eid celebrations, but being a vegetarian, he would not eat any meat dishes. This "Gandhian" behavior and thinking were not always well received by the community at large. In fact, the Chief Security Officer of JCW informed him that they had become aware of threats on his life. It was serious enough that my father armed himself with a British made 6-shot automatic pistol, which he always kept loaded and within easy reach.

Being the GM and a brahmin, my father was often required to participate in various Hindu festivals and rituals. Normally, he did not mind and that pleased many people. But then one day, a major issue erupted. On the Works site, which was still largely barren with small bushes and hardly any trees, there was one very old lone banyan tree and near its base somebody had created a Hanuman shrine a long time ago.

It was highly revered locally. But it was in a very awkward place and a key office building to hold large meetings was to be built there. Moving the tree and the shrine would create a major uproar, so it was a serious problem. Passions were strong and inflamed on all sides. Many solution options were suggested and considered, but they all required moving at least the Hanuman shrine. This was the main rub for all. The shrine was considered very holy and even had a dedicated local priest. Nobody cared much about the lovely old banyan tree, but moving the shrine was just not acceptable to anyone.

My mother used to visit and perform poojas *(ritual prayers)* at this shrine regularly with other ladies. So, she asked Pappaji, "It is an office building for meetings, is it not? Well, you are an engineer. Can you not change the building design and incorporate the tree and the shrine into it in some beautiful way? If you do that, everybody will be so happy. You will secure Hanumanji's blessings for many other things here as well." My father ran with this suggestion. The building design was modified in Bombay and both the tree and the shrine were made a lovely and seamless part of it. This building became iconic within ACC. As of 2017, it still exists and the shrine is as active as ever!

Then, on this lovely day, finally the railway came to the JCW! Until then, there were no railway tracks coming up to the Works and Jamul had no rail connectivity at all. This was a critical need for many things. All the major machinery and equipment would arrive at the Durg Junction railway yard. From there it would be hauled into the private railway yard of Bhilai Steel Works. But then what? The Jamul Works was 10 kilometers away. It was a horrendous problem.

The solution was to build a private railway line from the Bhilai yard into a new yard for Jamul Cement Works. This line and the yard took a lot of design, engineering, and construction work to complete. Then it was certified by the Indian Railways inspectors and put into operation. I still recall the day the first "goods" (*freight*) train steamed into the Works, bearing all sorts of critical supplies and materials. There was jubilation all around! The steam locomotive was covered with garlands and a special pooja was performed. This line would put the Works on the map of the Indian Railways network and now all sorts of things could be brought right in, and when ready, the Works could ship its cement out as well. The days of constant lack or shortages of various construction supplies and more, were finally coming to an end.

Another peculiar event surrounded the "greening" of the Works site. Pappaji was a lover of trees and gardens. But the Works site had hardly any trees, gardens, or even flowering bushes of any kind. It was a barren, hot and drab place. Further, the soil was ferrous, red in color, and not conducive to growing much of anything in it.

As the colony construction proceeded steadily, my father followed up with "greening" of all the finished parts. Better soil was trucked in. Fragrant bushes and saplings for shady trees were planted. Lawns were seeded in various public areas. He had a grand plan and followed it methodically. It helped that the people of Jamul knew a lot about growing things. However, the soil problems turned out to be formidable. It was low in nutrients, and fertilizers, like most things, were in a critical short supply all over India. The Works had none in the store house.

Well, on this day, the sewage treatment plant developed a major problem. It had to be shut down for a couple of days for major repairs. So, Pappaji turned adversity into an opportunity. He had the sewage sludge pumped out and into tanker trucks. The trucks then went around everywhere dumping it near bushes, tree saplings, lawns etc. It certainly delivered all kinds of nutrients to the soil to make things grow, but the whole site and the colony smelled like a broken toilet!

The air was just foul and totally disgusting everywhere. Everybody whined and complained, including my mother, but Pappaji just waved it all off. He said that as soon as the sewage plant was fixed, all the dumping would stop. And the odors? Well, they would just go away as the sludge naturally biodegraded in a few days. That did happen, but nobody forgot those stinking days.

These are but some of the stories on how a rural community blossomed as the Industrial Age arrived in India. Some decades later, India would enter the Information Age with its new set of challenges.

Those are very different tales.

Hosting Guests & Visitors

The GM Bungalow in Jamul was always a very unusual place for me. It was certainly our home, but many times it also felt like a fancy hotel. The constant stream of guests and visitors made it a lively place. It kept my parents occupied in a big way. Pappaji not only spent a large part of the work day with the guests, but also had to entertain them in the evenings. My mother spent most of her time running the household and managing the support staff in numerous activities. She also had to supply, run and maintain two entirely separate kitchens! This was a job and a half for her. And there were many reasons for it.

The primary reason was that my parents were vegetarians and conservative in their habits. While my father did eat eggs, my mother did not. And both of them had an aversion to any kind of meat. My Mom was also devoutly religious and practiced a variety of Hindu rituals, including visits to local temples, with great personal discipline. My father joined her as and when he could but that was not very frequent due to his intense work schedule and frequent travels. Further, my parents did not consume alcohol in any form whatsoever. These were their personal choices and they did not apologize to anybody for them. It was their lifestyle and they were quite comfortable with it.

But the needs and wants of the guests and visitors to Jamul were usually quite different. Many of them were away from home on Company business and wanted to have a good time. This included drinking alcoholic beverages and enjoying all sorts of exotic cuisines. The range of requests and demands could be wide and at times even unusual, depending upon who they were and where they had come from. If they were British or Parsees from Bombay, or Russians from Bhilai, they preferred western foods and drinks. If they were from the South, they wanted a vastly different menu of a southern flavor. And the people from the North or East, liked yet another kind of food and drink. Most of these cuisines involved cooking meat or seafood in some special way. For alcoholic drinks, my father had to keep a well-stocked bar of various spirits, mixes, and beer. Wine was not much in demand and not easily available in India at the time. What could be procured was of dubious quality at best, so most folks avoided drinking it.

So, to handle this vast array of potential requirements, a separate kitchen was setup to handle preparation of all non-vegetarian dishes. It had separate refrigerators, cooking utensils, and skilled cooks. The vegetarian kitchen was meant principally for us in the home, but would also supply various dishes to the meals as required. It also had its staff and cooks. These folks were supervised directly by my mother and sometimes she even assisted them in the cooking. Whereas in the "other kitchen" she kept an eye on things, but she never touched or handled anything herself. A major task was also to shop for and supply these kitchens. She would hold menu planning meetings with the staff and manage the supply chain for groceries, etc. with great skill in a world filled with constant and pervasive shortages for most things in Jamul.

There were 3 major meals served in the dining room each day. They were breakfast, lunch, and dinner. ACC's British heritage permeated all of them. They were all served in courses by properly attired Bearers. A food buffet was considered offensive and totally unacceptable. The dining table had a capacity to seat up to 12 people, with the expansion leaves, but typically was configured to seat 6-8 people. Every meal used to be quite a production and I would often watch my Mom perform like she was conducting an orchestra! The various courses had to be just right and served to the correct people in the right order. All meals were filled with of a variety of conversations that ranged from official business, to current events, news, and economic policy of the Government of India. Usually the guests were mostly men, but once in a while they had their wives along and that added a further charm to things. My Mom used to enjoy those visits the most because then she had somebody to talk with about other things.

Pappaji was also quite British in many of his habits and preferences. When he drank tea, it was always in the form of a "tea service" and he was very specific about how he liked to prepare and have his tea. My mother had also grown fond of it over time, but in the afternoons, she always had a bias for the Indian masala tea.

Pappaji had also prepared the grounds of the GM Bungalow, which was one of a kind in the colony, in a grand manner! It was designed to showcase ACC as a major Indian industrial company. Besides being the GM of JCW, he was also its brand ambassador in the Durg, Bhilai, and Raipur areas of the State of Madhya Pradesh. The Bungalow compound with its walls was huge. It had an attended security gate, long driveways with a turnaround at the far end, and a porch at the front entrance of the bungalow. There were many gardens, a vast lawn area with floodlights, where an outdoor reception could be held for 1000+ people, even at night! It was a site used for many a New Year's Eve and other major parties and functions. Also, he had a regulation size tennis court built on the grounds, with 40-foot tall steel mesh guard walls on both ends to stop the balls. He frequently played on it with guests or other senior managers of JCW. It was all designed to impress a visitor. And it invariably succeeded.

The Bungalow had, in addition to all the air-conditioned bedrooms, a large guest suite, which was reserved for VIPs. Pappaji decided who stayed with us. Other guests were housed at a large full-service Guest House adjacent to the bungalow. All the important guests were specifically invited to meals at the Bungalow. The most important meal was always breakfast. I can recall mornings when this meal was simply amazing to me. It always began with a glass of fresh fruit juice. Then, a course of cereal or porridge with hot milk and sugar or honey was served. For the main course individual orders were taken. Eggs would be served either soft boiled, poached, scrambled, or fried. They were accompanied by toast in carriers and roasted tomatoes and potatoes. Some would have omelettes to their tastes. At times, some folks ate dosas or idlis with sambhar and chutneys; while others had puris or bhatooras with subjis. The last course was always cut fresh fruit. I remember my mother getting up at 5am to arrange this meal at 8:00am with all the staff. Typically, I was not allowed to join in and would have my breakfast after everybody had finished their's and left for work.

Lunch was quite varied and the attendance was patchy at best. Many people would have it at the office or elsewhere and not come to the Bungalow at all.

But the dinner was something else. At 6:30pm, my father would serve drinks to everybody. He had a bar cart, a cute trolley with wheels, that he had custom built for this purpose. It carried all the spirits, mixes, beer and ice. The drinks were served to all and my mother would provide savories to accompany them. Curiously, there were rarely any hors d'oeuvres which were thought to ruin one's appetite for dinner. My father would join everyone with a glass of fruit juice. At 7:30pm, dinner would be served. It was always a multi-course meal and the entrees were split into non-vegetarian and vegetarian parts. Within each part, one was led to a choice of different desserts. This meal was also a grand production in its own right and was served with precision.

When the guests departed Jamul, my mother would get lots of effusive compliments. They would say, "Mrs. Yajnik, thank you for looking after us so well. The meals were superb. You are a great hostess!" My Mom's standard reply in Hindi was, "It is our pleasure. Do come again. And next time, bring along your family."

It was a lifestyle belonging to a different era in India. I was lucky to witness it firsthand.

A Rhino Hunt

The message came directly from the ACC Head Office in Bombay. Everybody in Jamul was shocked by what it requested. Pappaji was no stranger to the unpredictable ways of the Head Office. However, this one took the cake, as it were. He was totally unprepared for it and did not even know where to begin.

Mr. Sumant Moolgaokar (SM), the Managing Director (MD) of ACC, had won the bidding auction that year for the highly coveted single annual license, issued by the Government of India, to hunt a rhino! In earlier times, nobody cared much about conservation of various species in the animal kingdom in India. Hunting, as a sport, was practiced everywhere with great relish and all sorts of "kills" were a matter of celebration and joy.

But the times had changed a lot, and now, licenses were required for many hunts. Well, that having been said, an official license to hunt a rhino was an absolute prize, for which many wellheeled people yearned. These same folks sorely missed the good old days when you could just set out and kill any wild animal you desired. Big cats, especially tigers and lions, were a great favorite.

A rhino was always something extraordinary. Imagine having a mounted rhino head, with its great horn, as a prized piece of taxidermy display in the drawing room of your home! For many royal families of India, big game hunting was not just a sport, but also a family tradition. Sometimes it was also a part of the rites of passage into adulthood. Their hunting trophies adorned many rooms in their Palaces.

Issuing the annual license to hunt a rhino was an event motivated mainly by the money involved. While the official costs were not small, there were many more related expenses to benefit a vast array of people. All thoughts about controlling the size and location of rhino herds or taking care of their preservation were distant and foreign concepts at the time. In any case, what was not officially sanctioned was always handled by the poachers. They loved hunting rhinos, not so much for their skin, but because their bones and horns supposedly had special aphrodisiac qualities and could fetch a high price in the black market. So, an "official" rhino hunt was a widely known and an elaborate affair. There were a lot of players involved in it. Everybody, whether government officials or private parties, got a piece of the huge financial action, as it were.

In this milieu, the job of organizing a rhino hunt fell upon my father out of the blue. He knew Mr. SM very well and had worked with him closely many years earlier. But Pappaji was not a hunter. He was also a vegetarian. Well, he did start to eat and enjoy eggs after his training in Europe and England, but he did not eat meat of any kind.

Further, he did not believe in killing anything for pleasure. If one killed for survival or to save a life, that was one thing, but to kill for sport or recreation was anathema to him. The very idea of a "hunt for fun" was simply revolting to his values. But suddenly, this had become a part of his job as the GM of Jamul Cement Works.

I arrived in Jamul from RKC this year for the summer holidays to discover a frenetic beehive of activity surrounding this hunt. I was informed that it was a week away and would take place in the Bastar Forest, in the State of Orissa. The region was rural and backward, had dense forests, lots of wild life, and the trip would feel like going off on a serious camping trip. My mother had opted out from going, and Pappaji strongly discouraged me as well.

Then, I asked him, "Are you not going?"

My father replied, "Yes. But I have to go."

So, I said, "Well, if you can handle it, so can I."

Pappaji smiled and said, "That is exactly what I was afraid you would say! Okay, but remember that this is a highly dangerous activity. You must do exactly as you are told. You must follow and obey instructions without any questions. It is for your safety."

It turned out to be quite a hunting party. Mr. SM was the Chief Guest and he had brought a small entourage of his own with him. These people struck me as a bunch of lily-livered, pampered, city slickers from Bombay. I seriously doubted if any of them had tasted a "camping life" of any sort.

We left Jamul in a convoy of vehicles of various kinds and ended up at this huge guest house in the middle of nowhere in the Bastar Forest. Pappaji was not kidding. This forest was decidedly frightening. It was dense, massively overgrown, and just teeming with all sorts of insects, reptiles, birds, and wildlife. Unlike the Gir Forest in Gujarat, one got this crazy creepy feeling all over in Bastar. This forest reeked of danger.

Next day, we began the hunt in the early morning. I was shocked to see a convoy of some 8 elephants waiting outside! We were told that, according to the Game Warden and his trackers, the fields where the rhino herd was grazing that day, were accessible only on the backs of elephants! There were no roads leading there. So, we were all sorted into "fours" and assigned an elephant. Apparently, they were highly trained animals and well suited for the purpose at hand.

There was the big lead elephant #1, who was guided on an unmarked path in the dense foliage. Pappaji and Mr. Moolgaokar were on #2 and I was on #5. We set off as a slow-moving convoy in a single file formation. The foliage was so dense and high at times that it covered and brushed us on top of the elephant! One had to watch out for branches with thorns, and even snakes! There were a couple of stops for rest and water breaks, but they were mainly for the elephants. Nobody wanted or dared to get off them. The "mahouts", who guided the elephants, and the trackers seemed to have no such fears.

About a couple of hours into our ride, our convoy was slowly turning to the right, when suddenly a leopard leapt out of the thick brush and attacked the lead elephant #1. He was not a big cat and probably was more startled than anything else, but he clawed onto the side of the elephant. We had a clear view of all this and became highly agitated. But the big bull elephant did not even miss a stride! He just grabbed the cat with his trunk and flung him away! It vanished fast. I got scared crazy, because this was way too close for me.

Then in a while, the forest cleared and we came upon some beautiful open fields. Lo and behold, there was a herd of gorgeous rhinos grazing in them! Everybody stared at this awesome sight for a long while. The Game Warden shortly asked Mr. SM to take his pick and shoot. But then something beautiful happened.

Mr. Moolgaokar said to Pappaji, "Mr. Yajnik, I owe you a huge apology. You have organized such a magnificent hunt for me and I really appreciate it. But now, I cannot bring myself to shoot and kill such a lovely creature. Its home is here, not in some trophy spot in somebody's house."

My father replied, "Sir, you do have the permission to shoot. And you certainly need not apologize for your choice. But I agree with you completely."

Mr. SM put away his high-powered rifle with its telescopic sights. He picked up his cameras instead. Then he spent an hour taking pictures and shooting movies of the herd. He even went up close on the ground.

The Game Warden simply could not believe this development! Astonished, he asked, "Sir, but what about the expensive license you purchased?"

In reply, he heard, "I will let it go. These sights and pictures are worth more than anything I had imagined. I don't want a trophy anymore."

Our return home was slow, but uneventful. As a consolation prize, the Game Warden shot a deer from a herd he was trying to cull and gifted it to our party. Back home, the chefs created a great feast for all.

Everybody at dinner that evening enjoyed eating the "venison with lovely trimmings" and washing it down with chilled beer. My father ate his usual vegetarian food with plain water.

There was universal agreement that the whole hunt had been exciting and so thrilling. The leopard episode made it even more memorable and a key topic of conversation about who had been really brave. I was suitably teased about being so scared.

For everyone, the dangerous forest, its sounds, and all its vistas were so much more fun, than hearing gunshots and watching a gorgeous animal die.

A Strange Meeting

With shrieking twin whistles, massive hisses and puffs of steam, the powerful Howrah Mail train steamed out of the Rajnandgaon Station and picked up speed. In about 25 minutes, around 6:00pm, we would reach the Durg Junction Station which was my destination. The stop at Durg was just 3 minutes, so one had to be quite ready to disembark quickly. I was in the Howrah Bogey, which I had boarded at its origin at the Viramgam Junction Station, nearly two days earlier. I began to pull and drag my steel trunk and bed roll towards the exit door which was some distance away. In the crowded Class III sleeper bogies, moving luggage was always a challenge. I was nearly finished, when I noticed something.

About midway in the bogey, a young lady a bit older than me, seemed to be attempting to do the same thing! She was fair, trim, and had her hair in a long single braid. It was obvious that she was struggling with her luggage in trying to get it closer to the same exit door. So, I went over and offered to help her. She accepted graciously and we dragged her luggage slowly over near to the exit door as well. She thanked me, and went back to check if she had forgotten anything and to say goodbye to her fellow travelers. She had barely returned to the door when the Howrah Mail rolled into the Durg Station.

At the time, the Durg Station had no platforms. So, one had to climb down the bogey's short steel ladder and step down to the ground near the bed of the tracks. Luggage had to be slid out and lowered down to somebody, usually a "coolie" (*a porter*), on the ground one piece at a time. It required some effort and skill. So, I asked the lady to get down first and secure a coolie quickly. I would hand all our luggage down to him. She agreed and seemed relieved.

The train came to a stop with a jolt. She climbed down and promptly said to me, "Don't worry. My family is here and they already have two coolies ready." This was good news for me because usually finding a coolie during such a short train stop is quite a task. I quickly handed all our luggage down to the two coolies on the ground, and then facing the bogey climbed down the ladder myself. I stepped down to the ground and turned to see my parents waiting for me right there! There were squeals of delight and hugs all around, as I was warmly welcomed.

Then Pappaji asked me, "Was the journey smooth? I hope it was not too uncomfortable."

I replied, "Oh, yes. It was fine. It just takes so long. How are you doing?"

Just then, the mammoth Howrah Mail locomotive screamed with its twin whistles, and with a cacophony of steam and other sounds, the train rolled out of the Durg Station. It was a departure that sounded almost deafening since we were standing right next to the tracks. The ground shook, as the train quickly pulled away gathering speed, and soon vanished out of sight.

"I want you meet some people." my father said. Then we went over to the family standing nearby.

"This is Mr. Avinash Mehta. He is the Assistant General Manager of Bhilai Steel Works. This is his wife, Hansikaben Mehta. These are their young daughters Nisargi, Niyati, and Niraj. And this is their eldest daughter, Prakruti, who we are meeting today for the first time. The family is from Petlad also. They are Nagar Brahmins like us and we have known their extended family there for a long time. This is my youngest son, Vijay."

There were "namaste" greetings all around, and I said, "Well, we were not introduced, but I met Prakrutiben on the train by chance. I helped her with her luggage."

Hansikaben added sweetly, "Vijaybhai, we affectionately call her Kali."

There was a lot of chitchat and small talk about our journey and various things. The coolies were getting anxious about moving the luggage out to the waiting cars. So, the goodbyes soon followed, and we parted company.

That summer, we met the Mehta family quite frequently. In a while, Kashyap and Ajay arrived from Baroda, as the MS University vacations began. We used to play a lot of tennis in the late afternoons, after the peak heat of the day had passed.

One day, we had an intense tennis game under way. Because we were only three, one side would play doubles and the other would play singles. I was always placed for the doubles side, since I was the weakest player. I noticed that every now and then, Kashyap and Ajay would stand aside and engage in conversations in whispers. The set ended and they decided that it was time to call it a day. I wanted to play more, but they would not have it. Well, we all went inside and showered. Kashyap emerged very well dressed and wearing a lovely cologne. I could not figure out all these strange behaviors. Then, I found out from my mother that the Mehta family was coming over for dinner that evening.

It was a charming evening and the dinner was wonderful. I entertained the younger daughters as best as I could, with card games, checkers, etc. But Kashyap spent most of his time with Prakrutiben. It took me a while to realize that he was totally smitten!

177

Soon thereafter, Mr. Mehta was transferred to another assignment in Indore and the Mehta family relocated away. I did not get to see them much after that, since I was still studying at Rajkumar College, Rajkot.

Well, in about a year or so after that summer, Kashyap and Prakrutiben were engaged. In a few more years, Kashyap finished his graduate studies at Denver University in Boulder, Colorado, in the USA. Prakrutiben flew out to Denver. She got married to Kashyap, in a Vedic ceremony played on a tape recorder, in a local church. The bride was "given away" by Kashyap's Advising Professor. In attendance, were their friends, various faculty members, and the pastor. Unfortunately, nobody from India was able to come to attend this event.

In this manner, a lady named Prakruti, that I encountered by pure chance and assisted on the Howrah Mail train a while ago, became my dear Kalibhabhi!

My First Car Drive

During this summer, at the time I was all alone in Jamul. I think Kashyap had left for the USA already and Ajay was busy with his Medical School at MS University in Baroda. He did not have the vacation time to come home to Jamul.

This particular afternoon, I was totally bored. It was very hot and I had nothing to do. There was nobody to play tennis with and one can read only so much before one wants to go off and do something different. The hardest part of the day was always the afternoons. I had already read all my comics ten times over, finished all the books in Pappaji's study at least twice, and the latest Ian Fleming's James Bond novel had yet to arrive from Bombay. The Jamul Colony had no swimming pool. There was a 12-foot deep irrigation water canal flowing nearby and one could go for a swim in it, but I was forbidden to do so. The turbulent water was light brown and not considered safe because there were snakes and other reptiles in it. Also, it attracted a variety of dangerous wildlife that came to have a drink late in a day. The Clubhouse was closed until the evening so that option was not available.

I would while away my time somehow and eventually bug my mother. I would force her to wake up from her siesta and fix us some Indian masala tea. She would sigh, but she always smiled and got up for me. My boredom would often succeed in turning me into a pest.

Then on this day, Pappaji arrived home from work. He parked the car in the porch near the front door, and came in to freshen up and have his evening tea service. He loved this time of the evening. He would chat with my Mom, brief her on his day, and update her on upcoming events. He would engage me animatedly and talk about many wonderful things which used to leave me fascinated. He sensed also that I was suffering from intense boredom.

One suggestion he had for me was to join Vaalji on the "road roller" machine. It was a huge diesel-powered heavy roller with enormous steel wheels and it required great skill to operate it properly. It usually was supported by a near army of laborers working with dirt, gravel, tar and other things. They were laying down a key road next to a highly engineered gravel bed that would form the base for the upcoming placement of railway tracks into the plant. I could join and watch, but I would not be permitted to operate anything. However, it would be a great learning experience in seeing how key infrastructure for the cement plant was being prepared. I liked the idea, because I loved machines of any kind. If only I was allowed to operate them, it would be awesome fun!

179

With these happy thoughts running through my mind, I stepped out of the front door of the bungalow into the porch. And there stood the Hudson! It was a 1959 model and a well-appointed car. It was dark maroon in color with a beige leather interior. It had whitewall tires and the rear wheels were half covered by guards matched to its linear body lines. It was a heavy but spacious sedan, with lots of room inside. It had a large boot (*trunk*), and a large bonnet (*hood*), to cover the engine. On one side, it had an external flood light which could be moved around with a handle from inside the car. It had a steering shaft mounted stick shift, and a white steering wheel with an inner metallic ring, which was its horn. It was gorgeous! It was assigned to the GM of JCW because of all the VIPs that had to be ferried around from time to time and they needed a measure of comfort. The Hudson could seat 6 adults comfortably.

On an impulse, I opened the driver's door on the right side and sat inside. There was no ignition key in it since Pappaji had taken it into his study. I sat in it for a long time studying everything carefully and touching various knobs and buttons gently. Then, on a flight of fancy, I pretended to be driving it and turned the steering wheel back and forth going, "Vroom! Vroom!" I was tall enough that my feet easily touched the clutch, brake, and accelerator pedals. I remembered clearly how Pappaji used to drive it and all the sounds the engine made as he shifted gears. I also carefully observed how he pressed the clutch pedal, shifted a gear, and then gently released it. I used to be delighted by how a car was driven! Suddenly, my reverie was broken.

"What are you doing?" I heard Pappaji ask me. He was standing in the doorway.

"Oh, nothing. Just playing around." I replied. I looked at him and saw that he was amused and smiling.

"Want to drive it? Do you think you can?" He asked further, with a chuckle.

"Oh, Yes! Absolutely! I have watched you carefully and I know exactly how to do it." I said in an overly confident manner.

"Okay. Here is the ignition key. Start it. Stay in the first gear only. Go circle the turnaround, and come right back here. Move slowly. Let me see if you can handle just that much."

I was excited beyond belief! I took the key from him and then a few deep breaths to calm myself down. Then I put a sharp mental focus on the task at hand. I was determined to pass this test with flying colors!

I took a couple of minutes to orient myself properly in the driver's seat. I made sure that the car was in the neutral gear. I pressed the clutch and started the engine. I shifted into the first gear, and then I slowly released the clutch to get the car moving. She was so smooth. I quickly got a feel for the steering wheel and its sensitivity, and slowly rolled towards the turnaround about 100 feet away. At the turnaround, I took a proper controlled 180 degree turn slowly. Then I straightened her out and brought it to a gentle stop in front of the front door now facing the opposite way in the porch. I had no stalls, grinding gears, or erratic acceleration and braking. Pappaji was standing there throughout my drive, and watching me intently.

I shut the engine down and got out with the ignition key in my hand. I was full of smiles and beaming with joy as I came around the car and approached him. Then, Pappaji did something he had not done with me in a long time. He slapped me!

"When did you learn this? Who taught you without my permission? How many times have you done this? Why have you lied to me?" Pappaji thundered in a furious rage! He called out for my mother.

"Vijay ne kone shikhvadu chhe?" *(Who has taught Vijay?)* he demanded to know from my mother. She was just bewildered.

"Tame shu kaho chho?" *(What are you saying?)* she asked gently.

"Kaya driver pase gaadi challvata shikhyo chhe? Mari raja vagar? Ane Company ni gaadi ma?" *(Which driver has taught him to drive? Without my permission? And in a Company car?)* he asked sternly.

"Vijay kyan gaadi chalave chhe? Ene nathi avadtu." *(Vijay does not drive? He does not know how.)* my Mom replied.

An argument ensued. My mother told Pappaji repeatedly that I did not know how to drive and had never driven a car. But my father would not accept it. He summoned all the drivers, including Vaalji, to the bungalow to meet with him first thing in the morning. The entire evening and dinner turned into a complete disaster.

Next morning, Ramu, Binod Bihari, and Vaalji showed up at the bungalow at 8:00am sharp. My father interviewed them individually in his study first. It was more of an accusatory interrogation. He was hell bent on finding the culprit. The interviews finished and yielded nothing for him. So, he pulled them all together in a meeting to try one more time. All the drivers were confused by all the questions being asked of them and collectively said, "Sahib, hua kya hai? Yeh poochh-taachh kyun? *(Sahib, what has happened? Why all this questioning?)*

181

Pappaji grasped quickly that his tack had not worked. So, he changed it. He calmed down, and told all of them what had happened the previous evening. He explained, in utter disbelief, what I had done in driving the Hudson! He opined that what I had done was just not possible without somebody's training. And he was going to find that person.

Now, all the drivers started smiling and laughing! Ramu and Binod Bihari were the first to speak.

"Sahib, aap ka ladka tej hai. Woh dhyan se dekhta hai. Sau sawalein poochhta hai." *(Sahib, your son is sharp and quick. He observes with careful focus. Asks a hundred questions.)* they said.

And so, it went back and forth. Then, feeling gradually surprised, my father asked them, "Kya woh dekh ke sikha hai?" *(What, has he learnt just from observation?)* In response, both of them said, "Ji, Sahib. Beshak." *(Yes, Sahib. Without a doubt.)*. My father calmed down completely and became very reflective.

Then, he asked Vaalji for his opinion. Vaalji also smiled, and reminded him of all the compliments that he used to give him for the speed with which he had learnt to drive a car. He told Pappaji that it was largely because he too had learnt a lot through sheer observation!

Pappaji sent them all away. He sat quietly by himself for a long time. Then he summoned me. I was not sure what to expect, but my mother told me not to worry.

I went and sat near him. Pappaji was in tears! He apologized to me for his grave mistake and misjudging my abilities. Then, he just grabbed me and hugged me!

After that day, I was officially permitted to learn to drive. Ramu and Binod Bihari were designated as my main teachers. Over time, I got a driving license and began driving all of us around. By my demand, I became our family's designated social driver. And I loved it.

However, my very first car drive is what remained special and unforgettable for me.

Inauguration of Jamul Cement Works

(As Told to Me by Pappaji & Behn, Years Later)

It was a highly anticipated set of events, spanning two days. The preparations for them were extensive and detailed. After years of hardship, toil and labor, and countless sacrifices, the end result was almost at hand. While all sorts of trial runs had already taken place, this was the day that the Jamul Cement Works would officially launch itself into production of cement.

It could not have come any sooner. India was a country of serious shortages in everything. Anything that you could name was either in short supply or simply unavailable. It was more so for things critically needed. The little that was available was hard to get to, because of all the middle men and the pervasive graft that profited from these shortages.

For these two glorious days, many lovely events had been carefully planned. My father was the "Orchestra Leader" presiding over all these plans and activities. But there was one event that he trusted nobody with. It was the formal lunch, after the inauguration was done, at a swanky local hotel. There would be many important guests and dignitaries present, and it had to be handled flawlessly and with great care. The only person my father had faith in to achieve this was my mother.

My mother embraced this project wholeheartedly. She turned into a bit of a Field General herself. She created a team, trained everybody, and planned the lunch meticulously. It had a delicious mix of the Indian and British culinary tastes, among many things. There were rehearsals undertaken and then some. Then came the fateful days, which everyone had eagerly awaited.

But there was a massive surprise for everybody! My father was informed two days prior to the festivities that on the inauguration morning and at the formal lunch, the Chief Guest would be Pandit Jawaharlal Nehru, the iconic Prime Minister of India! Everybody was in a state of shock! My father wondered as well. Then it occurred to him that perhaps it was because of the synergies between the Bhilai and Jamul Works, or the presence of Russians? Regardless, it was a very welcome development, and everyone was overjoyed.

All the events on the first day went off smoothly. On the second day, in the morning, the inauguration went off flawlessly, many speeches were made, and Panditji did all that was asked of him. Around 1:00pm or so, all the guests and dignitaries gathered for the formal lunch that my mother had planned. But just as Panditji entered the premises, he was pulled away for an urgent call from Delhi. The lunch was delayed for more than 30 minutes Eventually, Panditji emerged from his phone call. The entire room was chock full of people and there was nowhere to sit. He looked around and spotted a sofa in an adjacent room which had some open space on it. He walked over and sat down.

My mother was never comfortable with English. She understood it, but was shy about speaking it. The wives of all the dignitaries present were highly educated and fluent in English, and that made her feel like a total outcast. So, she just found a spot at the end of a sofa to sit on, aloof by herself. She had no idea that Panditji would end up sitting right next to her!

Panditji sat down, but had heavy labored breathing. It was clear at once to my mother that he was feeling weak, and somewhat exhausted.

She observed him for a short while, and then asked politely, "Aap thake lagte hain. Kuchh pijiyega?" *(You seem tired. Would you like something to drink?)*

Panditji replied, "Han, Agar aap ko koi takleef na ho." *(Yes, if it is not of any trouble for you.)*

My mother waved over Krishna, our bungalow bearer, and said, "Krishna, ek gilaas sada paani. Usme thoda sa nimbu, aur ek chammach chini. Jaldi lao." *(Krishna, one glass of plain water. In it, some lemon juice and one spoon of sugar. Bring it quickly.)* The drink arrived in a flash.

Panditji drank it all and seemed to feel much better soon thereafter.

Then the lunch began. My mother took him along to the buffet, but nobody would leave him alone for even a moment. Everybody wanted a piece of this man. Mom then offered to fix a plate for him, which he graciously accepted. A little later, he was back on the sofa, with my mother, and ate a little bit.

Then he asked her, "Aap kahan se hain?" *(Where are you from?)*

My mother explained that she was from Gujarat, and that her husband, Mr. Yajnik, was the GM of the Jamul Cement Works.

"Achha! To kya Indulal Yajnik aap ke rishtedar hain?" he asked further. *(Good! Then is Indulal Yajnik a relation of yours?)*

The relationship between Indukaka and Panditji has spanned many decades and tumultuous events. They had been imprisoned together in Yerwada Jail in Pune with Sardar Patel, Mahatma Gandhi and others, by the British. They were colleagues in the long fight for the Independence of India and senior members of the Congress Party. Later, they were also political opponents in the fight for the creation of the State of Gujarat from the old Bombay State. Panditji had even offered Indukaka a cabinet post in the Central Government, but Indukaka had refused. As a long-term legendary Member of Parliament from Ahmedabad, Indukaka could pull more political muscle and public support in town than even Panditji. But, on a personal level, they were quite close and full of admiration for one another. Indukaka used to be a frequent guest for functions and meals at the Teen Murti House, the famous Nehru residence in Delhi.

My mother replied, "Han. Woh unke pitarai bhai hain." *(Yes, he is my husband's paternal cousin.)*

"Arrey, tab to yeh apas ke ghar ki baat hui." *(Arrey, then this is now a matter of our close homes and communities.)*

My mother did not understand this very well and just said. "Ji." *(A polite Yes.)*

Then the ADC *(aide-de-camp)* showed up and Panditji had to leave. My mother thanked him profusely for gracing the whole morning and the lunch. Everybody applauded loudly. My father could barely contain his pride at my mother's stellar performance!

As Panditji was leaving, he turned to my mother and said simply, "Shukriya. Woh paani or yeh khane ke liye. Indubhai ke saath, Delhi mein milane aiyega. Indira ko bhi achha lagega." *(Thank you. For that water and this lunch. With Indubhai, come visit us in Delhi. Indira will like it also.)*

Then he was gone.

The rest of the festivities went on to a great and successful conclusion. All sorts of dignitaries were entertained in a variety of ways. My father was totally preoccupied with all these things.

But for my mother, the inauguration festivities had ended with that lunch with Panditji. She had always just adored him and his entire family. She had no political convictions of any sort, and just figured that she would never get to see him, or meet him, let alone talk to him.

She was always so fond of the Nehru family and she would openly express her affection for it. She was enamored with their culture, heritage, education, and charisma. It was akin to how most Americans felt about John F. Kennedy and his family in the early 1960's.

In my mother's eyes, the Nehru family could never do anything wrong. No, she did not want to leave it to the judgment of history, or anything else, for that matter.

She knew for certain how she felt. To her, it was completely right in her way of thinking, that the Nehru family walked on water!

Four Major Exams in Six Months

It was 1965 and my final academic year in Rajkumar College, Rajkot. It was a crucial year because my entire future hung on how well I did in the graduation exams. It was going to be tough and it was all up to me.

In RKC, in those days, there were two tracks for students for matriculation exams. They marked the graduation from high school. The first track was to take the Senior Cambridge (SC) exams, later called Indian School Certificate (ISC) exams, which were held in December of the final academic year. One had to be selected for this track a few years earlier. These exams were considered to be quite tough. The subjects were Maths, Physics, Chemistry, English, and a regional Indian language. The exam papers were graded in England. In my graduating batch of some 50 students, there were only 5 selected for this track.

The second track was for the Secondary School Certificate (SSC) exams which were held in March of the academic year. This was the track followed by the entire batch. There were a few more subjects involved in these exams such as Civics, Geography, History and so forth. The SC track students were required to take the SSC exams as well, as insurance. This was due to the fact that the SC exams were considered to be equivalent to the exams at the end of the first year in a University and so one could skip it. If you just took the SSC exam, one would have to do the first year fully in a University. So, a student appearing in the SC exams had to do a lot of preparatory work and study really hard. This was quite a task at RKC.

We had all sorts of special tutoring sessions held for us over the months preceding the exams. The preparations were quite intense. Just as all these activities started, the India-Pakistan war broke out in the late summer of 1965. This made things even harder for us. All external lights on the RKC campus were shut off at night. In the Principal's Bungalow dormitory, where I was placed that year, we had to cover all windows with black paper to hide internal lights. It was a precaution to prevent aerial detection for potential bombing raids.

All sorts of jet aircraft could be heard during the night and it was a truly scary time for all of us. There were stories of aerial dogfights between air force planes in the skies around Rajkot. A Pakistani fighter jet had been shot down and the pilot captured we heard. But we were required to stay our course and continue with focus on our studies.

I vividly recall Mr. M.P. Chhaya, our Maths and Physics teacher, grilling us relentlessly late into the night on advanced topics. He was ruthless and gave no quarter to any slacking off of any kind. Mr. Pancholi, our Chemistry teacher, was no less of a tyrant. Also, I had Harukaka, who was our Gujarati teacher, and he worked me over really good as well. All this went on for a few months. The tough love was delivered with the best of intentions and to help us.

Then came that fateful week of exams in December. On the first day, Mrs. Kulkarni, the wife of our Vice-Principal, greeted us in the morning with an oil lamp, an arati, and some sweets to wish us good luck. Each exam was 3 hours in duration. There were two exams per day. When the 3 days ended, we all collapsed in sheer mental exhaustion. With me were Shahid Siddiqui, Vijay Ram, Mahendra Manek, and Amit Goradia. We celebrated by going off to play some tennis and had a swim in the pool.

Our normal school life resumed and we joined the rest of our batch in preparations for the SSC exams. These were comparatively easy, but we also had to prepare for our annual Tattoo & Prize Giving Day and that took a lot of time away as well. On a day in March, one late afternoon, I was playing field hockey when Mr. Ayaaz Khan came up to me and said that the SC exams results had arrived. Vijay Ram had scored #1 and I was #2! Both of us had a First Class with Distinction! Others had done well too. It was a foretelling of things to come.

In late March, we had another horrendous week of exams and then in early April the academic year ended with our glorious Tattoo. It was a sad day for all of us because our time at RKC had come to an end. There were lots of affectionate goodbyes and many tears all around.

My parents were in Ahmedabad and so I just took a State Transport (ST) bus from Rajkot to go there. But there was no time to relax. India had opened 5 University level campuses for studies in engineering around the country in collaboration with various foreign governments. They were all called the Indian Institute of Technology ("IIT"). They were located in Bombay, Madras, Kharagpur, Delhi, and Kanpur. These were premier institutes and offered rigorous studies in all disciplines of engineering and technology.

Admissions to their 5-year undergraduate programs were determined by common countrywide competitive entrance exams in Maths, Physics, Chemistry, and English. Each campus would take 250 students as freshmen, so there was a total of 1,250 seats available. One got to choose a campus and an engineering major based on one's national ranking in these exams which were offered all over the country in May. To be eligible to appear in the exams, one had to have completed the first year in a University. I was eligible since I had passed my SC exams. If you scored high enough, you were invited to an additional face to face interview at the nearest IIT campus before final admissions were settled. It was the purest form of a meritocracy and downright scary.

Pappaji encouraged me to appear in these IIT entrance exams, since I seemed to be interested in engineering. In those days, if you wanted a good job and make a decent living in India, the only routes were to major in engineering or medicine. Anything else relegated you to a life of economic mediocrity. So, I began to study for these exams promptly. The SSC results arrived in the newspapers. I passed with a First Class, but it was not material for me anymore.

The IIT entrance exams center in Ahmedabad was at the L.D. Engineering College across the Sabarmati River. The exams spanned 2 days. One exam from 9am to noon and another from 2pm to 5pm. There were some 150 or so students appearing with me. It was a very somber, morose, and hot environment. One memory I have of these exams is that in each paper, as the time ran out, there seemed to be only about 5 of us left still finishing up! All others had turned in their stuff and left. It made me feel really stupid.

But it was still not over. What if I did not make it in the IIT admissions test? That was a very real possibility. What was my Plan B? Again, Pappaji suggested that I should keep M.S. University, Baroda, as my backup. It made sense since my older brothers had attended it. However, MSU had its own entrance exams for the engineering school! So, in early June, I appeared in the MSU entrance exams in the same four subjects. They spanned 2 days as well. I stayed with Ajay in the Gajjar Hall in his room in Baroda. He was studying in the medical school and would take me on his bicycle to the exams center. Here it seemed that there were hordes of students taking it. In the summer heat, it was a grind to get through the 2 days. When done, I took a train to Ahmedabad in a state of complete exhaustion. I recall sleeping for 24 hours straight.

Well, to my utter surprise, I got invited to Bombay for an IIT interview. That year, some 130,000 or so students had appeared in the entrance exams nationally. I had ranked somewhere in the 700's. Pappaji told me that I should go to Kanpur since Kiritbhai was on the faculty there and could watch over me. The only major available to me there was civil engineering which I did not want to do. However, after a 3-year common curriculum, Kanpur permitted you to change majors, if your academic performance was good enough, so I took a chance and selected Kanpur. I did manage to change it to electrical engineering later on. Meanwhile, the MSU results came out and I got selected for chemical engineering, which was the hottest major there at the time. But with IIT admissions secured, my father suggested that I go to Kanpur. A little later, I discovered that Vijay Ram had secured admission at the IIT in Delhi!

The IIT in Kanpur was set up with help from a consortium of prestigious American universities. We had many professors from the USA on the teaching faculty there. Those associations led to many other vistas being opened up for me later on.

And so, ended the most defining six-month period of my young life and changed it forever.

"C" Bungalow

The Guest House

GM Bungalow

Ajay as "Joe Cool" *The Hudson*

At the indoor Courtyard Fountain – Pappaji, Dipak Dave, Ajay & Me

*Pappaji's Address
at
JCW Inauguration*

*Garland for
Dharamsee Khatau
Left-Mr. Sumant
Moolgaoker*

*Behn with Key
Dignitaries &
Wives*

Behn with PM Pandit Jawaharlal Nehru

Our "C" Bungalow - 2016

*The First Quarry - Now a lake
2016*

Our GM Bungalow - 2016

The Tennis Court – In Disuse
2016

Front Lawn – For Receptions
2016

The Railway Line - 2016

The Water Canal – Dry 2016

The Hanuman Shrine – In an Office Building

INDIAN INSTITUE OF TECHNOLOGY/KANPUR

Off to IIT/Kanpur & An Unfinished Story

There would come this fateful day when I had to finally leave for IIT/Kanpur to begin my 5-year program for a degree in engineering. The school did not begin till July, so I had some time for a little holiday. My parents suggested that I return with them to Jamul from Ahmedabad, so I had packed up and done just that. They were a few lovely weeks in Jamul and I finally got to relax after all the bruising sets of exams.

Then it so happened that on the day I was scheduled to leave Jamul for Kanpur, my father had to leave for some work in Bombay. Further, we were both on the same train! It was the Howrah Mail headed to Bombay. Pappaji was in the A/C First Class bogey and I was in a Class III bogey. While Pappaji's journey was direct to Bombay, my journey to Kanpur was a bit complex. I had to get off from the Howrah Mail in the late afternoon in Nagpur. From there overnight, there were 2 trains involved. I had to take a train from Nagpur to Jhansi. After a change of trains in Jhansi, I had to go to Mathura Junction which was on the main Delhi-Calcutta broad gauge tracks. At Mathura, I had to catch yet another train that would bring me to Kanpur in the afternoon.

At Nagpur, I got off the Howrah Mail and went to see Pappaji in his bogey and to wish him goodbye. We could spend barely 10 minutes together during the stop. He was concerned about my journey since I had never travelled in these parts of India before and I had never been to Kanpur. But I assured him that I would be okay and to not worry about anything. The HM thundered off shortly and now I was left to my own devices for the rest of my journey.

At the time, I did not know that as fate would have it, I would never be returning to Jamul. Before my first holiday break at IIT/Kanpur, my father was transferred to Dwarka and my parents relocated. I did not get a chance to say goodbye to friends and folks that I had grown close to in Jamul over my many formative years there. I received no form of closure at all. For me, Jamul remained an unfinished story of my middle and high school years for decades.

For now, however, I had to focus on my trains and all the crazy connections involved. These were lands I had never seen before in my life.

Jhansi was a storied city with its famous Rani who had died fighting the British. Mathura was always associated with the stories of Lord Krishna's childhood from the scriptures. The slow trains travelled through the fertile plains of India which were lush green from the monsoon rains. I enjoyed gazing at the sights and chatting with all sorts of people in Hindi. Eventually, I reached Kanpur.

The IIT campus was quite far away from the railway station. So, I hired a tricycle to take me there with my luggage. I recall the city of Kanpur as being quite unimpressive, poor, and old. I wondered why the campus was placed there. Could they not find a better town? We went 10 kilometers out of town to the village of Kalyanpur, where the campus gates were located. I was astonished to discover that large parts of the campus were still under construction! I was to report to Residential Hall # 3, which is where I would be assigned a room with a roommate. But even before I could finish my check-in, the "ragging" (*hazing*) began. Apparently, IIT/Kanpur had a tradition of sorts for it.

A few senior students engaged me and I was to follow their orders for all kinds of stupid activities. It was all in good fun of course. Well, after the RKC years, all this stuff seemed terribly trivial and timid to me. But I played along.

At dinner time, I was hungry and attacked the food with gusto, but there were others there who were feeling homesick and could not eat. They all had separation anxiety because they were apart from their families for the first time in their lives. Later, I settled into my room and wondered who would be my roommate.

Unknown to me, there were people checking me out to be a potential roommate. It was critical to find a good roommate that one not only got along with, but also one who could help and motivate you in studies. That evening, there was to be a show and a reception for the freshmen class thrown by all the seniors. This event would also signal an official end to the period of "ragging".

In the auditorium L-7, they put on a variety show of sorts with music, singing, comedy sketches, and even a little dancing. Then, the emcee asked the freshmen class if anybody would like to perform an act of some kind for the seniors. Everybody looked around, but no one signaled or got up. Then, the emcee added, "Come on, freshmen, does not even one of you have the guts to perform for us?"

Now, this is where my RKC training kicked in. We were taught to handle a dare. I could not let them get away with such labels. So, I volunteered. I performed the soliloquy from "Arms and The Man", written by George Bernard Shaw. I had delivered it a few months earlier at my final Prize Giving at RKC.

Suddenly, the whole place was abuzz! Who is this guy? His name is Vijay? Where is he from? Well, all these questions and more got answered in due course. But in the process, Viney Pal Aneja approached me. He wanted to room with me. He and his twin brother Arun, who was a year ahead at the IIT, were star track athletes. They had graduated from St. George's College in Mussourie. Vijay Kaul, an RKCian & Head Boy, a bit senior to me, was also in Arun's batch. VK had welcomed me and recommended me to the Aneja brothers as well. Thus, I found not only a roommate, but an endearing friend for the rest of my life. We shared an enormous number of things with each other over our lives.

The student body at IIT/Kanpur in 1966, including post-graduate students, was less than 1,500. Can you even imagine such a small student population at a world class university level institute in India? As a result, over the ensuing 5 years, many close bonds were forged among the students and with the faculty.

All these bonds remained strong and lifelong.

A Dog Named "Moti"

My mother and I tensed up as she walked gracefully into the family room. All conversation stopped and everybody just stared at her. She paused for a bit and then turned her head towards the sounds of all the squeals and yelps coming from just the other side of the open door. She was a gorgeous German Shepherd (Alsatian) that had recently had a litter of some 4 puppies. She was strong, her coat was soft, and her form was attractive like a show dog.

It was the summer of 1967. We were in Thasara, Gujarat, visiting Rameshbhai Trivedi and his family. He was an old friend and a business associate, who had worked with my father for many years.

"What a beautiful dog!" Pappaji said. He had always been very fond of dogs. My mother was not, and was actually quite scared of them.

"Saheb, ek layi jao." *(Saheb, take one with you.)* Rameshbhai offered.

A very animated conversation ensued. All sorts of opinions were being expressed. Then, this little bundle of joy weakly wobbled into the room. He was a barely 3-week-old male puppy. He was so adorably cute and seemed quite helpless. He came up to me, sniffed my shoes, looked up at me, and whined softly. Instinctively, I just picked him up and put him in my lap. He sniffed my shirt a little, and then put his head down for a nap. In the next 10 minutes, with Rameshbhai encouraging us, Pappaji and I were sold, but my mother would have nothing to do with a dog in the house.

"Eni seva kon karashe?" *(Who will take care of him?)* my Mom asked. "This dog is part wolf. He will need meat for his diet. Who will feed that to him? This will be like taking care of a child. Who will do all that work?"

Pappaji tried to convince her patiently. He told her that he would raise the dog as a vegetarian! The staff would help with the food, etc. He was so little that we could train him properly as well. After an hour of all this, my mother sighed and relented. So, we decided to take the little puppy home with us. Pappaji named him "Moti" *(literally, a "Pearl")*.

Rameshbhai gave us all the key supplies. We had a dog blanket, a tiny rug, a feeding bottle, milk, a very small leash, etc. So, with all this, and my mother's continuous complaints, we returned to Ahmedabad. The whole extended family, when they found out, made fun of Pappaji and me.

Little Moti was quite a handful. In barely a couple of days, we had to leave for Dwarka, which was a very long drive. This required special preparations.

We left early. Along the way, we had to plan "Moti breaks" so the little fellow could stretch a bit and relieve himself. Obviously, he did not know how to do any of that so my lap was the spot of choice. But he slept a lot and took his bottle feedings from me. It was a relief when we finally got to Dwarka.

Pappaji set things up beautifully for Moti in the huge GM bungalow. In a while, Ajay joined us as he finished his internship in Baroda. So, he and I had a grand time with little Moti who got very attached to us. Even my mother's heart melted for little Moti and she set about spoiling him like a little child over Pappaji's many objections.

Moti loved being with Ajay and me and running around like crazy on the beach nearby. He was so little that he could not keep up with us, and would stop and start whining, to call us back. He could not climb the large staircase to go upstairs and we would have to help his hind legs to climb the steps. Pappaji also started early obedience training and he seemed to pick it up quite fast. But soon the holidays were over and I left for Kanpur. I would not see Moti for a few months.

When I returned, Moti was so much larger and faster. He had also accepted his training very well. Also, the amazing part was that he was on a vegetarian diet! Well, my father would give him an egg once in a while, but never any meat. Any cooked thick vegetable slice was a meat substitute for him. He loved milk and rotis of any kind enormously. He had a natural instinct to hunt, but he could not kill. Apparently, this is a learnt behavior even in the wild. Whenever he managed to catch a squirrel or some such creature, he would bring it in and present it to us alive! It had never been killed.

Now, Ajay & I could not keep up with Moti. His ears were so sharp that he could detect Pappaji's car long before it entered the driveway of the compound. He would start jumping around and then race out to the car near the garage to greet him.

In 1969, my father retired from ACC, relocated and settled in his bungalow in Maninagar, Ahmedabad. This bungalow, named "Nikunj", had a large compound with a driveway and garden in the front yard. Moti used to love this area and was always running around in it. He was also fiercely protective of the premises. Locally, Nikunj was called "kutara valu ghar" *(the house with a dog!)*. Many folks also said, "Aa kutaro nathi. Aa to vagh chhe." *(This is not a dog. This is a tiger.)* Moti had quite a ferocious reputation in Maninagar. He did look quite intimidating to a stranger.

A Dog Named "Moti"

That year, my Nani Ma, Sushila Ba, came to visit us for a while. She was not in good health, walked slowly, and was simply terrified of Moti. So, if she was sitting outside on the swing in the veranda, we had to lock Moti up in a room near the stairs. She would do this mostly in the evenings when we often had guests visiting us.

Well, on this day, Moti somehow escaped from his confinement, walked out of the back door of the house and ran out to the front yard. Sushila Ba was sitting on the swing in the veranda by herself, dressed in her typical white sari. There were no visitors that day, so she was just relaxing with some snuff in her hands. She was an avid consumer of fragrant snuff and her clothes would always smell of it. Snuff is made from tobacco and if one is not used to it, it can cause a sneezing attack.

Moti was wandering about the front yard and suddenly spied this strange white form sitting on the veranda swing! With loud barking, he ran to investigate this creature. Poor Sushila Ba saw the dog racing towards her, concluded that she was about to be mauled to death due to her lack of mobility, and so just sat there quietly praying to Lord Shiva.

Now, Moti was used to people running away from him in fear, but this creature would not move! So, he stopped cold near her and started to smell her. Well, that got Sushila Ba's snuff up his nose and he had a major sneezing attack immediately! Moti quickly concluded that this white creature was not only unafraid of him, but also it was downright dangerous. So, he quietly sat down near Sushila Ba's feet, which she found just thrilling! With the steady motion of the swing, Ba began to caress him with her foot at the end of each arc. Moti really loved this! Since that event, Ba lost all fear of Moti and he became very attached to her. He could always be found sitting near Ba, having his fur caressed by her feet for hours on end.

On another occasion, a family had come to visit my parents and brought along their toddler son who had recently started to crawl. While everybody was busy with tea, this little "rug rat" crawled off towards the veranda. In those days, next to the swing in the veranda, there was an area of some nice lawn as well. Suddenly, Moti barked and raced out towards the veranda. I ran after him knowing that his body language suggested a serious danger of some kind.

As I came out to the veranda, I heard ferocious growling and barking from Moti. I could not believe the sight! On the lawn was a cobra, erect and hissing with a wide hood, the toddler was near the door, and between them was Moti snarling at the snake.

I screamed at Moti to come to me and get him away from the snake. He hesitated for a while, but I persisted and screamed even louder. Against a cobra, Moti had no chance of survival at all. Even with a mongoose, the survival rate is only 50%. Luckily, he obeyed, and I took both him and the baby inside promptly. Soon, the cobra was gone as well. In India, a cobra is considered divine, the Naag Dev, so typically nobody will kill it. Besides it is a key part of an ecosystem to keep the population of various creatures under control. But that day, Pappaji's training most likely saved Moti's life. And more importantly, Moti saved the baby's life.

Moti was also adept at sensing people who were afraid of him or just did not like him. For these folks, he reserved a special kind of wrath. Pramodkaki and Ushakaki, my two aunts who lived in bungalows adjacent to us, were examples of this behavior. They were deathly afraid of him and would yell a request to have Moti locked up before they came to visit. Moti knew their voices and would start growling promptly upon hearing them, because he knew that he would be locked up. Pappaji could never convince the Kaki's to change their ways.

In 1971, when I left for the USA, Moti was sad for a whole month according to my parents. The sense of attachment that develops in dogs is just amazing. Their emotions seem almost human at times. Then, when I returned for the first time in 1976, Moti went crazy for the whole day. He wailed, whined, and cried all day long and would not let go of me. But by then he was 9 years old and starting to slow down.

In 1981, when Nilima and I left India after our wedding, Moti was now 14 years and very old. He was arthritic and Pappaji used to give him medicine for his aches and pains. In the middle of that year, one day Moti's heart just stopped and he passed away. He was laid to rest in the center of his favorite front yard, with a Tulsi plant on top of his grave.

Moti was such a loving pet to me and our whole family. His passing was a total heartbreak for me.

It hurt so much that I could not bring myself to get another pet dog ever again.

Cultural Events & A Near Disaster

Perhaps it was due to my soliloquy from G.B. Shaw's "Arms & the Man" at the reception for freshmen at IIT/Kanpur in July, 1966, or for some other reason, but I fell in with a crowd of students who liked the performing arts. It was very odd, because the arts were very far from anybody's mind at this prestigious campus. The entire 5-year program was intensely focused on academic and technical learning. We did have a semblance of athletic and cultural activities programs, but for the most part they were viewed as distractions from the main mission on campus.

I was not inclined towards relentless studying so I was naturally drawn to the extra-curricular options available. Mostly this took the form of performing in student organized theatrical plays. There were two groups engaged in this. One focused on plays in English and the other on plays in Hindi. I was involved with the former. The plays would be performed locally on campus, or in the annual culture show, or even in the local communities if an opportunity was available. In some of our productions we were assisted by the wives of American faculty members who had received theatrical training in the USA. Mrs. Daisy Oakley, the wife of the Director of the Kanpur Indo-American Program, Dr. Oakley, was one such person that comes to mind.

Over the first 3 years, I participated in many theatrical productions. But two of them come to mind in particular. The first one was *Charlie's Aunt*, a comedy by Brandon Thomas. It is simply hilarious and I was cast to play the lead role of the aunt, in which a boy dresses up as a woman and pretends to be the aunt in order to court a girl he likes. This play has been performed worldwide in major theatrical venues. We premiered our production at the Inter-Varsity Cultural Show in March, 1968. It was a smash hit. The IIT/Kanpur team won the top honors! This was highly unusual since everybody thought of all the students there as serious nerds, something that was not too far from the truth. I won the prize for Best Actor, which was equally amazing. The play went on tour as well after the show. We performed in Lucknow at the Loretto Convent College and later at IIT/Kharagpur for charities and other competitions. We won various prizes and raised money for worthy causes at the same time.

Another play was Edward Albee's *The Zoo Story*. This was directed by Mrs. Daisy Oakley and fared very well as well in various performances. Many years later, I had the opportunity to see productions of both these plays on Broadway in New York. It was fascinating to see the difference between a collegiate production and a commercial production with professional and celebrated actors at work. In fact, the *Charlie's Aunt* production in New York had actors like Vincent Price and Roddy McDowell starring in it! I was left speechless.

During these years, I also got exposed to the IIT/Kanpur campus TV network. It had a small TV studio, a couple of TV cameras, a broadcast console, and a hard-wired campus TV network. There were black and white TVs placed in common rooms of residential halls and various lecture rooms as well. It was a highly unusual thing, because real broadcast TV had not yet arrived in India at the time. All this was quite a novelty, even if it was restricted just to the campus. I used to read the news and sometimes do topical interviews with well-known people or students on camera. It was great fun. The major highlight from this activity for me was when I interviewed Mrs. Indira Gandhi, then Prime Minister of India.

It was really weird. One day, we received word that Mrs. Gandhi was going to visit the IIT/Kanpur campus and address all the students and faculty. I cannot recall why she was in Kanpur, but the speech on our campus had been placed on her schedule. Further, I would get to interview her on our little TV network after her speech! I think this second part was to showcase some of our new student activities to her. I was excited by this opportunity beyond belief!

She came upon the campus like a tornado! There were support and security people everywhere all around her. I was positioned just near the dais steps prior to her arrival. On the other side of the dais, which I could not see, was the entire IIT/Kanpur student body and faculty seated on chairs in a theatrical layout. After her speech, I was to take her immediately to the TV studio for her interview. She arrived wearing a sari, walked in a remarkably fit manner, and nearly sprinted up the few dais steps to the microphones. She had been chatting with some people in English as she approached us, but as soon as she was on the dais, upon seeing a lot of white (American) faces, she switched to Hindi!

She spoke for about 20 minutes or so. As she concluded, there was a loud ovation. Some more people addressed the group with a few more short speeches and then the event quickly concluded. She turned and descended the steps, and then I was introduced to her. She smiled, did "namaste" to others standing by, but then she shook my hand. I escorted her to the TV studio and we had a huge crowd of people following us.

She apologized for all the people surrounding us, but told me gently that there was not much she could do about it in a public setting. Then, we entered the TV studio and relative calm prevailed. Security people cordoned us off and rest of the crowd was left outside to gawk through the glass screens. Well, there was one exception. Mrs. Vijaya Lakshmi Pandit, Indiraji's aunt, was allowed into the studio.

We were seated in chairs and I explained to Indiraji what we were going to do. I reviewed the list of questions that I was going to ask her, the camera angles, light signals, etc., and she listened to me with attentive amusement. I showed her the various monitors for cameras, "on air" lights, and so forth. And then I told her to standby as we were just a few minutes away from being on air! Then, I stepped aside to let the makeup lady touch up her face.

She got a patting and a slight dusting, but then she noticed her face on one of the camera monitors and started preening herself! I remembered my father's words, "Never put your mother in front of a mirror anywhere! She will start touching up her face and hair immediately".

Shortly, all the setup actions were complete and we were just waiting. Suddenly, Indiraji asked me, "Is Indulal Yajnik related to you?" I replied, "Yes. He is my father's paternal cousin. We call him Indukaka."

"How wonderful!" she said with a smile. "We call him Induchacha! I have known him a long time. He is a man, very dear to our family." Just then, we went "on air".

The interview went off smoothly. On air, she was so different from the lady I had been chatting with just moments earlier. The former was sweet, charming, warm, and affectionate. But the latter, seemed controlled, guarded, firm, and in command of each moment. You could sense immediately that this lady was used to being in the spotlight and highly experienced with the media scrutiny. As soon as we went off the air, she got up and took me over to meet her aunt, Mrs. Pandit. We chatted about Indukaka and our families, but not the interview!

When it was time for her to leave, she said, "Vijay, I have enjoyed this very much. My best wishes for you. And thank you." Then just like a tornado, she quickly disappeared from our campus.

Well, all these extra-curricular activities were fun and rewarding in many ways, but they also had a huge downside. It took time away from studies. IIT/Kanpur, like all IITs in India, was an academically highly competitive environment. Your Cumulative Grade Point Average (CGPA) mattered enormously for everything. It would be nearly accurate to say that you were judged almost singularly by your CGPA. It defined you as smart or dumb, a winner or a loser, and as acceptable for something or just rejected. It also defined how you were perceived by other students and even members of the faculty. The CGPA scale went from 0 to 10. At 6.5 or higher, you were considered First Class, but that did not get you any friends. Now, if you were 9.0+, or 8.0+, then you were liked. In the 7.0s, you were on the edge.

I remember my professor of design of electrical circuits, Dr. T.R. Vishvanathan, who was a truly gifted teacher. In his lectures, one would hear, "… So, as you can see, the voltage at this node of the circuit would be… Yajnik, can you tell us?"

I would jerk up straight in my chair and surely flub my answer. So, Doc TRV would say to the whole class, "Well, of course, Yajnik does not know the correct answer. He is busy rehearsing theatrical plays than studying!"

Another example would be where somebody asked a question such as, "Do you know Dipak Agarwal from the 4th year batch?"

In response, one would hear, "That is the 9-pointer, right? No wait, that Agarwal is in the 3rd year. It must be that other 8-pointer. But you know, I am not sure."

You were an "X pointer", and nobody much cared to even remember your name.

Well, in the spring of 1968, in the Maths 203 Class, I got an "F" grade. I bottomed the grading curve and failed. At IIT/Kanpur, if you failed a class, you could retake it in the summer holidays and the new grade would replace your failed grade. So, there was a shot at redemption, if one got into serious trouble academically. But one did have to face the embarrassment of failure at home. You would have to answer questions like, "Why are you going back to school during the summer vacation?" or "You failed? What? Why? What have you been doing? Are you not studying?" etc. There was no escaping any of these things.

So, the summer of 1968 became a summer of academic redemption for me. But besides fixing my F grade, it also made me realize that I simply had to forget about doing things I enjoyed and focus singularly on my studies. If I did not do that in the environment of IIT/Kanpur, I would be eliminated or dumped on the academic scrapheap. If that happened, all future academic and career possibilities would be closed for me, in India or anywhere else.

Getting admitted into an IIT was one thing, but performing poorly at any of them would be an almost certain death sentence for all future prospects.

My focus shifted. I turned deadly serious about my studies.

Meeting the Daughter

(As told to me by my Parents)

"**Y**ajnik sir, you have a call from the PMO in New Delhi!" the Secretary said aghast, to nobody nearby. He was forced to hang up, and then, he rushed off like a crazed man to find my father. He shortly did.

"What the devil are you talking about?" my father asked him. "Who or what is this PMO?"

"Sir, it is the Prime Minister's Office! It was a call from New Delhi!" he replied, in a hyper excited state.

"Okay, Sriram, fine. But first, you must calm down. Let's find out what they want and what this is all about. Does that not make sense to you?"

"Yes, sir." Sriram answered, rocking his head right-'n-left in agreement. "Most certainly, sir. I will get on it at once, sir."

It became clear rather quickly what the phone call from Delhi had been all about. It seemed that Mrs. Indira Gandhi, then Prime Minister of India, was going to pay a visit to Dwarka and nearby areas for some Government work and a few political meetings. Her schedule had been worked out in detail for the two days that she would spend in the area, except for one critical matter.

Nobody in Delhi could figure out accommodations for her for the night. There were no decent hotels to speak of in the Dwarka area at the time and there were no Dak Bungalows or Guest Houses available either. Also, a location had to be chosen carefully due to various concerns about her security and the needs of the sizable staff accompanying her. After much ado, it had been determined that the ACC bungalows were the only real option, and so my father had been politely approached.

As the GM of Dwarka Cement Works, Pappaji had done many favors for various folks and was used to getting such requests. For example, there was an Indian Defense Forces Encampment or Base near Scott's Point, with some 300 odd solders in it. It was mainly army, but also included people from the navy and air force. It had been setup as a "forward post" and "signals unit" after the war with Pakistan in 1965. My father knew the Base Commander quite well. Pappaji had offered free access to the ACC Sports Club for all the officers of the base and they were delighted to be invited to various social functions and events. Many times the officers were invited to our home for various meals as well. Whenever such visits occurred, my mother ensured that a full meal, including non-vegetarian dishes, was prepared for the guests. Further, alcoholic beverages were served by my father as well.

However, this visit by Indiraji would be vastly different. Pappaji had decided to give the 2 bedroom suites on the ground floor of our bungalow to her and her personal attendants. The rest of her support staff were all to be housed in the ACC Guest House. Some folks had to be put up in the spare bedrooms of the AGM bungalow as well. But, by and large, the whole party could be accommodated for the night in question in relative comfort.

An advance security detail arrived a few days earlier and inspected all the 3 bungalows. After clearance had been given, Pappaji commenced the rest of the preparations. It was decided that full meals, including non-vegetarian items, would be prepared for the whole PM party. My mother worked her head off with all the staff to get ready for this crucial visit. Then one evening, with great flourish, she arrived.

Indiraji flew into the Jamnagar Air Force Base on this brilliant sunny morning. She had a full day of events and activities en route to Dwarka. Then, at the end of a long day, she arrived in the porch of our bungalow. My parents received her and she was sweet as one can imagine! It was around 8:00pm. Everybody wondered about what she would like to do for food at this hour?

After she freshened up, Pappaji asked her if she would like some drinks and dinner. She replied that she needed something simple, because she had not felt well all day. So, my mother suggested a simple meal that she and my father planned have that night and Indiraji readily agreed! This meal consisted of kadhi, shaak, rotali, and bhaat. (*mild Indian soup, sautéed veggies, flat bread, and rice*). There was no meat or seafood involved at all. She declined drinks and simply joined my parents at the dining table, in a tired but relaxed manner. She told them that it felt like she was at home!

Soon, the conversation evolved into "Yajnik" relations, Indukaka, Pandit Nehru's visit to Jamul, etc. They talked about many things, except politics. Rather quickly, Indiraji understood all the connections. She was just thrilled to be with folks with such old relationships with her family.

"So, you are Induchacha's cousin!" she said to my father. "He has been so close to my father, and our family generally, for decades. I am so happy to be here and meet you tonight. You know, political life is hard, but if one has a calling, one must live up to it. It is always so rushed and busy. I have to travel a lot. If you come to Delhi, please do come and visit us."

As Pappaji said it, Indiraji was the very personification of grace. She dripped class in every way and showed great upbringing. She charmed everybody that she met! All politics aside, my parents became fans of Indiraji and it was not too much of a stretch for them.

She arrived like a storm, but she left like a gentle breeze. In between, she seemed to cherish the home of a simple Gujarati brahmin family, that clearly wanted to look after her like she was their own daughter. She certainly sensed it.

For the rest of their lives, even though she was close to my mother in age, my parents always thought of Mrs. Indira Gandhi like she was the daughter they never had. They believed in her affectionately and deeply.

It reflected a deep love, for the lady and her family, that was not difficult to understand. In lots of ways, I agreed with it as well.

Tales of Agra & Pavan Nagpal

Visit to the Taj Mahal

In 1966, as I began my freshman year at IIT/Kanpur, my roommate was Viney Pal Aneja. Then, I made another good friend. His name was Pavan Nagpal. He lived in the room adjacent to ours in Residence Hall # 3. He was affectionate, unassuming, and just so sweet. He was from Agra, the city known for the famous Taj Mahal. His manner and charm concealed some harsh truths and a life of incredible suffering. It took a person some time to learn about them. And to appreciate them was yet another matter.

The Nagpal family hailed originally from Peshawar, in British India. They were Hindus. After Independence from British Rule and the Partition of India, they chose to leave what became Pakistan for the new India. They lost everything in their home town. All land, buildings, business, etc. were gone in an instant and the family became "refugees" travelling slowly on bullock carts towards India. Along the way, they managed to survive the communal massacres that occurred all over. Eventually, and at great peril, they managed to find their way to Agra. In this city, with help from some other similar refugee families, they began to settle themselves and regain a semblance of their former lives. It was a horrendous transition, a huge economic loss, and it left the Nagpal family scarred for life.

It took me a long while to learn all this from Pavan, who would normally not talk about any of it at all. He was a bit introverted and shy, while I was extroverted and talkative. We were opposites and perhaps it was the reason why we got along so well. Shortly, there was some kind of a break for some holidays or such, and many students went home for 3 or 4 days, if it was nearby. But for a lot of us, whose homes were quite far and involved train journeys of 2+ days, going away anywhere was simply not an option. So, we would just hang around the campus and try to make the best of the break.

"Hey, Vijay, want to go to Agra?" Pavan suddenly asked me. "Have you been there? Ever seen the Taj Mahal?"

I was taken aback. I replied, "No, I have not. It would be a dream fulfilled to see the Taj Mahal!"

"Come on, let's go." Pavan offered. "My parents live there, and we will surprise them!" It was just too sweet to pass up. So, Pavan and I left by a train from Kanpur for Agra on this unforgettable adventure.

We reached Pavan's home in Agra in the late afternoon. His parents were shocked, but just delighted! I was accorded a typical warm Punjabi welcome by them. They were thrilled that I could speak Hindi fluently. His Mom, just like my mother, was obsessed with constantly feeding us! I suppose this was one consequence of having suffered through starvation during their migration to India. They were so loving in all sorts of simple ways. I just adored them.

We told them about our plans to see the Taj Mahal. At this, Pavan's Mom said to me, "Bete, Taj ko paheli baar to chandni mein dekhna chahiye. Kabhi bhoologe nahin." (*Son, Taj must be viewed for the first time in the moonlight. You will never forget it.*) Then, she continued, "Aaj Poonam hai. Aaj raat ko jaana." (*Tonight, it is a full moon night. Go there tonight.*) We took her advice and rode our rented bikes to the Taj at night when the full moon was out. It was surprisingly not crowded that night. There were some tourists, but mainly it was the local folks who were strolling around in the moonlit grounds.

I do not have the words to describe what I saw, or how I felt about it. It was a fantastic blend of ecstasy, breathless wonder, astonishment and awe, adulation, sadness, being drenched in beauty, and a severe jolt to the heart, if you can understand all my babble here! I felt all sorts of emotions just racing through me. It was hard to put it all together in a cohesive manner. We spent a couple of unforgettable hours and decided to return the next day. Pavan's Mom was totally right.

The Taj visit the next day was quite different. The tourists were everywhere and it was crowded. We walked the grounds again and took the guided tour as well. After being shown countless details and told all sorts of legends about this famous monument, the guide had us sit down in some shade for a little rest. Then, he posed an interesting question, "Do you know why the Taj Mahal is considered one of the Wonders of the World?"

In our group, people looked at each other to check if anyone knew. There were a few guesses, but none of us knew the answer. The guide then said, "Look around you. What do you see?" We all looked around, but generally were clueless. He continued, "Look, someone there is crying, somebody here is sitting quietly in thought, that couple over there seems distant from each other, while that other elderly couple cannot seem to stop holding their hands!" We all started looking around everywhere and noticed all sorts of strange behavior in people, regardless of race, color, caste, or religion!

The guide said, "The Taj Mahal is one of the Wonders of the World for a crucial reason. It generates a deeply emotional and passionate response within all who view it! Certainly, the edifice has magnificent architecture, amazing

212

construction, and is a legendary tribute to love. But it is this intensely personal response to it, by all who see it, that makes it unique."

Gift of Ivory Combs

As our visit to the Taj Mahal ended, Pavan and I emerged from its grounds into a busy market selling all sorts of wares to the visiting tourists. As we were making our way towards our stored bikes, I noticed the cart of a nearby vendor. He had all sorts of things made of ivory in it. I am sure it was ivory powder and not the real ivory. Regardless, the products for both types of materials would usually cost quite a bit. I saw some ladies' combs with intricate carvings on them. I thought of buying a couple of them as gifts for my Mom and family. So, I stopped and inquired about their price. They were expensive and I was on a meagre student budget.

I was about to start bargaining the price down with the vendor, when a large air-conditioned limo pulled up and stopped about 6 feet away, kicking up a considerable cloud of dust. It had Delhi license plates. Shortly, the passenger door opened and out came this enormous man. He was white with blonde hair, about 6 ft. 4 in. in height, and 250+ lbs. in weight. He wore a white linen shirt, blue jeans, leather boots, and a cowboy hat with a red scarf around his neck. Obviously, he was American and most likely from Texas.

"Jesus, Mabel, it is hot as a prairie shit house!" he said in a surprised and somewhat irritated manner. "You better keep your hat and sun umbrella handy. Hell, this had better be worth it. It sure was a long way to haul butt through that insane traffic."

"Now, now, JW (pronounced "Jay-Dubya"), you gotta relax. Did you take your pills this morning like I told you to? It's hot, because the limo was so cool. I am certain that you will like seeing this mausoleum, or whatever it is, because folks think it is so special. Why, Jenny and Bobby would not stop talkin' about it after their trip to India last year, remember?"

"Yeah, well, I reckon Jen and Bob are both just plain nuts! So, I am not holding my breath for this thing."

"JW, look over there! Such lovely things made of ivory!" the lady said, as she emerged from the car. She was 6 ft. tall, blonde, well fed, buxom, and with long shapely legs.

213

The American couple walked up to the same vendor I was about to start bargaining with. The vendor promptly brushed me aside and focused his full attention on the catch that had just walked into his net!

What followed was almost comical. Mabel fell in love with many items and promptly started shopping for friends and family back home. The vendor priced all the products at 20x higher than what he had told me. He winked at me slyly indicating that I should keep my mouth shut. When the final bill total came, JW converted the sum into US dollars and joyously announced that the prices had been such a bargain! Then, with the purchase completed, off they went to visit the Taj Mahal.

The vendor immediately folded shop for the day. He did not want to be around when the American couple returned. He had hit his goldmine for the day and he was done. Then, I asked about the ivory combs I wanted to buy. I pointed them out to him. He looked at me amused, and then just gave me 4 of them for free! I got my reward for keeping my mouth shut.

Shortly, he just vanished into the crowd of people and the various stray animals.

The Folk Dancing Club

My much older cousin, Kiritbhai, was on the faculty at IIT/Kanpur during the years that I studied there. To all the students, he was known as Dr. Yajnik. He was a professor in the Dept. of Mechanical Engineering and taught many subjects. With many of my friends, I used to visit Kiritbhai and Kalyanibhabhi at their home on many occasions and even for some parties. They were great hosts for all our crazy plans and activities.

Now, Kiritbhai was fond of folk dancing. He had acquired a taste for it while studying for his Ph.D. at the University of California, Berkeley. He had a lovely portable record player from America and many records of all sorts of folk-dance music. Most of us knew nothing about any of these dances or the music. But because it attracted the very few girls on campus, it became a celebrated event for all the boys! It became a place to meet and chat with the girls on our campus! Even though it was a lot of fun, nobody really cared much about the dancing, if you understand what I mean. Hey, I was certainly one of them. So was Pavan!

Now, the Folk Dancing Club met once a week, on Wednesdays, at the Guest House lawn at 8:00pm. While most folks would finish dinner and plan on showing up casually, Pavan would take a shower and lather himself up with some awful cologne to be attractive to the ladies! He took it all so seriously. But here was the best part. Pavan had no sense of rhythm at all. He could not keep time with the dance steps of any kind! That would cause a crazy chain reaction in the whole group. However, his goofy antics endeared him to all the girls! He became the most popular and sought-after dude of all! Perhaps it was because he seemed real to the girls. He just glowed with pride at this achievement.

It may seem trite today, but this "Folk Dance Club" in reality taught all of us Indian kids so much. We learnt rhythm, got exposed to famous dances from around the world, and got an understanding of international music. Most importantly, we learnt to be sociable with others, in an unknown setting.

Kiritbhai gave all of us an amazing gift. It paid dividends, in so many ways, during the rest of our lives.

Pavan Visits the USA

It was in the early 1990's. On a fine morning, I got a telephone call. "Is this Vijay Yajnik?" the voice asked. "Who wants to know?" I replied in a guarded manner.

"This is Pavan Nagpal." the voice said simply.

"Abbe, ... Saale! This is Yajnik! Tu kahan hai?" (*Hey! This is Yajnik! Where are you?*) I asked, bursting with joy at hearing the voice of my old friend after a very long time. He was on a business trip to the USA and was soon coming to Los Angeles, where I lived. We immediately made plans to spend some grand time together.

The Pavan I met in LA was a very changed man. Life had been hard on him. Unlike a lot of us, for many reasons, he had chosen to remain in India after graduating from IIT/K. He had tried some jobs but did not like them. Eventually, he started his own business in ceramic grinding stones. He had majored in Metallurgical Engineering at IIT/Kanpur and was quite knowledgeable about this subject, which had massive and emerging industrial applications. But he was an engineer by temperament and not a businessman.

So, all sorts of people got in his way. Nobody would let him succeed. The totally corrupt, inept, and parasitic environment in India did not give him any help or breaks of any kind at all. But he persevered doggedly. After a long slog, the tide went his way, he built a successful technology-based business, and became a wealthy man. He built himself 3 homes in Bangalore and bought many cars, but he never settled himself into a life of luxury or privilege. He was always on the hunt for the next scientific discovery or opportunity.

We reconnected, and despite all the time gone by, we became the same two kids on rented bikes in Agra from a long time ago. I showed Pavan around LA. He seemed nostalgic and emotional about things he felt he had missed out in life. He even expressed some regrets. But I reassured him that he had not missed out on a thing. Life is always about choices. We all make them based on our personal circumstances and reasons. There is absolutely nothing wrong with any of that.

"You remember the Folk Dancing Club?" Pavan asked, on the last day of his visit. "I used to put on that cologne to smell nice for the few girls. It was insane! When I think about it at times, you know, it feels so strange. But that was a long time ago, and now I am married and with children. You know, Bangalore is nice, but there are no beaches like you have here in LA."

"Oh, yes, we have some super beaches here all along the coast!" I replied. "So hey, let's go to Malibu! You will enjoy it!"

So, Pavan and I went off to Malibu. We walked on many beaches there and enjoyed the ocean air. Then we took a table at a nice outdoor restaurant to enjoy the sunset - a real California treat!

We chatted and laughed during the entire afternoon and into the evening. In California, one thinks nothing about such places, but Pavan did seem to be totally thrilled. He never forgot that afternoon. He struck an item off his bucket list, it seemed to me.

A Meeting in Bangalore

Many years later, in 2007, Nilima and I were in Bangalore visiting my dear old friend, Shahid (Sid) Siddiqui. We were hosted by Kiritbhai who was now settled there. Sid was very ill and we spent most of our time there with him and his wife, Shehnaaz.

But Pavan, who also lived in Bangalore, had heard about our presence and so he came over to visit with us. We all went off to a lovely dinner with him and his wife, Achala. It was a fantastic evening filled with stories of all sorts. We engaged in nostalgia, reviewed our current lives, and caught up on various lost friends and so much more.

"Vijay, I have to reciprocate for that lovely afternoon in Malibu!" Pavan said with a laugh. "I have a superb place picked out for us, so you must stay

216

for a few more days with us. Yaar, itni jaldi kya hai?" (*Yaar, why so much of a rush?*)

But unfortunately, we had to leave because of various other commitments. I sadly bid Pavan and Achala a fond farewell. Kiritbhai saw us off the next day.

I had no idea at the time that I would never see Pavan again. Within six months or so of our visit, after returning from a business trip to Europe, Pavan fell gravely ill. A virtual army of doctors attended to him and eventually he was transferred to AIIMS (All India Institute of Medical Sciences), in New Delhi. He was given the best care available, as I was told later. But all this was to no avail. Pavan succumbed to complications from a Hepatitis C infection. It is curable, if detected in time and treated properly. If it had been treated correctly, Pavan might have survived. For me, his death will always be a matter of grave doubt about the quality of his medical care in India.

But in this wind, known as Pavan (*his name literally means "wind"*), I found my life touched in countless and priceless ways. It also became a source of comfort and security. Pavan and I did not just share a past. We had something much greater.

We had something called a genuine friendship.

A Terrible Year - 1970

In the autumn of 1969, my father retired from ACC after 35+ years of service. My parents relocated from Dwarka to Ahmedabad. They moved into the bungalow, "Nikunj", in Maninagar. My father had built it many years earlier and they made it their new home. They settled their life into a comfortable mode, but there was a huge difference. My father had never lived in Ahmedabad while holding an important job locally. He was now retired. But, in Ahmedabad, nobody cared much for you if you did not have either political or economic power.

Pappaji was a near stranger in this town. In Ahmedabad, every aspect of life is "a trade". I will do this for you, if you will do that for me. The more favors you could grant to somebody, the more you were valued in society. Most relationships in this society, regardless of appearances, were based mainly on their economic value. Even within a caste, this aspect trumped everything else.

Then, on this fateful day, I arrived in Maninagar on the afternoon train from Bombay. I had been on a month-long mandatory national tour of India with my classmates from IIT/Kanpur. It was a requirement for graduation. We had a railway bogey all our own. We started off from Kanpur and a variety of trains took us all over India. It was like a travelling hotel. In each city, we would be placed on a siding and we all would set off as tourists to experience the sights, culture and the local food. It was just amazing. One got a perspective of what the real India was all about. My big takeaway was that even with different languages, dietary habits, and climates, we were fundamentally one people and one culture. We also accepted faiths of every kind into our communities without malice. This trip changed my thinking about India in a big way.

I arrived in Nikunj carting a bag full of dirty filthy clothes. My mother took care of all of it, but then conversations began about Pappaji's retirement. It was obvious that it had been hard on him so far. It was difficult for him to accept the loss of power and the lifestyle that went with his job. In Ahmedabad, he had no support structure of any kind and he did not even know the social customs of the town. But luckily, he did have one great friend to show him the way.

That friend was Anilphooa. He was a doctor and married to Pappaji's youngest sister, Shashiphoi. They had known each other for a very long time. In fact, my father was the one that had set them up on their first date, which led to them getting married a little later in 1940. Anilphooa told Pappaji to not worry at all. He would introduce him properly to all the key folks in the Ahmedabad society and also get him memberships to all the important social clubs.

Then, in February, 1970, when I was in Kanpur, all of them decided to visit the Ambaji Temple in northern Gujarat. It is a very prestigious and highly revered temple in Gujarat. Further, our caste of Nagar Brahmins had specific accommodations for staying there (the "Mahd") and special prayer service privileges at the temple. Well, the whole family went off and was having a grand time of everything. Eventually, they settled in for the night in the Mahd.

The next morning, to their utter shock, they discovered that Anilphooa had quietly passed away during the night. This was just unbelievable! Nobody could make any sense of it. But it was a fact, and had to be dealt with carefully. It was nearly impossible to move a dead body from such a holy place of high worship and religious rituals without being noticed. If a way could be found, how would one execute it without scrutiny or being questioned at so many places? It was a huge challenge on top of the profound shock and grief being felt by everybody.

Pappaji took charge of the situation immediately. He asked Pankaj, Phooa's son, to go fetch the car. He announced that Anilphooa was very ill and had to be evacuated to a hospital immediately. Phoi and my mother were ordered to show "No crying. No emotion. Instead, show concern. He is only very sick. Can you do that?" He was in control and totally devoid of any emotion at this critical hour.

Phooa's body was moved to the car and carried over laps in the rear seat. They sped off to Ahmedabad, some three hours away. Munikaka followed in a second car. Along the way, Pappaji informed all the relevant people in Ahmedabad about what had happened, what was going on, and the necessary funeral requirements. It was all so very dicey, because there were strict laws regarding dead bodies being transported in India. Anyway, it all ended fine eventually. The cremation occurred, the whole family fell into serious grief, and Shashiphoi went into a major depression shortly thereafter.

I have related this whole episode here in its essence, as it was recounted to me by Pankaj and Shridevi, who were actually there. Pankaj was in total awe of how my father handled such a complex, delicate, and highly emotionally charged crisis. Pankaj said to me, "Vijay, your father is a man's man. He is tough as steel. I do not know anybody who could have done what he did that day. He drove the car himself also."

Anilphooa's death hit all of us very hard. In the summer of 1970, we would often drive over from Maninagar to "Uttarayan", Shashiphoi's bungalow in Navarangpura, in the evening. We would spend a few hours with her and Pankaj to give them company. But Phooa's presence was always sorely missed.

Then on this evening, we returned from our visit with Phoi around 10:00pm. At that time, Sushila Ba, my Nani Ma, was visiting us for a few days. We all got changed into our night clothes and then Moti, our German Shephard dog, began wailing loudly. I tried to shut him up because my critical GRE ("Graduate Record Examination") exam was on the following morning and I needed to sleep desperately. But Moti would not stop or calm down, no matter what I did. It was very odd indeed.

Suddenly, my mother yelled for me. "Vijay, Ganga jal lav!" *(Vijay, bring the Ganga water!)* In every Nagar Brahmin home, Ganga jal is always present. It was required for a variety of reasons and it had to be in your home. Everybody knew where it was kept. I grabbed the bottle and ran into the room where my Mom was with Sushila Ba.

I could not believe what I saw! My dear sweet Sushila Ba was heaving for each breath! My mother was trying to comfort her. I gave my Mom the Ganga jal and yelled next door to summon a doctor really quick. My cousin, Vrajesh, was awake and yelled back that he would get a doctor at once.

Then, my Mom said, "Hold her up. I will administer the water." And I went, "Wait, what?"

I held Ba in comfort with her face close to mine. I loved this simple lady enormously. Then, she gave me a faint smile and passed away in my arms. My mother and I were left stunned and devastated.

Again, Pappaji came to the rescue. He, along with Behn and Munikaka, took Ba's body to Petlad immediately that night for cremation the next day. It was the most central place for everybody to get to so they opted for it. I was told, along with Vrajesh, to inform everybody in Ahmedabad about Ba's passing and to instruct them to go to Petlad if they wished to pay their last respects. It was around 1:00am.

Vrajesh was very nervous about our mission for the night and began to shake uncontrollably.

I asked him, "Are you all right?"

He replied, "No. I want a cigarette."

I said, "Heck, so do I! Let's get some." He smiled and visibly relaxed.

But it was equally clear that he was in a state of shock and did not know how to handle such an event. I was left to do the heavy lifting that entire night, while Vrajesh smoked uncontrollably. We did not sleep that entire night.

In the morning, I had to go give my GRE exam. It was an all-day affair, as I recall. Nobody was in Nikunj, as everyone had gone to Petlad for Ba's cremation. So, I just left to give my exam. By the time I returned in the evening, everybody had returned to Nikunj and it was a very quiet and somber place.

Soon, I had to return to IIT/Kanpur for my 5th Year. It was hard to leave my parents after all the recent losses in the family. I could sense that my father was extremely unhappy and disappointed with his life in Ahmedabad.

He began to dislike eveyhing about the city. He could not accept its conservative values, traditions, or its regressive norms. He had moved on and away from all that many decades ago. This was just not his concept of the beginning of his retirement years. In fact, it was a far cry from it. I had the sense that Pappaji would do something and soon.

In the autumn of 1970, Pappaji accepted the position of GM of the Port Okha plant of Carborundum Universal Ltd. My parents shuttered Nikunj and relocated away to Port Okha. In essence, they mainly just left Ahmedabad, a city in which they did not feel welcome or comfortable, in any way.

In this manner, the book on the ugly year of 1970 closed.

Applying for Graduate Studies

Options for a Future

“ **A**rrey, suna tumne? Prem ki toh lottery lag gayi!” the cry broke out. *(Arrey, did you hear? Prem won the lottery!)* The news was all over the Residence Hall # 1, where I lived, in a flash, as it were.

Prem Kapoor was a year senior to me at IIT/Kanpur and was also majoring in Electrical Engineering. He was bright, studied hard, but also enjoyed cultural activities. He was friendly, fun and a graduate of St. George's College in Mussourie, UP. We got along well and had become good friends since the summer of 1968, when we saw each other a lot on campus.

It was now spring of 1970. For all the 5th year students, admission results for various programs for graduate studies abroad were beginning to arrive almost daily via the post. A large part of this batch of students had applied to Universities in the USA. And now everybody would slowly learn of the outcome individually via letters in the mail. The anxiety level was at a near fever pitch. A favorable or a successful response from any University in the USA would be a definitive life-altering event with major economic consequences for one's life in the future.

Whenever an envelope arrived, each student would judge its contents by its thickness! If it was thin, it was nearly certain to be a one-page rejection letter. If it was a little thicker, that could suggest some good news. But if it was really thick, it would be a promise of great news! A thick envelope meant that there were "goodies" inside and various papers would have to be returned to accept and firm up whatever had been offered by that University. For some really academically bright students, this was almost a game of "how many thick envelopes can I collect?" It seemed that getting accepted at many Universities in the USA was the ultimate stroke to their egos! Some of this behavior bordered on intellectual arrogance, conceit, and in some cases, it was just self-centered and shameful. Regardless, what mattered to everybody was a successful end result.

Now, you may be wondering why all the students from a prestigious univeristy like IIT/Kanpur were so obsessed with going abroad, to the USA in particular, for further graduate studies? Why not stay in India and make a contribution to the building of the nation? These were valid questions that were often debated in open forums on campus. There was the conservative

222

nationalist view that felt that the IIT/Kanpur graduates owed something back to the nation for giving them such a lovely school to study in. Others felt that there was no such implied contract. The students should feel free to do whatever they liked and that their actions and achievements would eventually benefit the nation anyway. There were many other flavors of opinion as well. But, in plain truth, the IIT/K student actions were all based on the economic realities prevalent in India at that time.

A student graduating from the meritocracy of IIT/Kanpur faced stark choices, if he wished to stay in India. In the early 1970's, good and well-paying jobs were few and hard to come by in India. The public sector companies were run in a typical socialistic manner with strong political and labor union influences. Pay scales were low, highly stratified, and there was hardly any innovation going on. Many were some sort of a collaboration with a foreign government or entity.

In the private sector, companies, including those that were listed on the stock exchanges, were run essentially like "family owned" businesses. Their motive was profits and enrichment of the controlling family. There was hardly any professional management of any kind anywhere. That very idea was anathema to them and they were obsessed with retaining control within the family at all costs.

So, an "outsider" stood little chance of getting an important job within these companies. It was also the era of "License Raj" in India and only the politically connected families could get the licenses to either start or grow innovative new industries. On the occasions when this occurred, most families resisted the modern and innovative management practices. The concepts of openness, transparency, and product or process experimentation for improvement or efficiency were just too foreign for most of them.

Also, perhaps the Indian economy was not sufficiently ready. India had been playing catch up ball on nearly every front since achieving Independence in 1947. Its capital resources were limited and the economy had not yet reached a "take-off point" where it could self-sustain growth. However, it was valuable to acquire the latest technical knowledge and skills in almost any area, as it was expected that the demand for them would emerge sooner than later. So, naturally, a period of study abroad to acquire advanced technical skills was considered to be a worthy objective. Because of prevalence of English, the USA, Canada and the UK were considered the prized destinations. Unlike the trends in the 19th or early 20th centuries, the USA had now become the most attractive, due to its sheer size and a vast availability of renowned institutions of advanced learning.

That evening, Prem and all of us celebrated in a big way. He had been admitted by the University of Hawaii into their Master's program in electrical engineering. Not only that, they had also awarded him a Teaching Assistantship ("TA"), which would give him a monthly stipend in US dollars for his living expenses and covered all his tuition costs. This was a 2-year ride, in US dollars, that was fully paid for! It was just wonderful! Then, slowly other results trickled in. Many others got similar offers at other Universities in the USA and all sorts of celebrations became a frequent occurrence. It was the culmination of a long process that had begun for them in the prior summer.

You see, applying for graduate studies in the USA, or anywhere overseas, from IIT/Kanpur was not an easy thing. It was also a competitive process and it began the year prior to graduation in the summer. Everything was done by post or mail. First, you made a list of the Universities and their graduate program that you would be applying to.

Next, you wrote to them to get all their application forms and requirements. Some of them were obvious. Items such as transcripts, essays, basic application form were generally similar. One did have to copy and write the same information over and over again, depending upon the number of schools involved. The more difficult things were when a University asked you to explain or write things in a free form manner.

The hardest part of it all was the Recommendation Letters (RL). Each school would require 3 of them. If you were applying to 10 schools, this would mean you would need 30 such letters from your professors since you did not have any work experience. Also, a professor who had agreed to give you one would have to fill out his information 10 times, just for you! Nobody liked doing this at all. Further, the RLs would have to be signed and sealed by the professor, because you were not supposed to see what had been written about you. Then, they had to be retrieved so they could to be stamped and mailed properly. Even this was a pain.

One had to go to the post office with all the letters duly stamped and watch the postman place the seal on the stamps. This was to make sure that nobody would throw your letter away, steal the stamps, and resell them for money! The same thing applied when mailing the admission application packages.

On top of all these process issues, there was another major requirement to be overcome. One had to take the GRE ("Graduate Record Examination") exam in the prior summer and instruct them to send your results to your list of graduate schools. This was also a nightmare of a process, especially if one was taking this exam in India.

I had given the GRE exam in Ahmedabad under highly difficult personal circumstances (*There is more on that in another story*). The results had not arrived, but meanwhile my IIT/K batch faced a huge controversy over the application process. First, the professors were fed up of having to write endless RLs. Second, it would be foolish to have many applicants from IIT/Kanpur apply to the same University in the USA. It could hurt the prospects of all applicants. But then how should this matter be resolved? Who gets to pick which University in the USA? On what basis? How can it be equitable for all? How can the RLs be spread over a wider group of professors? There were heated debates and arguments all around. Finally, a process was agreed upon for the good of all.

In many ways, it was sheer madness. There was method to it, but it was madness none the less. It was fueled by everybody's desire to be the one to get a fully paid 2-year ride for a program of graduate studies in the USA.

In all honesty, while I hated it, I subscribed to it as well. There was no other choice. It was laborious and took way too much time. But, to be on the safe side, I also interviewed for jobs in India. There were companies like DCM, Avery, Hindustan Unilever, etc. that had interviewed students for jobs on campus. They seemed quite traditional in their thinking and business models to me. I did get an offer from Avery, so it was an option for me as well. But beyond this, unless one wanted to face the convoluted hiring process of public sector companies, there was little other choice.

In the spring of 1971, when my batch started to receive responses from the Universities in the USA, all those application difficulties were quickly forgotten. I received my share of rejection letters like everybody else. Then, North Carolina State University, in Raleigh, North Carolina, gave me admission to the Master's program. Shortly thereafter, the State University of New York, Stony Brook, NY, did the same and also gave me a Fellowship grant. I believe that my very dear friend, Bijendra Nath Jain (BN), who was a year senior to me and already there, had a lot to do with my getting this grant. He remained very dear to me. I am indebted to him in so many ways, life long.

Suddenly, it occurred to me that the option to go to the USA for further graduate studies had now become quite real for me. While I had followed the herd at IIT/Kanpur, now I wondered if I actually should go the USA? Both my older brothers were there already. Should I go also? And what about my parents? Who would be in India to assist them in their retirement years? Should I not stay behind for their sake?"

These and many other questions began to trouble me greatly. I had been chasing a dream really hard. Now, it had been realized. But somehow, it did not feel sweet to me. Suddenly, I discovered a lot of conflicts within my heart and mind that I had not been aware of until now.

During my life that followed, I was never able to reconcile myself to these conflicts. They have always remained with me forever, unresolved.

A Major Decision in Okha

On that fateful morning in the late spring of 1971, Kiritbhai, Kalyanibhabhi, and I drove off in their Ambassador car from the IIT/Kanpur campus for Bombay. The journey would take us a couple of days and we had an overnight stop planned along the way. I was accompanying them for the car drive, and was to go to Ahmedabad from Bombay later on by train.

Kiritbhai had accepted a new position with the National Aeronautical Labs in Bangalore and was relocating there. I had graduated from the 5-year program at IIT/Kanpur. My parents were in Ahmedabad at the time and I was to meet them there before proceeding to Port Okha, where Pappaji was working as the GM of the Carborundum Universal plant.

My mind was full of concerns, contradictions and a great measure of confusion. Should I go to the USA for further graduate studies? Or should I take a job and stay in India? I had to decide quickly because there were many arrangements to be made depending upon my decision. And time was running short.

In Ahmedabad, whoever met me would ask the same question, "Tu America kyare javano chhu?" *(When are you going to America?)* I could not give anybody an honest answer because no one would believe me! Well, nobody would ever pass up a real chance to go to America, so all other options were deemed false for me. As for the confusion, most of them wondered what was there to be confused about? It was pointless engaging anybody in a real discussion in Ahmedabad. I was steadily getting distraught and depressed.

We left for Okha and during the drive, it became clear to Pappaji that I was not myself. He engaged me in a lengthy conversation to understand what was bothering me. Then, he changed the subject and we talked about many other things. My mother also joined in trying to cheer me up.

"Will you come to my office at 11:00am this morning?" Pappaji asked me at breakfast the next day. "I want you to see some people."

"Sure." I replied. I had no clue as to what all this was about.

At the meeting, Pappaji explained to the two men present that I was there just to learn about things in general and to not mind my presence. It lasted about an hour. The discussion seemed to be about a proposal to purchase some equipment. It ended without a conclusion and a follow-up meeting was agreed upon. Then the men left.

"Do you know who those two men were?" my father asked. I shook my head.

"The younger man is the Sales Manager from the Rajkot office. The older man is the Region Manager–Western India and is from Bombay. They both work for Avery, Ltd., the company that has offered you a job. They are engaged in selling industrial weighing machines which are used at our plant."

"Wow! That is amazing." I ventured.

"If you join them and do extremely well in your performance, you may get the older man's job in 25 years or so. In these companies, technical selling is prized. Due to a joint venture with the UK parent company, there is little R&D done in India. Your job in India would mainly be a sales job."

I fell silent. In one swift stroke, my father had shown me directly what my job and career would be in Avery India Ltd. at its beginning and 25 years out. I saw selling, but no innovation, cutting edge technologies, or any of the things I had been exposed to in IIT/Kanpur. I would be selling myself seriously short if I went with this job offer, it seemed.

At home later, Pappaji engaged me on my other concerns. He told me that while it was sweet and thoughtful that I felt concerned about their well-being in their retirement years, it would be a huge mistake to let those feelings interfere with growth opportunities available to me. He said that the world was shrinking very quickly, travel and communications were getting much easier, and the future lay in embracing the new and emerging technologies. Even the Indian economy would move away from its current infrastructure oriented industrial focus, so it was vital to go abroad and learn the new things.

He further argued that my focus should be on building a great career for myself. I was at an age and at a point in my life where I should be taking calculated risks and plunging forward. I should travel, see, learn, and experience things, because therein lay some real education as well.

I should not be making compromises about silly things so early in my work career. A life lacking in serious effort, ambition, or tough goals, was a life not well lived. And a life of regrets was a life just not worth living.

So, it came to pass that I decided to go the USA to pursue graduate studies.

IIT/Kanpur Freshman - 1966

Party at Kiritbhai's House - 1968

Moti as a Puppy
With Pappaji –
Late 1967

Moti in Nikunj, Maninagar - 1976

Pappaji, Pankaj, & Munikaka - 1975

Ajay, now a Doctor, in Dwarka. Just before leaving for Ireland. 1968

My Batch Mates – After a tour of India

A GRADUATE STUDENT

Going to America

I sprinted at full tilt through the Ahmedabad airport. I thought I was a bit late, but I simply could not afford to miss this flight to Delhi on this strange morning. From Delhi, I was to connect to a flight to Kanpur, and then next day, fly to Bombay. It was all a crazy combination of weird circumstances.

"Sir, here is my ticket. Can you please check me in?" I asked at the counter with a tone of desperation in my voice.

The man at the counter was busy with some totally irrelevant stuff (in my opinion) and could not give a damn about me.

Eventually, in his own sweet time, he turned around, looked at me with disdain on his face, and said, "Yes?" I was just incredulous.

"Sir, is this not the Indian Airlines flight IC327 to Delhi? I have a ticket for it and I would like to check in."

The sign on the slate board above the counter read, "Delhi. IC 327." There was an aircraft on the tarmac just outside the dinky little terminal. It seemed that I was on time and there should be no problems. There was indeed a flight going to Delhi quite soon.

The man looked at my ticket, and without any explanation at all, said, "No, I cannot check you in for this flight."

"Why not?" I asked in a state of great irritation and incredible frustration.

"It is not your flight," he said simply. I just could not believe it and felt anger welling up within me.

"Wait, what?" I asked. "Is that airplane not about to depart for Delhi? Is it not Indian Airlines flight IC 327? Your sign at this counter says so. Then, why can I not be on it? I have a valid ticket right here?"

The man finally smiled with a grin of smug satisfaction. He said to me, "Yes, sir. You are quite correct. This is Indian Airlines flight IC327 for Delhi. And, yes, it will be leaving soon."

"Well then, why can I not be on it?"

"You see, sir, it is a full flight. And this flight, IC 327, is yesterday's flight. This airplane will go to Delhi and return later today. After it does that, the IC

327 flight for today will leave. And that is the flight you are booked on. I am sorry but we have had some problems lately. But, sir, why worry? You should just relax in the café. Enjoy some samosas and tea for a few hours. It will not be a problem I can assure you."

I felt like strangling the little shit! But there was nothing I could do about it. That was just the way things were in India at the time and you had to learn to just suck it up and deal with it.

I was used to travelling by trains. Flights were something totally foreign to me. This trip had become necessary totally out of the blue. I was due to appear at the US Consulate in Bombay for my student visa call and interview. A few days prior to it, I was informed that a key document was needed to complete my visa application. It had to be an original and issued by IIT/Kanpur. There was simply no way that I could achieve it by post. So, Pappaji told me to fly to Kanpur, get the document, and go straight to Bombay. He insisted that I should not miss my visa appointment. Any problems with a visa would create a domino effect for so many other things and it would all turn out to be way too expensive in the end. So, it was critical that I make my visa appointment in Bombay in full compliance of all the requirements.

Well, I achieved it! I got the Student Visa to go to the USA in Bombay! Hip, hip, hooray! It was quite an accomplishment given all the landmines along the way. However, there were still other problems to be faced.

Pappaji engaged me in an honest and forthright conversation about finances. This had never happened between us ever in my entire life. We had never spoken about money. It seemed that whatever money I needed, for whatever reason, it would just magically appear! I had no concept of the planning and sacrifices that lay behind all that. In retrospect, I think I was amazingly naïve and quite stupid about it all.

Pappaji told me quite honestly about the funds that he had available. Further, he said that I could have my 1/3rd share of them, in the context of his 3 sons, either now or as an inheritance after he had passed on. Beyond that, he could not offer me any financial support in the USA. Even with a Fellowship given to me at SUNY, Stony Brook, it was clear that I did not have the means to fully fund my education in the USA. I would have to find some way out on my own.

What made matters even harder was that Pappaji was strictly "Gandhian" in his thinking and principles. He would never do anything against the law, regardless of what others did. He had worked his entire life in the cement industry which was rolling in "black money". He could have become a very wealthy man if he had chosen to play in that world. He could have converted the black money into US dollars or UK Pounds via all sorts of "hawala" transactions, which he could have done with ease, given his connections in Britain. But he adamantly refused to do any of that.

He did not even use his influence to get Ajay admitted into Medical School at MS University in Baroda. He insisted on merit, while many of Ajay's classmates got in because they were well connected and used the proverbial "back door."

Many of my USA expenses were spread over time, so they offered some hope of being dealt with gradually. But there was one big expense which was immediate. It was the cost of my passage to the USA. It was common by then to fly instead of sailing on a ship, but the costs were considerable and had to be paid fully up front. I was trying to figure this problem out, when I received a letter.

The letter was from Lilyben Pandya, and it was addressed to me, and not my father. Lilyben was the mother of Kalyanibhabhi, Kiritbhai's wife. Lilyben had married Anant Pandya, a Nagar Brahmin man, who was very bright and a Partner of the celebrated Patel Engineering Co. This company had undertaken remarkable infrastructure projects in India and was based in Bombay.

Sadly, Anantbhai passed away at an early age, and Lilyben took over the family responsibilities. She was an amazing lady. She was educated, well travelled, cultured, refined, and classy. She educated her children abroad and groomed them to achieve great things. She was very active in the political and business circles of Bombay. I had met her a few times when she had come to visit Kalyanibhabhi in Kanpur. She was a person that left you totally captivated. I was immensely fond of her, because she could talk to anybody, about anything, and at any level. Her lifestyle was also quite British and that suited me fine because of how I had been raised. But this letter from her contained an amazing surprise.

The letter from Lilyben indicated that the Pandya Memorial Trust, which was set up in the memory of her late husband, gave grants to deserving students for further studies annually. If I was interested in such a grant, I should apply. Enclosed was also an application form. At the time, I had no idea that Lilyben was the Administrator of the Trust and decided all the grants personally. I showed it to my father and asked what I should do.

Pappaji smiled and said, "If you apply, I think there is a good chance that you may get a grant." Well, I did, and I got a grant! It helped with the cost for my air ticket to the USA. At the time, I just did not understand the nature of family connections and relations.

In effect, Lilyben gave me the grant to help me out financially. How she became aware of my problems, I never found out. But she was my White Knight at a crucial hour. I was overwhelmed by her generosity. I recall telling Pappaji that "One day, I shall reciprocate. And I will do so in a manner which is meaningful to Lilyben and the memory of Anantbhai." I did just that, but that is another story.

The summer of 1971 went by quickly and August arrived. It was time for me to leave for the USA. We drove over from Port Okha to Ahmedabad. The whole extended family gathered to say goodbyes. I was supposed to fly from Ahmedabad to Delhi on the morning flight.

Everybody went with me to the airport. In those days, it was indeed a big deal for somebody to be leaving for the USA. The day before, there were pujas done, flower garlands placed, visits to Mahadev temple in Maninagar, etc. But, alas, there was no flight to Delhi that morning! As usual, Indian Airlines had some sort of a screw up and the flight was indefinitely delayed. We all returned home with sad and deflated emotions. I was also getting worried.

Finally, in the evening, the delayed flight left and I was on my way. In Delhi, I was set up for the night at the swanky Ashoka Hotel, courtesy of BOAC airlines. Pappaji was not sure about my handling all this properly and dispatched Pankaj, my cousin, to see me off at Delhi.

Everything worked out fine, and the next morning in Delhi, I roared off from the Palam Airport on a jet airplane to a new life of adventure and discovery.

The Famous "Tea Bag Story"

The BOAC Viscount-10 jetliner thundered down the runway at Palam Airport in Delhi and shortly we were airborne. I was simply ecstatic! It was August, 1971.

Finally, after all the trials and tribulations, I was actually off and on my way to the USA! It was a major accomplishment for me and I was savoring it immensely. From the teeming sweaty millions in India, I had found a way out and was now jetting my way towards the Promised Land, the modern El Dorado. It was the USA, a land of freedom and gold, milk and honey, everything in plenty, no filth, and beauty everywhere. A place so wonderful, that even little babies did not cry, because they were always so happy. Wow, I was actually going there!

With me was my IIT/Kanpur roommate, Viney Pal Aneja. He was going to the USA as well and we had decided to travel together. We had designed a crazy itinerary, by working with a travel agent, who knew how to "game" the airline reservations system very well. Its key principle was "cover and see the most, while paying the least".

In those days, BOAC was advertising its flights on many billboards in all the major cities in India. I still remember the BOAC slogan, "Come, and experience our VC-10derness!" which was always slapped over a picture of a gorgeous young British girl. So naturally, we left on a BOAC flight from Delhi, headed to Tehran in Iran. From there, we were to go to Beirut in Lebanon; then to Frankfurt, Germany; and then on to London. We were deliberately booked on multiple airlines, and had free nightly stops with hotel bookings and airport transfers everywhere, but in London we were to break our journey for a few days.

My uncle, Atisukhkaka, was posted there and he had a nice house for a home. So, we planned to stay with him for a few days, and then fly onwards to New York on Air India, in its new and highly celebrated Boeing 747 Maharaja's "Magic Carpet" service!

In Teheran, we took in the Shah's Crown Jewels & the famous Peacock Throne, while enjoying the charms of the Intercontinental Hotel. In Beirut, we toured its famous caves and experienced the wonderful nightclubs. In Frankfurt, the German beer halls and sights were magnificent.

London was just amazing. We went to see the play *Oh, Calcutta!* because we had heard that in many scenes the entire cast, men and women, was totally naked on stage! We simply had to see this! Sharvari, Atisukhkaka's daughter and my cousin, took us to see the renowned Oxford and Cambridge with her siblings. It was all so grand. In a compressed span of time, we experienced and saw a lot on a poor boys' budget. But this BOAC flight out of Delhi was at the very beginning of all this.

As we climbed to cruising altitude, I noticed many things. The airliner was beautifully appointed in classic elegance. Everybody around us was white, dressed very well, and smelled wonderfully. The lovely fragrances were everywhere. This was very noticeable for me, because I was used to the smell of sweat or body odor all around me in India. People seemed to speak slowly and softly, almost in whispers. This was another world and I got lost in it for quite a while. Suddenly, I was yanked out of my reverie by a stunningly gorgeous young lady, who smiled at me, and leaned down towards me.

She said, in impeccable British English, "Would you like some coffee, or perhaps tea?"

I was a bit flustered by her beauty and radiant smile, but since I was used to drinking tea in India, I replied, "Yes. Some tea, please. Thank you." She nodded and floated away.

In a bit, she returned, and set a full tray down on my dropdown table. I looked at it in wonder.

In the tray was a cup of steaming hot water, a tea bag, a couple of packets of sugar, and a small sealed thimble of milk. I studied all this and wondered, "What is all this? I asked for tea, but I have a tray with all this stuff on it instead!"

I mean one does not just drink tea! Oh, my gosh, that would be sacrilegious! It is a ritual, to be performed with proper ceremony. Making tea is a sublime experience and one must be very particular in all its aspects. If spices are involved, one must be even more careful. A great cup of tea is like experiencing God!

When Pappaji had tea, it was a series of actions undertaken with great precision. He would warm the tea pot first by swishing hot water around in it. He would drain the pot and then throw his carefully selected tea leaves in it. He would add boiling hot water to it and cover it up with a "tea cozy". Then he would let it sit for 5 mts to cook.

Then he would pour a nice cup through a strainer, add warm milk to it, and just a little sugar. He would stir it all up, lift up the cup, and then smell the aroma. Oh, one must smell the aroma of a great cup of tea! Otherwise it would be an insult to the tea gardens where it was grown with loving care. And that first sip, it just changed your perspective on the entire day! You see, a great cup of tea is the very elixir of life. One simply cannot just drink any old cup of tea. Well, actually my mother did drink tea very differently, but that is not relevant here, and it is yet another story.

Then I caught myself. I thought that maybe things are different here, because we are on an airplane. Now, don't exhibit your ignorance, and just do what is normal. You have seen Pappaji have such tea a million times. So, be careful, but don't worry.

With confidence, I ripped open the tea bag and dropped the tea leaves into the cup of hot water. I added the milk from the thimble and looked for a strainer, but there was none in the tray. So, I figured that perhaps it was a minor oversight. I pushed the call button and the stewardess showed up promptly.

I said, "I am sorry, Miss, but it seems that I am missing a strainer for my tea in this tray." Her blue eyes widened and a look of total surprise covered her face.

She said, "Oh, dear, no. No! You see, this tea bag is a "flow through" tea bag. You do not need to tear it open, as it were. Just put it in the hot water, pump it up and down, and Voila! you have tea! There is no need for a strainer!"

Then she said, "Oh, well, let me just get you a fresh tray. That way we can get rid of all this and start off afresh." I accepted sheepishly.

But my mind started racing in all directions. The very idea of a tea bag! And a flow through one at that! How brilliant! Now, that is smart, really smart. It solves many a problem and avoids many a mess so easily. Why did we Indians not think of it? We grow the stuff! Why did we not think of packaging it in such a useful manner? We are so stupid sometimes. These Brits are thinkers, practical, and smart. Heck, no wonder we got conquered! And just look at the way things are packaged for an airplane!

If Indians had invented airplanes, would we have thought of all this? I really wonder. But our planes probably would not be allowed to take off until the stars were properly aligned, or some religious ritual had been performed with various Gods/Goddesses invoked. In the galley, somebody surely would try to fry samosas and stink up the entire bloody cabin! Sad, so sad… Again, I was snapped out of my runaway thoughts.

"Here we are! I have brought a fresh tray for you. Enjoy!" she said, smiled, and left.

Now, I approached this formidable tray with all my faculties and focus. I took the tea bag out of its jacket, put it into the cup of hot water, and pumped it up and down with the attached little string. I watched in total wonder as the tea formed in the cup! Then I added the milk from the thimble, put the sugar packets in and stirred it all up in the cup. Shortly, I tasted the tea. It was not sweet at all. And then this gooey mess floated to the top of the cup! I was astonished and thought to myself, "What now?" Oh, yes, it was quite obvious to my highly trained IIT engineering mind. The problem lay right before me! It was these sugar packets. They were clearly defective. So, again I pushed the call button and Lady Gorgeous showed up in barely a minute.

I smiled sweetly and said, "I am so sorry to bother you again, miss. But in this lovely tray, I think there is a slight problem. You see, I think I have here some defective sugar packets. It must be some sort of a manufacturing mistake. They do not flow through at all."

Her eyes bulged out in disbelief, and she could barely suppress her laugh! She said, "Oh, my goodness! No, no, you see, these sugar packets are not flow through. You have to tear them open!"

I looked at the tray in pure horror and my keen engineering mind could barely whisper, "What? I mean, really, Whaaat?!"

She gave me a radiant smile and said, "Oh, no worries. We shall have an encore. I will replace the tray for you immediately."

She went off to the rear galley with my tray again. I heard a male voice say softly to her, "Again? Goodness gracious, it will be a long flight today."

She replied to it, "That is quite alright. He is so polite, sweetly innocent, and quite cute, actually."

The male voice went, "Yea, I knew you would say that. But they would be much happier flying Pan Am, don't you think?"

Epilogue

I told this story for the first time in 1974 at an office party, one evening after work, in Detroit. The conversation had somehow drifted to talking about situations where everybody had embarrassed themselves in some way. The response to it was explosive laughter. Then it spread like wild fire.

Over the years, all sorts of folks, including my bosses, colleagues, and friends, would come up to me at various events and ask me, "Vijay, tell us that tea bag story!" They had heard about it somewhere. I would oblige and receive the same amazing response to it.

The crowning moment perhaps came when I was asked to tell it at a formal "black tie" function in Hong Kong, in 1997. It was just after its handover by

Britain to China. Around me was a crowd of European people, including lots of Brits, French, Swiss, and the "Taipan". (*He was a Scotsman, and head of the celebrated Jardine Matheson Group, where I worked on an Ex-Pat assignment.*) People were in hysterics upon hearing it! I became well known all over the Jardine Group quickly in some measure because of it.

It had never occurred to me that this little episode from my life would have such long social legs. I never fully understood the reasons behind its wide and universal appeal. Maybe it was because I was not ashamed of the faux pas I had made, or that I was quite comfortable, laughing along with others, at my own shortcomings.

Perhaps it was poignant, because of its innocent simplicity.

Adrift & The MBA Hustle

The Stony Brook Year – 1971/72

It was so very strange. I was enrolled in the Master's program in Information Sciences at the State University of New York, Stony Brook, NY in August, 1971. It was a prestigious program and I had even been granted a Fellowship in it. It had enabled me to come to the USA. I had some IIT/Kanpur friends there as well. My dear friend, Bijendra Nath Jain, who helped me so much, comes to mind. He was a year senior to me at IIT/Kanpur, just brilliant, and had a simply amazing career in his life as a scientist and an educator. But at the time, we were all just poor students, dealing with life as best as we could.

The differences amongst us began to show up quickly. Most of my fellow Indian students were incredibly bookish and would do nothing more than study their brains out every day. We all needed an American driver's license to deal with the basic aspects of life. But most of my friends did not know how to drive! So, we tried to learn on somebody's old beaten up car and then all of us went for a driver's license test in Riverside, NY. Everybody failed it, but I passed! So, for a while I became the designated driver for many an errand for all of us.

However, who could forget the great Darshan Singh? This guy was a piece of work. I have no idea how he got admitted to a US University for graduate studies. He was warm and sweet, but there was nothing normal about him at all. I will never forget the day that I met him.

"Ji, tusi change ho ji?" he asked. *("Ji, are you in good spirits?)* I replied, "Ji, yes."

"Aaj te saddi date hai, ji! Chinan nu picture dikhani hai!" he volunteered. *(Today, I have a date! I am taking a Chinese girl to see a movie!)*

I was impressed that he had managed to prevail upon a lovely Chinese girl to accompany him to the movies! Alas, it all turned into a total disaster. Poor Darshan! He knew nothing about the movie ratings system in the USA. He took this Chinese girl to see an "X" rated movie, which turned out to be a porno film, and she totally freaked out. She bolted from the theatre and Darshan was left there, shocked and completely bewildered! He had never seen such a film in his life either! This event became the stuff of local legend.

Throughout this academic year, I had serious economic issues to contend with. I needed additional funds in US dollars to cover the shortfall in living expenses and tuition costs. So, I started doing part time jobs of any kind that

I could find in and around the campus. I was determined to earn my way out of my money problems. In various combinations, I worked as a janitor, cleaning toilets and mopping floors; a grocery clerk, packing meat (including beef); and as a traffic cop for campus security. Every dollar earned mattered to me greatly. It was hard to do all this at strange hours of the day or night, but I pursued it with focused determination. This was on top of carrying a full load of graduate level classes!

Then came the qualifying exams for my M.S. degree and potential pursuit of a Ph. D. after that. I took the exams and did well. I passed my M.S. degree and qualified for the doctoral program as well. My advisor, Dr. Dollard, was thrilled with my performance and encouraged me to study further. But sadly, my heart was not in it. I did not enjoy academic work of highly theoretical nature. I was people oriented, extroverted in personality, and liked active interactions. Working in labs, or doing research, or even teaching others things that I had learnt via my studies, just did not excite me. Much to Dr. Dollard's disappointment, I declined to pursue a doctoral program. But then, what would I do next?

Perhaps it was due to my participation in the campus TV network and all the theatrical plays at IIT/Kanpur, I was attracted more towards learning about broadcast television. This industry held an interesting mix of engineering technologies and the performing arts. I arranged to meet people at the CBS Network in New York City. There were other networks based there as well, such as ABC, NBC and PBS. But CBS granted me interviews with key network producers and managers. In these meetings, I learned that any work option for me would be impossible without membership in the unions involved. This was the classic "chicken or egg situation". You needed a job to become a Union member and you had to have a Union membership card to get a job offer!

However, there was one exception in all this. If you had a Master's degree in "TV & Radio" from a USA University, the unions were required to give you a membership card by their laws. Well, this meant that I would have to enroll in yet another M.S. program and graduate from it to go anywhere with it. At the time, there was a wonderful program for this available at Michigan State University, East Lansing, Michigan. It was offered by their School of Communication Arts and it was considered quite prestigious. I decided to give it a shot and applied for admission.

To my amazement, Dr. Colby Lewis, Head of the Department of TV & Radio, replied to me quickly and asked me to come to East Lansing for interviews. It appeared that they were quite interested in enrolling foreign students into their program. I took the Greyhound bus from NY City overnight to East Lansing, Michigan. In this fateful trip, I secured not only admission to their program, but also a summer job at the WKAR-TV station, a PBS Network affiliate, on the school campus!

My electrical engineering and computer science backgrounds were deemed valuable for the new broadcast studios they were building and the installation of a new TV signal transmission system for broadcasting their local and network programs in color! I was thrilled by achieving this fateful break!

It made nobody happy. Both my brothers, Kashyap and Ajay, thought poorly of this option. They said, "Gosh, you have an MS degree already. Why don't you just get a job with it? Surely, somebody will hire you!" After many a discussion, they eventually decided to support my desires.

However, there were other factors at play as well. Kashyap had decided to return to India and further his career back home. Ajay had accepted a residency appointment for a year in Halifax, Nova Scotia, in Canada. It seemed that the summer of 1972 would see all of us moving around to various different places.

Indeed, it would turn out to be one of the most harrowing years of my life. It would be a year of promise, hardship, disappointment and disillusionment in sequence. But in the spring of 1972, I was optimistic and did not expect any of these things to happen.

The Summer of 1972

In June, Ajay wrapped up his residency year in NY City and I graduated with my MS degree from SUNY, Stony Brook. We packed up and drove in Ajay's car to Buffalo, in upstate New York and stayed with Atulbhai, one of our cousins, who was working there. Kashyap and Kalibhabhi met us there. They were driving from Denver to the East Coast. They had planned a driving holiday and were to leave on a ship from NY City for Europe and then onwards to India. Further, Kashyap had decided to give me his Chevrolet Malibu car for my use. It was a few years old, had some good mileage on it, but could be of great use to me in Michigan.

We had a lovely tour of the East Coast, saw them off on their ocean liner at the pier on the Hudson River in New York and then drove up to Buffalo in Kashyap's car. There Ajay and I parted company. He drove northeast to

Halifax in his Volvo and I drove west to East Lansing in the Malibu. Ajay had a clear sense about where he was going, but I was headed into the unknown.

After a lovely year of frequent meetings in NY City, we did not know when we would see each other next and in what circumstances. Ajay was concerned for me as always. He filled up the tank in my car with gas and gave me pocket money as well!

There is an old saying, "In life, 90% of it is just showing up." It proved to be so true in my case. I joined WKAR-TV for my summer job. Initially, it was filled with major real-world engineering challenges. Working as a member of the station engineering team, I was involved deeply in the installation of studio equipment, a new microwave link and controllers to our remote transmission tower. I worked on wiring and assembly of a variety of consoles, mixers, video recorders, and the high-power signal transmission equipment itself.

The Chief Engineer, Mr. Jorgensen, was a man of vast experience and a good teacher. He liked me because I would read up all the technical manuals quickly and execute the required tasks with efficiency. My ability to learn things quickly became something of huge value to the whole team. Also, since I had nothing better to do, I was willing to work long hours, double shifts, etc. without any complaints.

As the engineering work slowed down, the key station managers started using me for actual programming and "show" production tasks. I took on duties of a cameraman, stringer, master broadcast controller, audio recorder and mixer, lighting manager, and even production manager and director for our local shows and programs. In 3 short months, I covered a lot of ground and acquired priceless experience. But outside of work, it was a hard and dangerous summer for me.

Housing was my very first challenge. Since I would not be enrolled in MSU till the Fall Quarter started at the end of September, I was not eligible for student housing until then. Well then, where would I live? I found a cheap boarding house in Lansing, from some classified newspaper ads, and in sheer desperation grabbed the first available room.

It was an atrocious choice, but I did not know any better. This was just an awful place in a very dangerous area of Lansing. There were drug pushers, addicts, homeless people, pimps and prostitutes everywhere. It was a mixed neighborhood, of mainly black people, and quite unsafe at night. The house had a lot of ex-convicts living there. Most of them were on furlough from local prisons. By the time I became aware of all this, the landlord had taken my money and I was stuck in this small sparsely furnished room with a shared common bathroom down the hallway.

My biggest concern was that my Malibu car would be either vandalized or stolen by somebody. The car was my lifeline and I used to hide it in the alley behind the house and keep an eye on it at night.

Then came this long 4-day long holiday weekend. The TV station, except for broadcast activities, was shut down during it. Furthermore, I found myself without any cash in my wallet. Banks were all closed and I knew nobody in town that I could turn to for any help. So, I lived for 4 days on instant coffee and tea bags. It is almost funny to realize that I faced and endured starvation, for the first time in my life, in America!

Finally, the MSU Registration Day arrived. I enrolled and got my graduate student dorm room at the Owen Hall on campus. It also had a cafeteria so I could finally get some hot food on a meal plan. It was a massive relief to be back at last in surroundings that I was familiar with and where I had a sense of personal security. My days of living in the underbelly of an area of economic strife had come to an end.

The fall quarter commenced. It had barely been two weeks of classes when I realized that I had made the biggest mistake of my life! This MS program in TV & Radio was just pathetic! The courses were trivial and seemed to be aimed at high school level students. I was massively disappointed and completely disillusioned by what I saw and heard. I was also very angry with myself and had nobody else to blame for my predicament. Once again, in a state of near depression, I pondered about what I should do.

At dinner that evening, my roommate Walter Tung, who was from Singapore, sat next to me and we started to chat about our classes. He was having a blast in the MBA program and just loving all of his subjects! I poured my heart out to him about my difficulties.

Then, he suddenly said, "Vijay, forget this TV & Radio stuff. Why don't you switch to the School of Business and do an MBA instead? I think you are perfectly suited for it. You will love it and there will be serious career options at the end of it for you."

"Really?" I asked wide-eyed. This thought had not occurred to me. "But would they let me switch?"

Walter continued, "Look, you are already admitted to the MSU Graduate School. You now simply want to move to the School of Business, from the School of Communication Arts. Go see Dean Bryant tomorrow. He is a great man and Dean of the School of Business. I am sure he will show you the way to do it." My mood shifted dramatically immediately.

I went and met Dean Bryant the very next day. He reviewed my academic background and summer work thoughtfully. After a while, he said, "I can grant you admission to the MBA program, but only conditionally for now. You must take the required ATGSB entrance test (the current GMAT) for the MBA program & also take the courses I specify for you in the upcoming winter quarter. Based on your performance, we can then consider formalizing your admission. Agreed?"

"Yes, sir." I replied enthusiastically.

Dean Bryant smiled broadly and said, "Well then, welcome to the School of Business!" I was elated and took Walter out for a few beers at the Lizards Bar later that evening.

For the winter quarter, Dean Bryant assigned me courses in Business Law, Finance, and Accounting, subjects that I knew absolutely nothing about. The MBA program followed the "Case Based" studying method developed at the Harvard School of Business. This also was totally new for me.

These courses were tough indeed, but were full of real learnings as well. I did well in them and the ATGSB test. By spring quarter, 1973, my admission to the Eli Broad School of Business at MSU, was formally confirmed.

Dean Bryant had helped rescue me and redirected my career forever.

The Hustle

But now I had an even bigger problem to solve. How was I going to pay for my MBA program? To make things worse, it was a 2-year program, not 1-year like the other one. Unlike engineering programs, where one could try for a "teaching" or "research" assistantship, there were no such options in the School of Business. What little was available, was highly restricted at MSU.

So, where would I find the funds to pay for this program? I could not count on any support from India. I had no access to any real benefactor locally. Any kind of a student loan was out of the question for a "foreign student". I was nearly out of aces.

So, I gave this some really serious thought. My summer job would give me enough funds to pay for the fall quarter. I was still working at least 20 hours/week at WKAR-TV and expected to continue throughout the academic year. These earnings would pay for the winter quarter. But, what about the spring quarter? I had no idea about how I would fund it. Then, I would have to look for a really good job in the summer of 1973, and figure out things from there. The future for me quickly disappeared into the dense fog of uncertainty and the unknown.

I decided to focus on what I knew and could control, and not spend my time worrying about the future. It was a wise choice, but then the spring quarter came along. In sheer desperation, I called Ajay in Canada to ask him if he had any ideas. Ajay listened to me patiently, and then said, "Well, I can give you the funds from my savings for the spring quarter. I do not have much saved on a resident's pay, but what I do have, you can use. Beyond that, I am afraid I do not have anything else to offer you." So, Ajay became my savior for the moment.

As the spring quarter was winding down, I started looking for a well-paying summer job. On an Ad Board, I saw this offer for a job at the government of Michigan in Lansing. It required engineering skills. So, I applied immediately and got selected! It paid more than double per hour than what I was making at WKAR-TV. It was full time and for the entire 3 months of the summer! Heck, this was a divine lifeline clear out of the blue.

Then, I heard that a certain Dr. Able from the Department of Transportation in the School of Business was looking for somebody to help with statistics work for his Ph.D. students. I followed this up immediately. Dr. Able was young, very bright, and regarded as a bit of a whiz kid at the School of Business. He wanted someone to teach statistics to his Ph.D. students and to support them in their analytical research. They were to publish a paper by December in a prestigious journal.

"Can you handle these tasks? Dr. Able asked in the interview.

"Yes, sir, absolutely I can. I have spent a lot of time on these subjects at Stony Brook." I replied.

"Well, Vijay, I would really appreciate it if you can help us out here. We are in a jam. Unfortunately, the research funds are so tight that I am not in a position to pay you for your true worth." He continued.

He said he could sadly pay me only what was more than double my summer job rate! I could not believe my ears! But I kept my cool and poker face.

"Yes, Dr. Able, I understand." I responded. "But I feel such a sense of gratitude towards Dean Bryant and the School of Business in general, that I think I should do everything in my power to help you in any way that I can. I will accept whatever you are able to pay me. But could we just structure it a bit differently?"

"Sure. What do we need to do?" he asked, a little confused.

"Sir, could we classify this as even a ¼ time Assistantship? If you could, it would be of great help to me."

"How so?" he asked.

"Well, sir, any form of an "assistantship", whether teaching or research, would qualify me for "In State" tuition rates. This would save me a lot of money in tuition costs. Also, it does not hurt your grant budget." I offered.

"Absolutely, Vijay. Consider it done. I will speak with Dean Bryant immediately."

I held my mouth and posture till I reached Owen Hall. Then I screamed, "Yeeeehaah!"

Everybody thought that I had gone mad. I had, but not for the reasons that they thought.

So, now I was "in the money", so to speak, for a while. I banked serious cash during the summer of 1973. In the fall, I had the Assistantship. But there were still 2 more quarters to go. They needed serious "Out of State" tuition funding as well and I had nothing to fall back on.

It was December of 1973, a little after the Thanksgiving Holiday. I was sitting in the Owen Hall cafeteria when a colleague, Chuck Peters, decided to sit with me. He was very happy that day, because he had just graduated with his MBA! He was off to a lovely job soon and was happy as a clam!

I congratulated him on his success and wished him well. Then he asked me, "Vijay, how much more do you have to go?"

"Chuck, I don't know." I replied. "I am seriously short of funds and I am not sure that I can complete my MBA."

"What? Are you serious?" he asked in total surprise." Now, come on, you can figure something out!"

We chatted for a while. I shared my background with Chuck and all that I had done in 1973. I mentioned Dr. Able and statistics.

"What? You know Stats?" Chuck was elated. "Vijay, come with me. You need to meet Dr. Clarke De Haven. I have worked for him and he is looking for my replacement. I think you are it!"

Chuck set up a meeting with him. I had no idea who he was or what he did. But this man turned out to be another angel, under whose blessings and teachings, my life changed forever yet again.

A Savior – Dr. Clarke De Haven

C huck ushered me in and introduced me to Dr. Clarke De Haven. He was the head of the prestigious Nursing Home Administrator's Program offered by the MSU School of Business. This program educated these administrators, certified them, and generally promoted the causes of this key service industry. It was known and highly respected nationally.

"Thank you, Chuck. My goodness, Vijay, you have quite a CV!" Clarke exclaimed. He asked me a few questions and then said, "Vijay, you do know that this is just a formality. We have a tradition here. Every departing student is expected to bring in his replacement. So, welcome aboard!"

I was simply stunned by this turn of events. The job was a ½ time Assistantship with In-State tuition! I was to conduct training classes in Kalamazoo and Detroit on Saturdays. I would be given an MSU fleet car for these trips. I was expected to support all the session teachers in various administrative duties. When my exams came up, I was given free time to focus on them and not bother with the job. In an angelic way, I discovered that the rest of my MBA program was suddenly paid for!

With Clarke and his wife, Daisy, my relationship became almost that of a family member. They were incredibly sweet and supported me in everything. I was treated almost like a son that they never had.

One day, Clarke summoned me to his office.

"Vijay, we have a serious problem. Can you think of a way out?" Clarke asked looking very worried.

It seemed that the Department was engaged in conducting its annual survey of Nursing Home Administrators. It was an extensive survey. All the returned sets of survey forms were piled in heaps of boxes in a room. They were supposed to be analyzed and their findings reported at a prestigious conference in a couple of months. Every year, this exercise had been done manually. It was error prone and so the results were always a bit suspect. Also, it was an expensive and a highly time-consuming undertaking.

I looked at the problem and told Clarke, "Why don't you automate this whole process?"

"Automate? How? And where?" Clarke asked.

So, I said to him, "We could do this in a few simple steps. 1) Convert the data from these survey forms into computer readable punch cards at a data entry shop; 2) Read these cards and convert their data into an electronic data file, which can be processed on a mainframe computer; and 3) Use a statistical analysis software package to analyze the data, in a manner of your liking, and generate reports; 4) Use these reports to publish your results."

"Gosh, that sounds wonderful!" he said. "But nobody here knows how to do any of that!"

"Not quite. I do." I said simply.

Clarke gave me a free hand. I went about the project in earnest. I got the data converted and used the SPSS software package at the MSU Computer Center to analyze the data. It was all done in 10 days. When I presented the initial reports, everybody was just speechless! The reports generated more questions, and I could present answers to them on a nearly daily basis. The survey that year was a resounding success. And now we had a capability to do this easily every year after that as a bonus.

That year, Dr. De Haven was placed in administrative charge of a major conference hosted by the Department of Transportation in the School of Business. This conference was of a major scale and highly regarded, because the Department of Transportation was nationally known for advanced study of Logistics Networks, a new and emerging field.

"Containerization" was the major theme of the conference and all the key professors from the School of Business were going to teach various sessions to all the attending CEO's of major national companies. Well known names like Dr. Mossman, Dr. Bowersox, Dr. Able, Dr. Zwarenstein, Dr. Lewis, and other senior faculty members were on the program.

Clarke unleashed me on various organizational tasks. I worked closely with all the professors and Dean Bryant on session planning, materials development, housing, formal dinner at the Faculty Club, and local transportation for all the attendees. It was a lot of work, but I got a serious exposure to how such events were conducted in the real world, and to deal with all the complexities involved. As a consequence, I became well known to the entire faculty of the School of Business. This would have far reaching effects on my career later on, but at the time I was not aware of it.

One day somebody made a comment about me. "Who is this kid, Vijay?" a question was asked.

"He seems to be everywhere. He moves really fast and it is just remarkable how well our preparations have come along for the conference. Where did he come from? How did we get him here?"

Dean Bryant smiled and replied, "I may have had something to do with it!" He laughed when he told me this little story.

The conference was a huge success and the School of Business obtained a lot of "funding grants" from the corporate CEO's that attended it. I felt a sense of satisfaction that I had done something in return for the School of Business that had done so much for me.

My last final exam was on a Friday afternoon in mid-June, 1974. I said my goodbyes and drove out of East Lansing for Detroit on Saturday. I was to start my job at Advance Mortgage Corporation, a Citicorp company, on Monday morning. I could not stay for my graduation ceremonies or the various parties, because my financial condition required me to start work immediately.

On Sunday, I moved into an unfurnished apartment in Southfield near the office. My possessions comprised of a suitcase and a few boxes of my textbooks and important papers. The apartment was empty and I slept on the rug that first night on some sheets and a pillow that I had swiped from my dorm room. On my first day on the job, I had to ask for an advance against my pay so that I could buy some decent work clothes for myself!

But all these things aside, it was a fact that I had managed to complete my MBA. I had some debt to repay to Ajay and also pay Kashyap for his car, but 90% of all the costs for the 2-year program were funded by me along the way. Facing incredible risks, against formidable odds, and with many a strike against me, I had managed to survive, and achieve a successful start for my working career.

In many ways, in the past 3 years, I had lived the "American Dream". A precious dream, full of possibilities and opportunities, but without guarantees of any kind from anybody. Also, I had lived it on my terms.

It was an education all by itself.

Looking for a Job

I felt the icy snow melt and get into my rubber galoshes. It was around 7pm on a January evening, near the Placement Office building at the Michigan State University, East Lansing. It was very windy. I was bone cold and shivering. Was my information wrong? The recruiters from all these great USA corporations were to come out from the building around now. Where were they? I had been waiting for over an hour outside in the freezing cold. For me, it was a matter of "life or death" that I connected with at least some of them.

In 1974, foreign students at MSU were not eligible to apply for jobs with US companies. The thinking was that you had come to study, had now finished your studies, and were to shortly go home. So, the Placement Office was not meant for you. But, if you could get around the Placement Office, there was one exception available! If you could somehow secure a "job" for a period of "training" in your academic field, you could be granted a "training visa" for up to 1.5 years in 6-month increments.

Further, if you performed well, and did not displace a US citizen from a job, the company could sponsor you for the coveted "Green Card"! This GC, once obtained, would place you in the status of a "landed immigrant", and a world of opportunities was then opened up for you. Well, this American promise and the dream of a life of financial riches were at the heart of it all, but nobody told you about the pitfalls involved in realizing them. In reality, the risks were huge at the time. So big, that they could even cost you your life. Most folks in the US did not have a clue about these things. I know for a fact that many of my native-born American friends, who grew up in a comfortable and sheltered life, had no idea at all about any of this.

Among the friends I had made since arriving in the USA in 1971, this "Green Card" theme was a constant presence. Everybody seemed to want one. It was not from a burning desire to immigrate to the USA, or to escape from some form of persecution back home. It was pure economic opportunism on the part of most everyone. It was like, "Get the Green Card, make a bunch of money, and send a lot of it home to uplift the family back there. Then, marry a nice Indian girl who would be a wife, maid, cook, and cleaner for you. If she was skilled in something, well, she could be put to work as well! Bank the rest of the cash. Maybe return home after a while, but now so much richer!"

It was basic economic thinking born in a poor, under developed, and an over populated country that offered few opportunities. So, the key to this nirvana was to get the "Green Card" in any possible legal manner. Well, there was a quick way available also. The Vietnam war was going on and there was an active "Draft" system for new military recruits underway. However, if you joined the US Armed Forces voluntarily and put your life on the line in battle, you were given not just a Green Card, but a Citizenship automatically at the end of your tour of duty. Two of my friends liked this option much better and signed up.

After a 90-day boot camp, they got shipped off to Vietnam. In another 90 days, one of them returned in a body bag. The other one survived the war, became a US Citizen, and in 6 months committed suicide. So, getting a "Green Card" was something that demanded a severe price from you in many diverse ways. There were no guarantees of any kind along the way. As the expression went, "That's the deal, Lucille!"

Suddenly, the Placement Office building door opened. A middle-aged man stepped out and said, "Gosh, it is freezing cold!" to nobody in particular.

"Sir, please permit me. Let me help you with your coat, hat and muffler. Yes, it is quite windy and cold." I said.

"Why, thank you, young man. It has been a long day. I was hoping to leave much earlier today."

"Yes, sir, I know. I have been waiting here for you for a long time."

Then, I noticed his ID Badge, read the basic information, and smoothly said, "Mr. Hamilton, it is indeed a pleasure to meet you on this frigid evening. I know that you want to get out of this cold so I shall be brief. I have been waiting here for some time to give you my Curriculum Vitae (CV) because I believe that I could be of great value to your company, Advance Mortgage Corporation. Please contact me, if you agree."

"You have been waiting in this crazy cold weather for a long while, just to give me this envelope with your CV in it?" he asked in disbelief.

"Yes, sir. It is merely a reflection of my career interest in your company. I sense a great fit between us."

"Wow! Ya' know, I just spent a day talking with a bunch of kids graduating with an MBA. They all told me how great they were in many things. But you are the first one to actually ask me for a job! This is amazing! Let's get out of this cold. I will be in touch. Thank you."

Thus, unknown to me at the time, an endearing relationship began. The man I had met was John Hamilton (JH), EVP of Human Resources at Advance Mortgage Corporation in Detroit. AMC was a wholly owned subsidiary of Citicorp, New York. He handled personally all the MBA recruiting for the company. He was a highly skilled HR professional, rooted in mid-western values, and just charming. He called me up to Detroit for a day of interviews.

That day was followed by a handsome job offer. I just could not believe it! Then, he sort of took me under his wing and tutored me in things that I would otherwise have never known. Over time, he became almost a mentor to me as I made my first attempts at joining the real working world in the USA.

I had still not graduated from MSU with my MBA, when one day JH called me urgently from Detroit. "Vijay, you have to go to New York," he said. "We are having issues regarding assigning MBA recruits to various Citicorp companies this year. The Operating Group (OG) at Citibank wants to talk with you. I have strongly protested. I feel that you belong here with us and not in New York City. The OG is a very different world, not only by reputation, but also in reality. They are very picky, nearly insane, in their methods and selections. But, don't worry. Our job offer to you to join us after you complete your MBA is firm and unchanged."

I was shipped off to New York to interview for a new MBA recruit position at the OG at 111 Wall Street, New York City. At the time, the OG of Citibank was legendary in the banking industry. It was considered "Innovation Central"! They began in a novel way by treating the back office of a bank as a "paper factory". They employed manufacturing and industrial engineering techniques to bring about process efficiencies. Various electro-mechanical technologies were deployed for process automation. Where the technologies did not exist, they were invented using vendor partners.

It went to the extent that the OG managers even had a "lingua franca" of their own! For example, you would hear an OG manager say, "Let's team it, rationalize the channel, set the ROI, and then just paradise it." (*Translation: Let's set up a specific team, determine the process changes we want to make, understand the return on investment, and then fire the people whose jobs are eliminated.*) JH was so right. This was Citibank "Swahili"! It was spoken mainly by the "in crowd" of the OG managers. Admission to this exclusive corporate club was by a strange mix of merit, invitation, and "personality fit". It was a "dog eats dog" world in its purest form. Losers were wasted, winners celebrated, and egos were catered to with near pagan reverence for corporate power.

In this milieu, I walked in, filled with innocence and youthful exuberance, looking to firm up a job assignment. The day, filled with non-stop interviews, was planned in great and specific detail. I was to meet and talk with a wide swath of OG managers. But there was one rather vague part to the day. It was the lunch. The schedule only said, "Lunch at Noon. Executive Dining Room. Host - C. Pirelli."

After the last pre-lunch interview ended, I was ushered into the Executive Dining Room and brought to a reserved table. It was noon precisely. It was a lovely dining room with views of the city and a conservative mahogany motif in its décor. Nearly all the waiters seemed Italian, the tables had tablecloths on them, and the silverware was actually sterling silver! The ambience made one feel like one was in an upscale New York restaurant. A waiter offered me drinks, but I declined. I was waiting for this "C. Pirelli". I had no idea who he was and nobody had bothered to tell me. I figured that he must be some sort of a big "honcho" to be having me for lunch with him. Perhaps this was the acid test for me. But where was he? Nobody knew.

Now, it was 12:20pm. I was still sitting at the table wondering what I should do. Then, lumbers in towards my table, this giant of a man! He is 6ft. 3 in. tall, at least 275 lbs, very fat, grossly out of shape, and almost out of breath! He flopped into his chair and raised a hand, indicating that he needed a few moments to normalize and settle himself.

"Want a drink? he shortly asked. "Yo, Riccardo, get us a couple of vino rosso, prontamente," he said, without waiting for my answer.

Then he smiled, and continued, "Sorry I am late. A crazy and sudden process cock-up delayed me. The name is Charlie Pirelli (CP). Yeah, like the goddamn tires."

"Mr. Pirelli, it is nice to meet you." I said politely.

"No, it is not. And it is Charlie. Why is it nice to meet me?" he retorted. "You do not even know me. Why do people say such s**t?"

"Well, that is an interesting question. Social custom, perhaps?" I offered, not knowing what was going on at all.

"Yeah, well, may be. You havin' a good day so far? I hope so." Then, he studied me carefully for a while, and not much was said.

Our drinks arrived. And CP says, "Mille grazie, Riccardo." He replied, "Prego" and waited.

"You know what you wanna eat? 'Cause I do. Riccardo, per favore, take our orders."

Riccardo took our orders. I sat there looking at this monstrous Charlie Pirelli, who seemed to be losing control of all his faculties by the minute. It was simply bizarre.

"So, you are Vijay." he said finally. "You are from the "holy cow" country, eh? I will never understand it. You worship 'em and we eat 'em. Go figure." Now, I was becoming concerned. This was becoming quite insulting for me.

"And you did a MS in Computer Science, before the MBA waltz? Okay, so draw me a flow diagram on this napkin. How would you herd a 100 of your holy cows into the barn house in a wide-open Montana grazing field?" I am now getting really worried. This cannot be real! But I decided to go along for the moment, despite the obvious insults.

Just then, our food arrived. Riccardo was a wonderful server. Charlie loosened his tie, hooked the white napkin in his shirt collar, and began to attack his pasta with gusto. I was just staring at my fish fillet, because he was carrying on a one-way conversation of all sorts of gibberish. And I was steadily getting steamed.

"That is the trouble with all of you." he pontificated. "You have no plan of any kind at all. You all want just some dumb-ass slave job for a paycheck. You should have lived in another century."

By now I had received enough from this huge fat man. It was obvious that he was a racist and did not care about me at all. He also showed no emotional sensitivity of any kind. And I was fed up with his insults. Then, I wondered if he could take what he had been dishing out? Heck, since there was no job here anyway, why not give it a shot? Let's put this fat bastard in his place and give him a swift kick in his nuts. It might even be a little fun with this overgrown walrus!

"Oh, I am sorry, Mr. Pirelli, that you feel that I do not have a plan for my career. Because I think I do." I stated.

"What? And it is Charlie. You got a plan? For a career? Oh, yeah? Well, let's hear it!"

"Well, I actually have short-term, medium-term, and long-term plans. My short-term plan is to try and finish my lunch, if I may be permitted. My medium-term plan is to secure a job at Citicorp in one of its companies. And my long-term plan, if Citicorp places me at Citibank in New York, is to take your boss's job in 5 years." I wanted to be as insulting as I possibly could because this a**hole deserved it.

"Oh, that is great. And I'm sorry, please eat your lunch. But, long term, why would you want my boss's job?" he asked, without showing any hurt at all.

"Because I don't think you are going anywhere. And nothing would please me more than to be your boss!" I was wondering if he was realizing that I was now directly insulting him.

"Why?" Charlie said, showing no sign of being offended at all. "Why the devil would you want to be my boss?"

"Because then I could fire you on the first day." I said bluntly, shoving my spear fully into his chest.

"But why would you want to fire me?" Charlie continued, without even a flinch, or the slightest sign of feeling insulted.

"Because I do not like you." I opined, hammering the final nail in the coffin.

"Gosh, now that is the first thing you have said, that makes any sense to me." Charlie said. "And ya' know, just between you, me, and this table, I don't like me either! I cannot stand myself! But, hey, I gotta go right now. I am already late. Listen, this was a good lunch. Try the pasta next time. Their strozzapreti is exquisite. I will circle back with you later, if I can. You take care, bud. Ciao!"

Charlie waddled off into oblivion. I finished my day of interviews and went back. After much ado, it was settled that I would join Advance Mortgage Corporation in Detroit. Apparently, JH had won a major job assignment corporate fight.

Epilogue

Six months or so after joining my job in Detroit, I found myself at a Citicorp conference in New York. I met a ton of people during the 3 days it lasted. But strangely, whenever I met somebody from the Citibank OG, I would get a reaction like, "Hey, are you that Vijay? Aren't you at Advance in Detroit? Jeez, people often talk about you."

And I would say, "Really? Why? I did not think anybody would remember me."

"Are you kidding? The HR folks at the OG talk about you as a legendary reference point."

"But why?" I persisted.

"Well, you are the only MBA job candidate in the history of OG who had the balls to tell Charlie that you would fire him, if you got the chance! And it was because you did not like him! Nobody says that to Charlie ever and lives to talk about it."

"Gosh, I had no idea. But I do remember that he had managed to piss me off at the lunch we had. I figured I had lost the job anyway."

"Vijay, do you know what he wrote on your interview evaluation form? Everybody knows that he never fills them out for any job candidate. But in your case, he did! He just wrote, 'Get him!' The HR folks still talk about it."

A little later, I ran into Charlie himself. This man was totally different from the one I had met at lunch on that fateful day. He was so European, classy, polite, greeted me warmly in a typical Italian manner with a hug, and said, "Vijay, paisano, it has been a while! How is Detroit treating you?"

I said, "Mr. Pirelli, Detroit is fine. But I have always meant to apologize to you for my behavior that day."

"Hey, like I told you, it is Charlie. And apologize for what? Did you not know? I was just f**king with your mind! I wanted to see what you were like when I broke you. I never believed any of that crap that I was laying on you that day. But I loved the punch you threw! Yeah, I sure loved that! It was so Italian! Hey, you know what? Screw Detroit, come on over to New York. This city still awaits!"

Charlie and I met several times after that for various things. He went on to have a highly successful and revered career at Citicorp, but we did not become close as such. However, in many ways he was a formative and an influential figure in the early years of my work life.

<u>**Note**</u>: In this story, I must let you know honestly, I have altered names and characterizations, quite deliberately, to protect people and for creative reaons. However, all the factual and substantive elements of this story remain true and unchanged from the way they actually occurred.

Close Encounters of the Third Kind

In my years of living in the USA, I have been fortunate to have had some really strange "Close Encounters of the Third Kind". Unlike the Steven Spielberg movie with its aliens, mine were with celebrities! They all occurred purely by chance, in some of the most unlikely places and in peculiar ways. I have selected a few to write about.

A Teppanyaki Dinner

I had arrived in the US a few months earlier in 1971. Everything was new to me and Ajay, my older brother, was my guide and tutor. I adjusted slowly to graduate school; American diets, language, & customs; and the melting pot called New York City. He was a doctor and doing his Residency in Trauma Surgery at the Roosevelt Hospital in Manhattan. I used to visit him from the State University of New York campus in Stony Brook, for weekends in Manhattan, which was a fascinating place for me. There was so much to see and experience there when compared to Stony Brook, which was a huge campus, still under major construction, in the boonies of Long Island, much like the IIT campus in Kanpur in the late 1960's.

This evening, Ajay got out late from work, was still in his scrubs, and hungry. He decided to introduce me to Japanese Teppanyaki cuisine, and picked a spot in the Theatre District. We got there and the place was really busy. After much ado, the maître d' offered us a small table for 4 in a separate little room. Ajay grabbed it and we sat down. Soon another man was placed at our table also.

The chef came and the meal began. Ajay started to teach me to use chopsticks which then started some small chitchat among all of us. In a Teppanyaki restaurant, it is hard to ignore folks seated around you. The man guessed that Ajay was a doctor, given his scrubs. He also guessed that we were from India, due to our accents. Then I asked what he did. He said he was working in an Off-Broadway play. He was dismissive about it, but I persisted, and then he told us its name. At this, I blurted out, "Sean Connery is in it!" Well, that ruined nearly everything.

The man was totally bald, with a shaggy unkempt beard, badly overweight, drank lots of sake, and ate like a total pig, even though he handled the chopsticks rather well. Then, we recognized the voice! It was Sean Connery (SC) himself! Ajay saved the evening by just shutting me up, which relaxed him. We chatted about many things, but not much about the Bond movies, which he said were physically very demanding work. Despite his unrecognizable appearance, so unlike his Bond persona, he was a very well read, knowledgeable man, with a strong Scottish nationalist bent. He hit it off with Ajay because Ajay had spent a couple of years working in Ireland. It was all about the Irish and Scottish history and politics, about which Ajay was very well read also.

Towards the end, SC advised me to study hard at school and build a real career for myself. He said he was too poor to go to proper schools and considered himself "just lucky" to find work in films which became successful. He had to leave early and we parted company graciously. The only indication of stardom was a limo, which came to pick him up.

A lovely encounter, but it was also a sad one for me. It was so different from what I had conjectured in my star struck imagination. But still, he was a bright, polite, and an unassuming man. He was so Scottish, and he never forgot his roots and difficult days in poverty.

Sometimes, meeting up with reality is not a good thing. It ruins all that one's mind has created.

Sunday in SoHo, New York City

I was in New York City attending a weeklong conference for the Banking Industry around 1975 or so. It had an odd schedule. It went from Thursday to the following Wednesday. The Saturday and Sunday in the middle had been set aside for a massive show put on by a variety of vendors catering to the industry. Most attendees spent a long Saturday visiting various vendor booths on the show floor and in many sponsored breakout sessions and meetings. This was so that they could relax on Sunday, and perhaps do something fun to enjoy the city and is vast offerings of entertainment.

I was no exception. But that Sunday morning, Ajay was busy and said he would join me later in the day. So, I wondered about what to do with my time. We were close to the Greenwich Village area in Manhattan and I was familiar with it since Ajay had lived there. Close to the Village was the SoHo District, which at the time had a reputation for being quite Bohemian in its local culture and ambience. It was also full of bars, music clubs, and art galleries. On a lark, I thought it might be fun to go there, walk around, and see its various sights. It was a lovely sunny day and perfectly suited for it.

During this aimless walk in SoHo, I noticed an interesting large display window of an art gallery. It was about 20 feet wide and had many oil and water color paintings on show in it. The sunlight was also catching them just right. I suppose it was meant to attract you and pull you into the gallery.

I stopped to have a look starting at the left end. I noticed another man doing the same thing but he was at the far-right end. We were both looking at the paintings carefully and slowly drifting towards each other. Eventually we came up close and passed one another. He looked strangely familiar. I looked at him a couple of times, but could not place him. But the thought kept bugging me. He never looked at me or made any eye contact. He was writing in a little notebook in his hand and focused on the paintings. Now, where have I seen this man? Did I meet him somewhere? At the banking industry show perhaps? Was he with some major vendor? It began to bother me. Just then, he turned and walked to go past me and we were face to face.

He was wearing blue jeans, with a white shirt tucked in, and leather boots. He sported a light brown suede leather vest and had a baseball cap on his head. Also, he was strikingly handsome.

I said, "Excuse me, sir, but I have to ask you this question. You seem very familiar to me. Have we met before?"

He slowly broke into a grin, and replied, "I understand. No, we have not met before. It is a lovely day, is it not? I think this artist is going to have a great future. His work is striking and detailed."

"Yes, definitely. But, sir, if I may ask, who are you?" I continued.

"I am Clint Eastwood," he said simply. Then he turned and hailed a cab from the stand nearby.

I was speechless! He walked over to the cab, opened the passenger door, and turned towards me again.

"Sorry, but I've gotta run. I am late. Have a great day," he said. He smiled, waved goodbye, and was gone!

In the late afternoon, Ajay and I met up finally. We took a walk as well and soon it was evening. Ajay suggested that we have dinner at his favorite club in SoHo. Its food was renowned and one could also catch some live music performances. So, we decided to make an evening of it there.

It was a meal of superb "home style" Italian food, a New York City specialty. As we were finishing, a bit of a commotion started. I heard shouts of, "Come on, Bobby, just one!" and "Aww, Zimmy, do us a favor!"

So, I asked Ajay, "What is going on over there? What are all these shouts for?"

Ajay replied, "Oh, they always want Bobby to sing. He hangs around here a lot, especially on Sundays."

And I went, "What are you talking about? And who is this Bobby?"

Ajay said with indifference, "Oh, did I not tell you about it? That's Bob Dylan. But around here he is just Bobby Zimmerman, a local homeboy. Folks here have known him personally for years. He is great."

I was aghast! Whaat? THE Bob Dylan? Here in a SoHo club? A homeboy? This was too good to be true! This iconic musician, poet, and singer, who I was a total fan of, was just a few feet away from us? I went numb with a mixture of utter surprise, excitement, and wonder. But the best was yet to come.

After much ado, somebody got him a guitar. He sat on a stool and sang "Mr. Tambourine Man" just solo. All service and eating activities stopped during it. It was an unforgettable personal experience!

As he was leaving, he happened to walk by our table, and said, "Hiya, Doc!"

Ajay looked at him and said, "Bobby, great as ever. You take it easy now, ya' hear?"

He replied, "Yup," and left.

I was on "cloud nine" that Sunday night as I went back to my hotel! One close encounter was enough of a jolt, but two in one day? What is the probability of something like that happening? But then, it was New York City, I figured. Anything can happen there, on any day, clear out of the blue!

While I was easily blown away by such encounters, most New Yorkers were either too busy with their lives, or always in too much of a hurry. Or, maybe they just did not give a damn.

Flight to San Francisco

I made a mad dash from the curb, where I had been dropped off, towards Gate 800 in Terminal 7 at the LAX (Los Angeles International) Airport. In those days there were none of the security procedures of today and one could go straight to the gate, if there were no bags to check in. I was trying to board the hourly shuttle of PSA Airlines, a highly successful regional domestic airline, which operated planes that had a cute smile painted on their fuselage below the cockpit! I was returning home to San Francisco after a hectic 3-day business trip to LA.

I bounded up the escalators and sprinted towards the gate with my carry-on bag and a briefcase in my hands. Gate 800 was a "commuter gate" for PSA, and so was not far away. I reached the gate counter huffing and puffing, and I asked, "Can I make the flight?"

The lady smiled sweetly and said, "They may have closed the airplane door, but let me see what I can do." Oh, how blessed were those days, when air travel was actually personal and enjoyable! Well, she contacted the pilot who said that since they had not pushed away or started the engines, I would be allowed to board. The plane door was re-opened and I was boarded.

They shut the airplane door behind me promptly. The flight attendant said to me, "Sir, I will stow away your things, but please find a seat immediately and sit down, so we can push off. I looked around in the airplane cabin and it looked like a full flight. I could not see an empty seat anywhere.

Then I heard the attendant again, "Sir, right by the door, next to you, the middle seat is vacant."

It sure was, and I just plopped down in it and buckled up. We pushed off, taxied for a while, and then roared into takeoff. I was trying to settle my mind down throughout all this. It had been a long rough day, and I was so relieved to have made it to this flight, even if it was by a razor thin margin.

As we climbed, my nerves settled a bit and I looked around. Seated next to me, in the window and aisle seats were two enormous men. They were both wearing dark tuxedos and looked very handsome. After a while, I initiated some chitchat. It was something to pass the hour of flight time.

"You must be going to a formal event." I ventured.

"That is indeed true. Like you, we barely made this flight as well." said the tall man in the window seat. He had a great baritone voice with amazing diction. There was something familiar about it.

"I am glad it worked out for all of us." I continued. "You seem familiar. Did we meet at the Bank of America reception some time ago?"

"Yes. And no, I was not at that reception. But that does not matter. I am Greg Peck and that is Glenn Ford."

My jaw dropped to the floor, and I lost my voice and breath! I was thinking that it was simply not possible that I was sitting next to an iconic man who I had admired all my life! Scenes from "To Kill a Mocking Bird", "Guns of

Navarone", and "Roman Holiday" flashed through my mind in rapid-fire sequence.

"Oh, wow! It is indeed a joy to meet you Mr. Peck. My name is Vijay Yajnik," I babbled out without much control. I suppose he was used to seeing a lot of irrational behavior from strangers.

He continued, "We are to attend a black-tie event in San Francisco and there were flight problems. But we got lucky, and were placed here, finally. Now it seems that we will get there on time. And besides, we got to meet you!"

Goodness gracious! I tried to rapidly regain my composure. I decided to be just cool about it all, remain polite, and not gush like a totally crazed fan, which is actually what I really wanted to do! It was very hard.

These were living icons of Hollywood, but they were so unassuming! They wore their fame with ease, had no airs about themselves at all, and were very polite and friendly. We talked about many things. They even expressed interest in learning about what I did in my job at the Crocker Bank! Gregory Peck (GP) was very bright, incredibly well read, gifted with an amazing memory, and a superb conversationalist. Glenn Ford was relatively a bit quiet.

Then GP said to me, "You know, Vijay, I have actually been to India!"

I said, "Really? How come? A vacation?" *(I wanted to say 'holiday'? But that would have been too obvious.)*

"No. This was a long time ago, and I was in Bombay for a film industry event mainly. I was surprised to learn about the robust Indian cinema industry. The sheer volume of films made there annually was astounding! I recall meeting a major star of the Indian film industry during the visit. He was so famous in India! His name was Mr. Dev Anand. He was a very handsome and talkative fellow."

Then I went, "Oh, Gosh. Yes. He is now an even bigger and legendary star of the Indian cinema."

"Actually, I saw him again in Rome sometime after that. We were filming "Roman Holiday" scenes on the Spanish Steps, if I remember correctly. He visited our unit for a while."

And so, it went on for the hour. Sadly, and too soon, the flight landed and we had to part company. There were special people present at the door to hustle them off the plane first. Even in saying goodbye, he did not lose the slightest bit of grace. His words were simply, "Au revoir, Vijay."

And like a totally dumb idiot, I forgot to even ask for autographs. Regardless, I will never forget this amazing man named Gregory Peck.

California Dreaming

I t was the same PSA shuttle from LAX to San Francisco, but in the late afternoon on a Saturday. The plane was half empty.

We were about to depart and then the Captain said, "Folks, we have been asked to hold for 5 minutes for some passengers. Wait till you seem them. You are going to be surprised."

In a little while, a group of some 15 cackling and squealing 18 to 25 years old girls boarded the plane. They were all very fit, muscular, and wearing scanty bikinis which were still wet! Each one clutched a carry-on bag. They had no tickets for the flight. They showed their IDs at the door and proceeded to buy them on the flight! Everyone was shocked to see these nearly nude girls who just plopped down on various leather seats!

They cheerily announced that they had just come from a crazy swim at the Redondo Beach and had no time to change. Everybody wondered what was going on, but the sights were so enchanting that nobody complained! Then the Captain says, "Folks, there is a free drink for everybody on the flight!" There were hoots and cheers, and all the girls started screaming even more. Then, one by one, they all changed into their casual wear clothes in the lavatories.

Then we learnt that it was a big "bridal shower" party! One of the girls was famous and a bride, soon to be married, so they were all having one giant celebration. Well, the whole flight turned into a party! But I never found out the name of the bride.

Oh, how I miss those days when flying actually was easy and a whole lot of fun.

Troupe of Stars

W e were in the San Francisco International (SFO) airport. It was July, 1987. We were there to see off Morali, Nilima's sister, who was going to Chicago to start her medical residency program. Her flight had departed, and we were returning to our car in the parking lot.

With us were our little children. Neil was 3 and running around all over. Meghana was almost 6 months old and strapped into her stroller. The terminal was nearly empty on this late Saturday morning. There was only one more departing flight, which was preparing to start its boarding process. We were slowly walking past its gate.

I was trying to get Neil under control, when suddenly, a young lady slammed into me frontally. She was slim, fit, quite buxom, and had gorgeous large almond shaped eyes adorned with a liner and mascara. She had knee length hair tied into a single braid and was wearing the Indian salwar kameez. Apparently, she was also chasing some kid, who was running about the barren terminal, just like Neil.

"Sorry… So, sorry…" she said. And then she took off after the kid. She looked strangely familiar.

Just as I grabbed Neil and caught up with Nilima, Meghana decided that she was fed up with the stroller. She started crying a little. But Nilima did not reach down to comfort her. Her gaze was fixed on the passengers at the gate!

I followed it and asked, "What are you gazing at so intently? It is a flight about to start boarding. Let's go."

Nilima smiled and said, "Can you not see? Look who is over by that gate!"

I looked quickly and replied, "Oh, just some passengers waiting to board. But why are you staring?"

Nilima said, "Hon, you are so blind! Let me show you. Over by that counter, looking at us are Jeetendra and Prem Chopra. Next to them is Ranjeet. Over by that bench is Amjad Khan. Near the wall is Sridevi! God, she is gorgeous! And next to her I think is her sister, the girl who just now bumped into you. I think this is the whole performing troupe from the Bollywood Show in Berkeley last night. I had read about it."

I went, "Oh, wow!" I was aware of all these stars and had seen many of their films on video cassettes. Jeetendra and Prem Chopra I remembered from my days in India. Then, I asked Nilima, "Want to go talk with them?"

Just then, Meghana let off a full-throated shriek! She started to wail loudly and wriggle around in her stroller. And Neil ran off again. Meghana's crying echoed so loudly in the empty terminal that it caused all the heads at the gate to turn towards us!

I chased Neil again, while Nilima tried to comfort Meghana. Now, we had become "the show" for everybody at the gate! Meghana started bawling her head off and nothing would calm her down. Nilima was struggling and trying various tactics. Folks from the troupe started to come towards us. Even Sridevi got up and came up to the bench near us.

Everybody was now watching us with a fair measure of amusement. They seemed to be curious about how Indians handled crying kids in the USA. By now, they had all figured out that we were Indians, because we spoke to our kids in Gujarati. Nilima and I had figured that we should immerse them in Gujarati while they were very young, so that they would understand it and perhaps even learn to speak it. Later on, they would learn English anyway. We actually succeeded!

After a few minutes, when nothing else worked, Nilima had to pick up Meghana from the stroller. Calm was restored again and I had managed to lasso Neil too. Now, the whole troupe was standing there watching us, and wondering if we had recognized them. Nilima again started pointing animatedly, and now they were sure that we knew who they all were.

There was a sense of anticipation on their part it seemed. I was certain that in India they were used to being mobbed by people everywhere they went. But what might happen in the USA? I think they were curious.

With two cranky kids on our hands and no help, we decided that we should perhaps just get going before things got worse. So, we just waved to all of them, pointed to the kids, and walked on.

They all smiled and waved back too, as if they understood. After all, famous or not, parents with little kids face the same problems all over the world.

And that was a close encounter of the Bollywood kind.

Arrival in America – Visit with Kashyap in Denver - 1971

At State University of New York, Stony Brook, NY - 1971

A Year Later- Stage 12
SUNY, Stony Brook
1972

With Atulbhai,
Ajay, Kalibhabhi,
& Kashyap
Summer-1972

*With Prem
Kapoor, Mahesh
Anand &
Bijendranath Jain
1973*

*With Viney Aneja at SUNY,
Stony Brook, NY
1973*

With Walter Tung in Montreal, Canada – Summer, 1973

In Detroit - 1974

Dr. Clarke De Haven

EARLY WORK LIFE

The New Working World

The Initiation – Advance Mortgage Corporation, Detroit

I joined the "real working world" on a Monday morning in June, 1974. I was quite poor, but skilled, full of hope, and prospects for the future. On that first day, there was sort of a "reception" at lunch, in the Executive Dining Room, for all the new MBA recruits. There were 11 of us.

At this lunch, we were introduced to the entire "executive managers" cadre individually and in great detail. All of my colleagues were from Harvard, Sloan, Wharton, etc. all the "blue blood" or elite business schools. They were all received with great admiration and appreciation. And then came my turn. I was from Michigan State University, a school known for its Agriculture School programs! So, I was immediately branded as "that kid from the Cow College" and promptly made fun of in all sorts of ways. They were also amused that I was from the cow college and a country that worshipped cows at the same time! I was a joke for everybody at this lunch. None of them had any idea of what it had taken me to complete my MBA or to land a job on a foreign student visa. I felt hurt, but there was not much I could do about it. The only man who understood my feelings was John Hamilton, the EVP of HR at Advance, who had recruited me.

He said, "Vijay, they are simply ignorant. Do not be offended. All this has happened in too many situations, too many times before, in the history of our country. I want you to rise above their insults. You are the better one. Show them the way, by example."

I grumbled "okay" in some manner, because I had no idea at all of what John was talking about. And I did not really care, because I was royally pissed off at the whole bloody lot of them. Unknown to me, I had a lot of growing up to do. I was just a "babe" in the real-world woods.

In about 2 weeks after I joined AMC, I was told that I had to go to New York City for a 3-day conference for all the new Citicorp MBA recruits, worldwide. It was an important conference. Attendance was mandatory. So, I went, along with all my other AMC colleagues.

The conference was amazing. A lot of my AMC colleagues met their classmates and so forth. But I knew nobody. I felt totally lost and unconnected. I was just miserable.

In the 3 days, we attended many presentations from all sorts of senior executives of Citicorp, the parent holding company. But, one in particular, stands out in my mind. It was given by the EVP of HR for Citicorp, Worldwide, as the last item. He was the very "top dog" of all HR and commanded vast power.

His presentation was simple and brief. He put up a chart. It showed that 5 years out, only 10% of the current MBA recruits would still be around! The rest, 90% or so, would have left Citicorp for any number of reasons. They may have resigned, been fired, left due to stress, resorted to drugs, discovered religion, or just fallen apart. He had detailed statistics for all of these things and a lot more.

And then he said, "I want you all to know, that it is specifically that 10% after 5 years that we are really interested in. The 90% loss is merely the cost of acquiring the 10%. We think that the ROI is simply great. So, as all of you leave today, my question for you is, which group do you belong to?" The entire auditorium was filled with stunned silence! Nobody clapped for this freaky dude! He smiled and seemed to just love it.

Sidebar: Now, perhaps I am speaking out of turn here. But I did stay with AMC for close to 5 years. But, when I eventually left as well, there was only one another colleague present with me, from the original 11 of us in 1974! The other 9 had left for: another job, fired, marriage, drugs, and even a suicide. The HR guy was totally right, at least statistically.

In other ways, I was not so sure.

The Financial Services Industry – 1970s

These stories will have little meaning for you if you are unaware of the state of the Financial Services Industry in the USA in the 1970s. There is not enough room here for a treatise on this subject, but a general overview should suffice for the purpose at hand.

The entire industry was highly regulated in order to protect the consumer. The Glass-Steagall Act passed in 1933, after the market crash of 1929, was intended to prevent any recurrence of the economic carnage that had followed.

This Act of the Congress split the industry into 3 specific vertical silos of banking, insurance, and brokerage. Any company operating in one of these silos could not operate in the other two. In the banking sector, there were even more regulations.

Banks were restricted to operating their branches only in cities, or counties. Some states that were sparsely populated permitted a statewide branch network, but these were very few. All banking was mainly paper based. Any sort of technology use or automation in the branches or the back office of a bank was still in its infancy. ATM machines were a new phenomenon and generally not trusted by anybody. Also, the interest rates for all deposit and loan products were regulated. Hence, for any bank to compete effectively, it had to deliver superior customer service in the branches and be as efficient as possible in its back-office operations. In this environment, the arrival of "mainframe computers" became a highly significant development.

All sorts of electro-mechanical devices were invented for the branches and the back office of a bank. Nearly all of them had to be connected to mainframe computers to deliver their functionality. This was due to a simple but sound reason. All the "intelligence" to properly operate these devices resided in the mainframe computers. The devices, whether machines or CRT (cathode ray tube) terminals, were just "dumb" and had no intelligence within them. Local connections required extensive wiring and cable layouts. If they were remote, leased data lines had to be installed to achieve connectivity.

The advent of mainframe computers in the 1960s actually changed things in every industry, not just the financial services industry. The mainframe computers and the attached peripheral devices were physically huge, heavy, and consumed a lot of power. They required special climate-controlled rooms with raised flooring to handle all the cables and to remove the heat generated. All of this was housed in what came to be called the "Data Center" or "Computer Center". A veritable small army of staff, with assorted skills, was needed to operate, maintain, and upgrade all these technologies. It is in this era, that a new Corporate Division, named "Data Processing" or "Information Services" was born, as an organizational entity, in every major corporation in the USA. This birth was handled in a variety of fascinating ways. The issues and problems created in every corporation was the stuff of hilarious stories and legendary events. Hollywood even made films on the comedic aspects of many of these changes!

However, at Advance Mortgage Corporation there was a twist to all this. It was not a commercial bank. It was a mortgage bank! It was an entity legally permitted to handle just mortgage loans. It would borrow money from banks, underwrite and fund mortgage loans, then sell them off to large investors and pay the banks back. When it sold these mortgage loans off, it retained the "servicing" of the loans for a fee. Servicing of mortgage loans comprised all the activities like payment processing, collections, foreclosures, payoffs, reconveyances, etc. With a huge "servicing portfolio", it could be a great and profitable business. Also, and this was the best part, AMC could operate nationally! So, it had a large book of business in nearly all the 48 contiguous states! It is of little wonder that Citicorp chose to acquire the company in 1973. Citibank in New York City, the richest city in the USA, could gather huge deposits, and AMC could use that money to fund mortgages nationally! The larger the servicing portfolio, the greater the income generated for the company.

But for great profits, AMC had to be highly efficient in the way it did everything. It had made a strategic commitment to automation and the use of new technologies in all its activities. It had invested in a new mainframe computer, built a fine Data Center, and was starting to learn how to leverage these things for business advantage. They were still "baby steps", but it had certainly embarked on this unknown road.

It is at this stage, that I joined AMC, straight out of 2 consecutive graduate school programs.

David Guthrie

It was my 3rd week at AMC. I had just returned from a conference in New York. I was still going through my orientation sessions around the various Divisions of Advance. Suddenly, I was summoned by John Hamilton, EVP of HR.

"Vijay, I want you meet somebody." John said. "This is David Guthrie. He has joined us today in the role of VP of the Data Processing Division."

David and I exchanged the customary pleasantries.

"David, the vacant office next door is yours, and you can settle in there. We will have to get you an executive secretary to help you. Now, Vijay, we are going to have to cut your orientation program off short. I am sorry, but we have an emergency on our hands." John continued with a worried look on his face.

"Gentlemen, this Data Processing Division does not yet exist!" John said. "Its fragmented pieces are all over AMC, reporting to a wide array of people who know nothing about it. Your first task is to pull it all together as one organizational entity. David, it will all report to you. And Vijay will be your Financial Analyst, also reporting to you. I need specific recommendations from you in 10 days on a set of actions to create this Division immediately. I will present them to the Operating Committee and get its "green light" right away."

"But that is not all." John looked even more worried now. "Our annual fiscal budget is due in 30 days. We have to have it finalized for presentation in New York. Everybody else has been working on their budgets for the last 2 months at least. But nobody knows what to do about the Data Processing budget. Oh, I have seen some crazy figures tossed about, but nobody really knows what they are talking about."

"Surely, John, somebody is handling all the technical costs and budgets?" David inquired.

"That is exactly the problem! Nobody is! Let me tell you, otherwise you will not believe it!" John offered, his face now sweating.

"We have the data entry people reporting to the Servicing Division. The programmers report to two different Divisions in a split manner. All purchase orders, invoices, etc. are handled by clerks in Accounting. Yeah, can you believe that? The same guy, who buys pencils, is buying computers! And the Data Center, where the big machine is located, reports to me! Me, David? I did not ask for it. I know nothing about it. But nobody else wanted this headache, so it came to me. It is all crazy!"

"And then, there is this irritating fellow from IBM who bothers me daily! He is relentless! Apparently, something did not work, so an upgrade was ordered. It arrived on a forklift 3 days ago and cost $200,000! I had a near heart attack! I had to sign for it, but I am not sure what it is for!"

"Well, John, you should not worry about all this anymore." David said with a smile. "The cavalry has arrived!"

"John, I just remembered something." I said. "Yesterday, I met a young lady named Eva in the Payoff Department during one of the orientation sessions. She said she was a trained executive secretary, but was doing clerical work just waiting for a suitable opening. Maybe she should meet with David."

"I will arrange it at once." John said and picked up the phone.

David Guthrie was in his mid-30's, of medium build, blonde hair, blue eyes, and a receding hairline. He was incredibly bright, with a sharp memory, and a deceptively easy-going style. Just like me, he smoked cigarettes, ate mints or chewed gum to keep his breath fresh, and had acquired a taste for the lousy vending machine coffee. I had a good feeling about him and sensed that we would hit it off in a splendid way.

He had a chat with Eva and hired her immediately. She was 26 years old, a college graduate, very bright, fast at anything, and a natural self-starter. She had a ready smile and charming personality. So, while Eva set about settling

David's office and helping him through his relocation issues, I went off on a tear to deal with our short-term challenges.

I gathered all the organization charts of the fragmented units and built one chart. I gathered all the salary files to understand our personnel costs. Then, I went to Accounting to understand the balance sheet of all the Data Processing Division assets. Meeting people and gathering data was one arduous task, but then putting it all into a cohesive picture that provided information was quite another. I worked 16-hour days, 7 days a week, for the whole month straight. We announced the new Data Processing Division shortly, and published its organization chart to the entire company. As all the staff meetings concluded, everybody now knew that their new boss was a man named David Guthrie. And that he knew all the technologies at AMC cold, and a whole lot more.

But the Budget was something different all together. As I pulled our asset balance sheet together after days of labor and research in Accounting, I made a shocking discovery! The amortization or write-offs for our purchased equipment were completely erroneous. Technology assets had been treated like they were furniture! The classifications were haphazard. So, I proceeded to correct it all. It took many days. But the end result was the need for a huge "write-off". If things had been done right, this could have been easily avoided. Sadly, the accounting books were just flat wrong.

"Dear God, Vijay. This is a huge sum." David said, seriously. "It will affect the AMC earnings this year and hurt the annual bonuses tied to them for everybody. This is really bitter stuff. Jeez, what should I do?"

"I was taught in B School that, if you have to take a financial hit, take the biggest hit. Do it in one swift stroke and get it behind you, so you can focus on the future." I offered. "David, you did not cause any of these things. We simply discovered them. I suggest strongly that you confront this whole issue head-on with the Operating Committee. This year, it is not your issue. Next year, you will own it."

David took my advice. We delivered the financial hit. There was a huge reaction, but our budget presentations were a grand success in the end. The Data Processing Division now had an actual form and financial clout. It was to be the agent driving change at AMC in all sorts of ways.

As all this budget fracas came to an end, David sat down to chat with me. He said, "Vijay, I really do not need a financial analyst anymore. But I would love it and be grateful if you took over all the Applications Programmers of the Division, as Assistant Vice President, reporting to me. John Hamilton supports it totally!"

I was speechless and stunned. I was appointed AVP after about 3 months with AMC. Unbelievable, in every way! As a special privilege, I was given an assigned parking spot in the parking garage with my name on it. In snowy Michigan, this was a valuable benefit. But I lived nearby and walked to work, so it was mainly a huge stroke for my ego. For a "cow college" boy, I had bettered all the "blue bloods"!

And so, began one of the most amazing relationships in my life.

A New Way

"It simply does not end!" Ken Davidge complained. "The Loan Originations & Marketing guys want these reports in endless variations on a daily basis! We do nothing else but cater to them all the time."

Ken, David Guthrie and I were in a critical ad hoc meeting. We were at the urinals in the Men's Room! We continued in David's office. "You are right, Ken. This is nuts. There has to be a better way." David opined. After some thought, I offered a suggestion.

"Ken, aren't all these reports mostly in the same format? And we have individual Jobs scheduled to generate each one of them every night, right? But in this architecture, are we not doing the same thing repeatedly in each Job, for each report? So, why don't we try a different approach? Let's do things just once."

"What do you mean?" Ken and David both asked almost in unison and leaned forward with attention.

"Well, what if we did it differently? Instead of a "report based" architecture, what if we create a "function based" architecture? In Job 1, we read the Master Loans file once and write out separate report files for the reports needed. In Job 2, we crunch all the numbers required on each report file, based on "parameters" that they supply, and then write out print files. In Job 3, we just print the bloody files, and be done with it all. We handle everything just once. And since it would be parameter driven in Job 2, we also would not have to change our software code daily. It would save us a lot of time and effort, I would think."

I could hear the deafening sounds of silence in David's office.

"Vijay, I get Job 1 & 3. But Job 2 being parameter driven?" Ken asked with wide eyes. "I don't think it can be done. There are too many dependencies and risks. Also, our hardware resources are limited. It may not work for just those reasons. This is assuming that somebody can write the code for your approach."

"Ken, why not?" I asked. "Job 1 is I/O intensive; Job 2 is Processor intensive; and Job 3 is just plain stupid print work. We have a kickass IBM mainframe back there. Let's make it sweat a little."

Ken Davidge was AVP in charge of the Data Center and all its Systems Programmers. He was smart, old school, and had a back full of scars from data processing tragedies. He was always a tough sell on anything. And for good reason too. Often, he was the warning bell, just before you fell off the cliff.

"Well, let me give it a shot. If it fails, then we will have to think of something else." I offered.

David smiled, and said, "Vij, you are on. And, hey, if you need help, call me." It was a Wednesday morning.

I designed my ideas on paper first. I tried to validate the design with Ken, but he did not want to be bothered with a "sure failure", when he had real fires to deal with. David gave me great feedback and encouraged me. I busted the "midnight oil" for the next few days. By Monday morning, I had my code ready for Jobs 1 through 3. I asked for Ken's help in debugging, etc. We did all that and cleaned up my work. Now it was time to actually do a "production test" to see if it would work.

Both, Ken and David, decided to be present on this Tuesday night for the real test of my work. None of us knew if it would succeed. There were too many hardware and other unknowns at play. David bought us time by delaying various Jobs on a production night, and we decided on 9:15pm as the H-Hour for the test.

Precisely, at 9:00pm, Ken brought the whole national data network down in a controlled shutdown as the West Coast ended its working day. He shut everything down pretty much to give maximum resources to my test. At 9:15pm, Job 1 launched. The Master Control terminal of the IBM mainframe was talking to us via its printer and telling us what was going on. Job 1 being I/O intensive was expected to last about 35 minutes given the size of our data files. Ken's calculations were spot on.

Then, around 9:50pm, Job 2 launched. We could not believe what happened next! Every IBM mainframe computer had a key "Wait Light". If the light was on, the processor was idle. If it was blinking, it was doing things. But, if it was out, it was really busy. This would normally never occur. A mainframe computer's processor was simply never that busy. It would require serious software to make it that busy and most of ours was just too simple.

Well, as Job 2 launched, the Wait Light flickered and then just shut off! Ken, David and I looked at each other in a manner that said, "Say, whaat?"

"Well, okay Vijay, it is a processor intensive Job. So, this is not a surprise really." Ken offered. "But, damn it, I have never seen this in my life! A solid, hard shut off like this has never happened to me!"

"How long will Job 2 take? What's your guesstimate?" David asked perceptively.

"Well, by my calculations for today, because you know that each day is different, there is a wide range. The loan pipeline is changing all the time and so it is really hard to tell. But, on an average, generally speaking, my calculations suggest a time of 40 minutes or so for Job 2. But, hey, I could be totally wrong." Ken responded.

And so, our wait began. We hit 40 minutes, and nothing. We gave it more time, and nothing. We were coming up on 1 hour, and yet nothing. "Is it possibly in some kind of a logical loop?" David wondered.

"Nah! Because I can see that it is writing to disk at a steady pace. And the tapes are going well also. No, it is not in a loop, I am sure of it." Ken answered. "Well, how long do you think it will take?" David asked.

"David, we just don't know. Vijay has written the strangest reusable and re-entrant code I have ever seen. He is actually driving this machine at its full processing power in this Job. And it is still going. When is the end, I simply do not know."

We were now at 1 hour and 20 minutes. The Wait Light was still solid shut. David said, "Maybe we should abort it."

And then, suddenly, the Wait Light came on, with no blinking at all. The Master Control simply printed, "Job 2 End. Job 3 Start."

Job 3 launched and the printers went crazy spewing out the reports. Now, the mainframe processor was just sitting there, quite idle. The Wait Light remained fully on.

Ken checked the reports. He told David, "They seem fine. I think we may have a breakthrough here."

The next day, the reports checked out fine. We held classes on how to specify the parameters for reports and got out of the business of writing code daily to generate the reports.

The software I had written made some news in the industry. IBM software engineers came over to look at it. They took my code and published it under some IBM software product. I had no claim to it because I had no IP rights. I was told that it was the first case of "parameter driven" software ever written in the commercial world. And that it was also code that had tested the limits of actual mainframe processor performance in that era.

But what I did get was satisfaction. I was pleased that I could write something innovative, make a real difference in the lives of our people, and actually push an IBM 370 Series mainframe to it limits!

An Epic Crisis

Tuesday morning had started with what seemed like some usual production problems. The prior night we had experienced some weird hardware failures in the Data Center. Our folks and the IBM engineers had been working to fix things. Then, suddenly all hell broke loose.

Ken Davidge and John Sanders, the Manager of our Data Center, burst into the meeting that I was having with David in his office, with pure panic on their faces. "What has happened?" David asked calmly.

"We have a full-blown crisis on our hands, David!" Ken said breathlessly. "They cannot isolate the problem. It seems that something is corrupting all our data files! The entire production data sets and their backups are screwed up and unreadable! The national online network had to be taken down. We have no production going on in the Data Center at all. We are just dead in the water!"

"Also, the IBM guys are saying that it could be the core memory, or the controllers, or the data drives themselves, but nobody is sure. They need to run controlled diagnostics on every piece of hardware to find out what the hell is going on!"

It was time for "battle stations" in the Data Processing Division. George Rutland, EVP of Servicing, Finance & Data Processing, called a meeting of all the senior managers of AMC. With such a shutdown of the Data Center, nothing could function in any of its Divisions. In effect, the entire company was simply shut down nationwide!

"We all must support David and his team in this grave hour of crisis." George told everybody somberly. "Until they solve it, we must do what we can manually. We shall keep everybody informed."

With George's support, we focused on the tasks at hand. David said, "Ken, you should stay with the IBM team and the diagnostic work till we have the problem identified and a solution implemented. Focus on getting our Data Center hardware fixed and the whole thing back up and running again safely."

"John and Vijay, you guys focus on the recovery of our data sets. Obviously, we will have to do that at other Data Centers. I will find specific sites locally that we can go to physically in order to effect data recovery as fast as possible. Get your stuff ready to move offsite immediately."

We all moved at lightning speed. David made frantic phone calls and lined up time for us at the Data Centers of General Motors, Detroit Diesel, National Bank of Detroit, Ford, Chrysler, American Motors, etc. around the Detroit Metro area. We all had informal understandings in place about helping each other out in times like this. Everybody was helpful, concerned about the seriousness of our situation, and forthcoming with assistance. We grabbed any data processing capacity available anywhere.

With my small army of programmers in tow, we went from one Data Center to another carrying our disk packs, data tapes and decks of our source code. Using 1 day old and the last readable copy of the data sets, John and I began methodically.

The first step was to create at least 2 new backups of everything, in case we damaged things further. Then we had to run Production Jobs to catch up and bring everything to a current status. Finally, the latest data sets were backed up 3 times in case we had further failures at our Data Center again. It was a herculean challenge. We wrote code on the fly as needed and just kept going. Data integrity was the paramount concern. It had to be preserved. We knew that failure was simply not an option. The entire AMC, as a company, was in our hands that day.

We rotated the teams of programmers, but John and I had to be present throughout the whole exercise. We were the only ones with a full mental picture of the data sets and the architecture of various systems. We had to direct and verify all action steps with great precision and delicate care. It took us 2 whole days. We did not rest or sleep during Tuesday or Wednesday at all at the various remote facilities. David was everywhere with us as well.

By mid-day Wednesday, Ken had the problems identified and fixed at our Data Center, but we kept going where we were physically working. At 4:00am on Thursday morning, we returned to our Data Center and loaded up all the current data sets. Then we brought up all the various systems one by one and put them through detailed checks. By 7:00am all our systems were back up and running in our Data Center.

George Rutland called another companywide manager meeting and gave everybody a summary update on what had transpired in the last 2 days. We received a standing ovation from all! The best comment came from George Bender, EVP of Loan Production, when he said publicly, "You guys saved Advance Mortgage Corporation today. We cannot thank you enough."

Then, John and I received the sweetest gesture imaginable from George Rutland. He insisted that we be driven home by a designated driver because we had not slept in 2 days. He refused to let us drive home on our own.

A major crisis was resolved. But many lessons were also learnt about the handling of new technologies. While all computer technologies have changed and improved vastly since that era, those lessons remain as relevant today, as they were at that time.

The Green Card

Six months had passed since I had joined AMC. It was time for me to obtain my Training Visa extension. While the faculty at the MSU School of Business had been very supportive of my training visa needs, the time was at hand now to talk about a more lasting solution for me.

I approached David Guthrie.
"A Green Card?" he asked. "What in the world is that?"
David had never heard of such a thing. I explained it all to him and he promptly brought John Hamilton into the discussion.
"Yes, I know about it." John said. "Vijay, AMC would be delighted to sponsor you for an Immigrant Visa. Let us start the process at once. I will get our attorneys involved."
It was a long and slow saga to obtain a Green Card or an Immigrant Visa for me. They had to advertise my job to prove that I was not displacing a qualified US citizen. After obtaining the Labor Certificate, I had to wait my turn in the quota line. It took nearly 18 months from start to finish. During this period, I could not leave the USA for any reason or risk losing my job. Finally, the day arrived when I would actually receive it. Even that was quite eventful.

On that day, I had to undergo a medical exam. Then, I had to present myself at the Immigration Office in Detroit, with all the legal papers for verification and an interview. After that, I was sent off to yet another office that actually issued the Green Card which had arrived from Washington D.C. This office was attached to a Police Station in downtown Detroit.

The Officer checked everything yet again, and conducted another interview. Then he sighed and pulled out a file on me, which contained the Green Card. He had to separate it out and laminate it. Well, he did not know how to do that and messed it up! I stared at him in horror, wondering what would happen next.

"I guess I better get Andy to help me with this." he said carelessly. Thankfully, there was a spare copy, and Andy did not have hamburgers in his brain. He got it done with ease. My passport was stamped with the "Landed Immigrant" label, and I was handed the coveted Green Card finally. The Officer said dismissively, "You are done" and went off on his break.

He had absolutely no idea that he had just handed me my freedom! Or, what it meant for me.

At the AMC offices, it was a non-event as well. Nobody knew much about the Green Card. But three people did. They were John Hamilton, David Guthrie, and George Rutland. I was summoned to George's office and a bottle of champagne was popped for me.

In unison they said, "Vijay, welcome to America!"

The very next day, just to celebrate my "freedom", I left the USA. I drove across the Detroit River to Windsor, Canada. I had a beer at a bar, and crossed the border back into the USA an hour later. At the immigration entry point, I showed them my Green Card, and I was swiftly waved through. I was just delighted with the ease of it all!

Later that month, Dr. Clarke De Haven threw a party for me at his home in East Lansing. Speeches were made, and my "arrival" was grandly celebrated. But that is yet another story.

An Affair to Remember

It was love at first sight! She was stunningly pretty. She had the form, the curves, the lines, and that "come hither" look. From all around her, she was the center of a lot of attention. She was just too beautiful. Everybody ogled her, yearned for her, but nobody had the guts to approach her. Well, that is, until I stepped up. With total disregard for anybody around me, or their devious thoughts, I boldly strode forward towards her and looked directly at her without blinking an eye. And then, in a thrilling moment, we made contact!

She was a 1973 Datsun 240Z, an imported sports coupe from Japan, introduced to compete with monster machines, like the "Stingray" Corvette, that were made in America. She was petite, svelte, and quite muscular. She dripped class and just filled you with exotic promises when compared to the huge and vulgar American cars that were simply crude and too obvious. But here was the really amazing part. This Geisha was sent to make market in the very heartland of the auto industry in the USA, a town called Detroit, in the state of Michigan.

At the time, Michigan was the center of a long and explosive post-World War II economic boom, the like of which had probably not been seen anywhere in the world, in any century. In the Midwest region of the USA, there were three massive industrial sectors present. The first was agriculture, the second was automotive, and the third was transportation.

There were many sub-specialties everywhere as well. For instance, select companies focused just on gasoline or diesel engines designed to power huge train locomotives, or aircraft, or trucks and cars, or even small backyard well pumps. Others focused on agricultural machinery, or rolling stock for railways, and so on. There were also a lot of technological innovations underway everywhere, and a vast market available domestically to achieve a profit on the capital investments in them.

All the citizens, living and working in the area, took serious pride and interest in the local industrial products and manufacturing plants, including all their achievements or perceived faults. There was also a strong White Anglo-Saxon Protestant (WASP) Christian "work ethic" permeating the society at every level.

If you were a skilled immigrant to the USA and wanted to share in the fruits of this economic boom, you had to "assimilate" and "fit into" this society at large and its ways. In a country which cherished individualism on one hand, it went to a great extent on the other, to crush it when it came to sharing the economic fruits with the "new arrivals" in the land, or with people who were different in race, color, or religion. This was particularly hard for folks from Asia, or specifically India, which included me. I was at times openly referred to as "that brown guy from the land of holy cows." It did hurt, but I used to chalk it off to their ignorance, and just laugh it away.

One Monday morning in 1973, when I was still in school at MSU (Michigan State University, East Lansing) and working at the WKAR-TV station on campus, Paul Kazmirczak, one of the station engineers, came up to me and said gravely, "Hey, Vij, I worked on the new 98 all weekend long. Ya' know, they are crazy in their thinking. All of 'em!"

I replied, "Uh, Paul, what are you talking about?"

He was talking about his Oldsmobile 98 car, a top-of-the-line luxury sedan, manufactured in the nearby assembly plant in Lansing, Michigan. Their famous TV commercial tagline was, "Come to Lansing, and pickup an Olds, while the metal is still hot!"

"Well, ya' know that I got the new 98 last week, right? I jacked it up in my garage, and Tommy and I checked her out. The dual carbs are great, but the idiots at Olds Research got this newfangled thing called a "catalytic converter". Lemme tell you, because Tom and I figured it out by Sunday. It is a piece of s**t! Ya' know about it?"

"I am not sure, Paul. Does it not have something to do with controlling the awful emissions from cars to protect the environment?"

"Hoojamaflicks! That is crap, just like this word. Emissions? What emissions? If they are talking about the smell of gas and exhaust, dammit, they are missing the entire point!"

"I mean, what the hell good is it to have a car or a truck, with some real power, and not have the fragrance of gas, or diesel, or exhaust to go with it? Oh, and you know something else? These catalytic converters, they run the engine 20 degrees hotter! Yeah, Tom and I measured it. That is bad for the pistons, valves, gaskets, and the crank over the long haul. The MBF (Mean-time Between Failure) could drop by 20%, maybe. I have no doubt that you understand, Vij."

"Uh, yes, I do understand, I think." I replied, trying to hide the fact that I was mostly clueless.

"I knew you would. Tom and I are gonna go up to Lansing and teach the boys at Olds a thing or two about engine design. Wanna come?"

"But, hey, before I forget, my wife, Billy, said to tell you that she is expecting you to join us and the family, at the feast after church service this Sunday, okay?"

This was now 1975, and my life had changed dramatically. I had graduated from MSU with an MBA degree, had a great job in Detroit at a Citicorp company, and was in the market to buy a car. My trusty old 1969 Chevrolet Malibu, which Kashyap had handed over to me when he left for India in the summer of 1972, was near the end of its economic life. She had been my savior but was now banged up badly, had huge mileage on it, and was slowly dying. So, it was in this period, in a moment of pure emotional vulnerability, in fact during a lunch break, that I met my Geisha. And I just fell in love.

Unlike logical decisions, which are well reasoned and things that one should practice regularly, the emotional decisions, which can be simply disastrous, are just full of so much life, fun and joy. But they also present heartaches. Well, it has been a never-ending debate. Logic vs. emotion or function vs. form! Personally, at the time, I wanted to enjoy the various thrills of emotion, and screw the damn logic.

The "Z" (pronounced as in the American "Zee", and not the British "Zed"), as I called my Geisha, was simply lovely. She was blood red in color with a black leather interior. She had a "racing" stick shift, which meant that one could change gears with just a tap on the clutch and the shift. It had a manual choke and throttle to control the air fuel mixture for combustion, like in an airplane engine, and a rich instrumentation panel. The wheels were large and designed like racing cars. But foremost, she was bloody fast against anything on the road, a total joy to drive, and she also looked like nothing else on the roads of Michigan in 1975. Thus, began my problems.

None of this had even remotely occurred to me when I bought the Z. The sales folks also never gave me a "heads up" on what it would be like to own and drive a Japanese car in Detroit! I soon discovered that my colleagues at work, while very curious, would not ride in the Z with me! Many would say to me, "Vijay, how could you buy that car, when my brother is laid-off at Chrysler because of lack of sales?"

One day, late at night, in the countryside of Michigan, I stopped in my Z for some gas. The elderly attendant at the gas station would not sell me any gas!

I asked, "Why not?"

He said, "Just look at this! If you were a Jew, would you buy a Volkswagen?"

I apologized and pleaded with him. In the end, he said, "Oy, veh, you are just an ignorant kid. I will give you the gas, but promise me that you will read about the Holocaust." I promised and later on I actually did.

Then he said, "You know, for a while, I thought you were Jewish. Not Hassidic, mind you, but Ashkenazi. You are fair. Like my son. But then I thought that a Jewish kid would never drive a Nazi car!" I felt grateful, but totally humiliated.

Despite such difficulties, my love affair with the Z continued. I looked after her better than myself. It was a bit odd that, wherever I went to have basic things done for her, it seemed that nobody knew anything about this car. But I was a free spirit and did not worry about any of these things. In my mind, it was their problem, not mine. The Z provided me with some incredible experiences that I could have scarcely imagined.

One Saturday night I was returning from a party in East Lansing to Detroit. It was past midnight and I had a near 2-hour drive to get home. I had been drinking a little and everybody had asked me to crash with them for the night. But for some crazy reason, I had decided to drive back that night.

I got on the 96 freeway to Detroit, and was cruising on down, unaware of the weather conditions which I had not bothered to check. That night, the forecast called for light rain, freezing temperatures and a strong possibility of "black ice". About halfway home near Brighton, on this desolate freeway, I was crossing a short bridge when it happened.

Suddenly, I lost complete control of the Z! She felt like she was sliding on a long sheet of glass with soap water on it. There was no traction at all. Then I made another huge mistake. I downshifted. The high-performance engine raced up and my wheels spun. The Z went into a horizontal spin. I hit the clutch repeatedly to disengage the engine, and tried to steer her, at least to keep her on the freeway. But she kept spinning. I went through 2 full 360-degree harrowing spins with no control at all. Then suddenly, she found traction! After a massive jerk, she lunged forward. I hit my head hard on the steering wheel in all this, but then I pulled myself together and slowly brought her to a stop on the side. I was sweating profusely and scared out of my mind.

Just then, I heard a siren and a Highway Patrol car pulled up behind me with powerful headlights and flashing red and blue top lights. Shortly, a highway patrol officer walked up to my driver side window. I am thinking, "Oh, dear God, what now?"

"Are you okay? That was quite a stunt you pulled there, son! Don't you know that we got black ice everywhere tonight? What the hell kind of car is this anyway? Never seen one of these around here."

"Uh, thank you, sir. I think I spun out on some black ice back there."

"You sure did, boy! I was watching you in action. It's kinda late. You been drinking?"

"No, sir." I lied swiftly.

"Now look, son, these roads are all very dangerous tonight. I just finished with my 3rd crash and one serious injury. You do seem a bit shook up. So, follow me to the next exit, and join me for a cup of coffee. You need to relax a bit, okay?"

Officer Dombrowski was a kind and older man. He even "bought" me coffee. Well, nobody charged patrol officers near freeways in Michigan for food, let alone coffee. But he was also trying to ascertain if I was drunk. He satisfied himself and let me go home with warnings of caution on the road. I will never forget his stories of affection for drivers using "his roads".

I have many Z stories and may write some of them sometime, but I must tell you about the end of my "love affair". Because it just broke my heart.

One day, out of the blue, the Z started emitting a light smoky exhaust when the engine got warm. The manual choke lever did not seem to work like it did before. I took it to various mechanic shops in Detroit to have it examined, but nobody would even look at it! I would get a curt answer such as, "We only work on American cars here." The dealer I bought it from avoided me like the plague, saying, "We know nothing about these cars and cannot work on them. It came to us on a dealer swap, and we were glad to just get rid of it."

What was I to do now? Where could I go? Nobody I knew locally, at work or otherwise, would help me with my problem. I had become a pariah dog just because I had bought a foreign car! So, I thought about it, and soon the "Sabar Cola" (*water of the Sabarmati River which flows thru Ahmedabad, India*) kicked in. I devised a plan.

I waited till the end of a calendar month when all auto dealers are desperate to meet their monthly sales targets. I went with a friend in his car to a huge and high-volume Chevrolet dealer nearby in Detroit. I showed a strong interest in buying a Chevy and struck a deal with the salesman and his manager for the new car, loaded with many options, at a good price.

Then I sprang my surprise on them. I said, "Oh, I forgot to mention this, but I will be trading in my car against this purchase. I have my own financing, so it will be an all cash deal for you. I am sorry that I did not bring it in today." They gushed, smiled, and said, "Oh, no problem at all. Just bring it in when you come to pick up your new car and we will credit you its Blue Book value against the purchase price."

I drove the Z in when its engine was still cool and the exhaust smoke did not show. They looked at it aghast and made various urgent phone calls.

Eventually, they set its value, gave me the credit, and closed the deal. I caressed my darling Z slowly for one last time, and then drove off the lot in my new Chevy. Thus, my love affair ended. I never saw her anywhere again.

Epilogue

Some months or so later, I learnt from various sources, that the interest in my Z was huge all over Detroit! A lot of people knew about my car and its various metrics.

A vast community of mechanics, collectors, and auto lovers were incredibly interested in it and some were even keeping a track of it!

But it was a matter of public perception and shame to be associated with it in Detroit and so it was treated outwardly with scorn.

It was bought by an "anonymous buyer" within 24 hours of my turning it in! Its choke needed to be fixed and my guess is that the buyer was an auto mechanic, who probably did the job himself.

My Geisha vanished from sight forever. Like me, I am sure she made somebody very happy.

Two "Z" Stories

Almost Killed

I heard the screaming siren and I pulled over to the right side of the road. It was late at night, the police car was close behind and pulled up to a stop within a few feet of me. It was an amazing sight in my rear-view mirror. This police cruiser had its head lights on high beam and the two flood lights off its sides were also trained on me. The red and blue lights on its top and the strobe lights were flashing in addition. It was all designed to seriously intimidate.

I was thinking, "Gosh, what the hell did I do now?"

From behind me, on the same driver's left side, I saw in my left side mirror, an enormous African American man get out and start to walk towards me. His giant physical frame appeared to me in the form of a silhouette against all the lights, and it was scary. I felt that I had done nothing wrong, and so I had no reason to be afraid about anything. I decided to confront the matter at hand. I proceeded to open the door on the left side of my Z, and stepped out. Then, I reached for my wallet in the left breast pocket of my jacket, because I knew from watching police shows on TV that they would ask me for my driver's license.

"Freeze, Motherf**ker! Don't move!" a booming voice rang out, and I saw this huge black man drop to his knee, holding a drawn gun in both his hands, aimed directly at my chest. It was very frightening. Reflexively, in a wild snap, I put my hands up and out, with my palms facing the police car.

The voice firmly said, "Stay where you are. Stay still! Bobby, check her."

I sure did, because I was scared out of my mind. I had never had a gun pointed at my chest by a police officer, ever or anywhere in my life!

The giant black cop then slowly rose to his feet and approached me, still pointing his gun at me. As he came closer to me, I noticed a pair of white hands on the other side of the police car. There was a white cop there! I guessed he was his partner. He had a shotgun in his hands, which also was pointed directly at me.

The black cop came up to me and frisked me quickly but efficiently, while the white cop was checking out the insides of my Z to see if there was anybody else there. Shortly, he came around to the left side as well and showed himself.

He said, "Yeah, she checks clean. Joe, does he have any heat on him? Hey, Joe, you okay?"

Joe, the large black cop with greying hair, was not okay. He was sweating profusely and trembling. Then I heard him whisper, "Oh, dear Lord, forgive me... Sweet Jesus, please forgive me..."

Hearing this, I began, "You know, maybe we ought to... er..."

"Shuddup, you a**hole!" the white cop screamed at me. "Just shut the f**k up! If you so much as fart, I will blow your head off. Do ya git?" In pure fear, I replied, "Yes, sir." But I noticed that this white cop had also started to sweat and tremble. Beneath his tough façade, he seemed confused and scared.

I stood there in total silence for quite some time with my hands up, bathed in the police lights. By now, two other police cruisers had arrived. There was a "gawker's block" on the road as well. Soon, they cleared it all, and then, Joe approached me. All the guns had now been put away.

He said softly to me, "Are you okay? Put your hands down and relax. That Bobby is something. I am sorry for what happened. It should not have been this way."

I said, "Sir, I am sorry as well if I did anything wrong. But I have no idea about what just happened! What was all this about? And why did it seem to me like you were praying? Did you do something wrong?"

"I almost shot you dead! That is what almost happened. Son, tonight, Jesus saved me from taking your life. Yes, I was praying to him."

"What? Say... WHAAT? Why would you want to shoot me? That makes no sense at all."

"In Detroit, most cops get shot and killed stopping cars. We are usually chasing drug dealers, or pimps, and they will kill anything for a few bucks. They drive these tricked out cars which are very showy. Usually, we know these pimpmobiles. But tonight, we see this car! What the hell kind of a car is it anyway? It is so different, that we decided to stop you and check it out."

"But why all the guns?"

"Well, let me put it this way. I could have shot you dead tonight, claimed "self-defense under mortal threat" in a court of law, and they would have let me off. You would be dead, but I would be free and return to duty. That is how it would have gone down. The guns are entirely for our safety."

"For your safety? Hey, they were pointed at me! What reason made you do that? It still makes no sense."

"Well, let me explain. For a moment, let's play the tape back from my eyes and examine what I saw. As I approached your car, your engine was running. That is warning #1! They do that, so they can get away fast after shooting a cop. Then, you step out. Your jacket is open with your back to the lights. I cannot see your torso, and I don't know if you got a handgun or a machine gun against it! Warning #2! Then, you turn and face me. And at once, you lift the left lapel of your jacket and with your right-hand reach into your armpit area. That is where most guns are carried. Ever see a James Bond movie? That says, imminent attack! Warning #3! So, I drew my gun, dropped to one knee, and was at battle stations, expecting fire from you. We are trained to do this. But I yelled, and luckily you snapped your hands out and into the open, facing me. Believe me, I was a split-second away from pulling the trigger. If I had, this .44 Magnum would have blown you 6 feet away, and your chest would have a huge hole in it. These are nasty weapons with serious stopping power."

"Young Bobby here, is new and still learning. He gets excited quickly and needs to calm down. But his heart is in the right place. He yells and swears a lot, but most of the time, that is because he is also scared."

"So, son, the next time you are stopped by a cop, remember to do the following. Shut your engine, if possible. Stay in your car and don't get out. Keep your hands on the steering wheel and visible at all times. And NEVER make a sudden move of any kind. To us, it appears like you are reaching for a weapon. Our job is to protect and defend the public. But we are scared for our lives too."

Now, it was my turn to break out in a sweat and to start to shake and tremble. As I realized rapidly how close it had all been, I got even more terrified. Joe and Bobby also noticed this, like they were almost expecting it. They tried to calm and comfort me gently.

"Hey, what kind of a car is this? Never seen one like it around here!" Bobby said, trying to break the tension. "Ya' know something? How about we trade rides? If you let us drive this honey, Joe and I will let you drive a Detroit Police cruiser, with lights going and all. What d'ya say?"

Well, we did just that! They drove around my Geisha for a bit and were thrilled. Then, I got to take a genuine, high performance, twin carb, turbo charged, V-8 engine powered, monster cruiser of the Detroit PD, for one hell of a ride around town! I broke all kinds of red lights and stop signs, with its siren going, and all its lights blazing and blinking!

They were very surprised when I put her through a controlled 180 degree "wheelie" (a horizontal spin) on a wide street, with all the tires screaming and smoking, like they do in the chase sequences in the movies!

At the end of it all, Joe laughed heartily, and said it so very well - "Son, you are adorably nuts!"

I agreed, wholeheartedly.

An Unusual Ride

It was a late Sunday morning. I was hungry and did not want to cook breakfast. I decided to go over to the local International House of Pancakes (IHOP) in Southfield, where I lived. As I pulled the Z into the parking lot, a young African American man came up to my car. He said, "Please, mister, can you drive me to St. John's Hospital? It's nearby and I need to get there quickly." I wondered why he had approached me instead of calling for a cab. Then I thought that maybe he was just rushed. So, I relented and drove him over.

I dropped him off and as I was leaving, he returned in a hurry, and asked if I could drop him off at a nearby pharmacy, if it was not too much of a problem. I sighed and agreed again. Then things took a strange turn.

In a few minutes, he opened his coat and pulled out a large wad of cash. It had lots of $100 bills and I saw that he also had a gun tucked into his belt! Then he started to direct me in taking various turns.

So, I said, "I cannot do this any further. I will have to drop you off."

He replied quite simply, "Mister, you better just drive, like I am saying..." The tone of his voice had changed drastically and now there was a firm edge to it. Since I had seen his gun, or perhaps because he had shown it to me on purpose, I decided that it would be wise to just go along for now.

We did not go to any pharmacy, and it was turning into a much longer drive. He seemed to be very curious about the Z. He kept asking me relentless questions about her, which I thought was very odd. We seemed to be going towards Highland Park, a very dangerous area of Detroit at the time.

This neighborhood was a testimonial to the pathetic urban decay in parts of inner Detroit. It had many rundown, vandalized, or abandoned houses. Parts of it looked like a war zone. It was a den of drug dealing, prostitution, and some very unsavory people. Most folks simply avoided going anywhere near it. I was now becoming alarmed by my situation and the increasing danger all around me. I had to do something, and do it quickly.

But what and how, were the questions swirling in my mind. In a bit, a plan came together in my mind. It was tentative, risky, and a lot could go wrong in it, but then what alternative did I have? The man sitting next to me was getting more vocal, aggressive, and bolder by the minute. Also, I noticed in the rear-view mirror, that now an old beaten up taxi like car, a yellow Plymouth, was following us at a steady distance. It was all now becoming quite scary.

As we came up on an intersection, with a stop sign, I feigned a problem. I said, "Darn it, this is not right! What is happening here?"

The man looked concerned, and asked, "What? Whassup, dude? Is the car okay? Now, don't mess this baby up!"

I replied, "I don't know. She's pulling hard to the right. Can you check the front right tire for me? Maybe we got very low air, or a flat."

He said, "Oh, yeah, sure."

He did not know that the Z rode low and her seats were aft of center. You could not see her front tires at the end of her stretched out frame by just looking out of your window. You would need to actually step out of the car and lean out to be able to see them. I desperately wanted this man to be out of my car. Luckily, he took the bait.

He looked out of his window first and realized that he could not see the tire. Then he opened his right-side door, stepped out with one leg on the ground with his weight on it, and leaned out to take a look. My engine was running, the clutch was pressed, and the Z was in gear. I let go, gunned her, and took a screaming sharp left turn. The man fell out of the door on to the road in the middle of the interaction! I waited for nothing, and just took off. Shortly, I noticed in the rear-view mirror, that the Plymouth that had been following us, had actually stopped and picked up the man. Then this crazy chase began.

It was terrifying. The Plymouth was in my hot pursuit and I was in an area that I was not familiar with at all. I was thinking, "How do I get out of here? What streets can I take? Where can I find somebody to help me? God, please do not let me turn into a dead-end street! They have at least one gun. Maybe there are guys in that car with more guns. They could start to shoot at you at any moment."

I drove like a scared animal running for its very life. I broke all red lights, stop signs, and every traffic law imaginable, hoping that a police car would notice it, chase me, and arrest me. Therein lay one option for my safety. But there were no police cars around anywhere. Meanwhile, the Plymouth was steadily gaining on me and getting closer.

Suddenly, I came up on a major, divided street, heading west. I sensed that this street would hit the 10 (Lodge) freeway in a few miles, and I took a screeching turn on to it. The Plymouth was now about 50 yards or so behind me and made the turn as well! I was wondering, "Why such committed pursuit? What do these guys want? This is very brazen of them. Just who the hell do they think they are?" Now, I started to get angry. I felt it develop, and when that happens with me, on rare occasions, it is usually not a good sign.

I let them align their Plymouth behind me, in my traffic lane, at a near enough distance. Then, I downshifted the Z, red-lined her tach, and took off like a rocket! I tapped through all the gears fast, and was doing 70+ mph in just a few seconds, still hoping that a cop car would pick me up. That did not happen, but I left that Plymouth behind, almost standing still. I came up to the Lodge freeway, got on it, and seconds later, I was doing 100+ mph. My Z left those bastards in the dust. It was not even a contest. I never saw them again.

To this day, I cannot make any sense of this whole episode. What was it all about? I have more questions than answers. Perhaps these people were really interested just in my Geisha. But why? They seemed to know nothing about her. Maybe she was somebody's fantasy for a new pimpmobile!

However, at the end of that day, I was left with the distinct feeling that I had been set up by somebody and that it was not just a random event.

But they underestimated her. I believe strongly that my Geisha saved my life that day.

First Return to India

66 "I am led to believe that you are going to India, Vijay." Mr. Irving said on the phone. "May I request an appointment to meet with you?" I was shocked out of my wits!

The Irving family of Detroit had started Advance Mortgage Corporation decades ago. Mr. Irving, who had been the legendary CEO, had built the company into a hugely successful business and had sold it to Citicorp at a handsome price in 1973.

He was in his early 70's and desired a life of retirement. This move was timely for him and the extended Irving family. He was regarded highly and commanded deep respect as an innovator in the mortgage banking industry in the USA. He had a great presence about him. He was gracious, unassuming, and just charming. He had met me earlier on a few occasions socially, but a request for an appointment with me from such a man was just unimaginable for me.

"Sir, absolutely. I am available at any time convenient for you." I gushed. I had goosebumps about a formal encounter with such an iconic man.

We met in a conference room. He was so polite about everything. After pleasant inquiries about my work and extending sincere compliments about some of our recent achievements in the Data Processing Division, he came to the point.

"Vijay, I need your counsel." he said. "My wife and I are planning a holiday trip to India. Perhaps you can guide me on what we should plan and how we may go about it." I was simply stunned.

In the mid-1970's, India, as a holiday destination, was not on the top of many minds. In Detroit and in the US Midwest generally, you might as well be planning a visit to a different planet. For most folks, India was just a poor and strange land of holy cows, snake charmers, old palaces, and weird religious practices. When people met me, they thought I was from Iran, Italy, Egypt, or Eastern Europe, but never India. Sadly, ignorance about India at the time was quite pervasive.

Over an hour, I covered all the ground for him. I suggested an itinerary, recommended a travel agent, and answered a host of insightful questions from him. My information was current because a short while ago I had completed the travel research for my upcoming trip.

"Vijay, thank you so much. This information is valuable and quite helpful." Mr. Irving concluded. "Please tell your parents, when you visit with

298

them, that we are very grateful to them for letting us have you here at Advance Mortgage in Detroit. Do ask them to visit us here. We would be delighted."

It appeared that my impending trip to India had become a topic of news at Advance. All sorts of people would come up to me and ask, "Are you really going to India? Why?" Hardly anybody knew my background or my story.

I had planned to spend the month of July, 1976, in India. It would be my first return home after leaving in August, 1971. A lot of water had flowed under the bridge, as the saying goes. After 5 years of being away, not having seen my parents or extended family, it was a holiday I looked forward to with joy and also some trepidation. I wondered how it would all turn out. Perhaps India was still much the same, but I had become a changed person considerably. It weighed heavily on my mind.

However, before I could undertake such a trip, I had to deal with some financial realities. By nature, even though I was poor, I was a proud man. While I had accepted financial assistance, when I had no other choice, I never forgot the repayment of those obligations or the emotional gratitude. My creditors were my older brothers. With interest, I owed Kashyap a repayment for the value of the car he had given me in 1972. Similarly, with interest, I owed Ajay a repayment of the funds he had given me to cover expenses for a Quarter at MSU in 1973. I had meticulously saved money to achieve these objectives. One day, I wrote them checks of repayment.

It caused a major uproar! They said, "Are you crazy? This was a gift to you. There is no repayment required." But I would have none of that. I told them that it was certainly their privilege, as my older brothers, to give me a gift. However, we were not talking about gifts here. These were acts granting unsecured loans to me. These loans were the most difficult to get, since they were the highest risk. For a foreign student, they were impossible to obtain even for graduate studies. I told them that if I did not pay them back, I could not live with myself. After much back and forth, they relented and cashed my checks. I felt a major sense of financial closure.

But I was still not done. I still had one more obligation to deal with in India. I took funds with me for it, but more on that in a bit.

Finally, the time came for me to leave for India. But the day before, my dear friend from MSU Business School days, Ron Wilsie, who was also now working at AMC, came up to me. "Hey, are you all set to go?" he asked. "More or less." I replied. Then Ron did something very sweet for me.

He said, "Here, take this and either wear it around your neck or keep it with you. It is a silver pendant on a chain. St. Christopher, the patron saint of travelers, is embossed on the pendant. He will protect you. My Mom gave it to me a while ago. I want you to take it with you on this journey." It was such an amazing and loving gesture!

My departure from the USA was ordinary. I flew from Detroit to New York and then to Bombay. Then I took the late afternoon flight to Ahmedabad. In those days, the tiny airport at Ahmedabad had around 4 Indian Airlines flights per day, I think. There were two in the morning and two in the evening. They came from and returned to Bombay and Delhi respectively. It was still a sleepy little tiny airport.

I arrived in Ahmedabad and realized that there was nobody there to receive me! My parents were nowhere around. I figured that maybe they were a bit late and decided to just wait. But time went on and nobody showed up. The return flight left, the airport became barren, and they started to shut down the whole facility. The "chowkidar" (*security guard*) told me to take the Indian Airlines bus into town, because the airport was so remote that no other transport was available after the bus had departed. But I decided to wait it out and told him so.

Then he says, "Saheb, cha pisho?" *(Saheb, would you like some tea?)* I accepted graciously. He asked his wife to come over and fix all of us some nice tea. She was a sweet lady and made us some great "desi masala" tea *(Indian spiced tea with milk)* on a portable kerosene primus stove. I paid him and then offered him a cigarette from my pack of Marlboro's. He was delighted with the strange foreign brand with filter tips! His wife accepted one too and smoked it with us.

While all this was underway, my father was in the midst of a family storm. The Ambassador car had returned late from the shop after some repairs. So, he thought that I may have taken the Indian Airlines bus into town. My parents went to the IA office near Nehru Bridge and saw that I did not get off the bus. Where could I be? Pappaji figured that I must still be at the airport. After all, that would be the logical thing to do. But my mother disagreed.

She said, "E gher gayo hashe. Taxi ma." *(He must have gone home in a taxi.)* "Tame Shashiben ne phone karo. Tyan pan gayo hoy." *(Call Shashiben as well. He may have gone there also.)*

Well, dear Shashiphoi had no clue about what was going on. The moment she learnt about what was happening, she proceeded to lace into my father!

"Virubhai, tame kashu samajhta nathi. Tame moda kem padya? Chhokaro avyo chhe." *(Virubhai, you do not understand anything. Why were you late? Your son has returned.)*

"Shashi, reheva de. Vijay avyo chhe?" Pappaji asked. *(Shashi, let it be. Has Vijay come there?)*

"Na, mane kayi khabar nathi. Hun hamana Maninagar avu chhu." she said. *(No, I have no information at all. I am coming to Maninagar right now.)*

Then my mother lets loose. "Meh ketali vaar kahyu chhe? Aa gaadi kadhi nakho! Nakkami chhe. Pan tame manata nathi" *(How many times have I told you? Get rid of this car! It is useless. But you don't listen to me.)*

My father simply clammed up against all these verbal assaults. Even though it was now 2-hours late, he just drove to the airport. He was certain that I was waiting there. That is what he would have done.

In the fading light of this early July evening, the black Ambassador car came into view. Pappaji laughed out loud at seeing me sitting quietly on my luggage with a closed airport behind me. There were cheers, hugs, and even tears, as I met my parents after 5 long years. My mother was just beside herself! We loaded up the Ambassador and drove back to Maninagar in great relief. But it was short lived.

At Nikunj, our bungalow in Maninagar, there was a near war underway! A large group of people had gathered. Motakaka, Pramodkaki, Ushakaki, Shashiphoi, and lots of our neighbors were all there. There was an intense and loud debate underway.

"Aa kem thayu? Kem moda padya? Bus pase javatu hashe? Tamane khabar chhe, airport to bandh thayi gayu chhe? Vijay kyan chhe? Kadach avyo nathi. Ene America bahu gami gayu chhe!" *(How did this happen? Why were they late? How can you go to the bus stop? Do you know, the airport is now closed? Where is Vijay? Maybe he has not come. Maybe he has become very fond of America!)*

We walked in, but nobody noticed. Eventually, my father said, "Would you all care to meet Vijay?"

Heads turned, there were looks of surprise, and then shrieks of joy! All the crazy nonsense stopped promptly.

Such was my first return home to India.

July is a month of intense monsoon rains in western India. That year the monsoon season was strong and there were lots of disruptions in travel by roads. So, my time was confined mainly to Ahmedabad. I could not visit places like Rajkot or Baroda which was very disappointing. But I spent quality time with my parents and the extended family. Also, there was a shroud of sadness in Maninagar because my uncle, Munikaka, had passed away a few months earlier rather suddenly. His daughter and my cousin, Shridevi, was in New Jersey with her husband, Sumir, and so I brought news about their lives to Ushakaki, who was still quite distraught about the loss of Munikaka. I tried my best to cheer everybody up as much as possible.

My main source of entertainment was our dog, Moti. He was a big German Shepherd (Alsatian) and went nuts when I arrived in Nikunj. He remembered me very well and would not leave me alone! He whined and moaned for a whole day as if asking me, "Where have you been?" The environment was just amazing as well.

The sounds of birds, monkeys, and other animals were everywhere. In the mornings, I would wake up to the sweet musical calls of "koyal" or "maina" birds. The morning tea service and breakfast with Pappaji was always a real treat. I enjoyed all sorts of tasty foods and delicious dishes prepared by my Mom at various meals. I was emotionally overwhelmed as all the memories came flooding back to me. My life in the USA suddenly seemed distant and also trivial.

There was no television in Ahmedabad at the time so we listened to the radio music programs. In the evenings, on many days, my father had a very active "bridge club" underway and so we would play lots of bridge. But mostly we spent a lot of time talking about my 5 years away and reminiscing about countless things. Oh, and all the visits from various neighbors and family members were an ongoing phenomenon. It was just marvelous. The only serious problem I faced was with the insects and mosquitoes. They were everywhere, and I got bitten really well rather quickly despite all the fumigation efforts.

In a few days, I brought up with Pappaji my issue of financial repayment. He asked me, "What do you have in mind?

"Pappaji, I want to repay Lilyben for the grant she gave me 5 years ago. It was a sweet gesture on her part at that time. Now, I must pay her back." I said.

He smiled and replied gently, "She will not take any money from you. If you try to repay her, she will feel insulted. You must keep in mind that the Indian culture is different in these matters."

"But there must be a way." I protested. The conversation was inconclusive. I needed a new approach. I had to think outside of the "normative box". What could I do? It was all so confusing to me.

Then, I hit upon an idea. I wrote Lilyben a letter and enclosed a check with it in the amount of the grant with interest for 5 years and a little more. In this letter, I wrote, "Dear Lilyben, I was the recipient of a grant from the Pandya Memorial Trust 5 years ago. This grant was very valuable to me in enabling me to go to the USA for graduate studies. I will remain grateful forever to the Trust for this timely assistance. I feel strongly that such noble acts should continue in the future in providing help to other students who may follow. So, I would like to make a donation to the endowment fund of the Pandya Memorial Trust. It is but a small gesture on my part to assist in the continuation of this fine program."

I learnt much later that when Lilyben received my letter with the enclosed check in Bombay, she had tears in her eyes! It seemed that in all the years, I was perhaps the first grant recipient who had sought to donate to the Pandya Memorial Trust to support its mission of giving grants to students for further studies.

The only trip I managed to bake into the month was a quick visit to Delhi. I met my dear RKC buddies, Himanshu Jani and Vijay Kaul. Also, I visited with Ajay Kaushish, who was at MSU at the same time as me. The Kaushish family owned the famed Sheila Theatre in Delhi. We hung out for a couple of fabulous days and caught up on our lives.

The month in India flew by in what seemed like the blink of an eye. I insisted that my parents make plans to visit us in the USA and see our lives for themselves. They promised to do so in 1978. The goodbyes were painful and gut wrenching. I was sad during my entire return journey. I spent a couple of days in New York/New Jersey area to debrief with Kashyap, Ajay, and Shridevi/Sumir and then returned to Detroit.

When I reached my apartment, I remember checking my finances just to be certain about the state of things. All my financial obligations had been retired and I had also covered the costs of my visit to India fully and successfully.

After 5 hard and trying years in the USA, I was finally debt free, and full of hope for the future. I had $25 left in my checking account!

I felt a quiet sense of accomplishment.

San Francisco & Crocker Bank

The First Line Job

In Citicorp companies there was a widespread understanding of where lay the real corporate power. The various Divisions within all the companies could be classified into two silos. The first, and the most important, was a silo where resided the responsibilities for generating revenue. The second was a silo which included all Divisions that were supporting in nature. They were vital as well, but were viewed as "cost centers". For the people who worked in these silos, these differences were quite apparent in the expressed behavior, attitudes, and a sense of self-importance exhibited by the managers.

There were colloquial terms to describe these silos. The first was called the "Line" Divisions (or "Mainline" Divisions) and the second was "Staff" Divisions. In this "caste system", the Line Divisions were considered the most important. Well, if the company could not generate sufficient revenues, nothing else mattered much, did it? Further, all jobs or positions were also classified with the same nomenclature. You could be in a support position in a support Division. For example, a guy in the Finance Division (Staff), who managed the company bank accounts, would be in a Line Position, but a guy who printed the checks would be in a Staff Position.

For an MBA recruit, there was a typical career progression. You started in a Staff position in a Staff Division usually. Then you proceeded to a Line position in it. After that you were sent off to a Staff position in a Line Division. And if you did well, you got the coveted Line position in it.

In Line positions, you were usually required to manage people and be responsible for budgets and financial targets for your unit. These were the real experiences and key stepping stones to achieve senior executive positions. Also, the rotation program gave you training in a wide swath of functions and that was rightfully deemed necessary for your career development. Obviously, like most things in life, all these moves depended upon opportunities, openings, and at times just sheer luck.

After returning from India in 1976, I began to give my career some serious thought. While the Data Processing Division was great and I was involved in a lot of wonderful things, it would do little for my long-term career growth at AMC, it seemed to me at the time. So, I requested a change to a Line Division.

Well, there is an old saying, "Be careful what you wish for! It may be granted."

In the fall of 1976, I was offered the job of 2nd VP & Manager of FHA Section 235 Loan Servicing Portfolio at AMC. It was the stinking sewer of the huge Servicing Division! This portfolio was like an entire "mini" Servicing Division unto itself. The Section 235 loans were subsidized by the government. So, in every step, in every function, there were two parts to everything. One part was the mortgagor and the other was the government. Also, it was highly regulated and subject to endless process and financial audits. It was run as an entirely self-contained Unit.

It was in a serious mess, which desperately needed to be cleaned up. AMC was facing major penalties and fines from the Dept. of Housing & Urban Development (HUD) because of all the process and accounting issues. Nobody with a sane mind wanted to touch it, so obviously it was dropped into my lap! Instead of congratulations, I received messages of condolences. Many people privately thought that I had just gone totally nuts.

But all the portfolio issues aside, I faced many other challenges, for which I was totally unprepared. They left me even more bewildered. I was used to managing a staff of programmers, who were all professionals, and mostly men. But the staff of the entire Section 235 Unit comprised of some 100+ clerical women, most of whom were between 18 to 30 years of age. They were mainly high school graduates with no plans for further studies. Also, most were hoping to be married soon to their boyfriends and leave the AMC job quickly. There was no sense of any kind of loyalty or commitment to anything at all.

Oh, everybody wanted their paycheck, but nobody really wanted to work for it. Every day began with the torture of trying to determine who had not shown up for work and how we could compensate for it. The excuses I heard were just off the charts! I had to deal with young women having their periods (twice in a month!), sicknesses, abortions (two in 30 days!), lack of babysitters, domestic quarrels, religious holidays, exotic funerals, and on and on. Most of it was just blatant lies.

I grew up in a hurry and became one tough "son of a bitch". I gave nobody any quarter. I used the American Baseball analogy, "Three strikes and you are out!" One morning, I fired 10 women simultaneously because they had just had their 3rd strike. I did it publicly and in the full view of everybody. I wanted the rest to witness the carnage and remember it. They had a driven boss and I wanted them to know it. The news spread like wild fire through AMC that day. Folks started to view me with a sense of fear and I could not tell if that was good or bad.

There was this one tough lady named Lois. She was around 35 and quite a rebel rouser. She started a movement within the entire Section 235 staff to get me fired. She was openly defiant of my authority. But she was also highly knowledgeable and useful for our mission. I asked to meet with her, but she refused. I approached her to talk with her, but she would have nothing to do with me. She was Polish, very fair, and a redhead. I wondered if there was a racist twinge to all this, but I concluded that it was not so. Maybe she just did not like me or my methods? Regardless, I could not have any such behavior from anybody within the Unit.

So, I sent word to her that either she meets with me the next morning at 9:00am or she can leave AMC. Next morning, she was at work, but did not come over to meet with me. At 9:15am, I fired her. She made a huge scene and started crying. Apparently, she thought that I would not follow through on my statement. She considered herself indispensable to the Unit and just did not believe my words. She asked, "Why?'

I replied in a stone-cold manner, "Lois, you messed with a cobra. Now, get out of my sight." I never had any personnel problems after that. We focused on the tasks at hand, made huge progress, and actually started to have some fun as a Unit.

It was now February of 1978. Michigan was in the grip of a beastly cold winter. We had almost accomplished our critical mission of fixing the Section 235 loan portfolio and all its broken computer systems. A HUD audit team was on hand for our annual certification and senior management eyes were keenly focused on it.

Everybody wanted to know what the audit outcome would be after our massive efforts at clean-up of the mess over the past year and a half. Well, we sailed through the audit! We were given a clean bill of health and also a lot of compliments by the auditors. In particular, they said that our systems now set the standard for Section 235 loan servicing across USA. There was a huge celebration party. I ordered 25 pizzas for the entire staff! The Servicing Division EVP at the time, David Fusco, showed up to congratulate everybody.

I returned to my office and just then the phone rang. "Hello, Vijay. This is George Rutland." the voice said. I was shocked! George had left AMC some six months earlier for a great new job with Crocker National Bank in San Francisco, California. We had remained in touch off and on and he was quite familiar with the Section 235 loan portfolio debacle that I had been tasked with solving. I briefed him on our wonderful news of the day.

"That is fantastic, Vijay. Well done, and my congratulations! Yes, it sure was a can of worms." George said. "But I am calling you for a different reason. Here at Crocker Bank, we have some really interesting opportunities for someone with your skills. I would like you to visit us and have a look. If nothing else, it will at least get you out of the winter cold for a few days! Would you be interested?"

To say that I was stunned would be an understatement! We chatted for a bit and I accepted the invitation to visit Crocker Bank in San Francisco. I had not visited California since 1973 when I was still at MSU.

In such a manner, in the dead of winter in Michigan, began my adventure towards the West Coast of the USA.

Crocker National Bank

I flew into San Francisco on a Thursday evening after work. I had taken the Friday off and was to return on Sunday evening. George picked me up at the SFO (San Francisco International) airport. He started laughing when he saw me, because I looked like a clown! I had all the winter clothes on me from Michigan and it was all so out of place in gorgeous, warm, and sunny California! We had a lovely dinner at the Hyatt Hotel on Union Square where I was to stay.

George Rutland was EVP of the Operations Group of the Crocker Bank and reported to the CEO. George gave me an overview briefing on Crocker Bank and my schedule for the next day.

It was a full schedule of interviews and meetings. It was also an education for me on the various functions and workings of the Operations Group of a commercial bank in California. It was a different world from that of mortgage banking. Also, San Francisco was the center of West Coast commercial banking at the time. There were other major banks around as well. Bank of America, Wells Fargo Bank, and others were a major presence. Further, California permitted statewide branch networks, so these banks were quite large in terms of their physical footprint, and the size of their deposit base. It was quite fascinating in many ways.

My lunch was scheduled at 1:00pm with John Broderick, SVP in the Operations Group. Unknown to me, he had been receiving feedback on my interviews throughout the morning from all the folks I had met. So, this lunch turned into a sales pitch for me. He took me to the Fisherman's Wharf, and we had a fantastic lunch at a place overlooking the SF Bay.

At the lunch I realized that most folks I had met were all from Citicorp companies on the East Coast! It seemed that a near migration of talent had been underway for some time from the East to the West. Many people knew each other and there was even a strong New York accent present all around.

"Vijay, you belong here with us." John smiled and said simply. "This is a shot at a banking career on the West Coast and I am certain that you will find it to be a great fit for you. Besides, just look at this bay! Can you think of a better place to live? You can sail your weekends away!" John got carried away. We had a near 3-hour lunch! The secretaries at the office were frantically looking for us wondering if something had happened to us.

I was sold that afternoon. I told John and George that if all else worked out in terms of the financial package, I would join Crocker Bank. It did, and I accepted the offer.

The Union Fight

I relocated to San Francisco and joined Crocker Bank in a couple of months. After 6 years, it was bitter sweet to leave Michigan, but one must grab a passing brass ring when the opportunity is at hand.

In the very first week, I met Jim Jones. He had also recently joined Crocker Bank from Citicorp companies. He knew John Broderick from those days as well. Little did I know at the time that these would be very dear and long-lasting relationships for me over the ensuing years and decades.

Most of us new recruits were rapidly placed into Line Management positions within the Operations Group. I was handed initially the Area Proof Centers all around California and later on, all the Check Processing and related functions for Northern California. But at the time, we had a huge fight on our collective hands.

The International Longshore & Warehouse Union (ILWU), an entity of highly questionable methods and reputation, was engaged in trying to unionize the back-office operations at Crocker Bank in San Francisco. This was a serious and direct challenge for the management cadre at Crocker Bank.

Further, the Union had specifically targeted Crocker Bank and made great progress in obtaining sign-ups from our clerical and other staff members. It seemed that we would be headed for a unionization vote in a near span of time. To every manager, having a unionized back office in a Bank was just unthinkable. Imagine trying to run the back office of a Bank under the terms of a collective bargaining agreement, threats of strikes, protests, arbitrations, etc. It would be madness and could potentially shut the Bank down. This fight simply had to be won.

But there were all sorts of laws and regulations governing this whole process. It severely hampered our abilities at making meaningful changes and bringing about efficiencies in all our processes. The HR folks were everywhere, telling all of us about the various "do's & don'ts" all the time, to protect us from potential litigation. It was a highly toxic environment.

Every line manager in the OG had issues to deal with. In my area of responsibility, it was a highly volatile situation since I had people working 7 x 24 hours in shifts. I had to somehow make a connection with all the staff, and in particular, those on the "twilight" and "graveyard" shifts. They did not know me at all. I was generally written off as "management", not to be trusted, and so basically ignored. I thought about this problem gravely. I had to do something and I had to do it quickly.

I remembered my father's words when he had to confront labor problems in his career in India. He had said, "Vijay, always remember the human connection. Inherently, there is good in everybody. But developing trust is the first step. If you develop it, the human nature responds positively." On an instinct, I decided to leave my office, and drop right into the trenches with my staff. I decided to become one of them.

I started working with them during the twilight and graveyard shifts. I listened to all their issues and problems. It appeared that "management" was nowhere to be seen during these shifts. Their concerns ranged from important to trivial things. For example, many people complained about not getting their paychecks on time or not getting paid for overtime hours correctly. There was nobody to talk to about these problems during their working hours. Others whined about the "Coke" and "coffee" machines that had not worked for months. The cafeteria was closed during these hours so this was an important matter to them. I was astounded! I got with the HR folks immediately on the payroll issues. Then I called the vending machine companies and got a "Pepsi" machine installed, just to keep Coke honest. I kept at it doggedly on every matter, large or little. People soon began to notice. The murmur began that, "Go to Vijay. He will fix it." Well, it was at least a start.

One day, I found myself in the middle of a heated ad hoc meeting on the work floors at 2:00am. All work had stopped, people were arguing about something, and it was all "management's fault"! I made inquiries, but nobody would tell me anything. So, I decided to confront them all head on.

"You all keep complaining about management!" I said. "Who is this so-called management, let me ask you?" I did not get an answer, but everybody stared at me in wonder, and a little fear.

"Well, let me tell you bluntly. You are looking at management right now. It is called Vijay. I am the management. Whatever your problems may be, you must talk with me. I will listen and take action to solve them. I am here right now. I am here with you. There is a person, a body, a face, and a name. Let's deal with everything together, shall we?"

The mood and the tide turned dramatically after that. I received a flood of action items from them. I set about solving them methodically with the help of HR folks and support from senior managers like Jim Jones, John Broderick, and George Rutland.

In a few months, the ILWU gave up on its efforts, because they concluded that if a unionization vote was held, they would lose.

This whole episode was a genuine compliment to all the ex-Citicorp line managers, who collectively brought about a vital change in the mindset of the entire OG staff in San Francisco.

In many ways, they saved Crocker Bank and the banking industry in general on the West Coast.

A Performance Review

"Vijay, I am stuck here in this meeting and it is running way late." Lou said apologetically on the phone. "Most likely, I won't be back at the office till 6pm or so."

"No worries, Lou," I replied. "I am buried under stuff myself. Just call me when you are back."

"But listen, are you free this evening? It is Friday, and I was thinking that maybe we can do the review over dinner, if it works for you."

"That is a great idea. Let's do that. Just call me when you are ready to leave."

The man on the phone was my boss. His name was Louis Buglioli. He was a SVP, and responsible for a vast swath of back office operations across California, that supported the retail banking activities of the Crocker Bank. He was also ex-Citicorp and had joined Crocker from New York some months earlier.

Lou was obviously Italian in his lineage. He was in his mid-30s, tall, athletic in his build, had dark blonde hair and blue eyes. He was smart, aggressive, and innovative in his thinking. But he was also quite savvy about corporate politics and intrigue. He had an engaging personality and a powerful physical presence which he used very skillfully. Whenever Lou entered any room full of people, he just took it over in short order. Every head would turn to look at him at first, and in a few minutes, all power seemed to flow over to him and he would end up in command of whatever was under way. To top it all off, he was a good looking and handsome man. He was married, but all the ladies would still "swoon" at the mention of Lou's name! For the men, his charisma was captivating and his charm simply infectious.

Well, it was time for Crocker Bank's annual Performance Review exercise. Every employee, whether a manager or a staff member, would be given a written evaluation of their job performance by their supervisor or boss. Besides getting feedback on one's work performance, one also learnt about the aspects that needed to be improved. It was intended to be a positive activity for all. But at times, some folks would approach these reviews with a sense of fear and trepidation. I was not one of them. I always thought of the feedback as getting direction to pursue further learning and self-improvement.

Around 6pm, Lou called me and we left for dinner. He had reserved a lovely table at a restaurant in the Little Italy district of San Francisco. We settled down quickly for our meal.

A Performance Review

"Vijay, let's get the review bit out of the way first, so we can relax and enjoy a nice, easy going dinner." Lou suggested. He seemed somewhat uncomfortable. It was a little unusual.

"Well now, look, I have already given you a great written review on your work performance. Lots of compliments on things achieved and so forth. It is all here and you can read it." Lou continued. "But that is not what I want to talk about tonight. I want to talk about something else with you. It is something that I feel should not be written down."

"Really?" I asked in surprise and wonder.

"Yes. Well, there are a couple of straight forward things, and I think you need just a little coaching on them. So, let's begin there. The first is that you need to manage your time a little better. You tend to run late in things. Your work is great and thorough, but you never give yourself a little cushion of time before it is due. Whether it is a meeting, a presentation, or whatever, don't be so hurried. In fact, be a little early. Give yourself a cushion of some time. It will help calm you, make you feel more confident, and reduce the stress level."

"The second is to do with the way you speak. You talk very fast, and leave most people in the dust! I suggest that you learn to slow down your speech. It will make others understand you better, listen to you more, and even regard you with greater importance."

"Lou, I am surprised. I did not realize any of this. Okay, I will work on it." I answered honestly.

"But there is something even more important that I want to talk with you about." Lou said gently. "Now, I want you to take this feedback positively, and not feel offended in any way. okay?" I noticed that Lou was now even more uncomfortable with the topic at hand. It was so unlike him.

"It has to do with the way you dress at work. You seem to be fond of trendy clothes. Your work clothes are fashionable, colorful, and eye catching. Generally speaking, there is nothing wrong with any of that, because clothes are a matter of individual and personal tastes. But, in the corporate world, these choices can work against you."

I listened to Lou now with rapt attention, as he continued.

"You see Vijay, in most places, and particularly in the corporate world, how you are perceived matters a lot. Perception is reality! When people meet you, their first impressions are formed by how you appear to them. The clothes you wear will say a lot about who you are to their eyes and minds. In fact, there is an unwritten dress code which is ever present. Just look at how all the senior executives at the Bank dress themselves. They wear suites in a fairly conservative and traditional manner. This dress code reflects maturity, competence, and gravitas in all sorts of ways. It can even determine whether you are taken seriously in what you have to say or not. So, my honest and friendly advice to you is to think about this, and make adjustments as you deem necessary."

Lou seemed very relieved at having gotten this off his chest. We had a lovely dinner during rest of the evening. But that night, I could not get his advice out of my mind. It kept bothering me. Was I really not that observant? Was I really that far out into the left field in terms of my work clothes? How was I so unaware of something so important? And other than Lou now, why had nobody said something to me earlier?

Next morning, with a cup of coffee in hand, I laid out all my work clothes on my bed, to take a hard look. I was astonished at what I saw! It was all the fashions of the 1970s. My shirts were loud in color with large oversized collars; my pants were all bell-bottoms; my jackets were stylish and colorful; my belts were 2+ in. wide with fancy buckles; and my shoes were Italian loafers in suede leather! It was a nice wardrobe, if you were going dancing at a disco club of some sort. But I was wearing all this for work at a conservative Bank? Good God! I was mortified by the thoughts of how I must have appeared to most people at the office! I felt so ridiculous and totally ashamed.

On the very next day, a Sunday, I drove to San Francisco. At Grodin's, a men's clothing store on Union Square, I walked in and asked to see the manager. "Sir, is something wrong? Is someone not helping you?" the manager asked with a worried look on his face.

"No, not at all." I replied. "I wanted to meet with you today, because I am here not for just some new clothes. I need a new wardrobe. Can you help me?" He was just delighted. He assembled a small sales team and a tailor immediately for me.

Over the next few hours, I purchased a new and coordinated work wardrobe. I bought a dozen button-down Oxford cotton dress shirts in white or light blue solids; six European cut 3-piece suites in dark grey or navy blue, in solids or with thin pinstripes; half a dozen ties with small patterns or solids with a streak of contrasting color; two 1-inch wide leather belts; and 2 pairs of leather "wing tip" laced shoes. I was told to return on Tuesday evening for my fittings, and promised delivery of the whole set by Friday. I got a nice discount also and proceeded forward with this investment into my future. By the Friday evening of the next week, I took delivery of my new wardrobe. At home, I also set up a separate section in my closet for it, to make sure that I would never confuse it with anything else. Then came the fateful Monday morning, and a new Vijay walked into work.

Lou was the first person to see me. "Vijay, my God! Is that really you? From now on, I will have to call you Mr. Yajnik!" he smiled, gushed, and just glowed with approval. I could tell that he was really pleased because I had acted decisively by accepting his uncomfortable advice.

Everywhere I went that whole week, heads turned. Even John Broderick, our EVP, looked at me and said, "Have we met somewhere before?" and smiled. Most of my colleagues and subordinates were simply shocked. A most common question was, "Hey, Vijay, what is with the new threads?"

I was astounded by the overall reaction from everybody! My goodness, can something as simple as clothes make such a difference in perceptions? I was still very much the same person, but it was noticeable that everybody looked at me and thought of me a lot differently. In many cases, there were also changes in the attitudes and manner with which I was treated or regarded.

It is also interesting to observe how business dress codes have changed over time. In a few decades, with the arrival of the Information Age, a massive change occurred yet again. Many new and highly successful companies emerged out of the explosive growth in technology-based innovation funded by venture capital. The Silicon Valley, near San Francisco, became the Mecca of this growth phenomenon. Companies like Apple, Google, and Facebook, to name a few, became the new corporate stars and darlings of Wall Street. They brought with them a sweeping change in the corporate dress code as well.

The late Steve Jobs, a founder and savior of Apple, perhaps best exemplified these changes. At major public presentations, he was dressed in blue jeans, a dark sweatshirt, and sneakers! Others wore hoodies! This new dress code stated, "I am innovative, disruptive, and an agent of change. I am bright, skilled and creating the new economy. I am totally cool." In this era, anybody dressed in a business suite was regarded as "old school, traditional, boring, resistant to change, or even incompetent." Many venture capitalists looked at your clothes, before making a decision about funding your new company or ideas!

So, while the specifics have changed greatly, the existence of dress codes has remained as relevant in business life today, as in any other period of time before. Lou was so right. In life, perception is reality.

It seems contradictory, as it were, but often times, in order for one to stand out, one also has to fit in.

David Guthrie & Ken Davidge - 1974

My Geisha – 1973 Datsun 240 Z

Our IBM 370 Mainframe - 1974

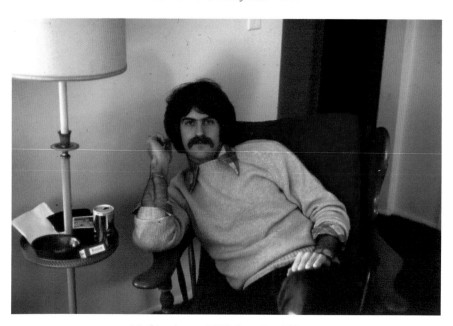

My friend since MSU days, Ron Wilsie - 1975

Kashyap, Ajay & Me – Detroit, 1976

Visiting Kiritbhai & Kalyanibhabhi – Bloomington, IN - 1975

"Nikunj" Bungalow,
Maninagar
1976

Pappaji at "Uttarayan" -
Shashiphoi's Bungalow
1976

Vijay Kaul – New Delhi, 1976

Bijendra Nath Jain & Madhu – New Delhi, 1976

Departure from Ahmedabad, 1976 – Ushakaki, Pramodkaki, Behn & Pappaji

Behn & Pappaji with me in California - 1978

With John Broderick
1981

Crocker Bank Party
1981

SVP at Crocker Bank
1982

Ajay & Me sailing around Manhattan, NY City - 1983

A 1982 Family Portrait-Sons/Wives/Grandkids
L to R Sitting: Nilima, Kalibhabhi, Behn, Mercy, Juhi
Standing: Me, Kashyap, Alay, Pappaji, Ajay

THE LATER YEARS

Adventures with Marv Rich

The Meeting

"**Y**ou know, I am not good at sitting on the bench." I offered. "I am like, either play me, or trade me." Marv burst into explosive laughter, and rubbed his palms.

"Yes, Vijay, I totally get it!" he responded, amused by my professional sports analogy. "But there is this thing here that I gotta deal with first. So, I am just saying, come on board. We will have some fun, and figure things out in short order. Trust me, because I played football in high school. I don't like benches either."

This was the beginning of what would turn into a long and endearing relationship with a highly unconventional and an amazingly talented man. On that day though, I did not know it.

I was interviewing for a job at California Federal Savings & Loan (S&L) in Los Angeles, California. It was a large S&L with branches in California, Nevada, Arizona, and strangely, Florida on the East Coast. It offered a full range of banking and related services via its vast branch network. I had been brought in by my former mentor, George Rutland, who was now Vice Chairman of the S&L. He had told Marv about me and introduced me to him.

Marv Rich was EVP in charge of IT Services, Branch Support Operations, & Corporate Strategy. He had risen quickly in the world of Information Technology because he was so good at understanding the needs of a business. His career had already exposed him to a variety of industries such as Retailing, Airlines, & Healthcare. He was thought of as a brilliant strategist and a driven agent of change.

In person, Marv was of medium height, slightly stocky build, had dark blonde hair, and blue eyes. He was fair in his complexion and possessed a radiant smile. In many ways, his looks and mannerisms reminded you of the famous Hollywood actor, Jack Nicholson! And Marv could be as evil in real life, as Jack was in so many of his iconic film roles.

Marv was always supremely confident in his ability to deal with just about anything. He was constantly restless at work. He liked to surround himself with a team of highly skilled people, who he placed in key jobs in his organization. He also unleashed them from time to time on various "missions" of corporate or business importance.

Marv, unlike what his name suggests, was not Jewish. He was raised as a Catholic, but did not practice his faith in a devoted manner. He was divorced, had no children, and did not want to have a family either. He liked the finer things in life. He loved upscale restaurants, good food, and fine wine. His tastes were always very expensive in everything, and he would spend lots of money catering to them. His favorite movie line was, "There are two kinds of class. First Class and No Class." He could be very charming if he wanted to, or ruthlessly cruel, if that is what was required. Women in general, found Marv to be a very attractive man and a serious catch, if they could somehow figure a way out to snare him.

"So, if I understand you correctly, you want me to join the S&L without a firm job assignment?" I asked.

"Yeah, like somebody held in reserve. But it won't be long before we place you. Oh, don't worry, this will not affect the financial package we put together for you." Marv replied with a gleam in his eyes and a smile on his face.

After some thought and further chats with Marv and George, I joined California Federal in Los Angeles in August 1987. I had barely come on board, when a massive earthquake hit LA, and nearly destroyed our Data Center in Rosemead. Everybody was deployed rapidly to work on this unexpected catastrophe. It was a huge challenge, and it took us many weeks to get things back into reasonable working order. This is also yet another wild story.

Now, it was Christmas/New Year holiday time, and I had returned to Walnut Creek in Northern California to be with my family, since we had not yet completed our relocation. On this evening, the phone rang and it was Marv. He wanted to make certain that I would be in LA on January 2nd. He wanted to see me at 7:00am in the morning. He said it was important and hung up.

I was left wondering what all that was about.

Cal Fed Mortgage Company

" **A** h, Vijay! Good to see you." Marv began, without any chitchat about the recent holiday break or even wishes for a happy new year. "At 9:00am today, we are announcing you as the CEO of Cal Fed Mortgage Company. I thought I should inform you, before that happens. The S&L will also issue a press release later in the day."

Cal Fed Mortgage was a wholly owned subsidiary of the S&L. It was a large mortgage banking company, based out of Los Angeles. It was well regarded in the industry and in the real estate brokerage community generally.

"Say, whaat?" I asked, stunned. "Marv, that is a large full function mortgage company with 21 offices in key markets across the USA. There must be at least 2,000 people working in it. It already has a CEO."

Marv laughed loudly, with an evil edge. Then he said, "It won't by mid-day. But the guy does not know it yet."

I was having a real hard time comprehending what was going on. Obviously, the current CEO of Cal Fed Mortgage was being replaced by me that day. I did understand that much.

"Jeez, Marv, that is a big job. Thank you. But why me? What am I supposed to do there?" I asked, still bewildered.

"Oh, you are going to re-arrange the deck chairs on the Titanic!" Marv clarified. "In a while, we will shut the company down. Nobody knows that yet either."

"Whaat? Shut it down?" I exclaimed. "If that is the case, then why involve me?"

"It is a strategic, delicate, and a damn tough job. It is also complex. We will consolidate parts of it with the S&L; we will sell off other parts, if we can get a good price for them; and shut down the rest. Our consolidated operating costs will drop a ton, and we will have a streamlined organization at the S&L for taking the next step. I would not trust this with anybody here right now, except you. Nobody here has your skillset." Marv answered, with his typical brutal and direct honesty.

"So, what happens after the mission is finished? I will also be out of a job. I get to ride off into the sunset?"

"Sorry, no such luck for you. You will move back to the S&L in a role we will create that is suitable for you."

It was an amazing project of incredible complexity. After a few months to understand the state of Cal Fed Mortgage and to formulate a game plan for the way forward, we went public with the announcement of our plans for the company. It caused a huge reaction in the marketplace, and in California in particular. All the employees were shocked and in disbelief at what was going to happen. I had to remain stoically on the bridge of this sinking and progressively dismembered ship, all the way till the very end.

Consolidation of select functions with the S&L was the relatively easy part. But the selloff of parts of Cal Fed Mortgage was a long and arduous process. All financial assets had to be curated and brought into regulatory compliance with formal audits completed, before a buyer would even step up to take a look. In many cases, after the sale terms had been finalized, it was a complex set of steps to close the deal and transfer the assets over to the buyer, without incurring financial liabilities. The last step of shutting down the few residual parts of the company was mostly a non-event by the time it occurred. It took a year and a half or so before it was gone. I was mostly sad about my first Captainship. It was not what I had imagined.

Because of the success of this whole effort, I was moved back to the parent S&L as SVP of Consumer Lending and Loan Servicing Divisions. I enjoyed the Consumer Lending Division the most. My responsibilities covered Secured and Unsecured lending, Mastercard & Visa credit card portfolios, auto/boat/aircraft loans, and so forth.

It was an amazing world, especially because we lived in LA, the capital of show business! Imagine approving credit cards or auto loans, for famous people in the movies, or Hollywood! California Federal had a lot of customers from the entertainment industry, which it catered to with great success. One became familiar with a lot of private information on celebrities. One could even approach them and chat with them! I did so with quite a few for sound business reasons only. It was a heady and just a wild experience. (No, I will not name these celebrities here for legal and ethical reasons. If I did, trust me, it would just blow away your mind.)

At this time, Marv launched a major and "top secret" initiative to bring together 3 of the largest S&L companies on the West Coast into one big company via strategic mergers. I worked tirelessly in helping him put the set of deals together. Then, we completed our "due diligence" activities, and got the final merger terms resolved as well.

It seemed like we were close to "ignition and lift-off", when suddenly everything just fell apart. Corporate politics and personal egos got in the way, it appeared. We even heard a story that the 3 Boards could not agree on who would be the CEO/Chairman of the new S&L or who would sit on the new Board of Directors! It was a huge disappointment with far reaching consequences. If it had gone through, the banking industry on the West Coast may have looked quite different from what it turned out to become.

After this event, the California Federal S&L got into its own internal upheavals. The aging Chairman retired, and a power struggle for succession and senior jobs ensued. Over a few months, many senior executives left or were laid off. Marv was fired one morning, and a few months later, I was fired on another morning. It was early 1990, and thus ended the Cal Fed story for me.

There is an old saying, "When one door closes, another opens." While this is mostly true, it does leave out a couple of important elements.

It does not indicate how long it will take, or how dark the room may get.

Entrepreneurship

I spent most of 1990 in free-lance consulting. It was hard and fun work, but a lot of time away from home. However, it was financially rewarding. In this era, functional "outsourcing" seemed to have come much in the corporate vogue. Everybody talked with great pride about how they had "outsourced" something or another in support functions for their businesses. Soon thereafter, another term also came into the business vernacular. It extended this concept to "offshoring" of various business process functions to take advantage of labor rate differences around the world.

Many countries became popular destinations for these activities. Philippines, India, and later Eastern European countries, became desirable places for things like Call Centers, Data Entry & Verification Services, etc. Further, there was a huge concern regarding the impact of the upcoming change in the century in the Gregorian Calendar. Many computer systems had to be checked for potential date change issues. The so called "Y2K" projects were becoming quite active in most major corporations in the developed world. They provided a huge impetus for further outsourcing of IT and other activities, and had a major impact worldwide.

At this time, I thought that I could bring about some seriously disruptive and beneficial changes to the mortgage loans industry and launched two companies along with a business partner. The first was a company called Silent Partners Inc. (SPI) and the second was called Loan Partners Inc. (LPI). In SPI, we set up shop to fully process mortgage loan applications for a variety of clients. They included banks, S&L's, brokers, and other folks in the business of generating mortgage loans. It was all an "outsourcing" play to handle not only the core functions but also overflow loan volumes. We rapidly built up a great book of business. In LPI, since I was a licensed real estate broker, we had loan agents generating loans for our own book of business. Both companies did amazingly well. Soon, I had nearly 50+ people on my payroll! I felt that I had hit the goldmine for some lucrative businesses.

Then, on this fateful day, Marv called me. He was in the role of EVP of IT, Finance, & Strategic Planning at Blue Cross in LA. He had landed in this big job, in the Healthcare industry, with amazing ease and rather quickly.

"Vijay, what the hell are you up to?" Marv asked in his typical curt manner. I explained it all to him.

Then he said, "Vij, are you nuts? Who the hell is funding all this crap you are engaged in? Have you not learnt anything? Never fund anything with your own money! Jeez, let me come over, and have a look." I agreed, but with some serious trepidation. I loved Marv, his methods, his brutal honesty, and his incredibly smart brain. But I was so afraid that he would visit us, and then just piss all over what I had worked so hard to create.

Marv showed up one afternoon in his Maserati coupe. He visited the whole facility and talked with everybody in great detail. Then, he pulled me aside in my office. I was mortified about the prospects of what he would tell me.

"Vij, I think highly of you, and you know it. Keep that in your mind, as I say this. This is a highly cyclical business. The rug could get pulled out from under your feet at any time. This could be due to variables that are completely out of your control. Then where would you be? I seriously admire what you have achieved here. It is amazing and just incredible. But you funded it by yourself? That is just plain stupid."

"Aw, Marv, come on. Am I that crazy in your mind?" I asked, looking for some validation.

"No. That is not what I meant. I am impressed and very proud of you. What you have done here, takes serious balls. It requires the ability to accept and handle risk. Not many have it. Anyway, I wish you the best in the future. However, one little bit of advice. Watch your cash flow. At the end of the day, in any business, that is all that really matters." And then Marv left.

It was a simple but serious lesson in life. In all my studies in B School and beyond, I had never fully understood the true value of "cash flow". Well, when it is your money on the line, this lesson is learnt in a hurry. It all came home to roost in my case in a most surprising manner.

In 1994, 3 years into it, when we were doing amazingly well and life was good, everything just fell apart, and with a speed that I could not even comprehend. The interest rates rose, mortgage loan volumes dried up, and we lost most of our clients. I tried buyouts, funding sources, and many other things, but nothing worked. Sadly, I had to close down both the businesses.

It was like killing my children! All the sweat, blood, and sacrifices were lost in a span of 3 months! I lost a boat load of my money, had nothing to show for it, and was left in a state of total despair, disillusionment, and utter desperation. I had a family to support, a home mortgage to make payments on, and I had meagre cash on hand. In fact, I could not afford to take my kids out to a meal at McDonald's. It was that, or a tank of gas. Times for me had become very hard indeed.

I called Marv to seek his advice and help. He asked me to meet him for lunch at a swanky place in Malibu.

"Ah, Vij, I am saddened to hear all this. I wanted you to succeed in the long haul. But listen, don't fall into the trap of blaming yourself. That would be totally wrong. Look, your businesses failed. You did not fail. Yeah, and you learnt some valuable things along the way." Marv said in a consoling tone, which was rare.

"Marv, thanks for the thoughts. But I need to find something and quick. If you know of an opportunity, please let me know." I pleaded.

"Well, there are some things afoot. I cannot talk about them right now. But I will be in touch soon. Just keep the faith." Marv replied with a devilish twinkle in his eye.

I had no idea what to make of this comment. Little did I know about what was around the corner.

Landing of the Space Shuttle

"**D**ad, you are simply not going to believe this! It is just amazing!" Neil and Meghana exclaimed in hyper excited voices. They had returned from school with some hot news it seemed.

I had been working ferociously long hours at my new entrepreneurial companies and I had not seen much of them lately. For some reason, I was luckily home that afternoon.

"My school has organized a field trip to see the landing of the Space Shuttle! And I am allowed to bring Meghana & parents along on it!" Neil said, just bursting with joy. "Can we please go? Will you both come with us?"

At the time, we were living in Agoura Hills in Ventura County, northwest of LA. Where our home was located, we were not strangers to seeing a variety of flight activities in the skies. The approach path of commercial air traffic heading to the LAX Airport was over the Pacific Ocean nearby and inbound airplanes were visible all the time. The Vandenberg Air Force Base was also not far away and we could often see the contrails of various rocket launches from there as well. To the north of us, at some distance in the desert near Mojave, was the Edwards Air Force Base. It had a mammoth runway which was used at times for Space Shuttle landings. Normally, the Shuttle would land at the NASA facility in Cape Canaveral, Florida. But on occasions, when there were weather issues in Florida, the Shuttle would be diverted to land at the Edwards Air Force Base. It was a huge Base and had been used extensively for various tests and trials during the development phases of the Space Shuttle program.

But the key issue was that the Shuttle landings at Edwards were mostly unpredictable. On any Shuttle mission, a change in the landing site could occur at the last moment from Mission Control in Houston. Nobody as a result would know anything about an imminent landing of the Space Shuttle at Edwards. Out of the clear blue and suddenly, we would hear the huge "double sonic booms" as it arrived from space. They sounded like loud and scary thunder. Everything around the house would shake a little, and someone would say, "No, it is not an earthquake. The Space Shuttle just arrived at Edwards." Later in the evening, we would get to see a video clip of the landing on the evening news on TV.

However, on rare occasions, Edwards was the designated primary landing site, and the news media would alert everybody locally about its date and timing. It would cause a wide reaction among the local residents and folks would try to go to Edwards to actually watch it land. This was not an easy thing to do, because Edwards was a highly secure and restricted area to the general public.

"Are you sure? Do you have an actual date and time for the landing?" I asked to ascertain that it was all for real.

"Oh, yes, Dad. It is scheduled, and our school has all the needed security clearances. We are to go there in 6 school buses! Our teachers will be with us as well," Neil replied with complete certainty.

"Gosh, this would really be something! Yes, we should all go. This is a rare chance," I said with a smile. "Let's sign up for it." I had still not fully understood the challenges of this special school field trip.

We were all required to report at the school at 2:00am sharp to check in and board the buses. The desert near Mojave is quite cold and windy at night, so we had to bring along warm winter clothes like parkas, caps or hats, mufflers, gloves, etc. For the kids and us, we had to pack picnic baskets with food and fill thermoses with hot coffee or tea and have cartons of fruit juices and water as well. The preparations were extensive.

The buses rolled at 2:20am or so, and we arrived at Edwards at 3:30am. After a long drive within the Base on this dark night, we were brought to a secure official viewing area. They had bleachers set up, with lots of "Port-a-potties" nearby for everybody as well. All around us, attached to tall poles, were many loud speakers. On them, they were playing "live" all the conversations going on between the Shuttle crew and Houston Mission Control. There were also many floodlights lighting up the whole area for everybody's convenience and security.

As we all bundled up against the cold wind and settled into the bleachers, an announcer from the Base came on the speakers. He welcomed all the schools, teachers, students, and parents to the Base. He informed us that while it was still quite dark, by the time the Shuttle came in for its landing, the sun would be up and we would be able to see it arrive and land clearly on the runway. We could not see the runway then, but in fact it was directly before us in the dark. Further, he added that at that moment, the Shuttle was still flying at its orbital altitude. In about an hour or so, we would be able to hear and follow the conversations during its key stages of: 1) Re-entry Burn; 2) Descent; 3) The Approach & Flare; and 4) Final Glide to Touchdown. He also warned everybody about the loud "double sonic booms" that would herald its arrival. He advised all of us to not get scared by them, because the intense shock waves were a normal event.

I began to feel goosebumps all over from the growing excitement. I remembered fondly my days of flying single engine airplanes at the Beech

Flight School in Detroit. But this was a totally different state-of-the-art. What this spacecraft was about to do was totally awesome to me! The sheer scope of all the technology challenges involved in it made my mind dizzy.

With us on this trip was also Dr. Sukumar, our neighbor and friend, and his family. He was a renowned scientist, an aeronautical engineer with a Ph.D., and engaged in advanced technical research in the field. He was an amazing source of information for my countless questions about everything.

Suddenly, I felt like I was of the same age as my kids! They were also wild with excitement, like all their classmates, and were just cackling away with all of them. We were all just delighted in this floodlit and cold but festive environment of building anticipation.

We started listening to the audio feed of the communication's "chatter" between the Shuttle crew and Houston Mission Control. They seemed to be engaged in all sorts of pre-landing procedures and check lists. There were endless technical terms and acronyms for various things that most of us could only understand in a general sense. Then, the Base announcer interrupted it again. He wanted to give us a quick briefing on what was going to happen in the landing.

"Well folks, just for your information, the Shuttle landing sequence is expected to begin soon. I want to give you an overview of what we expect to have happen. Right now, the Shuttle is still flying at its orbital altitude. When it fires its engines for the re-entry burn, which lasts less than 15 seconds, it will be over South Africa in the southern hemisphere. Its descent trajectory will take it across the entire Indian Ocean, all of South East Asia, and over the entire Pacific Ocean.

In its descent, it mostly drops like a rock. As it approaches Edwards, you will hear the double sonic booms and should be able to see it high up in the sky lit by the morning sun. It will then execute a 180-degree corkscrew turn and acquire its glide path to the runway. It will lower its landing gear and glide into touchdown. Then, it will deploy its parachutes to slow it down and eventually come to a stop at the far end of the runway where we have the receiving units already on standby. And here is something else to note. From the start of the re-entry burn to touchdown on the runway here, it is expected to take about 25 minutes. Our ETA (Estimated Time of Arrival) for this mission is 7:02:38am. Enjoy the landing!" He signed off and the audio feed resumed.

I was just stunned and speechless! In a bit, I gushed out loud, "Say, whaat? Only 25 minutes! Such a long descent trajectory and in only 25 minutes! Jeez, what sort of a spacecraft is this? This is a marvel of modern technology. And they have the mission ETA down to the second? I feel so ignorant and stupid.

But I am in total wonder and awe of it all. To think that not that long ago, to travel from South Africa to California would have taken months!"

"Vijay, it is not really that difficult to understand." Dr. Sukumar said casually to me. "You remember the equations that we studied in engineering school, don't you? This is just an actual example of the "ro" and "tau" variables in action."

"Doc, what the devil are you talking about? Yeah, I vaguely remember the equations from those classes a long time ago. But I have forgotten much more than that, since then. Good grief, "ro" and "tau" variables! Come on, seriously, are you not the least bit impressed? To me, this descent is just incredible!"

However, Dr. Sukumar did bring back some old memories for me. I remembered my days at IIT/Kanpur and Dr. T. R. Vishvanathan (TRV). He used to teach us electrical circuits, which he would pronounce as "sir...cute". He loved picking on me, because I was doing plays and dramas and he felt that I was not focused enough on my studies. He was right, but I did learn a lot from him.

He would often pose a question in his lectures. "What is real engineering?" he would ask. Then he would answer it also. "It is not these equations, and all this theoretical stuff that we study here. Yes, it is all necessary. But real engineering is when a Boeing 747 airplane takes off! That is when all the disciplines come together and into play, to create something truly useful for mankind." I never forgot those words. All my life, whenever I saw a 747 taking off, I would fondly remember Doc TRV. He was a brilliant man, and skilled at getting to the essence of everything.

While any technology is always fascinating, it is even more so, when one enjoys the fruits of it. That brings another event into my mind. Speaking of fruits, one day we were at the home of Dr. Sukumar attending a party. His wife, Jayanti, was a superb hostess. She made the best "dosas" in town. It was a treat to have a meal cooked by her. At this party, she was also presenting some great apples that she had acquired from some farm on the West Coast. In attendance, was also a gentleman who had 2 Ph.Ds.! One was in Horticulture, and other in Biology. It was a crowd of highly educated people, who were all scientists of great accomplishments. I was in some ways a bit of a misfit.

Anyway, Doc Hort/Bio began to explain why these apples were just fantastic. It seemed that the seeds were special, the pulp and nutrients were sweet, the skin quite delicate, and their size was just enormous. He droned on

333

about these apples and everybody listened with great attention. Soon, I began to get restless.

"Doc, this seems to be an amazing creation!" I said. "The technology involved is simply fascinating."

"Vijay, it certainly is." he replied with a smile of satisfaction. "But there are other interesting aspects as well…"

"Hey, they are after all apples, aren't they?" I said, cutting him off. "Well then, let's eat the damn things. Let's taste them and see what our palates have to say!" The whole room busted up in laughter. Everybody enjoyed the apples.

"Vijay, the countdown to re-entry burn is about to start." Dr. Sukumar said, yanking me out of my short reverie.

"Oh, yes. Thanks. I really want to listen to it all now." I replied.

What transpired next can only be described as a surreal experience. I listened with rapt attention to the audio feed. In cryptic terms, we followed the execution of the re-entry burn. The Shuttle began its descent, which struck me as a near free fall of an object from the heavens. But, in a short while, the audio feed died! Everybody gasped! We were told that it was a normal thing. Everybody waited, with baited breath, for what felt like a very long time. In a bit, the audio feed resumed, and there was a huge collective sigh of relief. By now, we were well past sunrise, and it was a gorgeous, bright and sunny morning at Edwards.

Some more time went by. Then, all of a sudden, we hear "BOOM… BOOM!" the deafening double sonic booms! Gosh, they were so loud. The ground shook, the bleachers shook, and my chest shook as well. The double shock waves were that intense. Like everybody else, now I was wondering about the location of the Shuttle. I looked at my 10 o'clock, but saw nothing. I looked at my 2 o'clock and still saw nothing. I mean, that is where you would normally expect to see airplanes that are coming in for a landing on a runway, right? Then, some kid suddenly screamed, "There it is! There it is! Look, it is above us!!"

I looked up. It seemed it was at our 12 o'clock, almost directly overhead above us. The sun gleamed off of it and we saw a small speck of light way high up. The speck rapidly got bigger, and it looked like it was just falling to the ground!

"Oh, dear God, it is going to crash! I thought that it flew, but this thing is just dropping like a stone!" I whispered softly to nobody nearby.

Suddenly, it banked, and went into a sharp turn, much like a jet fighter does in combat. It was a severely steep arc, and a nearly lethal tight turn of 180 degrees! As it finished it, it seemed to level out, aligned perfectly with the runway. We watched the landing gear drop down and it glided beautifully onto the runway. The rear wheels gently touched down with huge clouds of smoke, the chutes deployed, but its nose wheel was still in the air! Ever so slowly, the nose wheel came down in its cloud of smoke, and then it seemed to roll on forever. In the far distance, it eventually came to a stop. I looked at it through my binoculars, and could see flames coming out of its rear facing vents!

"Good God, Doc, I am seeing flames!" I exclaimed worriedly to Sukumar. "Is it on fire? Is there some problem here? This cannot be normal!"

"Yes, Vijay, all that is quite normal too." Sukumar responded in a comforting tone. "What you are observing is the exhaust of the Auxiliary Power Units of the spacecraft. These units work off and on at different speeds, as required. Sometimes, after a landing, this exhaust ignites, and shows up as pulsating flames in its vents. Don't worry. The crew is safe. In a bit of time, those flames will just go away." I felt so relieved.

In a couple of decades after that, the Space Shuttle program was ended by NASA. The whole nation, and perhaps even the world, was deeply saddened by this development. Folks remembered the successes, failures, and even the shocking tragedies that occurred in this program. Astronauts from all over the world had participated in it, shared in its incredible achievements, and many had even given their lives to it. It had advanced the objectives of scientific discovery and technology development in countless ways.

Towards the end, a Shuttle was placed on top of the custom NASA Boeing 747 and they made final "Fly By" flights in many cities, including LA, to celebrate and bid a fond farewell to this program. Everybody was teary eyed watching it that day all over California, which is where it was born. The Shuttle, Endeavour, was gifted to LA and it resides today in the California Science Center Museum at Exposition Park. One can visit it and even take a tour inside the spacecraft.

But for all of us in the Yajnik and Sukumar families, the Space Shuttle landing at Edwards that day remained special. I was so glad that in my life, I got the rare opportunity to spend one chilly morning in its company, watching it do brilliantly what it was designed to do.

Go into Space, and return safely with its crew, to Earth.

335

The Kmart Saga

The Retailing Industry – Mid 1990's

The S.S. Kresge Company, later renamed Kmart Corporation, literally invented "discount retailing". Its key tenet was "Hi-Lo" pricing, announced via weekly advertisements. It would offer greatly discounted items "on sale" each week to pull customers into its stores, and count on most people then buying other items as well at normal prices. The goal was always to preserve or improve the overall gross margin on sales. The company did well over most of the 20th century. Kmart became a huge company and an American icon, with a massive store network spanning all 50 states. Its success brought other players into the market, and they tried to improve upon the Kmart business model.

First, there was Walmart, which introduced the "everyday low pricing" business model. It became very successful with it. With the emergence of internet-based e-commerce, Amazon and others, entered the market with vastly different business models. Initially, in all these transformations, there were the usual doubters. They did not believe that these new business models would be successful. In Amazon's case, it took nearly 15 years, and massive venture capital investments, before its model was deemed a success. By the time the opinions changed and caught up with reality, Amazon had become a winning juggernaut in retailing and other things.

If one examines the history of all this carefully, one can see that there are many vital lessons to be learned from it. First, regardless of the business model involved, "retail is detail". Doing things in a planned, methodical, and specific way is a key requirement. A focus on details is crucial. Second, one must keep up with the times and consumer tastes. Consumers tend to be fickle and one must have a keen sense of their ever-changing wants and needs.

Third, new and internet-based technologies were having a profound impact on every aspect of the retailing industry. Every retailer had to recognize this and develop a new vision for its business. Also, it had to execute it, along with the necessary changes in its work practices, in order to stay relevant and competitive. If a retailer was stuck in its old ways, ignorant about the changing business practices or emerging trends in customer tastes and desires, it would face hard times. Being averse to new technologies and their impact, moving slowly in their adoption, or changing with the times, it faced the considerable risk of failure and even fading into oblivion.

While it is a complex and long history, Kmart as a company, had started into this downward spiral when the stories following played out. But a new management team had come together and it did manage to save and turn the company around significantly for a period of time. However, this team then dissipated, and the decline of Kmart appeared to resume all over again. Many other management teams have come and gone since those days, but a sustained improvement in Kmart's fortunes has remained elusive.

So, it is hard in many ways to believe today, that there was a time, when the prospects for Kmart in fact did look quite bright. Once, for a few years back then, it did seem like there almost was a Camelot.

I was fortunate enough to get to experience a good measure of it.

The First Visit

It was late October, 1994, and I had just come home from work, where I had a short-term consulting gig underway. The phone rang.

"Vij, this is Marv." the voice said.

"Heyyy, Marv, it is great to hear your voice! I was thinking about you just the other day." I said. "How are you?"

"Cold! Goddam cold!" he replied. "I need some new clothes. My nuts are freezing!"

"Gosh, that is surprising! Where are you? Are you up in the Sierras?" I asked. "But it is not so bad there right now."

"I am in Detroit." Marv answered. "I took this job at Kmart 2 weeks ago, running IT, Finance, and Corporate Strategy for the CEO. I am freezing my butt off in the weather here! Maybe you did not see it, but there was a press release on it."

"Ah, I am sorry, but I did not see it. Hey, congrats! That is a big job, and at a big place." I said. "But I think I read somewhere that Kmart was in some kind of trouble. Is that true?"

"Yeah, it is true and quite serious. Either we fix it, or it is 'adios, baby'!" Marv said quietly. "Listen, I want you to look at something for me. Can you come to Detroit?"

"Sure, I can. I will need to rearrange a few things. How about next week? When do you want me there?

"How about we have dinner tomorrow at 6:30pm? I will pick you up in the lobby of your hotel. My secretary will call you shortly and make all the arrangements. See you tomorrow." And he just hung up! It was classic Marv, who never waited for nobody.

Yes, she called, and we got all our arrangements sorted out quickly. Next day, I flew to Detroit. Marv arrived in the hotel lobby at 6:30pm sharp. He looked good, but was still cold. We set off for dinner.

"Tell me, is cashmere wool really warm?" he asked, during our meal. I told him that the genuine thing was the best. I also gave him a quick lesson on Pashmina, Shahmina, and Shahtush, which was actually banned worldwide. A lovely meal ended and Marv dropped me back at the hotel. In the lobby, he handed me two 3-ring binders.

"What are these?" I asked puzzled.

"Oh, the keys to the kingdom!" he replied. "Look them over tonight. Let's meet at 7:00am tomorrow in my office. I want to hear what you think. G'nite." And he left.

Back in my room, I settled down to look casually at the binders. In minutes, I sat up ramrod straight! I could not believe what was in my hands! One binder was the Balance Sheet and the other the Income Statement of Kmart Corporation Consolidated, and individually in tabs, all its wholly owned or public Subsidiaries! This information was so sensitive, that if leaked, it could move the prices of shares of many companies in the stock market.

I focused on a detailed review of all this financial information as best as I could, because there was a lot about Kmart that I did not really know. A picture began to form in my mind. Sadly, it was not a good one. I stayed awake almost the entire night studying the binders.

I reached Kmart HQ in Troy, an iconic building designed by a world-famous architect, at 6:30am. I could not figure out a way to get in! After much ado, a passing security guard helped me out, and I reached Marv's office by 6:55am.

"How the devil does one get into this place?" I asked, bewildered. "It is just nuts!"

"Ah, Vijay, now you have faced it too! Did you notice the huge 40-foot sculpture out in the front? It is modern art, supposedly. Serious money was doled out for it. Yes, it is a man's head with a hole in it. Quite revealing. Well, welcome to Kmart!" We made some hot coffee in the kitchen, and settled around a conference table in his office. "So, tell me what you think," he asked simply.

"Well, I am not sure that you are going to like hearing what I think. It may also cost me a potential work opportunity here. But I cannot figure a way to sugar coat it. So, are you sure?" I responded, with real concern.

"Yeah, give it to me straight. And say it, just as you are thinking it," Marv replied, with a steely edge to his voice.

"Okay. Well, Kmart seems to be a train wreck, which will happen in 4 to 6 months, unless some drastic action is taken, pronto! I simply could not believe my eyes last night! This company has $34 billion in annual sales, 2,400+ stores in 50 states, and it is operating at a negative cash flow? It will run out of cash, unless action is taken immediately to stop the bleeding. Also, all the subsidiaries seem past their prime. None is a cash faucet." I noticed that Marv had started to smile.

"Your focus has to be hyper short term right now! Cut costs immediately, and buy time. In this bought time, figure out the medium-term and long-term actions. Further, since you can do little to reduce fixed costs in the short term, you will have to look mainly at variable costs. The stores already seem quite lean. So, most of these costs are in administrative or overhead functions. I would focus on reducing costs there. This mainly translates into reducing managerial and support personnel." Marv was now just beaming and rubbing his palms!

"You know Vij, we are on the same page! But I have to convince the CEO about this at 8:30am today. I already have some notes on a yellow pad to share with him on all this." Marv said. Upon hearing this, I was simply horrified.

"You have an 8:30am meeting with the CEO today?" I asked aghast. "And you are planning to present such a Kmart crisis action plan to the CEO via yellow pad paper notes?" I asked, incredulously. "No. Not while I am here. Where is the nearest computer with PowerPoint on it? We still have 30 minutes."

I banged out 5-6 slides for Marv real fast. A key question came up. How much could one save through staff reductions? Marv wanted to use an impressive "swag" (*scientific wild ass guess*) number for now. But I said, "Well, let's quantify it. In staff reductions, at 10%, it is a "gimme"; at 15%, you make a few choices; and at 20% you make real decisions. Aim for 20% and you will likely get 25% in the end."

The rapid exercise yielded a "lifesaving" annual cost reduction target of $100 million! Marv and I iterated the short slide deck a couple of times to clean it up and then he went to meet the CEO at 8:30am. I waited in his office wondering about the outcome. The Executive Floor was now a beehive of activity, as others and all the secretaries were now also at work.

He returned in barely 10 minutes! He was smiling and laughing at the same time. The CEO had rejected his proposal totally and completely. Marv was told that there was no crisis at Kmart. Everything was just fine.

"We have to find a new CEO, I guess. Somebody who gets it. What we have here is someone in total denial of reality." Marv said in a deadly serious tone.

"Vijay, I need your help. I can put you up in a furnished apartment here, pay your travel expenses from LA, and I will honor your billing rate. We can figure other things out later, but I need you here quick. Do we have a deal?"

"Sure." I replied. This was not a man one turned down flippantly. "But you are aware that I know nothing about the retailing business. I have never worked in it." At this, Marv laughed heartily!

"Hey, do you know what a SKU is?" he asked, barely containing more laughter.

"Yes. It stands for Stock Keeping Unit. I learnt that in B School years ago. It is used to identify and track all products bought for sale in a retailing business." I replied.

"Well, then you know retailing!" Marv exclaimed. "The rest of it is just mouse nuts. You buy stuff, put it in stores with a price markup, sell it, make profit, pay your expenses, and bank the rest. It is that simple."

"Then why do retailers get in trouble?" I wondered.

"They complicate things by doing them all wrong." he replied. "They buy the wrong stuff; build the wrong kinds of stores, in the wrong places; set the prices wrong; advertise products that they do not have; and manage expenses in a wrong way. Do it right, and financial magic happens!"

"Vij, I've got to give your position a name or a title. Kmart cannot function without them. HR is certain to go crazy. It needs to be something that I can use without Board approval, because that will take forever. Got any ideas?"

"No. And I really don't care." I replied. He came up with the important sounding title of Director, Strategic Planning. Well actually, I did no planning and nothing strategic. In reality, it was all tactical execution, at a furious pace, for the sheer survival of Kmart. But it did give me a bit of gravitas on occasion with some difficult people.

So, began a saga of some truly amazing experiences in my life.

Consultants & HR

In less than a month, a major cost reduction initiative was approved by the Board of Kmart. It was broad and deep in its impact, which was mainly a staff reduction at HQ and Regional Offices. In Detroit, a city of strong labor unions, such an event had never before occurred at Kmart. Its timing was also just dreadful. It was 10 days prior to Christmas of 1994. We were thrashed badly in the local media. The whole week in fact was a surreal nightmare.

Marv had asked me to deal with all the consulting companies working at Kmart. All the Big 8 firms and others had many people on assignment at Kmart everywhere. They were a serious cost, and it had been decided to end this expense. I had been handed "the axe" by Marv to carry out this dirty kill job. I scheduled meetings with Partner level folks at each firm for 30minutes on this Tuesday. All these meetings had a flavor quite similar to the first one.

"Thank you for meeting me at such a short notice." I began. "I am presenting you this formal notice of termination of all engagements with your firm by Kmart, effective today. Please advise your personnel that all ID cards will be deactivated at 6pm today. If somebody needs more time to vacate premises, please give me a list and I will make the necessary arrangements. However, all financial obligations of Kmart under our current contracts will cease, as of the end of business today."

"Whaat?!! Say, WHAAAT?!! Vijay, you cannot be serious!" said the Senior Partner, who was clearly shocked out of his wits, and in near cardiac arrest. "We have major and important projects underway, and you cannot just terminate them like this!"

"Well, guess what? I just did." I replied. "We have completed legal reviews of all our contracts with you and this action is perfectly within our legal rights."

"But why? We have done such good work for Kmart over so many years!"

"The costs are far greater and certain, while the benefits much less so and obscure. There are other perspectives on your consulting work as well. In every project, you provide great analyses and advice, but take responsibility for nothing. You have no skin in the game of achieving results, while your billings remain sacrosanct. Anyway, I don't want to discuss this further. The ride is over, and this is the end of the line."

"This is just impossible! I will have to talk with Marv Rich, or the CEO, immediately."

"Well, Marv is with the CEO, as we speak. They are handling many other moving parts right now also. I suggest that you request a meeting for next week sometime, and instead focus on discussing this notice and next steps with your staff immediately."

Meeting after meeting, it went on and on, the whole day. Every consulting company had its sets of whines and moans, and the fault was always on the part of the client, Kmart. Collectively, in just the previous year, Kmart had paid $30+ million to consulting companies! It had tomes of PowerPoint decks to show for it, but not much else. Nothing had changed or been made better. But they all kept working Kmart. Some had even placed their staff in management positions at Kmart. This ensured that a permanent "employee replacement" would never be found. Also, more consulting people would be placed in that unit. Well, a big shame on Kmart for letting all this happen as well. There was no accountability anywhere, and rampant opportunity everywhere for consulting companies to further their billings. It was a step just shy of semi-approved larceny. Who knows what other arrangements may have been at play behind the scenes.

I would typically go home to LA on a Thursday evening, every 2 or 3 weeks, for a long weekend with my family. At the Detroit Metro Airport, it would be a sight to behold! About 30 to 40 consultants working at Kmart would be waiting to board flights. They were doing this every week. Kmart was billed for their travel time to Detroit on Monday and return home on Thursday. It also paid all travel and living costs for these folks. It was a great lifestyle for the young and single College or MBA graduates. But in it, they would not learn the real meaning of business responsibility and accountability for achieving results.

So, in one day in that fateful week, at the last count, I fired 150+ people from various consulting companies. It saved us a lot of money in expenses. At Kmart, projects stopped in mid stride; manager and staff positions fell vacant overnight, but were consolidated away; and many managers were forced to start thinking and acting for themselves. The best part of it all was that the absence of all these consultants had no negative impact on anything at all! In fact, all the muddled thinking, born of "consultant speak", vanished and folks began to communicate clearly and simply. It never ceased to amaze me how a consulting service, which can be useful and does have a legitimate place in business, can lose its way so badly due to revenue considerations.

Then we had the great Kmart Human Resources (HR) organization! I am sad to admit it, but in my life, I have met few HR people that I would consider worthy of any respect. Most are by nature chameleons, tuned into the prevailing political winds, obsessed with reading corporate tea leaves, and fond of basking in reflected executive power. They also tend to be wily, devious, manipulative, and devoted mainly to self-preservation and promotion.

The HR Group in any company is typically a valuable asset charged with providing highly necessary and useful services in a wide range to its business units. But at Kmart, this was not the case. Oh, while it did provide all the key services nationwide, HR at Kmart was also a roadblock to almost any executive action.

Some examples: 1) We need to reduce staff. (*You cannot for 90 days. A review process has to be followed.*) 2) We are going to sell this business unit. (*You cannot. The Unions will oppose it.*) 3) No salary raises this year. (*Oh, you cannot do that. Due to Union contracts.*) 4) Ok, so no goddam Coke in the cafeteria! How's that? (*No. They will strike for Coke.*) 5) Is there anything that we CAN do? (*No. Welcome to Detroit.*) Obviously, I am exaggerating greatly here, but you get my general drift.

"It is a total stonewall." I said to Marv in frustration. "They have a block for every action. I don't know what to do."

He thought for a few minutes. Then he picked up the phone and called the SVP of Kmart HR. In a sweet voice, he said that he needed two things: 1) A list of folks to be laid off to achieve a 20% reduction in HR staff; and 2) A meeting with the entire HR Division staff at the HQ to answer their questions on what was going on. Later on, in this meeting, I would witness the depth of their reaction. Oh Gosh, HR nearly blew up like a repressed volcano!

The SVP responded with the typical, "Marv, how can I do that? It is just not possible. This is a most difficult and involved process and will take considerable time."

Marv replied, "It is really not that hard. For each job grade, let your people get into a line on their own. Then shoot every 5th person. It will be a self-selection and you will achieve the 20% reduction! Go ahead, put your mind to it."

Soon, Marv took on the persona of a corporate T-Rex! He was greatly feared everywhere. I was thought of as one of his Velociraptors and considered even more lethal. Terrible as it all was, nobody was trying to win a popularity contest. It was a brutal fight for the sheer survival of Kmart. Few people understood this stark reality at the time.

At a huge meeting at HQ, Marv was asked pointedly, "Mr. Rich, how could you remove so many jobs at Kmart HQ? And that too, just before Christmas?"

Marv's answer was a blunt "I am not in the business of removing jobs at Kmart HQ before Christmas. I am trying to save the jobs of over 200,000 people who still work at Kmart, in every season, all over the country."

Harsh as that statement was, its poignancy was not lost on anybody.

Flying in Style

"**I** have to see him, Alice." I pleaded. "I have orders from Marv to prep him before he meets with the Goldman Sachs people at dinner in New York City tonight."
"Vijay, I know. But something is afoot this morning. Floyd is in an intense series of meetings with all the merchants. I will get to you when I know more." Alice replied.

Floyd Hall was the new CEO and Chairman of the Board of Kmart Corp. He was tall, handsome, silver haired, and simply charming. He was smooth with employees, vendors, and stockholders. He was highly regarded in the retailing industry. He embodied the promise of turning Kmart's fortunes around.
Alice was his Executive Secretary, a new hire. She was tall, athletic, and gorgeous. Her looks reminded one of the famous Hollywood actress, Doris Day. Like Doris, Alice was also German in her lineage, with the blonde hair and blue eyes to match. She possessed a smile that can only be described as dazzling. However, all her physical beauty aside, she was smart, efficient, and many steps ahead of everybody in anything. She was a true professional at her job.

"Alice, that is not good enough." I said. "I need just 30 minutes with Floyd. Surely you can find them for me? If I do not achieve this, Marv will certainly kill me! You know that he is away on a trip today, right?"
"Vijay, I could never think of disappointing you. Just stay near your office. I will get to you as soon as Floyd is free."
Just then, the office door opened and Floyd emerged. "Alice, I have lost all control today. Oh, Hi Vijay! I know that we have to chat. I promise I will

344

do it before I leave. But right now, we have a huge issue that I must resolve at once. So, just stand by, okay? Alice, we need a working lunch in my office for 10 people."

"A lunch of sandwiches and drinks will arrive in 10 minutes. I ordered it an hour ago." Alice replied, with a twinkle in her eyes.

Then, the day turned even crazier! Floyd's meetings seemed endless. Even Alice eventually lost it and said to me, "Vijay, I am going to need a martini after this day! Wanna join me?"

At 4pm, Floyd was shoved out of his meetings by Alice, and told to head to the Pontiac airfield for his flight to New Jersey. She overruled everybody, and insisted that Floyd had to leave immediately. As she hustled him off to his waiting limo, Floyd noticed me standing by and said, "Ah, Vijay, sorry about all this. Come, get in the car with me. We will talk on the way to the airport." Alice looked dead straight at me, smiled knowingly with a barely noticeable wink, and waved me on.

Just as Floyd and I settled into his huge limo, the phone rang. It was the satellite phone of the limo. Well, Floyd got into this phone call which seemed to be awfully important and about many critical things. It lasted the entire 40 minutes to the airport. So now, the limo pulls up directly near the Gulfstream 5 jet, which was the airplane from the Kmart fleet assigned to the CEO. The limo stops within 10 feet of the door/ladder of the G-5. A couple of people put away Floyd's luggage in its hold and he had to walk just a few feet to board. Then Floyd says, "Vijay, sorry about that call. Why don't you just come with me? We can review your material on the flight. The plane returns immediately and will bring you back."

Kmart at the time had a corporate fleet of 7 airplanes. Six of them were Beech business jets. And one was a Gulfstream 5, the absolute Cadillac of business jets of that era. All the Beech planes had twin jet engines and were nicely appointed, but the fuselage was such that one could not stand fully upright in them. Also, their galley was limited and the toilet setup was a bit sketchy. These airplanes were used heavily by various senior executives for store, regional office, and vendor/supplier visits around the USA. With a network of 2,400+ stores, where many were in tiny communities not well served by commercial airlines, this fleet was of great value in supporting travel needs of many people from the Kmart HQ.

However, by contrast, the G-5 was a total dream. It was also powered by twin jet engines but had a larger fuselage so you could stand up fully in it. It could seat 12 people, had a lovely galley for hot and cold food, and wonderful toilets. Its interior layout was a fascinating and brilliant puzzle. It could be

345

configured for seats with tables for 2 or 4 people; a group seating of 8 people; and even 2 full size beds for long haul flights. Its flight crew comprised of a pilot and a co-pilot who also functioned at times as a steward. This aircraft was sleek, sheer elegance, and richly appointed in everything.

Also, with the G-5, there existed a "club" of sorts to support the maintenance schedule of the airplane. All G-5 airplanes would substitute for each other to accommodate service outages, as required. The owners/lessors did not seem to mind these substitutions at all. I flew the G-5 on many occasions later on and I remember flying on many different airplanes belonging to other people. Once, we had the G-5 belonging to Jack Welch, CEO of General Electric. On another occasion, the G-5 belonged to Ted Turner, CEO of Turner Broadcast System. Ted's G-5 was decorated with lovely and personal photos of his trophy wife and Hollywood actress, Jane Fonda. The world of flying in a G-5 jet was about "as good as it gets" in luxurious air travel at that time.

So, I got on the G-5 with Floyd Hall. We sat down and the door promptly closed. There was nobody else to wait for! The pilot spoke to Floyd and verified the "wheels up" clearance time of 5:00pm. In minutes, we were taxiing for takeoff. At 5:01pm, we lifted off. We were headed to the Teterboro Airfield in New Jersey, just across the Hudson River from Manhattan, New York City. It was a flight of about 1 hour and 20 minutes.

En route, I reviewed my materials with Floyd and got him fully prepared for his crucial dinner meeting. We barely finished and it was time to descend and land. We taxied to the apron at Teterboro. Floyd got off the G-5, and walked straight into a waiting limo. It took him directly to Manhattan for his dinner engagement. The pilot now asked me for my permission for "wheels up" clearance time, which was only 5 minutes away. In just that much time, we left to return to Pontiac.

I was left stunned by the whole experience. On the flight back, I had a cold beer, ate my dinner, and spent a lot of time with the pilot learning about the G-5 cockpit and its various control systems. I had the whole G-5 to myself, so I explored it all. But, sadly, when we got back to Pontiac, I was jerked back to my own different reality. There was no limo waiting for me. I had to call for and take a beat up old "yellow" taxi back to the office. Then I had to find my car in the vast parking lot on a dark cold night, remove snow from it, and drive myself to my little one-bedroom functional apartment.

However, this flight remained etched in my mind. It was my first time in a G-5. It was unforgettable.

An Unusual Lunch & Dinner

In the retailing business, one has to keep up with the changing fashions and trends. One has to remain tuned in, open to new ideas, and be amenable to stepping out of one's comfort zone. The learning process is continuous and ongoing, in the never-ending quest to stay informed and relevant. Sometimes people forget this bit of wisdom and face sorry results. This story is about one such person in particular.

"Hey, it is time for lunch!" I said. "What kind of food would all of you like to eat? There are many places nearby."

I was driving back with 3 Kmart merchants/buyers, two men and a lady, from a vendor show in downtown Detroit. It was half past noon and we could either have lunch outside, or settle for the usual cafeteria food in the HQ building.

"So, what shall it be?" I went on. "We have American, Italian, Mediterranean, Middle-Eastern, Indian, Chinese, or Japanese. Hey, I can go on! There are still more choices." In reply, I got mostly silence, and a few soft grumbles.

After some quick discussion, it seemed that everybody favored Italian food, but there was an exception. I will call this man, Robert or Bob. He was born and raised in Michigan. He had lived his entire life there as well and did not want to eat any "foreign" food. He just wanted his meat and potatoes, which at lunch translated to "a hamburger and french fries".

I asked him, "Bob, don't you want to try a different taste? You know, you may actually like it! Also, it would be good for your health."

"No, not really. I don't care for all those cuisines. They are too fancy, weird, and expensive. I like food that I know."

I realized that it was pointless trying to convince this man. He had no desire to discover anything new, unfamiliar, or different. It seemed that this attitude of his extended into almost everything in his life. I wondered how he had become a senior merchant/buyer at Kmart? How in the world did he do his job while remaining blissfully ignorant about it? The irony was striking.

So, out of respect for Bob, we settled for a local Burger joint for our lunch. As we were seated, suddenly Bob asked me, "Vijay, you are from India, eh?" I replied, "Yes, sir, that is correct."

"Is it true what they say about how Indians worship the cow? That Indians do not eat beef?"

"Yes, that is right. In the Hindu religion, the cow is a sacred animal. So, those Indians, who are Hindus in their faith, do not eat beef."

"Oh, are there other kinds of Indians too? Are there black, yellow, or oriental looking Indians? They follow pagan religions, don't they?" I could not believe my ears. This was from a senior Kmart buyer! But for now, I just went with the flow of the chat.

"Bob, India is a very old country with a rich history. It has an ethnically diverse population, many languages, and ancient religions. The major faiths would be Hinduism, Islam, Sikhism, Christianity, Buddhism, & Jainism. It is amazing how, despite periodic upheavals, it has all managed to co-exist in India for centuries," I replied in a short summary.

"But they worship idols, don't they? That's kind of pagan, to my way of thinking," Bob continued. Now, I was in grave disbelief. Is he putting me on, or is he serious? Then, he asked me, "So, how do people live over there? In buildings, or in huts?" My jaw nearly dropped to the floor! Then, I decided to tease and test Bob a bit, for the sheer fun of it.

"Oh, Bob, India is way different from anything you could imagine. It is primitive, exotic, strange, and even frightening for visitors. Did you know that my house is up in a tree?" I offered. (*I wondered if he caught the joke.*)

"No kidding, Vijay! That is amazing. I can only imagine all the problems that one would have with that setup. I mean, a house up in a tree? That is just incredible. Anybody that can climb, could get up there. So, how does one provide security for it?" (*Now I am thinking, dude, are you serious? I am just messing with you! Do you still not get it?*)

"Well, Bob, one can never be too careful in these matters. So, we have an old-fashioned solution for the security problem. We just have our pet Bengal tiger guard the base of the tree. No climbers can get by that big cat!" I replied. (*Oh, come on, Bob, surely you get it by now?*)

"Oh, wow! That is really something." Bob said, genuinely impressed. "It is surely an exotic country. The house up in a tree, and a Bengal tiger guarding its base from unwanted climbers. Man, that is just awesome. But it must be so difficult for everyone. How do you get up and down from that tree house?"

"Oh, you just take the elevator." I said simply. (*I had totally given up by now.*)

That evening, I was to have dinner with Marv. He had made a booking at the "Phoenician" in Birmingham. As we drove out to this restaurant, I told him the story about Bob. Marv said, "Remind me to fire that son of a bitch. They are the reason why Kmart sucks."

We got there and Marv was just horrified by what he saw. Their tables had tablecloths with glass sheets on top of them! Marv had a thing about tables. They had to have proper tablecloths on them or he could not eat there. The maître de' asked, "Sir, is anything wrong?"

Marv said, "Yes, very much. We need a table with a proper tablecloth on it, instead of glass. You see, it is against my friend's pagan religion to eat off of glass! Can you fix it?"

We got the tablecloth and had a divine meal. Nobody cared a rat's butt about any pagan religion.

Epilogue

It had been 3 amazing years of consulting at Kmart. They offered me a senior job at the HQ in Detroit with a great financial package. The catch was that I would have to move from LA to Detroit. Nilima outright refused.

So, in June 1997, I returned home to LA, once again unemployed, and looking for the next gig. But first we took a grand holiday, after 3 brutal years of back breaking travel and work. We went off on a cruise to Alaska from Vancouver with our kids and Nilima's parents. It was a novel thing at the time and it was a total blast.

I returned from the cruise to discover a strange DHL package waiting for me. It was sent from Hong Kong and it had just a "tea bag" in it! But that is another story, which I will get to in a bit.

Marv and I remained in contact over all the years after Kmart. His career took him from Kmart to the East Coast in various things. Eventually he retired in Malibu, California. I was also back in LA by then, and we met from time to time. Retirement was a hard adjustment for him. He was not prepared or cut out for it. He struggled with regaining a purpose in his life.

Sadly, in late 2015, Marv suffered a massive stroke, which eventually felled him. I had known his wife, Cheryl, since 1987, when they were not even married, and we had all been through so much together since that time. Marv wished to be cremated and I was with Cheryl at the "ash dispersion" ceremony later on in the Pacific Ocean, off of Santa Monica, California.

As the Pacific Ocean accepted Marv's remains, and the roses offered floated away with the ocean swells, I cried uncontrollably. It was for the loss of a mentor and a brilliant man. A person who had meant so much to me, taught me a lot, and who had done so much for me in my life. An honest man, who had also been an honest friend to me.

Marv Rich, without a doubt, was the finest teacher that I ever had in my work life. He was dyslexic and could not even dial a phone number, but he had a photographic memory and a razor-sharp mind. A difficult man, who suffered no fools, and who was driven beyond belief in anything, to achieve results. There were always one of two camps that you fell into, when you met him. You either liked him, or hated him.

I loved him.

Global Experiences

An Arrangement in Code

In the Spring of 1997, Ron Floto, EVP of the Super Kmart Division, announced that he was leaving to take a new job as the CEO of the Dairy Farm Group, a subsidiary of the storied Jardine Matheson Company in Hong Kong. The news hit the executive suite at Kmart like a sledgehammer. Many people were quite shaken up since Ron was a widely liked and respected senior executive.

"Vij, wanna go for a smoke?" Ron asked me with a smile. I smiled back and said, "Sure." It was quite cold in Detroit, Michigan, and we still had a lot of late snow on the ground. We went down to the ground floor, stepped out of the building, and into the snow drifts from a side door. Outside, in the open and frosty air, was the only place available to smoke at Kmart. Covered in thick hooded parkas, we lit up and started to chat. I congratulated Ron on his new job and asked him if had ever worked in an international setting. He confessed that, outside of his US Army deployments, he had not, and that this was going to be a real adventure for him.

"I envy you," I said. "You know, Ron, ever since I came to the USA from India many years ago, it has always been my dream to work in an international assignment. You are fortunate to have such a great opportunity. In Asia at that! It is wonderful! You will love it, I am certain."

"Vij, you really think so?" Ron asked. "I mean, would you seriously consider working overseas in Asia, of all the places?"

"In a heartbeat," I replied without any hesitation. "Why? Do you have something in mind? What are you implying?"

"Well, I gotta get there first and get the lay of the land," Ron said. "But I already know this much. I am going to need some serious help in this mission. Help that I know and can trust. Come to the house for dinner this Saturday. Nancy likes you and she likes steaks. I will cook for us." Out of sheer curiosity, I accepted the invite graciously.

Nancy, Ron's wife, was a lot younger than him. It was a second marriage for Ron. She was blonde, blue eyed, vivacious, and engaging. She had been a buyer at a major retail chain and so was an astute judge of people and knew how to handle them. She was a huge asset for Ron. At this dinner, she was terribly excited. She carried on about life in Hong Kong, all the comforts and trappings of a privileged life in Asia, the charms of China, and the joys of the American Club! It was hard to stop her.

"Nancy, please relax. It is alright. I get it," I said. "Well, all this is obviously quite new for you. So, your reaction is understandable. But do remember that I grew up in Asia, and all these things were actually present in my life. None of it is a surprise for me. It is all quite familiar, and even a matter of some nostalgia."

She batted her eyes at me and said, "Really? You do? Okay, Ronnie, he is all yours."

We all had a good laugh over Nancy's aggressiveness and she turned a bit coy. Then, she came over and said, "Ronnie, tell him!"

Ron said, "Vij, Nancy and I feel that you belong with us in Hong Kong. We have been together here for nearly 3 years. We are moving on and we think that you should too."

"Why, I am quite flattered by your words, Ron." I replied, somewhat surprised. "I have enjoyed our many gatherings over these past years and Nancy has always been just wonderful. But, what do you exactly have in mind?"

"Well, in a few months, after I get to Hong Kong and get a grip on the situation, I will send for you. It will be "in code" that only you can understand. This is for reasons that I will explain later. But, when that happens, contact me immediately. Deal?"

"Yes, deal!" I gushed. I had no idea what this "deal" was all about. It was a wild shot in the dark with no assurance of any consequences. But it was a passing opportunity and predictably, I went for the risk.

In early-August 1997, we returned from a fabulous holiday in Alaska. I had left Kmart and we were celebrating my homecoming after 3 years of brutal commuting to Michigan. As a family, we took a cruise from Vancouver, Canada, to Seward, Alaska, on the "Inside Passage", visited the Denali National Park, and had a blast. We had Nilima's parents with us and obviously our children, Neil and Meghana.

In the "stopped mail" stack, there was a DHL package from Hong Kong! I opened it with great curiosity. Inside the envelope were a tea bag and a note. Written on it was, "A Hong Kong phone number. R."

Such was the beginning of my many adventures in international business in the years that followed.

A Formal Introduction

Ron Floto engaged me for a brief consulting project. He wanted some help on valuation questions regarding an acquisition that the Dairy Farm Group (DFG) was contemplating in Indonesia. My solo work was up against formidable competitors such as Goldman Sachs, Price Waterhouse, etc. with their highly skilled and vast resources.

Well, my work was well received by the DFG Operating Committee and Ron offered me a senior level job. I remember meeting him on a rainy night at the old Kai Tak Airport in Hong Kong. I was on my way back from visiting my Mom in India. Ron gave me a package with the written offer inside and told me to call him once I was back in LA. I was sitting in the Business Class lounge, waiting for my flight and thinking about Ron's offer. I was partially watching the TV as well. Suddenly, the story broke that Princess Diana had died! I sat up, was overcome, and my eyes teared over. She had married Prince Charles about the same time that I had married Nilima. It broke my heart to see her life cut so short. It all seemed so grossly unfair. Like millions around the world, I adored her too.

The name of the Dairy Farm Group was a misnomer. DFG had nothing to do with either dairy or farming. The name was derived from a rich history dating back to the colonial era, when in fact it did have farms and sold dairy products around the territory of Hong Kong. In the late 1990's, by contrast, it was a major retailer with a vast footprint around all of South East Asia.

Geographically, it owned retailing companies from India to Malaysia, Singapore, Philippines, Thailand, Indonesia, Hong Kong, Taiwan, China, South Korea, Japan, Australia, and New Zealand. In these countries, it owned retailing companies that operated chains of any combination of grocery stores, convenience stores, health & beauty stores, pharmacies, do-it-yourself stores, hyper-markets, specialty stores, etc. Further, it also owned the vast logistics, transportation, warehousing, and distribution infrastructure to support them. It was known mostly by its country specific "chain store brands", which locally were household names, but not many folks knew the name Dairy Farm Group.

DFG was a publicly listed company with the controlling interest held by the Jardine Matheson (JM) Company which was famous for its storied past in the entire region from the days of sailing ships. JM, while also publicly listed, was a tightly controlled and mainly family owned Scottish company. Its origins dated back to the 1700's when William Jardine, a daring Scottish seafarer, established it with an Indian partner from Bombay, Jamsetjee Jeejeebhoy. He made it a huge success with sheer guts, a keen sense for commercial trading, and fearless sailing skills. In Hong Kong, in a throwback to that celebrated past, the Managing Director (MD) of the Jardine Matheson Company, was locally always referred to as the "Taipan" (*the chief executive or leader*). James Clavell, the celebrated British novelist, had noticed this and had incorporated it into some of his hugely successful books and films about China and Southeast Asia.

"Mr. Vijay! You go to lunch today at noon, yes?" Kay Li sternly admonished me. She was my executive secretary. She was smart, efficient, and highly dedicated to my welfare.

"Kay, dear, try to understand this. Informally, it is Vijay, my first name. However, in a formal sense, it is Mr. Yajnik, my last name. But it is never Mr. Vijay. That is just wrong! Do you follow me?" I tried my best to set her straight. It never worked.

"Yes, Mr. Vijay, I understand. But now you must go. Lunch with Taipan, ok? Cannot be late." Kay said firmly, with no understanding at all about what I had just said.

I went in a car arranged by Kay to the "Jardine House" (JH) in the Central District of Hong Kong. It is an iconic and legendary high-rise building. While somewhat dwarfed today by the newer and taller buildings, it is still highly noticeable, because all the windows on its 50+ floors are round in shape! No other building in all of Hong Kong has this feature. When one sees it for the first time, one does a "double take" because it is so unusual. But the local folks in Hong Kong, who are smart and so clever, had this building figured out very quickly. In the Cantonese language, spoken in Hong Kong, the JH was a widely and well recognized address. It was known by a simple phrase in Cantonese. It was the house of "a thousand assholes"!

So, in this famous venue, on this fateful day, I had a date for a formal lunch. It was intended to introduce the 4 new "Americans" actually to the Keswick (pronounced "Kessick") brothers, since we had met the Taipan already. Besides Ron, our group comprised of Bob Neslund (North Asia Director), John Pearl (Group HR Director), and myself (Group CIO & Director). I did not know what to expect of this august meeting.

We were ushered into an executive dining room on the top floor of the Jardine House. I was taken aback by the décor and trappings! What century were they living in? Did they know that Queen Victoria was long dead? These were my impulsive thoughts. In this incredibly ornate room, there were waiters dressed in formal attire. There was a board on an easel showing the seating arrangements for a table of just 6 people! I was immediately offered and served a dry martini. We had barely 10 minutes before we were "invited" to sit down at the dining table. Soon, the hosts showed up from seemingly nowhere.

From a well concealed side door, in walked the two Keswick brothers. They were Henry, who was about 70 years old, and Simon, who was about 65 years old at the time. Both Henry and Simon were the direct blood descendants of William Jardine. They were the living scions of a family that still controlled the vast JM empire. Unlike the earlier eras, the Taipan of JM today was at times a hired hand. However, the Keswick family owned and controlled everything. The two brothers had absolute power, and they never hesitated to exercise it. But at this lunch, I knew none of this.

Our drinks were summarily dismissed. We were seated promptly. The Keswick brothers took the end seats and the other four of us took the lateral seats. After the perfunctory pleasantries, the formal introductions began. The Keswicks spent precisely a few minutes with each person, before moving on to the next one. I was just amazed by all this. It felt like we were at Court, before some sort of a monarch, from some bygone times.

Then, Henry turned towards me. He said, "Ah, Vijay, you hail from India(r), eh?" Clearly, he had read the dossier on me. I was sure that one had been prepared in detail for both of them.

"Yes, sir. I do," I replied honestly. My hard-earned American citizenship was obviously nowhere in this picture for them.

"So, tell me, what did your father do in India?" Henry inquired. I was simply stunned, and also a bit annoyed by this question. What the hell did my father have to do with my working in his companies? My ugly American side began to rise up quickly. But, because I was still quite ignorant about all this, I decided to play it cautiously.

"Well, Mr. Keswick, my father was a General Manager in a British company which built and operated cement plants all over India. It was hard and rough work, given where they made cement."

Henry Keswick nodded with approval, and smiled, like he was remembering something from the past. Then Simon spoke up.

"Vijay, that is wonderful to learn. But, tell me, what did your grandfather do in India?" To say that I was shocked more, would be an understatement. I was appalled, incredulous, and now getting downright angry on the inside. I mean, who the hell did these guys think they were? What the heck did my father, or my grandfather, have to do with anything? But I decided again, with great effort, to control my rage, answer the question, and just shut up. It turned out to be a wise choice.

After questioning everybody at the table and having our meal, we were invited to join the Keswicks for a digestif and a cigar in an adjacent room. It was a very old, single malt, Scotch whiskey and the cigars were of a rare Cuban variety. We were welcomed, and then shortly the Keswicks just melted away.

As we left JH, I quizzed Ron, Bob, and John, "What the hell was all that about? I mean, all those crazy questions."

Ron said, "Vij, relax. You all passed the test today. They select one from two check-off boxes in their minds. One box says "Acceptable", and the other says "Not Acceptable". In the former, you are welcomed, but in the latter, you are shot."

Well, over the ensuing years, I got to meet Simon and Henry on many occasions. I even had some business interactions with them, given the ever-growing threat of internet-based commerce. In everything, their thoughts were always about their "family". They also held strong beliefs in family values. They would fight aggressively to protect any and all of their employees from any harm from anybody, especially if it involved China. They hated China with a passion, and spoke about it at length on occasions. This was because the Communists had grabbed all the vast JM holdings there, after Chairman Mao's revolution, without paying any compensation. "A bunch of thugs" Henry would call the Politburo of China. However, they were always very gracious to us. I recall offers to visit Scotland during conversations on a couple of occasions, to attend something within their family. I thought that these were incredibly sweet gestures on their part.

The Keswicks were a devoted Scottish clan. They were conservative, but also open to new ideas. They held few prejudices that one could discern. They never seemed to discriminate on the basis of religion, race, color, sex, or lifestyle.

They admired greatly the religion of "aggressive business competence." For that, in essence, had been their family history and legacy over the past 3 centuries.

A Home in Beijing

It was December 1997, and it was very cold. With Ron Floto, I was on my first visit to Beijing from Hong Kong. The trip had a loaded agenda. We were trying to figure out many things. As Americans, we had many strikes against us. We were looking at retail grocery stores, hyper-markets, convenience stores, etc. in China and it was a strange world indeed. From products, to retailing formats and intellectual property copyrights, nothing about it was normal. We were also followed every step of the way by somebody.

Ron and I were a bit uncomfortable with this type of scrutiny. We had landed in the pathetic Beijing international airport in the evening. It was actually worse than the dinky airport in Ahmedabad, India, at the time. We emerged from it and I had noticed promptly that we were being tailed. Anyway, we chose to ignore it all and settled in for the night at our hotel. The next day, we had a full itinerary. We visited many places. It was all intended to orient us to China and the state of the retailing industry in it. With its vast market, every international retailer was trying to figure out its strategy for China at the time. The Dairy Farm Group was no exception. But everybody was wary of China as well. The business playing field was never fair by design and intent. One had to also contend with a strange web of regulations and political control as a foreign company.

We were driving along on the Chang An Lu (*Chang An Avenue*), near Zhongnanhai (*the Politburo complex*), when our guide suddenly said, "Oh, you must see the real China. It is not what we see here or around the Tiananmen Square. It is so different." Ron agreed with delight and asked him to show us around.

Hector Lee was with the Jardine Matheson office in Beijing. He was smart, informed, and well connected. He offered to show us his ancestral home which was nearby. Shortly, we left the major road and went down many narrow streets and ended up in the front of his family home.

"Here we are! This is the home of my grandparents, who still live here. It has belonged to my family for as long as anybody can remember or see in the records. It is authentically Chinese," Hector said. Ron and I stepped out of the car to have a good look. I felt a strange emotional vibration immediately.

In another moment or two, much to my surprise, I felt a growing sense of familiarity! Actually, even that would be an understatement. I felt like I was being pulled back in time. I just could not believe my senses. "Hector, may I tell you what this house is like? I have never been here before, but I know this house very well," I stated in near disbelief.

357

"What? You know this house?" Hector replied in total amazement. Ron wondered if I had gone completely nuts.

"Yes. I know it fully and precisely. This is the same home as that of my grandparents in India. Without ever having seen it, I can describe it to you in exact detail."

Hector was shocked and so was Ron. So, I was put to a test immediately. I just blew them away! I knew the overall design, orientation, adjacencies, and the purpose of every room, etc. in great detail. We walked in and met Hector's grandparents. The home was exactly as I had described it. It was indeed strange that people of different cultures were connected in such an incredible way. Perhaps building design and construction technologies in the ancient times were somehow mutually known or shared.

Over the next few years, I witnessed this entire neighborhood of centuries old, priceless, and classic Chinese homes, get bulldozed for more modern high-rise buildings. Was this supposed to be progress? In its quest to compete with and equate itself to the West, somewhere along the way, I felt that the Communist Party of China had managed to lose not only its national heritage, but also its very soul.

Landing at Kai Tak Airport, Hong Kong

I was returning to Hong Kong from a business trip to Auckland, New Zealand. It was a 10+ hour flight and I was travelling in First Class. Out of sheer curiosity, when the stewardess came around, I asked her if I could join the crew on the flight deck for the landing at the Kai Tak Airport in Hong Kong. I told her that I was a licensed private pilot and would love to experience this celebrated landing. She smiled graciously at me and said that she would try to see what could be arranged.

The old Kai Tak Airport at Hong Kong was legendary. This was due to many reasons. For one, it had only one short runway which stuck out into the Victoria Harbor. Many airplanes had overrun it and some had ended up in the water as well. Also, the approach to this runway was just nuts! The airplanes had to follow a crazy narrow path of descent adjacent to hills. There was a lot of wind shear. On both sides there were tall high-rise buildings with people in them.

The airport runway was known for fierce crosswinds, which were ever present, across from the harbor. It was ranked as the most dangerous commercial airfield in the world. All commercial pilots, flying for any airline, needed a special certification and clearance in order to land at Kai Tak. Further, it was going to close within a year, as Hong Kong had built a brand spanking new airport at Chek Lap Kok. So, Kai Tak's days were numbered, but all the "fly boys" just loved the challenge of shooting the last few landings on its single runway!

I had actually forgotten about my request when the stewardess came up to me and said, "Mr. Yajnik, Captain Murphy requests the pleasure of your company on the flight deck." I bolted upright, thanked her profusely, and pulled myself together. She broke out into hilarious laughter. She told me that she had never had a request quite like mine in her entire flying life! Then, she took me to the flight deck.

Now, on this particular flight we were flying a Boeing 747-400, the stretch version, of Air New Zealand. It was their premier daily flight to Hong Kong from Auckland. They were very proud of it and advertised it everywhere it seemed. I entered the cockpit from the upper deck and was given the "jump seat" behind the captain on the left side. To the captain's right was the co-pilot and to my right was the flight engineer.

359

"Well, hello! This bird is a bit bigger than what you are used to, right?" Captain Murphy said in the headphones. Everybody had a pair on. "Listen, I am Nick. Mind if I call you Vijay?"

"Not at all, sir," I replied. "I am so grateful to you for this gesture. You have made my long-held dream come true!"

"It is our pleasure, Vijay." he replied. "We all feel that you deserve this, before they shut Kai Tak down forever. By the way, we are all on a first name basis here."

"Fine, yes, thanks. But is it as bad as they say it is?" I wondered. "I have heard many stories."

"Well, there is nothing predictable about it, that is for sure. I have seen it easy and awfully difficult. What you get is just the luck of the draw. So, you play it, as you face it. Oh, and is it as bad? How shall I put it? Well, let's say that nothing in my life has scared me more. If that helps you."

"Five minutes to start descent," the flight engineer informed us. We were flying at flight level 390 (*39,000 feet*), our cruising altitude. Our descent would be long and slow.

"Vijay, we will go west during descent and approach Kai Tak heading east. Just follow the radio traffic and you will get a great sense of what we are doing. We may not talk much, but do listen real closely."

Soon, all the passengers' cabin announcements were finished and the cockpit got deadly serious about the impending landing. The steady descent continued. I began to feel a building sense of tension about what we were about to do in this enormous and fully loaded commercial airplane.

"NZ 423 Heavy, maintain descent and heading. Wind shear reported 5 miles out. Crosswinds gusting 40 mph," the Kai Tak Tower warned us in a crisp British accent.

"Let's power up by 10% for wind shear, just in case. We may come in a bit hot, but that is okay," Nick said.

I felt the engines rev up a bit. Now, there were hills to the left and tall skyscrapers on both sides nearby. We were flying a ridiculously narrow path in between them. There were people in apartment balconies staring at us and pointing at the plane. We could even see their facial expressions!

Then, Nick says, "I am taking her." In a moment, we felt the auto pilot disengage and now Nick was flying this ginormous bird with his bare hands, feet, and his brain, just like me in my little Beechcraft 150 Sundowner years ago.

Suddenly, a buzzer went off! We had clipped the Outer Marker. This is a physical point, in 3-dimensions, where 3 radio beams intersect, and it tells the pilot exactly where he is in relation to the runway. Normally, at this event, the pilot looks up and sees the runway before him. Typically, his glide path is also indicated by streaming strobe lights to assist him.

So, given my prior flight training, I instinctively looked up. All I saw was a huge hill directly in front of us. There was no runway and no strobe lights. And we were flying straight into it! Reflexively, I blurted into the mouthpiece, "S**t, where's the runway?"

"At 2 o'clock... strobes in a 90-degree arc due south... we turn to "final" directly and line up..." Nick said cryptically. "Joe, we got 40-mile gusts... southwest crosswinds... nose right at 30-degrees... prepare for a 3 pointer..." Nobody else said a word.

Nick banked the giant 747 to the right at a near 45-degree incline like it was a little toy. As he completed the turn, the nose of the huge plane was pointed 30-degrees to the right of the runway. We faced directly into the crosswind, but our ground track was dead center of the runway and strobes.

"100 feet... 50 feet..." the terrain warning system intoned. As we came up to the "flare", Nick swung the nose of this huge plane 30 degrees to the left, while simultaneously banking it to the right. In a split second, the right landing gear made contact, then in a bit the left, and eventually the nose gear. The engines roared in massive reverse thrust, but we missed the last turnoff. We came to a stop barely within 20 feet of the end of the runway and the water just beyond it. Nick handed the plane to his co-pilot to turn it around and taxi it to its gate.

"Well, Vijay, just another landing at Kai Tak!" Nick said with a smile on his face.

But I was shaking in my shoes. "Jesus Christ, where the hell did you learn to fly this thing like that?" I asked. "I mean, doing this in a dinky little Beech airplane is one thing, but this is a monster 747 stretch! And she is as big and heavy as they can get!"

"Ah, well, they are all just airplanes after all," Nick said. "I hope you enjoyed it."

"Enjoyed it? My God, I shall never forget this! It is an experience to last a lifetime. I cannot thank you enough." I gushed.

Little did I know at that time, that the era where this type of flying was even possible would shortly vanish forever. After 9/11, everything changed.

Experiences such as this became the stuff of memories and stories just like this one.

Madam Zhang in China

At the Dairy Farm Group, my initial responsibilities were quite diverse. Among many things, I was also responsible for handling the affairs of some non-traditional businesses that had little to do with modern retailing. The question always was about what to do with them. Do you grow them, or merge them with something complementary, or do you sell them? Or in the worst case, do you just shut them down? In Hong Kong, unlike the USA, the answers to such questions were never easy and always quite complex. Even doing a business deal, as I soon discovered, was a strange opera of many acts and players. There were a lot of cultural variables that one had to deal with carefully and delicately. Success could elude you on the basis of the smallest of things.

However, I had a shining star in this entire mix. It was the Sims Trading (ST) Company. Its MD, who was a Brit, reported to me. This company was a classic trading business, that had exclusive "agency" relationships for Hong Kong & China markets, with major global FMCG (*fast moving consumer goods*) companies. The diversity of these agency contracts was amazing. For instance, Sims represented Kraft Foods, Heineken Beer, Guinness Beer, Lavazza Coffee, Toblerone Confectionary, Monte Blanc Pens, Chilean wines, and Italian Parma Ham, to name a few. The agency contracts spanned the globe, and ranged across consumer products, beverages, dairy, wine & spirits, fashion accessories, etc. Further, Sims also offered logistics, warehousing, and marketing/sales support services to its clients, who were mainly the sellers. It had a highly significant book of this centuries old and traditional "agency" business.

Sims had offices in all the major cities in China. Also, to further its reach, the Chinese operations were actually structured as a Joint Venture (JV) with a huge State-Owned Enterprise (SOE), headquartered in the city of Guangzhou (*formerly Canton*) in the province of Guangdong. In this JV, Sims held a 51% interest and the SOE 49%. In real terms, the JV deferred every decision to the Sims management team. Sims had the products, marketing, and technical knowhow, while the SOE had access to a vast market, huge demand for foreign products, and a network of cheap warehouses. It was an arrangement of great mutual benefits.

The laws in China required the JV to have monthly Board Meetings. So, every month, Glenn Smith, the MD, and I would go to Guangzhou by an elite non-stop train from Hong Kong for a day to do this meeting. Sometimes we went the prior evening and had dinner with the JV managers. It was at my first such ornate dinner that I met Madam Zhang. I had no idea of what was about to happen.

Madam Zhang was a powerful lady. She was the General Secretary of the Communist Party for the Guangdong Province (which was like the size of the state of Gujarat in India or California in the USA). She was a person of high rank in the scheme of things and could get difficult things done, as I learnt later. She was about my age at the time. I was 48 years old and she was perhaps 50 or so. This suggested strongly that she had been a Red Guard during Chairman Mao's Cultural Revolution in the 1960's, and had probably been a part of many horrid things done in that era. She never talked about her past life. She spoke only Cantonese & Mandarin. Her knowledge of English was limited to just a few words which she did not like to speak either. She was of typical height for a Chinese lady (about 5ft. 3in.), physically strong in her build, with features and a manner that suggested a hard peasant upbringing. She was smart, but lacked a formal education. I could only converse with her through an interpreter, who was always nearby.

"Ah, so you are Vijay!" Madam Zhang said. "But I am so confused. You look Indian, but they tell me that you are American. You live in China (*Hong Kong*), but work for a British company. Who are you? What am I supposed to think?"

"Madam, it is an excellent question!" I replied. "Many times, I have wondered about it myself also. But, as you know, these are mere labels. For you, I am actually a valuable colleague, and I hope also a friend."

"A clever answer! But also, a good answer." Madam Zhang opined. "Now, work can wait until tomorrow. Tonight, you must have a good meal and peaceful rest. I have planned a lovely menu for Mr. Glenn and you. I am sure that you will like it. Please eat lots of food. It is good for you." It was obvious that Madam loved feeding everybody around her like a concerned mother. I wondered if she had lived through starvation in China in her younger days, like my mother had in her youth in India. In a few months' time and after some more meetings, Madam Zhang seemed to slowly warm up to me. At times, her formal demeanor would relax a little bit with me. But she always appeared somewhat stern.

One day, Glenn & I had to stay the night in Guangzhou, since we had some further key meetings the next day. Upon learning about this, Madam Zhang insisted that we have dinner with her. She selected her favorite place, which also had a karaoke bar in it. A bunch of us gathered for dinner and Madam insisted that everybody take their turn in making a fool of themselves on the microphone! I was never a good singer, but on my turn, I sang "Tai ki mein jhuth boliyan?" (*So, am I lying?*) from an old Indian film called "Jagte Raho" (*Stay Awake*), much to Madam's surprise and delight. She seemed to love karaoke singing, and actually had a good voice. She sang a couple of nice songs in Mandarin for us.

As the evening came to a close, Madam approached me rather nervously, and asked me if I could identify an Indian song that she would hum in my ear! She said that she had been looking for it for years and did not know its name, lyrics, or the singer. But it was from an Indian movie! I replied that I would certainly try it. To my amazement, Madam Zhang hummed not one, but several songs! They were "Mera joota hai japani", "Awaara hoon", and "Ghar aaya mera paradesi" from the films of the great Indian film maker and actor, Raj Kapoor! I laughed out loudly and told her that I knew all the songs very well and would try to obtain them for her. She was just thrilled, started giggling like a teenager, and even gave me a quick hug!

I waited till it was Madam Zhang's birthday. A huge party had been organized after the Board Meeting at, where else, but her favorite karaoke lounge! At the end of a lovely evening, when it came to offering her toasts, I got to the podium and gave her a present before the whole crowd of some 200+ people. It was a box DVD set of classic Raj Kapoor films like Barsaat, Awaara, Jagte Raho, Shri 420, etc. that I had bought for her in Singapore. I also announced to everybody that all her favorite Indian songs were in these movies.

When it was her turn to speak and thank everybody, she singled me out. She said that her childhood had been very hard. The only joy she knew in her remote farming village, were these movies and the songs in them. She did not understand the lyrics, but loved the music, and their stories that she kind of figured out. She said that she must have watched them a 100+ times, since there was no other entertainment around at the time. Then, she was so overcome emotionally, that she cried openly. I went up to her and gave her a hug. She just held on to me, sobbing uncontrollably.

It was a genuine tribute to the genius of the great Raj Kapoor, who brought so much joy, to so many people, living a hard life all over the world. He also proved the power of music as a universal language of the heart.

Madam Zhang in Hong Kong

As time went on, Madam Zhang and I became closer. She shared many things about her life with me. For some reason, she felt comfortable with me. She told me that she had organized a huge party for her family to view the movies that I had gifted her. She had her teenage daughter, and a few cousins still left alive, come to Guangzhou along with their families to see these movies! Everybody sang the songs and cried a lot during the screenings on TV, with all remembering their difficult days gone by.

"Vee Vee, I cannot thank you enough." Madam Zhang said during my next visit. She had used the Chinese practice of repeating a name twice for my name. This is why we see names like "Ling Ling" or "Xing Xing", etc. In my case, I had actually been given a Chinese name, according to a common practice in China. It was written in Mandarin and printed on the backside of my business cards also. My Chinese name was "Yung Wei Jiu". Yung, as my last or family name, was a play on Yajnik. And Wei Jiu, which actually meant "young and handsome", was also a play on Vijay. In all this, most Chinese folks forgot Vijay. Wei was adopted and repeated twice. As a nick name, then Wei became Vee! It is considered a sign of great affection in the Chinese culture.

"Madam, you need not thank me. It was my honor and great pleasure to do this for you," I said.

"But, Vee Vee, you do not understand. Things are difficult and hard here. Life is not like what you know in Hong Kong or the USA. Well, I have only heard about all that. In these things, TV is no good."

"Madam, are you serious? You have only heard about it? But you are a senior Party official! Surely, you get to travel and see things around the world?" I asked incredulously.

"No, I have not," Madam said simply. "I have never left China. I have not even gone to Hong Kong, ever in my life. I have family there from a long time ago."

"Oh, my God!" I responded in sheer disbelief. "We must fix this at once. I promise you, Madam, that I will arrange it for you. I will find a way."

Being a senior Communist Party official, Madam Zhang was under constant scrutiny about everything. She was guilty by suspicion. That was the way their system worked. It was insane! I tried everything in my power in Hong Kong. We thought of conferences, vendor visits, speaking arrangements, festivals, etc. where we would get her an invitation. None of it worked. Her visa application for Hong Kong was denied every time. At this time, even though Hong Kong had been handed over to China by Britain, people from China had to get a visa to visit Hong Kong. Glenn and I were now at a total loss about what to do. One day, I felt inspired.

"Hey, Glenn, I have a totally wild thought. Consider this... This JV of ours with them... What if we held a Board Meeting in Hong Kong? It is their law. Could they deny a visa to her for that?" I asked.

"Vijay, that is simply brilliant! Heck, why did I not think of it? I will get on it at once," Glenn replied, as he was quite fond of Madam Zhang as well.

In short order, a JV Board Meeting was scheduled in Hong Kong. As a consequence, Madam Zhang was granted her visa to Hong Kong, and she showed up on the elite train from Guangzhou just beaming with joy! Glenn and I had asked everybody at Sims to treat her like true "royalty". We wanted her to have a grand time. But we had to also deal with political constraints. A formal dinner was required for her, as a condition of her visa. We had to somehow figure a way out to fulfill it.

My boss, Ron Floto, came to our rescue. He organized a lovely dinner party for Madam Zhang at a swanky place and also invited all the key Chinese luminaries, living in Hong Kong, to come to it. Ron pulled out all the stops. People were shocked at the honor accorded to Madam Zhang by the business elite of Hong Kong. No doubt, reports were sent back to Beijing immediately and her stars shot up considerably politically. The dinner was formal and filled with Chinese traditions.

However, it was also a politically delicate time, because China had just implemented "salary caps" for foreigners working in China! This was a greatly unpopular move and it was hotly debated everywhere in the media and in the various Expat communities.

The formal dinner began. Madam Zhang looked lovely. She knew that she was on a stage. After some normal chitchat, she was asked, "Madam, China has just announced salary caps for foreigners working in China. Do you think that this is fair?"

"Foreigners working in China are paid very generously. Much more so than the native citizens." Madam Zhang replied smoothly, as if she had rehearsed her answer or had been provided with it by somebody. "This increased salary expense, reduces the profitability of these companies. So, they pay less taxes to the Chinese Government. This is not fair. So, the salary caps limit this rampant abuse," Everybody at the dinner seemed somewhat bewildered by this response.

Ron looked at me with an expression that said, "Vij, come on, you don't buy this crap? Damn it, boy, answer her!"

"Well, with all due respect, Madam, there is another perspective on this matter," I offered. I had to say something.

"Mr. Vijay, we are always happy to listen to different perspectives," Madam replied in a sly manner.

"Well, Madam, it can be argued that these foreigners possess skills that are vastly beneficial to China. They help various enterprises grow and achieve more. So, that causes the overall Chinese economy to grow. And the government of China gets a lot more tax revenue from this growth, than it would by putting caps on salaries of foreigners," I summarized gently.

"You do have an argument. But I do not have the data to debate it here. We shall have to defer it to another occasion," Madam replied, smooth as ever. I heaved a sigh of relief. I almost heard Ron say, "Vij, you crafty dog! Nice jab, nicely done!"

The dinner went off very well. Madam Zhang was received with great fanfare by all. But the next day was very different. Glenn & I told her to forget about the Board Meeting and spend the day just enjoying Hong Kong. She was quite nervous and distraught about this offer.

"Vee Vee, will it be okay? I am worried," she asked me nervously. "I am always watched by all sorts of people."

"Yes, Madam, I know." I responded. "But you have no worries today. Johnny has my car and he is my driver. He speaks Cantonese & Mandarin fluently and is a native of Hong Kong. He can be trusted totally and will help you all the way. He will find your lost family today. He will take you shopping also. Buy whatever you like for yourself and your family. Johnny will pay for everything. You will not need any Hong Kong money. I will take care of all the bills later. So, do not worry about the costs. Just promise me that you will relax and have a good time."

She blushed, gushed, and gave me a big hug and a kiss on my forehead! Then, she took off like a little girl visiting Disneyland for the first time! She had a great day. She met her long-lost family after 40+ years, renewed contacts, shopped her brains out, bought gifts, etc. She returned home simply beaming. In fact, this trip set the stage for many a subsequent visit by her to Hong Kong, but now she was not bothered by the authorities as before.

In due course, my tenure with DFG in Hong Kong came to an end and I returned to the USA. My contacts with Madam Zhang slowly diminished. Later, I heard that she had continued to grow in her stature and eventually she had retired to a quiet life in Guangzhou.

Sadly, with time and distance in play, I lost contact with this truly beautiful lady, with an amazing and historical past.

E-Commerce in Asia

In the early summer of 1999, e-commerce came to Asia like a tidal wave. In fact, it could be characterized more as a highly disruptive commercial war in Hong Kong in particular. I was away on holiday in the USA with my family. We were in Las Vegas, when I was summoned back to Hong Kong immediately. There was a development that had arrived clear out of the blue.

E-commerce, as defined in the "B-to-C" (Business to Consumer) segment in Hong Kong, was older than the invention of the telephone. Before that, actual "message runners" were used. Later on, the phone and then the fax machine came into vogue. But the idea had essentially remained the same and it was vastly popular.

Nearly all significant businesses ordered their supplies, groceries, prepared foods, etc. from their suppliers using the traditional methods. Orders were written out on paper, and then sent over to the supplier, to be fulfilled by the date and time specified. At first, runners took the orders over, then they were conveyed over the telephone, and later they were sent out by fax. The supplier fulfilled and packaged up the order and delivered it to the address specified. Payment was settled either by cash on delivery, or via central monthly billing for a large enterprise. In Hong Kong, a city where commercial and residential space was always way too expensive, storage of anything in any kind of volume was always difficult. So, these services provided an attractive and vital level of support for all types of consumers.

In the segment of groceries, dry & packaged goods, fresh foods, dairy, and beverages, Hong Kong had a duopoly for a long time. While there was a large unorganized market of small "Mom & Pop" stores everywhere as well, two huge chains of stores controlled the organized market completely. They were "Park n' Shop" and "Welcome". The former was owned by the famed tycoon Li Ka Shing, while the latter was owned by the Dairy Farm Group, a Jardine Matheson company. Despite many attempts by others, these companies had managed to ward off any new arrival into this business space for decades. Well, that is, until now.

The trouble for any new entrant was always the inability to acquire suitable locations to build a store network. The duopoly, through its contacts and connections, would prevent anybody else from obtaining sites to build stores. However, the new business model offered by the internet-based B-to-C e-commerce capability, eliminated the need for a vast store network, at least in concept. A new entrant into this space could compete without a store network.

Amazon was blazing the trail in this regard, and in the euphoria of that period about "disruptive business models", many folks were willing to take the risk for a slice of the huge business pie.

One such company was Apple, Inc. which had nothing to do with Apple Computers Inc. of the USA. This Apple, in Hong Kong, was actually a publishing house or a media company, which ran many tabloid newspapers in Hong Kong and South East Asia in general. They were all tawdry rags, quite racy, and full of lurid photos of celebrities, but had large circulations in their various markets. Well, Apple decided to enter the grocery business in Hong Kong without a store network. It built a big Web Store quietly and one day just arrived with huge discounts on all sorts of products. The idea was to become well known and acquire market share quickly, without any capital investment in a network of stores. It did invest in a modern warehouse and fulfillment facility, and a distribution service. In its first 30 days of operation, it was hugely successful.

Well, alarm bells went off in the HQs of the duopoly. While both companies had internet-based service offerings, they were mainly experimental and subordinate to the robust store-based retailing. Neither was prepared to confront a frontal assault by a new market entrant, which was a media company, that had no regard for morals, decency, or traditions of any kind. At the price points offered by Apple on a vast array of products, it was an all-out commercial war! It was also clear that this war could never end in a draw. It had to cause the death of somebody. That somebody was targeted to be, Apple and its hated CEO, by the duopoly.

At the Dairy Farm Group's Welcome chain, its internet-based service offering came under intense and massive pressure, for which it was not prepared at all. It tried to fight back, but failed miserably in every aspect, since its service had not been designed to scale up by several fold. Very quickly, the signs of failure began to show up publicly. Orders were backlogged, many went unfulfilled, or were completed with errors. Customer complaints skyrocketed and its small "call center" was just overwhelmed. Inventory management fell apart and there were intense staff shortages to handle the work in every task. And to add insult to injury, its website could not handle the transaction load, and swiftly just crashed. Besides having a huge negative business impact, all this also became a public relations disaster of significant proportion for the Dairy Farm Group.

"Vij, sorry to yank you back like this from your holiday," Ron Floto began, at our first meeting after my return to Hong Kong. "But we have a massive crisis on our hands. And there is nobody here with your kind of skill set to tackle it. I am appointing you as the head of this internet business immediately. We have to fix it quickly and start to take on these crazy people at Apple."

"Okay, Ron. But please give me a day. Let me get the lay of the land first, and I will get back to you on the next steps," I replied with a worried feeling. In my gut, I felt that this would be a seriously difficult task.

Within 24 hours, I completed my assessment, and addressed the Operating Committee of DFG and Welcome jointly. My message shocked everyone, but I withheld no punches. I told them that "Welcome Delivers", the internet business, would have to be shut down for 30 days to clear its order backlog, and reset its inventory. It would take a further 30 days, to get it ready to scale up to the order volumes being currently experienced. When all the facts were laid out, the issues understood, my plan was fully supported by everybody. But down in the various trenches, the closure of a business was just anathema! That was just not the Chinese way, and there was widespread disapproval and resistance.

I had no time for such internal politics and took charge of things aggressively. I quickly assembled task forces using borrowed resources to fix key issues: 1) Fix the website and restructure it for much greater transaction volume; 2) Link fulfillment center inventory system to the parent system for critical product replenishment; 3) Size up and retrain the Call Center; 4) Beef up logistics capacity to handle much greater volumes of order deliveries and so on.

But foremost, I setup a special team to clear the backlog of orders. That was their sole focus. In 30 days, I asked them to drive the backlog to zero. If it is a valid order still, process it. If it is not or it has been cancelled, then close it out. Every team was put on a 7 x 24 rotation schedule so that we would keep moving forward. All such actions are not particularly difficult for folks who are used to executing things, and have a common way of thinking. But to do this in a world, where there are huge mismatches in skill sets and different cultural variables is quite difficult. Also, language barriers, which can cause incredible misunderstandings, are a challenge of massive proportions.

One day, I was leading a meeting of Region Managers of Welcome. I was briefing them on the problems and the progress that we had been making. Suddenly, a Chinese lady says to me, "Mr. Vijay, why are the orders not handled on time? Why did the business have to be closed? This is not supposed to happen! We have lost a lot of "face" with our customers." It seemed that she had not heard a word of what I had been explaining for the last 30 minutes. I was irritated, but also wondered about how to make these folks understand.

On that day, as it so happened, that a jetliner had crashed at the new Chek Lap Kok Airport of Hong Kong. Many people had been injured, the incident was under investigation, and there was intensive media coverage of the tragedy. So, I asked the group, "Why did the jetliner crash at the airport today? It is not supposed to happen! Many planes fly and there are no problems. But this one crashed today. Why?" People looked at each other, simply bewildered.

"Well, because sometimes s**t just happens," I explained bluntly. "I am sure that there are reasons for it and they will figure them out. Meanwhile, one has to simply clean up the mess and move on."

The Welcome Delivers business did get fixed in record time and returned to the e-commerce wars valiantly. Within a few months, the duopoly succeeded in toppling Apple, as its business model was not sustainable for the long term and the e-commerce war in Hong Kong came to an end.

But even in Hong Kong, the profitability of the Welcome Delivers service remained elusive. Eventually, the dedicated fulfilment center was eliminated. All orders were fulfilled from the nearest store which already had a robust inventory and staff. The service turned profitable. It was replicated in similar "avatars" in Singapore and New Zealand as well over time.

It is fascinating to realize that the financially successful models for B-to-C e-commerce had been tried and adopted successfully in South-East Asia, way before the USA. They had been implemented there at an industrial scale. We were way ahead of the times, because of the nature of our markets, and achieved many a breakthrough, well before all this became fashionable in many an industry all over the world.

I was fortunate to be not only a part of it, but also to be an executive leader, to cause its realization.

Medical Crises in India

A Heart Attack in Ahmedabad

One fine morning in LA, in March of 2008, I received a call from my cousin, Dr. Pankaj Divatia, in Ahmedabad, India. He got straight to the point.

"Vijay, Damayantimami had a heart attack this morning. She was given emergency treatment at Nikunj in Maninagar, and then moved to the ICU at the Apollo Hospital in the City by an ambulance. I have been with her and she is under good care. She is also responding well to her treatment, but she will have to be kept there for a few days."

To say that I was shocked would be an understatement. I had always harbored this odd feeling that since my mother had chosen to live out her life in India, after my father passed away, I would one day face a medical emergency of some sort there. And I would have to figure out how to deal with it from across the world. I had anticipated that it would be difficult, certainly stressful, but manageable. I was so terribly naive in all these judgements, as I learnt the hard way, later on.

As Pankaj hung up, I thought about what to do. My brother, Ajay, was in Ahmedabad at the time, and I thought that perhaps he could step in and assist Pankaj with medical and other matters for my mother's care. But Ajay had suffered from a couple of strokes a few years earlier, and even though he was a doctor, he was not all mentally there anymore. So, I had a limited level of confidence in his abilities to assist.

However, I was scheduled to go to India within 3 weeks or so, on a business trip. At the time, I was the CEO of a venture capital funded software company in LA. We had a wholly owned offshore engineering & development center in Pune, India, which had some 60+ people working in our dedicated facility. I used to visit it twice a year, for a week or so, take care of matters there, and then visit with my mother for a few days in Ahmedabad. This had been going on for a few years by this time.

My mother, affectionately called "Behn" (*Sister*) by all of us, was 89 years old that year. She was in reasonably decent health for her age. She was now stooped over, walked slowly, and she needed assistance for many activities. Her hearing in the left ear had reduced a lot, and her vision had also suffered due to macular degeneration. But her mind was still quite sharp. With time, the Nikunj bungalow had turned into more of an "assisted living" facility for her. We had to deal with finance and all the proverbial staff issues constantly. Everybody tried to prey upon our frail emotions, whenever any of us showed up, with the intent of obtaining some sort of financial gain for themselves. It was an awful and vicious cycle.

Well, I had foreseen all this and had actually tried hard to avoid it. I had pleaded with Behn many times to relocate to the USA, and live with me. It would have solved a ton of issues. But she would have none of that option. She told me that she and my father, after touring most of the USA, and coming to our homes on 3 different visits in the 1980's, had concluded that they preferred to live permanently in Nikunj, their home, in Ahmedabad, India. Furthermore, they were also quite candid in their reasoning behind this profound decision.

They felt that they were not comfortable with the lifestyles that us 3 sons lived in the USA. Besides, it was a country for young people, where youth was the highly prized thing, while they were facing their twilight years. They disliked and disagreed with the moral values exhibited in the American society and preferred to be in country and surroundings where they felt socially, emotionally, and culturally comfortable. Also, in the USA, they were a nobody, but in India, they had their entire extended family, friends, and even social status. Oh, it would sadly mean living far apart from the 3 sons, all the grandchildren, and missing out on many precious life events.

But then, even in India, ours had never been a "joint family". That was a way of life that my father intensely disliked, almost hated. He understood its purpose and value historically quite well. But in the context of the 20th century India and its economic future, he thought that it was outdated and regressive, especially if one had a choice in these matters. He felt that it simply perpetuated mediocrity or incompetence within a family.

However, in spite of such strongly held views, my parents never asked any of us to return to India, to look after them or to take care of them, in their old age. They did not want to be "roadblocks" to or "burdens" for our career decisions and wished all of us great success in our lives. Oh, they would miss us immensely and sorely, and would always welcome visits to India from any of us and our families, as frequently as possible. However, beneath this strong, tough and an independent exterior, there were equally intense, difficult, and delicate emotions at play, on the part of all of us.

All this was a seriously traumatic debate for me. Its conclusions, I will freely admit, left me emotionally scarred for life. But against this backdrop of such a clash of values versus desires, and strong will power on the part of my parents, I did not have any better solutions to offer.

Perhaps there were none. Perhaps this was the lot of most first-generation immigrants to the USA. This or similar dramas had played out countless times before, over the many decades of history, within every sort of an immigrant family. The only difference for us was that we were not running away from persecution of some kind in the old world, or escaping a brutal war. While the specifics and urgency were different, the issues were the same. Even to this day, whenever I think about it, I am overwhelmed by a huge cloud of deeply felt sadness and regret. If there was "a better way", as a family, we surely were not able to find it.

It had been barely 24 hours, and the phone rang again. "Vijay, just a quick update." Pankaj said. "Mami is doing fine. Within the next 2-3 days, we will move her to my home from the hospital. Tanvi and I can take care of her much better at home than in a hospital room. But I do not think she should return to Nikunj as yet. Do not worry. She will be fine with us."

I was greatly relieved to hear this. I called Kashyap, my eldest brother, right away. "I am going in 3 weeks to India. She should be okay at Pankaj's house, don't you think?" I asked him.

"Oh, yes. I agree. But we will have to figure out the way after that!" Kashyap replied.

I spoke to Behn almost daily at Pankaj's house over the next 3 weeks. "Behn, kem chho? Tabiyat kevi chhe?" I asked. (*Behn, how are you? How are you feeling?*)

"Saru chhe. Pan jail jevu lage chhe. Tu kyare avu chhu?" she replied and wondered. (*I feel okay. But this feels like a jail. When are you coming?*)

My mother was a fiercely independent lady. Other than my father, nobody could control her. Well, even that was debatable! She was conservative, traditional, vocally opinionated, and a free spirit that would always refuse to be confined by anything. And she loved life. Especially, she saw joy in the smallest of things. It was an attitude born out of a life of dire poverty, in her childhood, when she had often gone to sleep hungry, so her younger siblings could eat.

Pankaj, who was Shashiphoi's son, was an orthopedic surgeon. He was UK trained, headed the department at his hospital, and was regarded highly as an innovative professional. He had published many surgical papers, which he had been invited to present at various medical conferences worldwide. By temperament, he was more of a professor and scientist, than a businessman.

This was key, because a "medical practice" of any kind in Ahmedabad, as it turned out, was big business! An MBBS degree in India (like an MD in the USA) was more of a license to mint money. If you cured people of ailments along the way, then that was good, but cash was always king. Often, the poor were given a bit of a free ride, but the "middle class" or the "rich" got shafted in a big way. It was like, "Pay cash now, God & treatment come later". Furthermore, this entire industry was an eco-system of its own. Each doctor, lab, hospital, pharmacy, rehab facility, etc. took a "cut" of the referral or service fees paid. These were mainly in cash, and so largely unaccounted for, to avoid the taxman. Nobody in this eco-system ever talked or explained anything, to anyone, about any aspect of it. There was this unique version of the Sicilian "Omerta" Code, as it were, in place in the context of Indian medical practices.

Well, I had been away from India for a long time and I did not know any of this. So, when I asked blunt or direct questions in sheer desperation, I would get all these strange responses. Oh... and shhh... you are not supposed to talk about any of this. "Avu na bolaye! Loko shu kaheshe?" (*One cannot say such things! What will people say?*) I was always left confused and totally bewildered.

"Vijay, she refuses to listen to me. She insists on going back to Nikunj!" Pankaj complained to me on the phone.

"What is bothering her?" I asked.

"I don't know. She wants to be in Nikunj when you arrive here," Pankaj replied.

"Let me talk to her," I asked.

"Tu kyare ave chhe? Tu avish tyare hun Nikunj ma haish. Apde majha kareeshu!" Behn said in a cheery voice! (*When are you coming? When you arrive, I will be in Nikunj. We will have lots of fun!*)

"Behn, tame Pankaj nu kahyu sambhalo. Hun be divas ma avu chhu. Nikunj javani shi utaval chhe?" I asked. (*Behn, please listen to what Pankaj has to say. I am arriving in two days. What is the hurry to go to Nikunj?*)

"Mare gher javu chhe. Arrey, maro chhokaro ave chhe. Nikunj ma taiyari karvani chhe. Pankaj ane Tanvi nahi samjhe." Behn replied forcefully. (*I want to go home. Arrey, my son is coming. I have to ready things in Nikunj. Pankaj and Tanvi will not understand.*)

Who were any of us to argue with my mother, when she turned into Amba Ma herself? Against all medical advice, she prevailed. She returned to Nikunj and set about fixing things so that her home was "ready" for the arrival of her "prodigal" son. Yes, over the years, she had always chastised me about my spending money on her.

From the moment I arrived, it was a time of hilarity and fun! Behn cooked great food, ordered special "take-out" items, and we also drank lots of tea. She loved the "adu-vali cha" (*tea with fresh ground ginger*) and would just delight in drinking it. We laughed at times till we had tears in our eyes, and we also shared some amazing memories. She did not look or behave like a lady who had just emerged from a serious cardiac event! Pankaj was astounded and cautioned me.

"Arrey, aa to jail jevu hatu! Hospital ni room, Tanvi ni room, ane aa badha manaso! Sha mate? Hun to kantali gayi!" Behn explained to me. (*Arrey, it was like a jail! The hospital room, then Tanvi's room, and all those people! What for? I got fed up!*) "Ha, mane khabar chhe ke aa badhu mare mate kare chhe. Saru. Pan pachhi shu?" (*Yes, I know that they are all doing these things for me. Good. But then what?*)

Our good times rolled on. I decided to defer the Pune visit and spend my time with my mother instead. It was a grand time and Behn seemed to be in such great spirits. And then suddenly, it happened.

Out of the clear blue, Behn developed a shortness of breath and general anxiety. We laid her down on the diwan and I sent for a local doctor. It seemed like a real emergency to me. In about 20 anxious minutes, our servant found this Dr. D. He shows up and wants to do an EKG. But he does not have the gear and it must be ordered from a local lab. After much ado, since Pankaj was in surgery, these people show up and do an EKG and draw blood for some tests. Nobody explains nothing to me about anything. Behn is looking at me like, "Beta, tane to khabar chhe ne?" (*Beta, you surely understand all this?*) I was just aghast.

"What does it say?" I asked Dr. D, who was looking at the EKG print out. "Uske liye to MBBS karna padega!" he replies. (*For that, you will have to get an MBBS degree.*) In any other environment, I would have directly choked this damn arrogant son of a bitch! He would not have lived. It would be like, "If my mom dies, you die. Do you understand?"

But for now, I am running around like a mad man. I dash to the bank to get cash. Lots of it! I am doling cash out left and right, to try and get my mother stabilized. I asked Dr. D, "Does she need any urgent medication for her condition?" "Han, mein davai likh deta hun. Usko mangva ke shuru karen. Badme dekhenge." (*Yes, I will prescribe some medication. Get it and start her on it. Later, we shall see.*)

Luckily, Pankaj emerged from surgery and called. He informed me promptly that this Dr. D was a bloody quack and to forget everything he had said. Pankaj then asked to see the EKG results. The lab managed to send them to him somehow. Pankaj then got a very eminent cardiologist of Ahmedabad to examine the data. Then, Dr. J, asked to examine my mother. "Can you bring Mami over to his clinic?" Pankaj asked.

"Well, I am not sure. She is still quite uncomfortable. I don't know what to do! Perhaps the only option is an ambulance to take her over?" I replied, nearly frantic.

Dr. J was this celebrated cardiologist in town. It was almost impossible to see him unless there was a referral from another renowned doctor. His reputation had placed him in the annals of legendary doctors. He was considered nearly divine (Yes, I am indeed exaggerating!). It almost seemed like he could cure any cardiac ailment, by just "farting" in your face! It cost you a boat load of money, but hey, you were supposedly cured! Lots of folks believed this crap, and paid up.

However, it was a critical time for my mother, and I was feeling that I was losing this race against time. I rushed around all over trying to find a solution that would work. Dr. J would not come to our side of town. We could see him in his clinic only. I finally managed to find an ambulance, but it would take almost an hour to show up!

Meanwhile, Pankaj prescribed some medications, which I shot off like a crazed animal, to acquire from the local medical store. I brought them home quickly and started Behn on them immediately.

I was very distraught and just furious internally. It was because I knew that it did not have to be this way. I had access to much better options, but all that was in a land quite far away.

Immersed in all this intense and frantic activity, as I was struggling with making something work for us, I lost some valuable time. But during this time, the medications prescribed by Pankaj began to show some positive results. My mother's condition seemed to stabilize. Her breathing became normal, her discomfort disappeared, and her anxiety nearly vanished. She actually smiled at me! Oh, dear God, did I breathe a sigh of relief.

"Behn, have kem lage chhe?" I asked her. (*Behn, how are you feeling now?*)

"Have ghanu saru chhe," she replied. (*I feel much better now.*) "Tane bahu chinta thai?" (*Did it cause you a lot of worry?*)

So then, I proceeded to brief her on all that had transpired. I also told her that Pankaj had asked that she be examined by Dr. J, across the river, and that I had arranged for an ambulance to take us there soon.

"Mare nathi javu." Behn stated in a matter-of-fact manner. (*I don't want to go.*) "Hun Pankaj ne samjhavish." (*I will explain and make Pankaj understand.*)

377

"Behn, aa barabar nathi. Apde doctor pase javu joyiye. Tamara sara mate," I pleaded. (*Behn, this is not right. We should go and see the doctor. It is for your good.*)

"Hun tane ek vaat kahu? Chaal, hinchke basiye," she said, and held her arm up. (*Can I tell you something? Come, let's go and sit on the swing.*)

"Hun samjhu chhu ke tane mari chinta chhe. Pan sha mate? Vadhaare shu thavanu chhe? Hun mari jayish, bas? Arrey, ek divas to marvanu nakki chhe. Mane Amba Ma bolavshe, tyare hun jati rahish," she said, after we were seated on the swing, in a clear voice and with a smile on her face. (*I understand that you worry about me. But what for? What more is going to happen? At most, I will die, right? Arrey, it is certain that one day we all will die. When Amba Ma calls for me, then I will go away.*)

"Pan atyare chinta sha mate? Chaal, apde adu-vali cha piye." she said with a twinkle in her eyes (*But why worry about all that now? Come, let's have some tea with fresh ginger.*)

Behn was a lady of remarkable strength and spirit. She never lost a moment in life that she could enjoy in some way. It was usually in little things, and they often involved food. She loved good food, both cooking it, and serving it to others. She lived for another 4 years in steadily deteriorating health. But her spirit remained strong as ever.

One day in May 2012, she decided on her own, that she had lived long enough. She threw away her false teeth, all her medications, and went on a "Santharo" fast. (*a fast to death, without any food or water.*) She passed away 3 weeks later. She was 92 years old.

She lived her life, for 20+ years after my father passed away, all alone and on her own terms. In 1993, she even came to visit us in the USA, all by herself. She came to spend precious time with all of us and our families. It was amazing for a lady, who could not speak English, or another western language. But it was a promise she had made to us, and she kept it.

I will always retain, for the rest of my life, many painful regrets about the later years of Behn's life. Quite often, I blame myself, because it did not have to be this way. What went wrong? What was amiss? Why? I guess I shall never fully understand or know.

However, there is something that can be said with great certainty. All members of my family, at various points in time in our lives, made choices for various reasons. The significance of these choices became apparent much later, when we lived out their consequences.

A Massive Stroke

I had been slaving like a dog at trying to get my "startup" business off the ground in Burbank, California. It was brutal work and I was burning a lot of hours on it, away from my family. My children were little and I was not able to spend time with them like I wanted to. It was an awful price to pay indeed. My wife, Nilima, was holding down the fort brilliantly for all of us. If she had not done that, my business idea would have failed right at the starting gates. It was July 1991.

"Vijay, this is Kashyap. I have some very troubling news for you. Pappaji, it seems, has had a stroke! He has been taken to the ICU at the LG Hospital in Maninagar, Ahmedabad. It is serious and we do not know the prognosis for his recovery as yet. Pankaj, as you know, is the head of Orthopedics there, and he was the one to call me today. Ajay and I are flying out to Ahmedabad tonight to be there with Behn."

"What? Say, whaat? What the heck is a stroke? I don't even know what that is!" I asked in a state of total shock. Kashyap quickly explained it all to me and I decided to travel to Ahmedabad immediately as well. Pappaji in the ICU? It was an incomprehensible thought.

A journey to Ahmedabad from LA was not a simple or an inexpensive matter in those days. There were few flights, and last-minute plans were particularly difficult and costly. Also, I had no paycheck to count on. I had no income, as I was working on a startup funded by my own money. It had yet to show any cashflow.

It was a surreal scene at the LG Hospital in Maninagar, Ahmedabad. It was a municipal hospital, with all that it implies. Even at that time, things were so different in this hospital, from a private one. At least, due to Pankaj's position of power, my father was placed in a nice room after being moved from the ICU facility. When all us 3 brothers arrived, one by one, it became a truly warped situation. I had never seen anything like this in my life. I was seriously traumatized.

My father had a private room, with a washing area behind it. My mother was standing guard like a hawk over my father. He had lost his cognitive functions, speech, and seemed paralyzed on the left side of his entire body. He was totally bedridden and needed full-time complete nursing care. Initially, it was all provided by my mother, various members of our extended family, and Tanvi, Pankaj's wife. It seemed incredibly difficult and complex to me. It was certainly that for everybody who pitched in to help.

Meanwhile, the Nikunj bungalow, our home, had turned into an "ashram" for all sorts of people. The kitchen was non-functional, the staff seemed to be on a free paid holiday, and the whole house was a mess. Various strange people showed up, and parked wherever they wished, without anybody's permission, under the guise of "visiting" my ailing father. The pantry or "kothar" of the house was looted for all sorts of things, since there was nobody around to check on anybody. The 3 of us brothers came home to sleep in shifts, but we spent most of our time at the hospital. For food, we just ate out at any eatery near the hospital. Throughout all this craziness, the central question on our minds always was, "Is he getting better? What is the prognosis?"

Each day in the morning, Dr. A would come on his "rounds". He was the neurologist attending to my father. He would spend 5-10 minutes doing various things with my father, while we watched anxiously. Then he would pronounce to all of us "Saru chhe. Badhu barabar chhe." (*It is fine. Everything is normal.*) Kashyap would receive this information in a somber manner; Ajay, who was a doctor himself, never said much; and then there was the loud and mouthy me! I was much younger than my brothers, and would just shout out after Dr. A had left. "What the heck does that mean?" I would ask in exasperation. "He has said the same thing the last 3 days, which is basically nothing. What the hell is going on here?" I was overwhelmed with worry, feeling helpless, and I could not control myself.

"Let's go for a walk," Ajay suggested. Kashyap and I readily agreed, in order to get away from Dr. A's visit for a while. We walked over to a "paanwala" stall, outside the hospital gate, and bought ourselves some Cokes. Then, Ajay spoke.

"Okay, both of you whine in your own ways constantly. But surely, you understand that Dr. A will never tell us what he honestly thinks! We are facing a huge cultural difference here, in the way medicine is practiced. In the Indian culture, speaking the truth in medical matters, is not proper or respectful. So now, let me ask you bluntly. Do you want to know the truth?" Ajay questioned us in a steely manner. "Are you prepared to listen to it? Can you handle it?" We nodded anxiously, but affirmatively.

"Pappaji is gone! He is never coming back." Ajay said in a matter-of-fact way. "His cerebral hemorrhage was severe. The damage is permanent. He will not recover. It is only a matter of time, before he passes away."

Kashyap and I stopped sipping our Cokes. Neither of us was actually prepared to hear this. I felt all the air leave my lungs and my stomach just collapsed. I turned numb. I could not even cry. All I recall feeling is confusion, bewilderment, and a steadily building intense anger.

"Vijay, control yourself!" Ajay admonished me directly. "You are not alone. We feel it too. But all of us have to be strong for Behn. She will be hit hard. We are going to have to make some difficult decisions and plans here, in a short span of time. We need to prepare ourselves."

In this story, while I would like to tell you much more about it, it is difficult. It is too painful for me to recall it, let alone write it down. You see, it was a time of incredible stress, heartaches, confusion, conflicting demands, and huge sadness. To this day, I harbor strong personal feelings that all us brothers failed our mother at this crucial time. Why? Oh, for many reasons.

Mainly, I think that we were selfish or self-centered, could not handle the reality on the ground in Ahmedabad, or we did not make the required effort. But in her days and months of critical need, in caring for our father, none of us was near her. We were all gone. Oh, we all had our reasons, I suppose, but in retrospect, I think we were wrong in what we did. I know that I tried my best, but I still think that it was not good enough. I should have done much more, somehow, and in some way.

The timing for everybody was also strange. Ajay had to leave in a week because he had a medical practice to attend to and could not be away for too long. Kashyap had to return to his job as well for his reasons. But who would stay with Behn? Well, since I had no commitments, or even a real job, I was deputed. After both my brothers departed, I was left to spend the entire month of August 1991, supporting my mother in the care of my father. We received amazing support and help as well from Tanvi, Kavita, Anupama, Nisha, and other members of our extended family. But I recall it as being one of the most painful months of my life.

We all soon got a schedule of sorts worked out. Who would stay at the hospital, for what hours, who would fetch the tea or the food, who would substitute for another at what time slots, etc. And soon, it became a practice of sorts.

Then one day, something incredible happened.

The Old Man with a Fever

During all those days, and it was strange, but a lot of folks confused me with my cousin, Dr. Pankaj Divatia. A lot of people thought that we looked alike! Yeah, we were similar in our physical build, facial features, and so forth, but this aspect had never before occurred to either of us. Now, mind you, there is a huge difference here. Pankaj is a renowned orthopedic surgeon, with a huge reputation in tow, and I am a goddam nobody in the world of medicine. He is a man of worldwide reputation, who teaches orthopedic surgery, and for whom people in India kissed his feet. While I am someone, who people in India would not even give a hoot about. In the presence of Pankaj, my dear cousin, I was so inadequate. There was nothing comparable between us. Well, that is, until now.

"Aa dava aje apo." Dr. A prescribed. (*Give him this medicine today.*) As soon as he left, I rushed out to the medical store to fetch the medicine for my father. As I got to the store, I found myself standing next to an old man. He seemed very sick. He had a fever, he was shivering, and had no idea about what to do. But then, he suddenly seemed to recognize me! "Arrey, Doctor Saheb, kanyi karo. bahu taav chhe." (*Arrey, Doctor Saheb, do something. The fever is intense.*) I was simply shocked and wondered about it all. Why was this old man asking things of me? Did he think I was a doctor? Good God, why would he think that? Did he know Pankaj? Was he confusing me with Pankaj for some reason? This is just awful, and it makes no sense at all. What should I do?

In milliseconds, I gave this intense and serious thought. I said many things to myself. Vijay, observe carefully, and try to understand this situation that you face right now. This old man thinks that you are a doctor! Whether in fact you are one or not, is not the issue. He believes that you are a doctor. He desperately wants help for his condition. Now, what are your choices for a response?

Well, let's examine the options carefully. First, you could just tell him honestly that you are not a real doctor and that he should go and find himself a real one. But would he believe you? Most likely, he would think that you did not want to treat him for some reason. No, most likely, he would not believe it at all. Second, you could suggest a local doctor. Perhaps one in the hospital. Now, would he believe that? Most likely, he would think that you just pawned him off to somebody who could not care a damn about him. He would have serious doubts about getting any treatment fast. Well, Vijay, it seems that there is simply no way to make this old man believe your recommendation, now is there?

Well now, come to think of it, there is in fact a third option! It is the most impossible and a totally insane one! It can be titled as, "Why fight it?", or "Just cater to the belief!" So, filled with regret and full of trepidation, I set about doing the totally "wrong" thing. I took a piece of paper, wrote "Acetaminophen" on it (it is branded "Tylenol" in the USA & "Panadol" in India), with an "Rx" at the bottom, scratched an illegible signature, and gave it to the old man. To my utter amazement, the old man was thrilled! He promptly handed the paper to the pharmacist, got the medication, and took off. He seemed thrilled beyond belief. I was at a total loss about what I had just impulsively done.

Well, a couple of days later, I happened to be at the same medical store, when the same old man showed up! He shouted that he was cured by my medicine and was healthy as can be. He started singing my praises. "Arrey, aa Doctor Saheb gajab na chhe! Badhu saru kari de chhe. Jadoo chalave chhe." (*Arrey, this Doctor Saheb is incredible! He cures everything. He works magic.*)

When I related this episode to Pankaj jokingly a couple of days later, he admonished me sternly. He said, "Vijay, never do that again! I will show you another way. But what you did was just wrong." Well, that is clearly what Pankaj thought. But I must say, I did not entirely agree with him. He seemed to lack empathy, in this case, I thought. But then, this was India. Many things were done in strange ways in the Motherland. So, who was I to dispute Pankaj's views?

As a reader of this story, what do you think? Well, I seriously wonder. What would you have done, if you had been in my shoes, facing that shivering old man? Do give it some thought. Try to answer this query in your own mind, to yourself.

It will surely reveal something about yourself to you.

You Think You Have It Bad?

The month of August 1991 dragged on. There seemed to be no perceptible change in my father's condition. We were still in the same private room in the LG Hospital, in Maninagar, Ahmedabad. I was doing all that I could to support my mother, Tanvi, and the rest of the extended family, but I was also getting steadily despondent. There seemed to be no hope.

Also, strange events never stopped happening. One afternoon, when my mother and others had barely found the opportunity to take a nap, an elderly gentleman showed up. He was loud, very vocal, and full of drama about my father's condition. I stopped him in the lobby outside the room and told him that this was not a good time to visit, because everybody was exhausted and taking a well-deserved nap. Oh, but he would have none of that! After much ado, he says, "Tame kahejo ke hun avelo." (*You tell them that I had visited.*) I found this statement to be just bizarre. This man seemed to be more concerned about the perception of his having visited, than about showing any real concern for the situation at hand. I wrote him off as a "certifiable jackass". But he had a lot of company, as I came to discover. In social norms and practices, India or Ahmedabad in particular, could be a very cruel place indeed.

Then there were the fumigation activities. It was August, for God's sake. It was very hot, humid, rainy, and just unbearable. There was no air-conditioning at the hospital. Where we were located, there was not even a breeze. The insects and mosquitos were everywhere and it was just miserable. So, every other day, this fumigation van would drive thru the premises. It unleashed an awful smoke which was supposed to get rid of the mosquitos and such. But it was a relic of the colonial times and achieved none of its objectives. Besides, it stank up the place for at least an hour after it was gone. However, nobody questioned it, and it was just blindly accepted. Gosh, are we really that ignorant, gullible, tolerant, or just plain stupid? As a culture, have we forgotten to think independently? I could never understand it.

Anyway, with time, I began to get depressed. I saw no hope. The awful and intolerable climate, the hospital situation, Pappaji's condition, etc. all seemed hopeless to me. I witnessed my mother's pain, felt my own, and looked for something positive. But I could not find it. I became very despondent and told Pankaj about it.

384

"So, you think you have it bad, eh? You think that you are the only one hurting, and that all is well for everybody else, eh?" Pankaj asked me, in a furious rage. He was 3 years older than me and, as Shashiphoi's son, he qualified as my elder cousin. But, much more than all that, we also were really close. We could be quite blunt with each other.

"Arrey, gadheda, chal mari saathe. Hun tane batavu!" Pankaj thundered at me. (*Arrey, you idiot, come with me. I will show you.*) Pankaj grabbed my arm firmly and walked me over to the next hospital wing. It was the orthopedic ward.

What I witnessed there was not just surreal, but downright horrifying. I had never seen such trauma or suffering of people in my life anywhere. There were hordes of patients everywhere, who were on beds, floors, mats, etc. recovering from their surgical procedures. "Look at all of them. My surgery teams and I are the doctors who did all this. Yes, they are uncomfortable and many are still in pain. We try to do the best we can, but this is the real India." Pankaj explained. "And you are whining about your father in a private room?"

Just then, an old lady cried out plaintively, "Doctor Saheb, maro chhokro chalshe ke nahin?" (*Doctor Saheb, will my son walk or not?*) Pankaj looked at me directly and said, "Come, this is a very good example of what we do."

The old lady's son had a fracture in his leg. It required putting a plate in it surgically to fix it. But such plates and the required procedures were very expensive. Most folks in India could not afford them. So, Pankaj had come up with an innovative surgical procedure. It had not been approved by any medical authority as yet. Pankaj was so confident in his novel approach, that he had proceeded to simply build ample case-based evidence for it.

"Maaji, maru kahyu karsho? Tamane jovu nahi game. Pan chhokaro chalto thayi jashe," Pankaj offered to the old lady (*Maaji, will you do as I direct? You will not like seeing it. But your son will be able to walk.*) She smiled joyously and readily agreed. She came forward, hugged and blessed Pankaj, with the priceless "ashirvaad" (*blessings*) of a mother.

Pankaj's innovative technique was to put the "plate" outside of the body! He put anchors into the bones, and secured them to a plate outside! It structurally held things firmly in place, just like an inside plate, to facilitate bone healing. After the required healing period, the plate and anchors were easily removed, the holes sutured up, and the patient just walked away.

Pankaj's method was least invasive, highly effective, and it cost less than 5% of other procedures. Yes, it looked awful, and one did have to handle post-operative recovery carefully, but it was a quantum simpler than all the other approved procedures. For patients in India, it was a game changer. Later, Pankaj travelled the world presenting papers on his various new surgical innovations and a litany of patient case studies.

I returned from this ward visit with a whole new and sober perspective. Remarkably, I saw this same old lady, some days later, with her son, as they both slowly walked out of the hospital. She recognized me and told me that they would do the rest of the recovery at home and then return to have the external plate removed. I was blown away. Pankaj had indeed made a difference in countless lives with his intellect and daring.

Soon, the month of August came to an end. My father was moved from the LG Hospital back to Nikunj. What followed was a nightmare of a nursing situation. My mother bore the brunt of this incredible effort.

Nine months later, in February 1992, my father passed away. Ajay's prognosis had proven to be true. With that, a very difficult chapter in our lives came to an end.

While the chapter closed, I never recovered personally from its overall psychological fallout.

The Charms of Rajasthan

Palaces of Udaipur

I believe it was December 2000, and we were visiting India as a family. Our children were young and so travelling with them was akin to moving along an army, which needed lots of stuff. Nilima, my wife, always harangued me about various things, that I seemed to be totally incompetent at, and more. But somehow, I managed to rise to the occasion, whatever it was, eventually. For a father, it should be obvious, that this was a tough road to hoe.

In this visit to India, we had decided to take a trip to Udaipur, Jaipur, & Jodhpur, in Rajasthan. Other than Udaipur & Chittod, very briefly many years ago, I had not seen anything else, and in my mind, these were places of legendary significance. Over the years, like many other visitors, I had romanticized everything about the kings, kingdoms, and the people of Rajasthan. I had desperately wanted to see it all for myself. Nilima had agreed with me, and so with some trepidation, we set off on this adventure along with our kids.

We checked into the Lakshmi Vilas Palace Hotel, Udaipur, in the near center of town and right by the Pichhola Lake. It was a palace that had been converted into a hotel and it was just magnificent. We had a grand time there. A part of our package was a tour of the old City Palace of Udaipur. It was a celebrated old palace, various kings of the Mewad dynasty had lived there over the centuries, it had a rich history, and it had also been filmed in many Bollywood movies.

Now, during this entire City Palace tour, I was like a kid in a candy store. I kept asking endless questions of the guide. For example, why were the arched entrances that connected various rooms so small and short? They were barely 4 feet in height! I was informed that it was a security precaution. Under an attack, everybody would have to pass through these small openings by bending down. And that left them open to being "beheaded" by someone on the other side!

Then, towards the end of the tour, we came into a room which was appointed in a rather plain manner. There was not much in it, except for a simple armoire which had glass doors in the front of it. Within it, in plain sight was something that looked like a battle tunic, mostly in chain mail, of a very large person. We all wondered about what it might be, or its history.

"Please, all of you, gather near me," the guide requested. "This is the "bakhtar" (*the battle tunic*) of Rana Pratap. He was the celebrated King of Mewad in the 16th Century. He fought tirelessly with Akbar, the Mughal Emperor, who never managed to conquer him. To this day, all of us in Rajasthan, revere his legacy."

To say that I was stunned or speechless, would be an understatement. I was actually shocked out of my wits! My dear God, I was within a few feet of the battle tunic of Rana Pratap? This King was a man of legend! As a child in India, I grew up hearing all sorts of stories about his intellect and smarts in battle. He was a huge man physically, ferocious in battle, very clever, and always managed to confound Emperor Akbar, who so desired to vanquish him. Then there was the horse that Rana Pratap rode. His name was Chetak. This horse had saved the Rana's life in many a battle by just riding off with him quickly to safety, sometimes when he himself had been wounded. Chetak was also legendary. The horse eventually gave his life in yet another successful escape from battle, in which he saved Rana Pratap's life! He has been celebrated as a beacon of loyalty and dedication to a master, ever since in Rajasthan.

The legends about Rana Pratap said many things. Like most legends, I am sure that they were based on a considerable measure of facts and events, that actually occurred. However, legends typically tend to embellish the events and amplify the people involved, which actually form the basis of their origin. But in the case of this magnificent tunic, I was stumped. I mean, unlike typical legends, here was real physical evidence. This was a far cry from a bunch of childhood stories. I went up close to it and took a slow and detailed look. My heart was filled with feelings of deep reverence, I will admit. Then, quite suddenly, something struck me as being quite odd.

"This does not make any sense to me!" I asked in earnest of the guide. "Such a valuable artifact of the history of India, and it is stored in this simple armoire?"

"Hukum, what seems to be the problem?" the guide responded. "It has been this way for as long as I can remember. What is it that is troubling you?"

"Gosh, can you not see it?" I asked in an agitated manner. "This is a priceless object. It is our national treasure. It is protected only by this silly glass faced cabinet?"

"I am confused. I do not understand your concern," the guide replied. "You seem worried about something."

"You are damn right, I am!" I replied. "Somebody could break this glass here and steal this priceless tunic. Then, they could sell it on the black market for such things. It is not protected at all. Nothing is guarding it. Can you not see it? This item is invaluable. Some devious people may want to steal it and take off with it. How can it not bother all of you?"

"Oh, I see. I think I now understand your worry," the guide said, with a smile of amusement. "Well, let me explain a few things to you. They may help ease your thinking."

"Yes, it is a priceless tunic. But, what or who do you think is guarding it? Do you think it is this "almaari" (*a cupboard or cabinet*) with its glass covered doors? Oh, it is easy to break the glass, or the cabinet, and steal the tunic, but then what? It is very heavy. Where and how would you go with it? Who would assist you?" the guide continued with a broad grin.

"Hukum, this tunic is not guarded by this simple almaari? It is guarded by all of Udaipur! It is easy to physically steal it, given where it is kept. But whoever attempts it, I promise you with my blood, will never leave Udaipur alive! There will be no court case, no trial, or any such thing. That person will be killed immediately and publicly, to avenge the insult to the kingdom of Mewad. Nobody will bear witness to it in a court of law. We are Rajputs, and this has been our way for centuries. Everybody here knows this. So, please relax, this historic and priceless tunic is quite safe where it is."

I felt numb, and totally cut down to size. These thoughts had not even occurred to me. A sense of awe came over me as I realized what it was to be in Rajasthan. Its proud people, ferocious in battle, yet soft and gentle in their hearts and ways, and so rich in their various traditions, just amazed me. In so many ways, they seemed to represent all that was grand about India. And, to be honest, I did sort of fall in love with it all in a romantic sense.

Another strange realization for me was about something that most folks would not think of normally. I asked the guide, "Why are many kings in India called Maharaja, while here in Mewad, they are called Maharana? Raja or Rana, is there a difference?"

"Oh, yes, hukum. There is a big difference!" he replied. "A Raja typically sends his key generals to lead his armies into battle for his kingdom. While, a Rana leads his armies into battle himself! In Mewad, all our Rana's put their lives on the line personally in battle. So, they are celebrated as truly brave kings and given the moniker of Maharana!"

There are many legends about Rana Pratap and his reign. Many of them conflict with the so-called "known" or "recorded" history, and nobody is really sure about the truth. Well, one says, that he rarely got to stay in his capital, Udaipur. He was always on the move with his forces. He fought the huge armies of Emperor Akbar constantly with guerilla warfare techniques. He lost most of his kingdom at first, but then he fought back, and managed to also regain most of it back. Well, it seems that Fort Chittod remained elusive.

Also, there are many legends about how he died. A popular belief holds that he died from "Dhanurvaa" (*Tetanus toxicity*), acquired from his many battle wounds, and the various complications derived from them. Another legend says that when Akbar learnt of the death of Rana Pratap, he cried like he had lost a member of his own near family! Akbar respected Rana Pratap in every way imaginable enormously. A period of mourning was announced in the entire Mughal Empire to respect the passing of Rana Pratap.

As I stood inches away from his tunic, peering at it and recalling all this, I felt a strange chill creeping up my spine. Oh, what a man! Oh, what times he had lived in. What amazing strength and endurance he must have possessed to fight the Mughal power to preserve his kingdom and its ways. I was in total awe.

It is truly a sad epitaph that within two generations after Rana Pratap passed away, in the era of Emperor Jahangir, Mewad became a vassal state of the Mughal Empire. There were many reasons for this development.

In essence, in the times of Rana Pratap, independence and honor were primary, and so they justified war. In less than 50 years or so later, peace was primary, and so it allowed subservience to the foreign and Muslim rulers in Delhi.

The Royal Hunting Lodge, Udaipur

"❝I am extremely sorry, sir. But there has been a terrible mistake on our part and I would like to request your assistance in resolving it suitably", the Manager of the Lakshmi Vilas Palace Hotel spoke to me with great sincerity in his voice and concern on his face. We had just finished a grand tour of the famous Lake Palace Hotel in the middle of Pichhola Lake and were now having lunch at the adjacent Shiv Nivas Palace Hotel in Udaipur.

"Oh? And what is the problem?" I asked.

"Sir, it is the peak of the tourist season. The palace is fully booked out every night. Tomorrow we have a large guest party arriving for a destination wedding. I know that you were booked with us for 3 nights, but I am afraid that we do not have a room for you for tomorrow, your 3rd night!"

"Good Lord! I have my family here with me and we have young children. All our remaining time here has been planned out with tours and so forth. What do you suggest we do?" I reacted politely.

"Yes, sir. This is most embarrassing for us. Well, may I offer you accommodations for tomorrow night at the Royal Hunting Lodge? It is not far from here. It is in a wilderness area, but the accommodations there are very nice indeed. The guests of the royal family usually stay there. Obviously, we will take care of all transfer arrangements and your stay there will be complimentary." he offered.

After some discussion, and in the interest of mutual peace, we accepted the offer. Well, there was not much choice in the matter anyway. Besides, who knows, we could discover something new at this Lodge. Afterall, we were in Rajasthan!

The Royal Hunting Lodge was deceptively rustic. It had a main building with various amenities offered centrally. All the guests were housed in individual cottages located all around the nearby area. To make matters interesting, all this was located in a protected wilderness area, which boasted of a vast array of wildlife, including major predators. Everything in the cottages was beautifully appointed and we were made to feel special indeed. But there was one catch. We were advised bluntly that no movement around the grounds was permitted without an armed escort. You could call for one at any time at all. Ignoring this advice was dangerous and had even proven fatal in the past. Well, we got the message in a hurry.

"Sir, please be sure to be in the main building this evening," our Lodge attendant said. "Cocktails start at 5:30pm in the Drawing Room. At 6:00pm, the show begins. Oh, you will love it! And at 7:00pm, dinner will be served in the main Dining Room. Please be on time to really enjoy it all. Welcome to the Royal Hunting Lodge!" Then he left.

Nilima and I looked at each other with, "What was that? What show?" It was very curious indeed.

We were escorted over to the main building around 5:30pm or so. As we entered it, I felt like I had entered a time warp! It felt like I was in the 19th or 18th Centuries! The whole building and its décor dripped royalty. The waiters and staff were dressed in "period" outfits, there was taxidermy everywhere with huge creatures, and large oil portraits of the Mewad royal generations all over. It just took my breath away.

The Lodge this evening seemed to be quite full. There were a lot of people there. Many white foreigners, some Asians, and a few Indians. Not many children around. One heard many different languages. It was obvious that this was a crowd of well-heeled people.

"Sir, a gin & tonic, perhaps?" the waiter asked.

"Sure, why not? Please bring one for my wife as well. Thank you." I replied. I was already beginning to like all this very much. I must admit, it suited me enormously.

Soon, we heard, "Ladies & Gentlemen, please move towards the veranda. Do not lean over or go past the marble railing. Please, be totally silent. No talking, noises, or light flashes of any kind. They tend to scare off our guests. The show is about to begin."

Some 20-30 of us slowly drifted over to this veranda, which I had not noticed till then. The Drawing Room opened on to it. It was semi-circular in shape. Perhaps 20-30 feet in diameter and 15 feet in radius. There was an ornate 3-foot-tall railing around the circumference of it. The entire veranda was made of exquisitely carved or tiled marble.

On the other side of the railing, about 6 feet below, was the waterline of a magnificent lake. It was teardrop in shape and we were at the tip of the broad end of it. The narrow end vanished off somewhere into the distance. Around both sides of the lake, nearby and at various strategic locations farther away, floodlights had been placed to illuminate the water's edge. And thus, was created a natural stage for this amazing show.

In the balmy quiet, all of us observed all sorts of wildlife come to the lake to get a long and cool drink of water. We were facing West and the sky was a grand yellow/orange to add charm to it all. Slowly, the light faded away and darkness descended. But the floodlights kept the show going.

The initial batch was all sorts of birds, fowl, rabbits, and raccoons. Then, came the deer. Lots of them. We even saw many "Neelguy" come by. The foxes and wolves came along also and finally the large cats. There were quite a few of them, but they were far away. Perhaps tigers or leopards, but I cannot remember it specifically today. They were in different places far away around the lake. But the strange part of it all was that we did not see a single hunt or kill. It seemed that the whole animal kingdom was focused on quenching its deep thirst after a long hot and dry day. The critical need for the life sustaining drinks of water had become primary over the presence of mortal danger nearby.

In an hour or so, it slowly ended. We returned to the Dining Room for a sumptuous meal and the veranda was closed off and secured. After dinner, we were escorted back to our cabin.

In my life I have been lucky enough to see wildlife in many diverse settings. But this one remains truly exceptional in my mind. In the violent world of nature, where it is survival of the fittest, I witnessed what appeared to be an acceptance of others brought about by something so necessary for everyone's survival. It was drinking water.

I have always questioned if there was a lesson here for mankind? When weapons, economics, politics, religions, and a desire for domination over others, have all failed us collectively, will we be sensible enough to revert to what nature has been teaching us every day? Will we learn to look after and protect our climate, forests, wildlife, oceans, waterways, farmlands, etc.? Or will we just over breed ourselves, abuse all our resources, and destroy our planet into oblivion?

I truly wonder.

Umaid Bhavan Palace, Jodhpur

We flew into town and were taken to the Umaid Bhavan Palace, which had been in a large measure, converted into a 5-star hotel/resort. It catered largely to the foreign tourist traffic and was a site famous for ornate destination weddings. We had a suite booked there for our stay.

"I am sorry, sir, but there has been a serious mistake with your booking. The class of suite you were booked into, has been unfortunately sold out." the man at the Reception said, with a sincere and an apologetic look.

"Dear God, not again!" I thought. It was one travel agency, one agent, and one multi-city tour in Rajasthan! How difficult could this be, for Heaven's sake? After endless faxes and phone calls, everything had eventually been confirmed, many times over. But the reality on the ground obviously was totally different. I felt like the victim of a "bait & switch" ploy. Or was it that even now nothing in India functioned in any kind of a predictable way? With consistent regularity, your hopes were dashed, promises were broken, and one seemed to easily get booted from something at the drop of a hat!

The demand for anything and everything greatly outstripped the supply, and so your money really did not matter. What mattered in reality were your connections with people who could "fix it". All my contacts in India were old, stale, and dry. Also, I had nothing to offer to them in return, unless they travelled to the USA which was rare, so I was not of "much value" to anybody.

This was vital, because India was a culture in which reciprocal social and financial obligations were measured and tracked in minute detail by everybody. So, in other words, the more favors you could grant others, the more favors you could obtain from others. I had little to offer locally, and so sadly, I had to fend for myself, which can make life truly difficult in India.

The country can suddenly and entirely lose its charm, warmth, and attraction in your mind and heart. Shockingly, when this happened, you wanted to just get the hell out of there and simply bloody well leave. It is amazing how intense this reaction can be, even within a native-born son like me.

"We are disappointed, to say the least," I responded. "What do you suggest we do? My wife and our children are with me."

"If you do not mind, sir, we can offer you the Maharana Suite. Normally, it is a highly desired upgrade and gets sold out quickly. But under the circumstances today, we will make some adjustments. Also, we will waive any additional charges," he offered.

"Fine. But let us have a look at it. Then, we can decide. I presume that there is no other option?" I asked.

"No, sir, I am afraid there is not," he replied honestly. "But you will not need it, I can assure you."

We were escorted to the Maharana Suite of the Umaid Bhavan Palace. As we entered it, my lungs lost all the air in them! With one small step, I entered not a suite in a palace hotel, but the 19th Century India itself, it seemed!

The Maharana Suite was, in one word, incredible! It was actually a 4-bedroom apartment. All the bedrooms had attached bathrooms, which were very ornate and western. There were additionally a drawing room, dining room, kitchen, a walk-in pantry, and more. But all that was not as important.

The whole suite was appointed royally! There were oil portraits, fancy rugs, antique furniture, and so many unique decorative things from all over the world, everywhere one looked! Oh, and further, it was filled with taxidermy animals! There were entire large cats, heads of various animals, and skins with intact heads, all over the place. I was sure that these had all come from various hunting events in the past. The display was unimaginable. I was just delighted, thrilled, and awestruck. But my joy was short-lived.

"Papa, I am scared here!" my little daughter, Meghana, complained. "This place is frightening. Can we go somewhere else?"

"Gosh, now how do I deal with this?" I thought. Neil and Meghana both had a terrible reaction to the suite. Their senses were overwhelmed and they were frightened by it all. I decided to take them on a walk of orientation, hoping to establish some level of comfort.

"Now, guys, there is nothing to be scared of here. All these creatures are dead. Their bodies have been stuffed with things to make them look alive. That also goes for all the animal heads with the skins. But, hey, look at these oils! And how about these grand bathrooms, eh? Is it not just amazing? Look, there is history of all sorts associated with everything and the people who lived here! They were royalty! Come on, is this not fun?"

"No, not really," Meghana replied with wide scared eyes. "Can we sleep with you and Mom tonight?"

My attempt failed miserably. Nothing would calm down the minds of my children. They were scared out of their wits. I had to figure out something, but I was not sure about what that could be.

"Well, let's check out the palace and its amenities. We can walk around and then later get some dinner," I offered, as a distraction. Thankfully, everybody agreed and we set out. We got to a central foyer and I needed a "bio-break", so I told everyone to look around while I found a rest room. A nice man nearby even gave me some general directions towards it.

I thought I had followed the instructions correctly, but soon it became apparent that either the directions were flawed or that I had made some sort of an error somewhere. The upshot was that I was totally lost. All the hallways and turns felt like a maze and I could not figure my way out. Then, I took this turn and found myself looking at an armed guard standing near an ornate door. Just as I walked up, the door opened and a man emerged. The guard saluted and shortly vanished. All this was very curious.

"Good evening. May I be of some assistance?" the man asked me with a warm expression on his face. He was tall, fair, athletic, well-dressed, and had a radiance in his face and eyes that were captivating.

"Well, perhaps. My family is in a foyer like area. I was looking for a restroom, and now I am lost. I am trying to get back. Do you know this palace hotel?" I asked.

"Yes, in some ways, you might say," the man replied with a gentle smile. "Come with me. I will take you there."

We engaged in a lively chat on the walk back. The return was not easy at all, but the man knew his way. At last, we entered the foyer and I saw my family standing there waiting for me. "Papa, what took you so long?" Neil asked.

"Oh, your Papa decided to visit me, and we got carried away chatting." the man replied to Neil.

"Then, he must have told you about the frightful place we are staying at tonight? Neil continued. "It is very scary. All those animals. It is the Maharana Room, or something like that."

"Oh, you surely do not mean that! A tough young man like you!" the man said with a laugh. "I bet that you could shoot any of those animals in a hunt. Many children of your age have done just that here in the past."

"Really?" Neil reacted in total awe of the very concept.

"Hukum, we have a table ready for you. Would you like to be seated?" the maître d' of the nearby dining room inquired politely.

"Oh, the dining room here is simply lovely. But I would not do that tonight, if I were you and liked to eat meat." the man said with a twinkle in his eye. "There is a fantastic bar-b-que hut, just outside the palace gates, which is open only on select days. Today is one of them. I have known the cook for a long time. His "junglee maas" (*wilderness meat*) is unmatched. It is an easy walk to get there. Anyway, I must get going. Well, it was a pleasure chatting with all of you. Enjoy yourselves, and have a lovely stay."

As the man slowly walked away, I thanked the maître d' for the dining room offer. Then I asked him, "Who is that guy? He suggested that we eat outside the palace gates at his favorite bar-b-que hut!"

"Oh, Sir, you cannot be serious! Do you not know him? That man is the HH (*His Highness*) of Jodhpur himself! He is Gaj Singh Ji!" he said in disbelief. "He owns all of this, but lives quietly in an apartment in the palace. He has turned his holdings into things that people at large can enjoy. We just adore him."

I was at a loss for words and felt totally stupid. To think that the HH had been so gracious to me, while I was carrying on like a complete idiot. And I swear, I have never had bar-b-que food, quite like that night, ever since. The HH was so right!

That night, the children snuggled with us in our bed for a while. Then, they got too sleepy to care and we managed to put them to bed in the adjacent room. Next day, in the beautiful glow of the morning sun, all the fright was forgotten. We enjoyed every aspect of this magnificent suite, with all its royal possessions and history, for the rest of our stay.

It was an amazing experience. We truly made memories as a family.

Amber Fort, Jaipur

Jaipur, the "pink city", was full of extra-ordinary charms of all sorts. We had booked a suite at the Ram Bagh Palace Hotel, because I wanted to stay at the palace where the gorgeous Maharani Gayatri Devi had arrived as a bride with the HH of Jaipur a long time ago. The palace was renowned for its amenities and rich history. It had been converted into a luxurious hotel a few years earlier, but they had preserved the ambience of the palace, as it might have been as a private royal residence. It was amazing and unforgettable in so many ways.

We took in all the highlights of Jaipur and had many delightful tours. Just when I thought that nothing could top any of this, the day arrived when we were to visit the Amber Fort (or Amer Fort). I was not prepared for what we were about to experience.

Well, for one thing, it was at a bit of a height. For another, I was not expecting to ride up to it on top of an elephant! It was certainly by design. The clear intention being to charm all the tourists and set the mood for them before their visit to this amazing fort and the palace within it. It also greatly helped smooth out the flow of the visitors. I was later informed that this elephant ride was so famous that it had been filmed in a major Bollywood production (*Movie - "Hum Saath Saath Hain", Song - "Mhare Hiwda Mein Naache Mor"*). By the time we all got up to the top of the hill and got off the elephants, we were just ecstatic and could not contain our joy at the thrill of it all. My children were just shrieking in delight.

As we got off our elephants, our tour guide came up to us and we began our tour of the Amber Fort. We were escorted inside through an ornate gate of sorts and soon found ourselves in what looked like a temple of the Hindu Goddess Kali, or Durga. Everything around us was just amazing and full of history. I was, as usual, asking too many questions of our guide, who was very knowledgeable and responded very well.

Then shortly, a man approached me out of nowhere! He had the appearance of a Brahmin Pujari (*a Brahmin Priest*) of the temple and was dressed as such as well.

"Hukum, aap maante hain?" he asked. (*Sir, are you a believer?*)

"Kis baat mein? Kaun poochhta hai?" I asked in return, a bit surprised and confused. (*In what matter? Who is asking?*)

"Ji, Devi ke naam, ek Pujari poochhta hai. Aap maante hain?" he replied with a gentle smile on his face (*Sir, in the Devi's name, a Priest is asking. Are you a believer?*)

I was totally flummoxed. I had not a clue as to what this was all about or how to handle his question. I knew that in Rajasthan such things had deep meanings and I did not want to offend anybody. So, how do I play this? How do I respond to this priest? Perhaps, when in doubt, the best option is to main line it, and play it safe.

"Pujariji, dharm se to Hindu hun. Ma ke mandir mein khada hun. Ab aur kya kahoon? Han, mein maanta hun," I said. (*Pujariji, I am a Hindu by faith. I am standing in Ma's temple. What else can I say? Yes, I am a believer.*).

The Pujari broke into a broad smile of approval. He said, "Ji, aiiye mere saath". (*Sir, please come with me.*)

My family tried to follow me, but he stopped them. He indicated that mothers and minor children were to stay in the part of the temple we were in at the time. I would be taken to an adjacent section, which was "segregated" for adult males only, by religious custom.

In this section, I prayed like I normally did at any other Hindu temple. The Pujari performed additional holy rituals on my behalf. Then, he offered me "charanamrut" (*a blessed holy-water based elixir*) in the palm of my hand. I was supposed to drink this offering and I proceeded to do so. Then, in a purely reflexive act, I almost spat it out! I am glad that I actually did not, because that would have been an insult. My surprise and shock were due to the fact that the liquid in my palm actually was whiskey!

Then, the Pujari offered me "prasad" from the morning Puja. It all seemed quite normal. But as I ate it, I darned near choked in surprise! Again, I simply could not believe what I was consuming. It was small pieces of cooked and spiced goat meat! The Pujari had been watching me intently. He noticed, with great satisfaction, that I had indeed consumed both the offerings. I was obviously very surprised, but my actions were those of a believer, according to his eyes and thinking.

"Aap yeh sab kaise karate hain?" I asked delicately. (*How do you manage to do such things?*) The Pujari laughed with great amusement.

"Bhai Sa, yeh Rajasthan hai. Yeh Sila Devi (Durga) ka mandir hai. Yeh reet aur rivaaj hamari parampara hai. Delhiwale apna wahaan karte hain or hum yehaan apana. Har Poonam ki raat, vadh hota hai, aur bali chadhaya jaata hai" (*Bhai Sa, this is Rajasthan. This is Sila Devi's (Durga's) temple. These are our traditions and heritage. Folks in Delhi do their things there, and we do our things here. Every Full Moon night, there is a sacrificial offering here.*)

So many thoughts were racing through my mind upon hearing all this. Oh, God, I could have gone ballistic in so many different ways and about all these weird practices and thoughts. My years in America were now becoming shamefully apparent, even to me. Wisely, I did not vocalize any of my thoughts.

As the prayers came to an end, I thought that perhaps all this was a ploy to get some money out of me. Regardless, strong feelings of guilt overcame me and I offered a generous amount to the Pujari. He refused to accept it. He took only a small token cash note so that I would not feel rejected or have my sentiments hurt. Then he put it into the offering box on my behalf. Then, he turned and looked at me with an angelic and a benign expression. He seemed to be mentally far away.

"Khamma ghani, Sa." (*Many blessings, Sir.*) he said shortly, and then disappeared quietly through a door nearby into an inner sanctum. The mandir was now empty. Other than my family and the guide in the section next to me, there was nobody around.

Crazy as all this may seem to you, at that moment, I recall sensing a strong energy field all around me and even going through me! I have no idea what it was at all. All I can say is that I recall feeling it very distinctly and being aware of its intensity. Perhaps, it was because nothing like this had ever happened to me before, anywhere in the world.

So, what was all this about? Among the tourist groups going through Amber Fort that day, why was I approached? Did something about me tell them something? Was this Pujari a good guy or a bad guy? In the Hindu faith, nothing comes along scarier or fiercer than the Goddess Durga. She is strong, vicious, blood thirsty, dominates everything around her, and always needs to be pacified. She is the very embodiment of "Shakti" (*divine strength*). But she is also a belief, a philosophy, a moral code, a way of life, and much more. So, why was I subjected to these things in her mandir? I was perplexed.

I had more questions than answers. But curiously, at the end of it all, I did find myself in a state of relative mental peace. My normal irritability, angst, and short temper with most things in India, seemed to have greatly subsided. I was a lot calmer about everything, at least for a while.

We had a grand tour of the Amber Fort and the palaces within it. The Sheesh Mahal (*Mirror Palace*) took the honors! I recall fondly about being reminded of one of my favorite Bollywood classic films, "Mughal-e-Azam" (*The Great Mughal*).

In summary, this whole trip to Rajasthan left me dazzled and with a sense of colors. Jaipur, the pink city; Jodhpur, the blue city; and Udaipur, the white city, were all unique and fascinating. But all these colors aside, everything about Rajasthan and its amazing history, just made me fall in love with it.

Yes, the forts, palaces, and monuments were all great. But the greatest charm of Rajasthan was its people and their ways. They were proud, but always warm, welcoming, and wonderful. They touched your heart and your emotions deeply.

Oh, we went to a few other places as well, but I will leave those stories alone for now. Maybe I will write about them, perhaps on another inspired day.

Behn & Pappaji with Neil in Walnut Creek, USA - 1987

Mortgage Industry Exhibit – Georgiana Yoshioka, Jan Duffy & Lisa Vargas
1993

Kmart Auto Center Outsourcing Agreement Signing – 1995
Seated (l to r): Roger Penske, Michael Penske, Floyd Hall, Marv Rich

With Richard Rosenberg,
Art Gonzales, & Steve
Sears.

Marv & Cheryl

With the "Taipan"
Alasdair Morrison
(right) – Hong Kong
1997

With Ron &
Nancy Floto -
Hong Kong
1998

With Marlene & Bob
Neslund – Hong Kong
1998

Dairy Farm Exec Assts: Kathy Leung & Kay Li - 2000

At Hong Kong Formal Functions

Chinese New Year Dinner 1999 – Sims Trading Co., Hong Kong

Reception Dinner for Madam Zhang (3rd from left) – Hong Kong 1999

*Meghana at the
Mahadev, Maninagar
2016*

*Hatkeshvar Temple
in Vadnagar
2017*

*With the Pujari:
(R to L) Rajivbhai,
Me, Astikbhai, Doc
Utkarshbhai, Nina,
and Gnanesh.
2017*

*Hatkeshvar Mahadev
Shiva Linga
Vadnagar, 2017*

*With Ramesh &
Chandrakant
Kotecha
Jamnagar, 2017*

*Somnath Mandir
2017*

FINI

A Ranking Question

I
t is an amazing feeling. I do not know how to give it any sort of a body, but it has been captured brilliantly by William Wordsworth, the British Poet Laureate, in his trilogy of poems about the River Yarrow. In my little stories here, I have drawn great inspiration from his writings.

All of us, at some time or another, have thought of places that we would like to visit. Let's call one, a "Place Unvisited". Then, let us add to this an actual visit to it sometime later. Let's call this experience, a "Place Visited". Now, let's say further that a long time later, we get to visit this place again! Let's call that, a "Place Revisited."

My question for you is "How would you rank these experiences? And why?" It does not matter what the Place is and you have no further information about it. Based on just what you have been told here, how would you rank these experiences? And why?

It is a popular riddle amongst various literary circles. Oh, there is nothing arrogant about it. Folks choose a variety of rankings for many reasons. Let me share with you mine, and the reasons for them.

My ranking is as follows: 1) Place Unvisited; 2) Place Revisited; & 3) Place Visited. Why? For some sound reasons.

Well, a Place Unvisited, is to me all about imagination. It usually is reflective of things we desire and want. So, it presents to us a utopian view of a Place, that is just lovely and fulfills all our dreams. It is our concept of a Place where all we want is satisfied and everything is near perfect.

A Place Revisited, is next for me, because it is all about nostalgia. This is a powerful human emotion. We tend to embellish and praise the "days gone by", when life was so great. We are inclined to remember all the positives and forget the negatives. As such, the "old days" invariably have a great charm and attachment to them. This emotional edge adds something fascinating to a revisit.

A Place Visited, is the last for me, because it is about disappointment. It is a sad thing to say, but reality rarely lives up to what our imagination has created and it has nothing by way of an emotional attachment. As wonderful as it may be, the Place as it actually is, simply cannot compete with human imagination or nostalgia. And so, it ranks the last.

So, you may be wondering by now, what does any of this have to do with my stories? Well, as you will see shortly, it has a lot to do with them.

Shopping Trip to India

It was December-January 2016-17, and I was in India on a "wedding shopping" trip for my daughter, Meghana, who was going to get married that summer. We were travelling as a family. We had spent a gorgeous time in Hong Kong reminiscing about the "old days", when we lived there and the life that we had enjoyed. Then, we wandered all over Mumbai, looking for this very particular Parsee white lace "sari" that my daughter wanted for her bridal outfit.

It drove me bonkers! I even had help from Madam Cooper in Lahore on this topic! She weighed in so sweetly, but Meghana would listen to nobody. Shop after shop, the offerings were just not right. I threw my hands up eventually, and said, "I give up, honey!" At that very moment, she shrieks, "This is it, Dad! We found it!!" I am like, "Say, what? Hallelujah, you found it? Somehow I don't believe it." It was simply gorgeous! It was Parsee, Indian, classy, a sari, and much more. However, it was pure white lace and had no red color in it and so some folks objected. Meghana said, "It's okay. My shoes, lipstick, and nails will be red! It is covered."

It is also significant that all this was going on in the midst of a monetary crisis in India. Cash was very hard to come by since various currency notes had been eliminated by the Government. For folks shopping for a wedding, this was a certifiable disaster. We did suffer a lot, but my trusty debit card saw me through in many a dicey situation.

Also, we were all short on time. We had to get things done in a hurry. So, my family made all the choices and decisions, and left me straggling behind as the "sweeper" to clean things up. However, this gave me an opportunity of a very different kind. There were short blocks of time, after everybody had left India, where I could do things for myself!

Visit to Vadnagar, Gujarat

For as long as I can remember, since I was a child, I had heard about Vadnagar. I was told that we were by our caste, Vadnagara Nagar Brahmins and that we were the "genuine" article. All other kinds of Nagar Brahmins were a later and lower phenomenon. They were different offshoots born out of politics and key events in history, and so were not deemed to be as "pure". Our main deity, or "Ishta Deva", was Hatkeshwar, a form of Lord Shiva. Our main temple of worship was in Vadnagar itself. We were supposed to visit there, and pray at least once in our lifetimes.

"Vijay, have you never been to Vadnagar?" Utkarsh asked in disbelief. He was soon joined by Rajiv, Astik, Anal, and Gnanesh. They were all either Nilima's first cousins or their spouses. We were at a dinner party at Doc Utkarsh's home, and were steadily getting "well lubed".

I was talkative about many things that evening. I have a tendency to speak in Hindi a lot, with English and Gujarati mixed in, which at times unnerves some people. With my parents and friends, I had done this for years, so it was not strange for me at all. However, in Ahmedabad, this was not the norm. The language was conservative and mainly Gujarati. In general, folks hardly talked openly about much of anything in their lives. It was the nature of the local culture.

"Chalo, kale apade jaiye," Utkarsh said. (*Come, let's go there tomorrow.*) And so, it happened. My dream was realized! A trip by motor car was organized and we paid a visit to the famous Vadnagar and its Hatkeshwar Temple the next day. I must say that at first glimpse of this temple, I felt let down. I was expecting a grand and ornate temple, but that was not the case here. It was nice though.

As we entered the well-sculpted complex, I was informed that it had been restored and renovated recently, after years of neglect. We were greeted by the main Pujari (*priest*), who turned out to be Doc Utkarsh's patient. They promptly went into medical consultations about his health. His priorities were quite clear.

Actually, as I got to know him, the Pujari struck me as a wonderful and learned man. He also knew our extended families very well, which did not surprise me at all. He helped us with the Rudri puja (*prayers for Lord Shiva*), and organized a small "Abhishek" (*a ritual worship of Lord Shiva involving cleansing ceremonies*) for each of us in the main inner Shiva temple. But there was a key requirement.

One could not do the abhishek without being dressed in a silk "abotiyu" or "solu". (*a silk dhoti*) They loaned them to us and we changed into them before going into the inner sanctum. He also explained in detail what the ritual ceremony was all about to me. My respect for him increased greatly.

The whole abhishek ceremony was in Sanskrit and an amazing experience for me. This was for many reasons. For one, I had never done one, and I did not understand the meaning of all its rituals. I realized soon that they were profound and represented many great concepts.

Second, I could not get over the location where I was doing this. My whole family had worshipped this temple, however remotely, for generations. I recalled my mother often saying, "Jai Hatkesh!" after telling "goodbye" to someone. Now, here I was wearing a silk dhoti, sitting in its inner sanctum doing an abhishek! How incredible is that? Perhaps, it was my "karma". (*divine duty*)

Third, perhaps due to my overall psychological state, I felt again an energy of some kind flowing through me. I cannot explain it and it was rather wierd. It disappeared, as suddenly as it appeared. To this day, I wonder about it.

This trip was and will always be remembered as an unforgettable visit for me. Perhaps my initial disappointment was because my expectations were sky high. Based on all the stories I had heard, I had imagined something quite different. Still, it was a wonderful surprise.

I will remain indebted to Nilima's cousins for arranging it and taking me there. If you get an opportunity to go there, do perform the abhishek. Also, try and understand the ceremony, before you perform it.

It might give you a different perspective on many things in life.

Closing an Unfinished Story – Jamul

I had always wanted to return to Jamul Cement Works (JCW), in the new State of Chhattisgarh. This was due to some deeply personal and emotional reasons, from a long time ago.

Prior to leaving for India in December 2016, I had done some research with the help of Kiritbhai in Bangalore. I had found the name of the current GM of Jamul Cement Works, a Mr. Gupta, and contacted him with a request for a visit. I had explained my purpose, and he had graciously offered to facilitate it for me. It was sweet of him indeed.

So, on this fateful day, I took a flight from Ahmedabad to Mumbai, and from there I flew to Raipur, Chhattisgarh. I was picked up by a car with a driver, who informed me that he would be with me for the next two days and would take me wherever I wanted to go. I was thrilled about it and looked forward to the visit with great hope.

On the drive from the Raipur airport to Jamul, a distance of some 30+ kilometers, we passed through the city and it brought back memories of all the families that we used to visit there often. "Where were they now? What happened to them?" I wondered. We passed the famous Rajkumar College, Raipur, a public school that I was almost transferred to, until my father resisted all those attempts. Its entrance gate was ornate and there was a horse-riding class underway just on the inside. The students were learning to ride English saddle!

We arrived at the JCW and I was taken directly to meet Mr. Gupta at his office. We introduced ourselves and he was quite surprised at my memory about various things within the cement plant, the residential colony, and the times past.

"Mr. Vijay, it is a pleasure to meet you. Welcome to Jamul Cement Works." Mr. Gupta said. "You see, we are close to launching our new plant into production. It is based on totally new technologies from Germany. It has been my project for the last several years. Would you like to review it?"

"Mr. Gupta, first of all, I want to thank you profusely for permitting me to visit here. You have helped me in ways that you cannot even imagine." I replied honestly. "Please do not think that I am being rude or ungrateful to you, but I have no interest in the cement plants at all. I am here on a purely personal and nostalgic visit."

"This place was my home during my childhood, in its most formative years. One day, I left not knowing that I would never come back. I never got the chance to even say goodbye to anyone or anyplace. It has left a huge void within me, which has not left me, even with the passage of so much time. I am here to achieve closure to a personal and an unfinished story in my life."

"Really?" Mr. Gupta said, in total surprise and with a bewildered look on his face! Then, as he slowly understood, he broke into a broad smile and welcomed me warmly. "Mr. Vijay, I will help you in every way that I can to fulfill your hopes. A room has been booked for you at the Guest House. Mr. Mehta, our Chief Engineer, well oversee your visit and facilitate it as you wish. I have some commitments today, but I will see you later tonight. Please, feel free and do enjoy your visit."

Mr. Mehta was from Uttar Pradesh. The first thing he did, after we were introduced, was to ask about my caste! Once his suspicions, that I was a Brahmin were confirmed, his tone and manner changed to amazing levels of warmth and friendliness. When I shared with him the purpose of my visit, he was just blown away. He promised to stay with me for my entire visit. According to him, it was the very least that one Brahmin could do for another!

Actually, all this caste nonsense aside, Mr. Mehta proved highly valuable in dealing with all the security around JCW. This situation was totally new for me. The whole place was bristling with security and guards with assault guns everywhere. I suppose it was for good reasons. A terrorist organization could cause some serious harm in a place like JCW, if allowed to move about unchecked. Mr. Mehta got us through with great ease.

We started with the colony. What I saw just amazed me. There were lots of buildings, from the 1960's, in various stages of decay, that were in the process of being replaced by new ones. The soil was still red, but there was lots of greenery everywhere. There were little parks for kids and lots of huge tall trees throwing wonderful shade everywhere (I thought of my father). The old Sports Club was still there! Its auditorium, badminton courts, billiards/table tennis tables, and the ladies bridge room were still intact. But there was nobody there. The caretaker said, "Sahib, bahot kum log aate hain yahan." (*Sahib, very few people come here anymore.*) I remembered my parents, the Balan's, the Pradhan's, the Rao's, & the Moolarpattam's, and the hey days of the Sports Club when it was the very center of all social activity at JCW.

We drove out to the quarries. The first one, from my father's time, was now a pristine lake, with a man-made island in it where families came for picnics (I remembered Vaalji). They were now on to their 4th pit. Then, we went to the railway tracks near the packing house. I walked around taking

416

photos of the yard and the tracks. Then a man, from its repair crew, came up to me.

"Sahib, aap is patari ke photo kyun le rahe ho? Koi khas baat hai?" he asked in wonder on behalf of his whole crew. (*Sahib, why are you taking photos of these tracks? Is there something special?*)

"Han, khas baat hai," I replied. (*Yes. There is something special.*) Then, I went up to all of them. I told them about the past and the laying of the original single track. I talked about how difficult it had been to achieve, due to a lack of infrastructure, construction equipment, and supplies. Also, I shared with them some details about what it had meant to the whole JCW community. I described the arrival of the first "goods" train and the "puja" done for its steam locomotive in that very yard. They were enthralled!

Then, to my disbelief, one man asked me, "Kya aap Yajnik Sahib ke bete hain? Mere dada unki bahot batein karate the!" (*Are you Yajnik Sahib's son? My grandfather used to tell all of us a lot about him!*) They invited me to come to the Jamul village, which was now a city, for dinner. I thanked them and politely declined due to a lack of time. But it touched me deeply.

Perpendicular to the tracks was the famous irrigation canal! The bridge over it for the tracks was so cute. I remembered when they were building it with manual labor! I jumped around taking all sort of photos. At the time, the canal was dry. Apparently, this was due to the new water supply management protocols, and the water flow was not in season.

"Let's have tea at my house," Mr. Mehta offered. Obviously, I could not decline such a request from this wonderful man. I accepted and we drove over. As we pulled into his driveway, I just froze! Then I began to tremble a bit.

"Vijay sir, I wanted to show you one of the original Type C bungalows. I thought that you may recall it. Today, this one is my home," Mr. Mehta said with a smile. I was welcomed warmly by Mrs. Mehta and their lovey 20+ year old daughter. They had prepared some lovely tea for us. Then, Mr. Mehta inquired, "Sir, aap yeh ghar dekh kar kuchh ghabrah gaye? Mujhe aisa laga. Kyun?" (*Sir, upon seeing this house, you seemed a little perturbed. That is what I sensed. Why?*)

"Mehta Saheb, aap ne theek socha hai," I replied (*Mehta Saheb, you have sensed it correctly.*) "Now, you will probably not believe me, but this very bungalow was my first home at JCW in the early 1961! I know, because it was the first bungalow built of this original design. After building about 4 of them, for some reason the design was changed. I am sure it has been improved further over the years, but I know this bungalow and this location completely. There is a Type B bungalow across the street and to the left. That was Mr.

417

Balan's bungalow. It was also the first one built. Yes, I know this bungalow very well. I used to play in the dirt in this front yard, even in the awful summer heat. My mother often scolded me for getting all my clothes full of this red colored soil."

The Mehta family looked at me in total awe. They could not even imagine what I was saying. "Aap yahan rahete the?" Mrs. Mehta asked in shock! (*You used to live here?*)

"Ji. Phir uske baad, GM ka Type A bungalow bana, aur hum wahan chale gaye," I explained. (*Yes. Then after that the GM's Type A bungalow was built and we moved there.*)

Then, Mr. Mehta took me on a tour of the GM's bungalow grounds. It was like an estate, and had been my home for most of my time in Jamul. We entered the walled compound, which now had armed guards on duty 7 x 24 hours at the gate. The west side gardens and the driveways, with their brick lined borders, all looked somewhat the same. The huge lawn in the front was in a reasonable shape. However, the tennis court seemed to be in disrepair. It looked like nobody was using it. The old roundabout was gone. All the servant's quarters and the garage areas had been redone.

The east side patio, with its gardens and outdoor swing, where Pappaji used to enjoy his evening tea service were also gone. In some ways, I was not surprised. Afterall, things change with time. However, while it was still a large and lavish estate, it seemed to lack the life and vibrancy that I remembered.

Then, Mr. Mehta got called away for something, so I asked the driver to take me to the Durg Railway Station, some 10 kilometers away. This was the dear place where I had arrived after an amazing train journey from Rajkot, so long ago. When we got there, I was really surprised. The tiny and quaint station, which was only a small building, besides the main double tracks, that I remembered so well, was gone. In its place was a new station with platforms and all the modern amenities of a Junction station!

On our drive back, I asked to go through the various "Sectors" of the colony of Bhilai Steel Works. They seemed nearly the same. But I could not find the Chitra Mandir. It was this grand cinema theatre, where I had seen movies like "Junglee" (*Animal*), "Bees Saal Baad" (*Twenty Years Later*) and "Come September". Actually, Kashyap & Ajay, my older brothers, had tricked me into going to see "Bees Saal Baad", a murder and horror mystery film. I had been scared out of my mind for weeks, with nightmares about the killer's claw like hand! Chitra Mandir was gone also. In its place was some sort of a Multi-plex theatre complex, which had no character or soul at all.

In the evening, Mr. Gupta & Mr. Mehta came to visit me at the Guest House. We sat around in an empty guest room, and had a couple of drinks, with some savories served up from its kitchen. As the evening came to a close, to my utter surprise, Mr. Gupta invited me to visit the inside of the GM's bungalow! We walked over and I met his family. They threw open the whole house for me and I went around each room telling them all sorts of stories of events past. They were fascinated. Mr. Gupta even took over my Nikon camera and took photos of me and us everywhere.

The bungalow was quite different from what it used to be in Pappaji's time. It had lost all its British panache, and the feel of being a special social place for important visitors. It had turned mainly into a typical Indian home, which was still lavish but did not seem to entertain anybody much. The look & feel, the ambience, and its setup, were vastly different and inwardly focused. It was indeed the highlight of my entire visit.

Next morning, Mr. Mehta came to see me off. He suggested one final stop to me. It was a Hanuman Shrine "in the middle" of an office building. "Vijay sir, I can assure you that you have never seen anything like this!" he offered. We visited it and it looked well maintained. After a while, I told Mr. Mehta about the history behind it. He nearly lost his mind in total shock. He took me to the Pujari (*the priest*) promptly and told him all about it. This man was stunned as well.

"Aap Yajnik Memsahib ke bete hain? Mere dada unko Damayantiben kehte the. Woh hi hai na?" the Pujari asked in amazement. (*You are Yajnik Memsahib's son? My grandfather used to call her Damayantiben. Is it not the same person?*)

"Han, aap thik kehete hain," I replied (*Yes, you are right in what you say*).

"Arrey, Sarkar, aap aiye yahan. Aap ki Ma ke bina yeh mandir bachta hi nahin!" he said (*Arrey, Sir, please come in here. Without your mother, this temple would not have survived!*). We chatted for a bit. Then, in the memory of my parents, I prayed there with the Pujari's assistance. I left a generous donation as well. However, he seemed more thrilled about meeting me.

With that final stop, I left JCW for the Raipur airport. As we began our return drive, I felt a churn of various emotions within me. It was an intense mix of nostalgia, sadness, and even disappointment.

While change is inevitable in life, I was not sure that I saw positive change here. The whole area seemed to have become too industrial, urbanized, over-populated, and filled with too many stresses of daily living. The feeling of being in a rural place, with a simple life, and a close-knit society, appeared to have all vanished. Even though life was not easy by any means even then, it seemed that we enjoyed it much more.

A major factor certainly was our human relations and daily direct social interactions. It was a world without the internet or television and with limited radio and telephone. Our entertainment was interacting with each other, talking about and sharing our lives, and reading lots of different things. As often as possible, we enjoyed delicious food prepared by someone or the other, in so many ethnic variations.

So, was this visit worth the effort? Yes, definitely. While everybody I knew from my time in Jamul was long gone, in more ways than the obvious, I was glad that I had attempted this pilgrimage. I did feel sad, surprised, and disappointed about many things, but then I had changed a lot as well since 1966.

As we drove out of the gates of JCW, I turned around for one final look back. It was a sight I had seen countless times in the past. It was quite distinct in my memory. It had always told me that I had arrived home.

As I held my gaze, my eyes moistened over, and the tears began to flow. Then, with a heavy heart, I turned the last page, on what was now a "finished story".

A Nostalgic Sprint – Saurashtra Calling

I returned from Jamul and discovered quickly that I still had a gap of a few days, waiting for delayed delivery on things, before I went back to the USA. So, by way of an extension of the Jamul visit, I asked myself, "Why not do Saurashtra as well?"

That is how this adventure began. Kshitishbhai, my father-in-law, with whom we were staying in Ahmedabad, offered me his car and driver. Based on this opportunity, I devised hastily a travel itinerary, which can only be described as a "fast sprint" through Saurashtra.

On an early morning, we left Thaltej, near Ahmedabad, and headed for Dwarka. I stopped in mid-morning in Rajkot to pay a visit to Ayaaz Khan Sir at his home, and then left for Jamnagar. Here I was received by Ramesh Kotecha, my RKC batchmate, who took me to his home for lunch. During the two hours or so, I met Chandrakant & Narendra, his older brothers, who were luckily around that day. We caught up on our lives and about many other things. It was great to see them after so many years. Chandu was still just as crazy about Shankar Jaikishan, the Bollywood music duo!

Then we drove on towards Dwarka through terrain which was familiar to me. However, it had changed so much! All the highways were so improved and wonderful. The old roads were still nearby, if one had an eye to spot them. I startled my driver many times by making him stop so I could take photos of things like low causeways on old roads, which were now used mainly by cattle. Back then, we used to spend many hours on their banks, waiting for the flood waters to recede in the monsoon season. In a couple of places, I spotted a siphon dam, which he had no idea about at all. Then, as we got closer to Dwarka, I saw something quite unusual. Windmills! Lots of them. This was certainly something new. Well, soon Dwarka approached and we stopped to get directions to our hotel.

"Jaate keva chho?" the oily man slithered up and smiled, as he inquired. (*What is your caste?*) Normally, I would have replied rudely to this sort of a question with, "What the heck is it to you?" But I managed to control my reaction.

"Hun brahmin chhu," I replied. (*I am a brahmin.*)

"Keva brahmin?" he followed up further. (*What type of a brahmin?*) I was getting annoyed, but I stayed calm.

"Nagar Brahmin," I responded. "Vadnagara."

Hearing this, he broke into a broad grin of great satisfaction and joy. It was a smile that said, "Gosh, did I land a great big fish today! And, boy, am I going to work this one over really well or what?" He promptly started selling me on doing various pujas at the Dwarkadhish Temple. I chatted for a bit, offered him hope, extracted the directions to my hotel, and then we drove on. Now, it was his turn to be bewildered.

We got to the hotel fine, and then I set out to find the bungalow which used to be my home in Dwarka. There was no information about it anywhere at all. We asked all sorts of people about it, but nobody knew anything about them. Then, at this place, an old sadhu, sitting in semi-meditation, overheard me.

"Saheb, ACC na bungala shodho chho?" he asked. (*Saheb, are you looking for the ACC bungalows?*) "Ha. Tamane khabar chhe kyan chhe?" (*Yes. Do you know where they are?*) He did, and he gave us good directions. A sweet man. I gave him an offering.

After much ado, we found the place and I could not believe what I was looking at! I was pulling out my camera when a security guard hurriedly approached us. He said that we could not be on the premises without proper permission.

"Koni raja levani chhe?" I asked him (*Whose permission do I have to get?*). "Saheb, malik ni." he replied (*Saheb, the owner*). The owner was in Jamnagar and the guard called him on his mobile phone. I introduced myself and told him about my desire to just shoot some photos of the place.

"Vijaybhai, tame Yajnik Saheb na dikara chho?" he asked suddenly. (*Vijaybhai, are you Yajnik Saheb's son?*) When I confirmed it, he goes "Arrey, apdo to bahu juno sambandh chhe!" (*Arrey, we have a very old relationship!*) Shortly, all the roadblocks were cleared. The security guard actually became our most invaluable guide about the whole property and what had actually happened there. His version, was sadly also the truth.

ACC had closed down the Dwarka Cement Works many years ago. All that could be salvaged had been removed and sold off. Now, the old plant, the residential colony, and all support buildings were in ruins, literally. The whole society had been destroyed. Folks had not been allowed to buy anything and settle down anywhere nearby on their own. They had all been forced into a collective exodus.

The reason given was, according to the guard, something called "Ozone". He had no idea what it was, but even the 3 managerial bungalows in the compound by the seaside had been abandoned. The AGM and the Guest House bungalows had been demolished the prior year. The GM bungalow was still there standing in a very fragile state. It was falling apart and crumbling away on its own. It was now considered a highly dangerous structure. The guard had been actually worried about our physical safety.

To show my warmth, I told the guard many stories about the times when we had lived there. He was fascinated and wide eyed. Then, just for his own closure, I told him about the long-term dangers in areas of high levels of Ozone.

It is a gas which is found in higher concentration in places that generate pollutants, like manufacturing plants. While it could be harmful to human health, it was also corrosive to many things over time. It was capable of destroying the structural iron in buildings over time, which could cause buildings to just collapse due to lack of reinforcing support. Long term effects of Ozone were never good. Perhaps that had a lot to do with the closure of the whole cement plant.

The GM bungalow was a sight to behold. It was a ruin, with all windows and doors gone. The building was literally crumbling, even though its form was still intact. There was debris everywhere. I went in cautiously, took my photos quickly and got out of there. It made me feel so sad, because every room held precious memories for me.

Next morning, I went on a nostalgic visit to the Dwarkadhish Mandir. It was teeming with security everywhere. There were guards with guns, snipers, etc. all over in visible sight! I think it was intended to send a message to anybody wanting to engage in any kind of mischief.

The temple seemed much the same as I remembered it. Strangely, as I was walking around by myself, one group of Pujari's looked at me and said, "Jai Hatkesh!" It was weird and I replied in kind. But I must admit, I thought of my Mom, who just adored this temple. I prayed in her and Pappaji's memory.

From Dwarka, I went to Port Okha to see if I could visit the GM bungalow there. My father had worked for Carborundum Universal for a few years there after retiring from ACC. That was the home from which I had actually departed for America in 1971. Unfortunately, I had not made prior arrangements and the current GM did not permit me anything more than a cursory visit.

From Port Okha, we left for Porbandar. Near the Harshad Mata Mandir, there was now a lovely bridge to drive over to Miyani! No more transfers by boat, which I remembered so well. From there the road to Porbandar was great. My host in town was Sanjay Thakrar, an RKC old boy, who was a lot younger than me. He had graciously offered to show me around town and had even arranged a lovely lunch at his home. He took me around to see the Villas,

Navyug Vidyalay (my elementary school), the Palace by the beach, and the old ACC bungalows. My mind was flooded with memories.

It took some doing to find the bungalows! Like Dwarka, Porbandar Cement Works had also been closed many years ago. Its property and land had been nearly sold off, but the 3 managerial bungalows were involved in some dispute so were still there, but also in ruins. I could not get near them and took photos from some distance. It was all so sad to see.

From Porbandar, we continued our drive south to Somnath. All my life in India, the Somnath Mandir had been under endless construction. I was told that it was now complete. Gosh, it was a sight to behold! I must admit that the end result is just fantastic. It is a newer, but a grand temple nonetheless. One should definitely visit it. We managed to attend prayers and arati there as well. The architecture was amazing. I wanted to look at it more, but we could not linger. We had to drive on to Sasan, in the Gir Forest, which is where we had booked our hotel for the night. By now, it was also getting dark.

As we entered the Gir Forest, Prahladbhai, my driver, started to get scared. As the forest grew denser, he grew more tense. "Saheb, aa to jungle chhe. Anhi ghana sawaj chhe. Apdi pase bandook pan nathi," he informed me with wide and scared eyes. (*Saheb, this is a jungle. There are many predators here. We don't even have a gun.*)

Then, to make things livelier, we got lost! Prahladbhai had boasted to me that he knew all the roads around Saurashtra very well and had driven lots of folks around everywhere, so he was a safe bet. But now, he was hopelessly lost in the dark of the night in the Gir Forest. There were no lights or signs of any kind, and the real possibility of predators of all sorts being near us. Soon, he became nervous and very agitated.

"Saheb, mane samjhatu nathi. Apde mate ghana jokhum no vakhat chhe," he said with audible fear. (*Saheb, I am not able to understand this. It is a time of great danger for us.*)

"Prahladbhai, tame ghabharasho nahi. Hun tamne rasto batadu chhu," I said in a comforting tone. (*Prahladbhai, please do not be afraid. I will show you the way.*)

"Saheb, kevi reete? Phone pan nathi chalto. Signal nathi," he asked. (*Saheb, how? Even the phone does not work. There is no signal.*)

With some foresight, I had downloaded some Offline Google Maps of Saurashtra on to my phone. It had a near full charge. So, I set the navigation for our hotel and hit "Start". The girl, with a British accent, started talking to us and giving us very precise directions.

But, Prahladbhai would not believe her! "Saheb, aa chhokari sun bake chhe? E khotu bole chhe. Hun rasto janu chhu," he pleaded. (*Saheb, what is this girl babbling? She is telling us wrong things. I know the way.*).

"Prahladbhai, aa chhokari apan ne hotel layi jashe. Tame bharoso karo," I stated. (*Prahladbhai, this girl will get us to our hotel. Please trust her.*)

And get us to our hotel she did! We went through the village of Sasan to the north. After some strange small roads and various crazy turns, we ended up at this charming hotel! They even had rooms and food for drivers. At the Reception, we were informed that we should only move about with an armed guard, especially at night. We were accompanied respectively to our rooms and now Prahladbhai seemed quite relieved. It was an entertaining evening.

Next morning, we drove around the Sasan village. I looked for and asked various people about old guest houses or "dak bungalows", but nobody seemed to know what I was talking about. Also, I could not recognize one single thing anywhere. It did feel bigger and more developed. There were a lot of folks there who wanted to see the Gir Lions, the main attraction of the Forest. The tourist industry was doing brisk business it seemed. This was just with the domestic travelers!

Soon, we left Sasan to head back to Ahmedabad. The drive out of the Gir Forest seemed to get Prahladbhai perturbed again. It was now daylight, but he reminded me, "Saheb, haji badhu jungle chhe. Sawaj game thyan thi avi jaye" (*Saheb, it is all still the jungle. A predator could come from anywhere.*). Then, all these fun times passed.

We drove through Junagadh, which was a treat for me after a long time. I recalled many a trip there with my parents. Then, we raced on via Rajkot to Ahmedabad.

It was, as I explained earlier, a mad sprint through Saurashtra. So, was it worth it? Yes, definitely, but not for the same reasons as Jamul. There was a huge difference.

In the Dwarka, Porbandar and Port Okha era's, I was either in KG/Elementary school or at a University. While, in Jamul, they were my middle & high school years at RKC, the most formative time of my young life. My emotional development and maturity were vastly different.

However, I could not help noticing a few things about Saurashtra. The roads were much better, the connectivity between places had greatly improved, there was better infrastructure, and many more services were available than I could remember. But there was also loads of plastic trash everywhere, even in the holiest of places! There was also a distinct impact of "terrorism" in the experience at many monuments. However, the people were warm, sweet and affectionate as ever.

My nostalgia about it all was also not the same. I felt sad about the various bungalow ruins, but I did not cry. However, one thing was abundantly clear. A lot of water had passed under the bridge, since I had last crossed it. The people, places, and circumstances that I knew and remembered, were a memory of the times past, from a different era.

And like most times, in any era, to borrow a classic title from Margaret Mitchell, they were all "Gone with the Wind".

Who Am I?

I have thought about this question many times. If for no other reason than to convey to the generations that follow me, a few things about myself, that they would otherwise perhaps not know. At the very outset, I will admit that this is a difficult mission. It is a complex question, and the answer to it is not simple either.

Also, there are mental and emotional tussles involved here and they are hard to sort through. But for the sake of posterity, I have given it an honest shot. I hope and trust that no reader of this book finds this particular narrative offensive in any manner. If I do offend you in any way, please forgive me. That is not my intent.

My life can be broken down into a few simple phases or chapters. The stories in this book generally suggest what they were to the reader. Every phase was different, formative, and went a long way towards developing me. However, what was created in the end, is a different matter altogether. I believe that I became a "synthesis" of these diverse experiences and influences. In my case, I think this was more so, than for many of my contemporaries.

As a young lad, born and raised in a Nagar Brahmin family in Gujarat, India, I had not a rich, but a comfortable upbringing. I was immersed into the various Hindu religious rituals, as practiced in any Brahmin family, at a young age. I memorized prayers, practices, and customs, in Sanskrit, because I was told and required to do so.

But as I grew older and was eventually sent to Rajkumar College, Rajkot, I came to realize that all those rituals really did not mean much to me. I had internalized little of anything. I had done things obediently, because my family had demanded that I do so. Then, how much of me was a true Brahmin boy? Why did I not feel the various religious beliefs deeply and intensely within me? I could not understand this.

Rajkumar College, Rajkot, proved to be a highly formative place for me. Besides the academic training, it also taught me discipline, the English language and its related British culture, the ways of the Indian royalty, physical fitness, and various sports. Along the way, I also acquired a taste for non-vegetarian food. But when I left the cocoon of this lovely school, I discovered that I was bit of a misfit in many places.

In my case, this was perhaps due to the emphasis that was placed in my family on further education in specific fields. Careers in engineering or medicine were highly prized at the time. The sciences, government services, or the military, came in second. While the arts, commerce, or law, were dead last. In contrast, a lot of my fellow RKC graduates faced different realities.

A huge lot of them were from Indian royal families. As such, the RKC training was a great start for them to prepare further to take on family responsibilities. There were many others who came from business families, either in India, East Africa, or Asia. Again, they also received a great start at RKC to prepare them further to assume vital roles in their family businesses.

However, I was from a family of mainly educated professionals. As such, I was expected to educate myself further and become a career professional in some chosen field. This meant that I would have to study further at colleges or universities, where my well-rounded RKC education was not necessarily a significant asset.

I would also face intense competition from others who had maintained a largely academic focus during their prior years. I recall being in Ahmedabad and Baroda, giving various engineering entrance exams, and feeling like I did not belong there. There were no known public-school or RKC boys with me during those exams! So, how would an RKC education help me? It took me a long time to fully understand all the lovely things that RKC had actually done for me. But who was I at sixteen, when I graduated from RKC? Was I prepared for further challenging studies? I was not really sure.

IIT/Kanpur came my way quite surprisingly. I did not think I was that smart or gifted. But I made it. So, it started a new adventure for me. I am truly grateful for the opportunity to get an IIT education in India and there were tons of great things about it. The whole experience over the 5 years was grand and I made lifelong friends out of it. But the raw truth for me was that I was not constructed for an IIT education at all. By my temperament and nature, I didn't think I was meant for engineering or the sciences. I was more of an artist. I loved the arts, but an IIT campus was certainly not a place for them.

Perhaps more significantly, I really did not know what I wanted to do with my life or career. I had more questions than answers. But IIT was not a place to go searching for answers to questions on self discovery. It was an intensely competitive, "dog eats dog" world, where your worth was largely determined by your academic grades. So, besides learning a lot about sciences and engineering, and acquiring a certain "brand value", what else did it do for me? Well, in fairness, I did benefit from an IIT education in many other important ways also. But it took me a long while to truly discover all of them. Then, was I this grand and illustrious "IIT product"? Was I now an engineer headed for a sterling future in the world of engineering & technology? Or, was I another confused Graduate with a degree, but without a Mrs. Robinson?

It was in America, that I actually found the freedom to discover my real calling. I invested time and effort, at great personal and economic peril, to find myself and determine what I wanted out of life. It spanned the years from my graduate studies, to my early work career, and more. I assimilated into the American culture in the Midwest, and lost a lot of what was Indian about me in the process.

However, it did not bother me at all at the time. I was now driven towards a purpose, with goals, and committed to achieving success in them. I was deeply immersed in my quest. When it took me to the gorgeous West Coast, I was enamored with it even more. It was interesting that the American society at large seemed to accept and embrace me warmly.

At this stage in my life, I did not "feel" very Indian at all. I had little by way of an Indian lifestyle. In many places, at work or otherwise, people would often say to me, "You are Indian? From India? It is hard to believe. There is nothing Indian about you at all!" Well then, what happened to that long-lost Indian boy? You may be surprised, but it has a name. The name is Nilima.

Out of the blue, I was setup to meet her by my cousin, Pankaj, living in Ahmedabad. She was living in Austin, Texas, at the time. It was a most improbable pairing, if I may say so. She represented everything that I had long forgotten. But in a weird way, it was also kind of appealing. She woke me up gradually from a dream of sorts to re-connect with my inner self.

I had not seen that fella in years! It was nice to meet him again. Well, the essence of it is that Nilima got me grounded again and we decided to get married. The rest is history, to use a cliche. But what does all this say about me? What had been really going on with me during all those years? Was I simply messed up, or was I just incredibly driven? I do not know for sure, but in truth, perhaps it was a little of both.

After my marriage with Nilima, there came all these bewildering situations and questions. These were things that I had never truly known, understood well, or paid much attention to. They were matters dealing with the various aspects of the Indian culture. I had been away from its social customs, norms, and values for quite some time. I agreed with little of it and disliked the rest. I would protest, but Nilima ignored it and continued to re-educate me and reset my thinking.

Well, what does all this suggest? Yes, I had certainly become quite a "firang" (*a foreigner*), to use an Indian term, but it seemed that I was still very much a "home boy" in my core. So, what were my values? What did I really believe in? At this stage, it was hard for me to answer these questions with clarity.

When the children arrived, something even stranger happened to me. I got sucked into the "Indian-ness" of things even more! Initially, I rebelled. But slowly, it dawned on me that the ways of the "old world" were not so wrong after all. In fact, in some things, they were actually brilliant. With support from our extended family in the USA and our parents, I gradually adjusted myself to my new environment. However, I did remain elusive, resistant, or indifferent to many things. Why? I do not know. I still ponder this question.

With young children, we socialized naturally with other families in a similar situation. It so turned out that a lot of them were Indian. There was inherently nothing wrong with this and they were all lovely families from all over India. However, at times I would find things a bit difficult, due to significantly different beliefs on my part. Clearly, I was in a minority.

First, most Indian families seemed to "coddle" their children endlessly. The children were permitted to do whatever they wished without any restraint. Does loving a child mean allowing a complete lack of discipline in most things? The parents never seemed emphatic in "teaching" their kids right from wrong, or disciplining them when required. It was rarely a case of "Sweetie, no, that is not what we do. We do it this way. And if you do that again, Mommy (or Daddy) is going to smack you!"

Is this cultural? Is it the result of a belief that, since "Bal Gopal" or "Nand Lal" (*names for Lord Krishna as a child*) got away with whatever he wished, their kid should be allowed to do so as well? I don't know. But Indians generally, either refuse to understand or choose not to accept, the old adage that "spare the rod, and spoil the child."

In various "kiddie" parties, I would encounter all these Indian kids running amuck, screaming their heads off, and driving everybody berserk! Now, I strongly believe that not only is it perfectly fine, but also in fact a great necessity, to let kids be kids. It is vital for their development. Yes, they should scream, run about, fight, tumble, express themselves, get filthy, and more.

However, there must be a time and place for everything. In my view, parents should "teach" their kids to know the difference. Further, they should also be teaching them, in a firm but encouraging way, proper manners, behavior, social etiquette, and the correct manner of speech, to name a few more things. If the parents do not, then who will? The default answer here is that it will be the society at large and that may generate highly questionable results.

So, what do these beliefs say about me? Am I anti-children, a heartless person, or just an awful parent? Well, with many of my friends and even within my family, these views of mine were received skeptically.

Second, it seemed that many Indian families we knew had suddenly begun focusing on various practices of the Hindu religion. While some of them had been devoutly religious all along, there was now this whole new cadre that had recently become highly interested in religion. Perhaps the arrival of the children had caused a spiritual awakening of sorts. Curiously, I felt no such thing. I continued to do what I had always done before. I prayed at the small mandir in our home, and later, I introduced our kids to it.

However, suddenly there were Pujas (*ritual worships*) being done, Kathas (*religious story recital-based worships*) held, etc. for various reasons and occasions, and your attendance was strongly expected. The kids involved had no idea of what the heck was going on and would have preferred to be at a playground or Disneyland. Perhaps it was all a reaction to feelings of some type of guilt, or a newly discovered sense of responsibility. So, due to my indifference to all this, does it suggest that I had no religious convictions at all? If I did have them, what were they? How did they manifest themselves? These are all great questions.

Third, I call it my aversion of the ubiquitous Indian "KPD" behavior. In Gujarati, it stands for "karvu pade". (*It must be done, as a social custom or practice.*) This is something that I truly abhor. It is not only meaningless, but it also lacks real emotions of any kind. It almost enshrines "an absence" of true thoughts or genuine sentiments. It is a medieval practice, but it is still widely followed all over India, and in particular in Gujarat.

I know that I am in the minority here again, but I was always of the opinion that, "You should do something because you want to do it. Not because you have to." And you should decide its "when and where", as you see fit. This produces a more truthful and honest behavior.

For example, I believe that if one wants to extend greetings and wishes to people because of birthdays, anniversaries, religious holidays, funerals, etc., it is totally fine to do so. However, doing so because it is a "karvu pade" (KPD) act is plain wrong. But nearly everybody does it like automated robots facilitated by the latest technologies.

Also, what makes this truly absurd is that there are some really sorry people, who actually keep score of this robotic crap! Oh, on my birthday, so-and-so did not send me a robotic greeting. Or, I am the senior or the elder person here, and they should have at least sent me a moronic automated greeting.

Instead, I would rather get a call or a greeting that says, "I was thinking of you today. How are you?" Or, "I bought a gift for you today, not because it is

Christmas, Diwali, or Eid. I did it because it is a sunny Monday in LA, I saw this item, and it made me remember you!"

If this happens to you, I promise you that you will feel seriously touched, maybe even overwhelmed. If you want proof, just do it for someone, who is dear to you, and watch their reaction. Neither of you will forget it.

So, what do these beliefs say about me? Am I a social misfit, or another egotistical self-centered "jerk"? I will leave it to you to determine the answers on my behalf.

In terms of my work life, I have been fortunate enough to experience many diverse things in the USA, and internationally. One concept permeates all the things that I have done. I like to think of it as my "comfort with risk". Some people think that handling risk in life is a matter of one's personality, upbringing, training, values, and more.

Maybe that is true, because there are some people, who simply cannot handle risk. They need a secure environment to bring out the best in them. However, I was never comfortable in any situation that did not have a measure of calculated risk in it, with an associated upside. Furthermore, I was equally comfortable with the notion of danger. I could accept danger, even mortal danger, without much trepidation. So, what does this suggest about my personality? It makes me wonder.

All my life, I have been an intellectually curious person. I was always excited about discovering and learning things that I did not know or had not experienced. I was always looking to see what was around the next corner. If I had to stay tethered to the tried, known, and predictable, I would have gone insane! However, with some luck and considerable effort on my part, I was able to facilitate my choices.

Travelling and visiting places that I had never seen, learning about new languages, exposure to different cultures and their history, tasting different cuisines, and experiencing a world in constant change, was the essence of my motivation for living. Words or expressions like "steady state", "quiet and peaceful", "routine", "comfort zone", "badhu apda jevu" (*everything just like us*), suggested to me a state of existence, which was akin to being just dead. Well, not physically, but certainly mentally. I could have none of that.

This nature of mine caused me to spend a lot of money and time catering to it. So, am I just a hedonistic and profligate person? What does it say about my definition of "a good life"? (I used to have this debate with my late mother frequently. We would argue, laugh endlessly, and then hug each other! God, it was wonderful and I loved her so immeasurably.)

As one gets older, spirituality begins to slowly manifest itself in one's life. I watched Kshitishbhai, my father-in-law, turn steadily more spiritual over the last two decades of his life. He was a highly educated, well-travelled, and a widely respected man of sharp intellect. In his 80's and whenever he was with us in LA, he and I would sit outside in the backyard garden in the evenings. He would sit on the swing, and I parked in a chair nearby. We would talk about lots of things endlessly, over a glass of wine. One topic, among the countless ones in our discourse, used to be spirituality.

He turned me onto some amazing books by Swami Vivekananda, Chinmayananda, C. Rajagopalachari, and others. I did a lot of spiritual reading because of his encouragement and re-discovered our ancient scriptures in many new ways. No, I did not turn into some sort of a fanatic for religious rituals, etc. Well, I do "fast" on two separate days during the year in the memory of my parents. They are Maha Shivaratri (*Lord Shiva)* and Janmashtami (*Lord Krishna*) for Pappaji & Behn respectively.

For me, all my reading was more a study and pursuit of spiritual knowledge, from our celebrated ancient texts. It is a journey that still continues. So, am I a near atheist? Or an agnostic? What am I spiritually? I continue to grapple with this question even today.

In November 2019, we are expecting the arrival of our first grandchild, a daughter. As all parents know too well, the children arrive, and in the blink of an eye, they are older and asking you myriad questions about everything. At times, they ask questions about things that you may not have thought about or even considered.

So, I wondered about this the other day. My children, Neil and Meghana, have a pretty good idea of what sort of a person is their father and what he is all about, I believe.

But what if my granddaughter were to ask me, "Grandpa, who are you?" How would I answer her? This question really vexed me. After a lot of thought, I settled on an answer that I would give her.

"Sweetie, that is a great question!" I would say to her. "Well, this may seem a bit weird to you, but I think your Grandpa is an enigma! Even to himself!" Most likely, she would not understand either the word, or my answer.

However, I hope that someday, when she is a lot older, she reads this book. It is quite likely that I may not be around to witness it.

When she does, I believe she will understand.